Communications in Computer and Information Science 2381

Rationale

The CCIS series is devoted to the publication of proceedings of computer science conferences. Its aim is to efficiently disseminate original research results in informatics in printed and electronic form. While the focus is on publication of peer-reviewed full papers presenting mature work, inclusion of reviewed short papers reporting on work in progress is welcome, too. Besides globally relevant meetings with internationally representative program committees guaranteeing a strict peer-reviewing and paper selection process, conferences run by societies or of high regional or national relevance are also considered for publication.

Topics

The topical scope of CCIS spans the entire spectrum of informatics ranging from foundational topics in the theory of computing to information and communications science and technology and a broad variety of interdisciplinary application fields.

Information for Volume Editors and Authors

Publication in CCIS is free of charge. No royalties are paid, however, we offer registered conference participants temporary free access to the online version of the conference proceedings on SpringerLink (http://link.springer.com) by means of an http referrer from the conference website and/or a number of complimentary printed copies, as specified in the official acceptance email of the event.

CCIS proceedings can be published in time for distribution at conferences or as post-proceedings, and delivered in the form of printed books and/or electronically as USBs and/or e-content licenses for accessing proceedings at SpringerLink. Furthermore, CCIS proceedings are included in the CCIS electronic book series hosted in the SpringerLink digital library at http://link.springer.com/bookseries/7899. Conferences publishing in CCIS are allowed to use Online Conference Service (OCS) for managing the whole proceedings lifecycle (from submission and reviewing to preparing for publication) free of charge.

Publication process

The language of publication is exclusively English. Authors publishing in CCIS have to sign the Springer CCIS copyright transfer form, however, they are free to use their material published in CCIS for substantially changed, more elaborate subsequent publications elsewhere. For the preparation of the camera-ready papers/files, authors have to strictly adhere to the Springer CCIS Authors' Instructions and are strongly encouraged to use the CCIS LaTeX style files or templates.

Abstracting/Indexing

CCIS is abstracted/indexed in DBLP, Google Scholar, EI-Compendex, Mathematical Reviews, SCImago, Scopus. CCIS volumes are also submitted for the inclusion in ISI Proceedings.

How to start

To start the evaluation of your proposal for inclusion in the CCIS series, please send an e-mail to ccis@springer.com.

Asad Safi · Anabel Martin-Gonzalez ·
Carlos Brito-Loeza · Victor Castañeda-Zeman
Editors

Intelligent Computing Systems

5th International Symposium, ISICS 2024
Sharjah, United Arab Emirates, November 6–7, 2024
Proceedings

Springer

Editors
Asad Safi
Higher Colleges of Technology
Sharjah, United Arab Emirates

Anabel Martin-Gonzalez
Universidad Autónoma de Yucatán
Merida, Mexico

Carlos Brito-Loeza
Universidad Autónoma de Yucatán
Merida, Mexico

Victor Castañeda-Zeman
Universidad de Chile
Santiago, Chile

ISSN 1865-0929 ISSN 1865-0937 (electronic)
Communications in Computer and Information Science
ISBN 978-3-031-82930-7 ISBN 978-3-031-82931-4 (eBook)
https://doi.org/10.1007/978-3-031-82931-4

This Springer imprint is published by the registered company Springer Nature Switzerland AG
The registered company address is: Gewerbestrasse 11, 6330 Cham, Switzerland

Preface

Current technological development, along with faster computer processors, has promoted the generation of an enormous amount of digital data. The capacity to create and store information increases the need to implement and improve intelligent systems that automate the analysis and understanding of new datasets to overcome real-world challenges and enhance human life. Capable of perceiving, reasoning, learning, and acting rationally, intelligent systems can make decisions to solve complex and multidisciplinary problems automatically, giving support to the decisions of an expert. Their applications can be numerous and of great variety, including biological sciences, computer vision, robotics, search engines, and data mining, among others. Every year, new algorithms and applications are introduced, including deep neural networks, optimization techniques in learning, and evolutionary computation, among others.

This book contains papers presented at the Fifth International Symposium on Intelligent Computing Systems (ISICS 2024) held at the Higher Colleges of Technology (HCT) Sharjah, UAE during November 6–7, 2024. ISICS 2024 was an international conference intended to attract computing professionals to discuss recent developments and trends in software and computing with their research communities. ISICS 2024 aimed to further increase the body of knowledge in this specific area of computer science by providing a forum to exchange ideas and discuss state-of-the-art results. ISICS 2024 was committed to the promotion, preservation, and collaboration of research and practice, focusing on the fields of artificial intelligence, computer vision, and image processing.

For this edition of the conference, we received 71 papers from 15 different countries around the globe. Each submission was evaluated in a double-blind review process by at least three members of the Program Committee, and based on these reviews, 25 papers were included in the conference program as long oral presentations. In addition to the contributed papers, five keynote speakers were invited to give plenary talks.

We would like to warmly thank all the authors who submitted their work to ISICS 2024. Their contribution to the conference is highly appreciated, and we kindly invite them to continue contributing to future ISICS conferences. We gratefully acknowledge the professional work of the international scientific program committee members, and we also greatly appreciate the contribution and participation of our invited speakers, Luc Verburgh (CAO, HCT UAE), Saeed Al Dhaheri (UNESCO co-Chair, UAE), Dr. Veljko Milutinovic (University of Indiana in Bloomington, USA) , Faisal Ameer Malik (Huawei Enterprise Business Group, UAE), and Semih Kumluk (PwC Academy, UAE).

We are very grateful to the Universidad de Chile and Universidad Autónoma de Yucatán for their support in the organization of ISICS 2024.

November 2024

Carlos Brito-Loeza
Anabel Martin-Gonzalez
Victor Castañeda-Zeman
Asad Safi

Organization

General Chairs

Alhosban, Fuad	Higher Colleges of Technology, UAE
Aoudi, Samer	Higher Colleges of Technology, UAE
Tamimi, Hatem	Higher Colleges of Technology, UAE

Program Committee Chairs

Brito-Loeza, Carlos	Universidad Autónoma de Yucatán, Mexico
Castañeda-Zeman, Victor	Universidad de Chile, Chile
Martin-Gonzalez, Anabel	Universidad Autónoma de Yucatán, Mexico
Safi, Asad	Higher Colleges of Technology, UAE

Program Committee Members

A. P. Saleel	Higher Colleges of Technology, UAE
Abdelmajid, Nabih	Higher Colleges of Technology, UAE
Abu Rahmeh, Osama	Higher Colleges of Technology, UAE
Adnan, Muhammad	Higher Colleges of Technology, UAE
Akpinar, Mustafa	Higher Colleges of Technology, UAE
Akre, Vishwesh	Higher Colleges of Technology, UAE
Al Barghuthi, Nedaa	Higher Colleges of Technology, UAE
Al Shehhi, Abdulmunem	EDGE, UAE
Al-Aqrabi, Hussain	Higher Colleges of Technology, UAE
Al-Hassan, Munther	Higher Colleges of Technology, UAE
Alawadhi, Ibtesam	Zayed University, UAE
Alazzam, Azmi	Higher Colleges of Technology, UAE
Alkouz, Akram	Higher Colleges of Technology, UAE
Almiani, Khaled	Higher Colleges of Technology, UAE
Alrefai, Ammar	Higher Colleges of Technology, UAE
Amin, Anang	Higher Colleges of Technology, UAE
Arabyat, Eman	Higher Colleges of Technology, UAE
Aranda, Ramón	Centro de Investigación en Matemáticas, Mexico
Atassi, Reem	Higher Colleges of Technology, UAE
Ayyal Awwad, Aiman	Higher Colleges of Technology, UAE

Badreddine, Said	Higher Colleges of Technology, UAE
Benlamine, Mohamed Sahbi	Higher Colleges of Technology, UAE
Bibu, Gideon	Higher Colleges of Technology, UAE
Brito-Loeza, Carlos	Universidad Autónoma de Yucatán, Mexico
Castañeda-Zeman, Victor	Universidad de Chile, Chile
Dessi, Rima	Higher Colleges of Technology, UAE
Durrani, Usman	Higher Colleges of Technology, UAE
El Zabadani, Hicham	Higher Colleges of Technology, UAE
Elsersy, Mohamed	Higher Colleges of Technology, UAE
Espinosa-Romero, Arturo	Universidad Autónoma de Yucatán, Mexico
Estrada-Lopez, Johan	Universidad Autónoma de Yucatán, Mexico
Fares, Elie	Higher Colleges of Technology, UAE
Flores, Pedro	Higher Colleges of Technology, UAE
Guerdelli, Fethi	Higher Colleges of Technology, UAE
Hernández López, Francisco	Centro de Investigación en Matemáticas, Mexico
Hevia-Montiel, Nidiyare	Universidad Nacional Autónoma de México, Mexico
Hitam, Nor Azizah	Higher Colleges of Technology, UAE
Kasem, Asem	Higher Colleges of Technology, UAE
Khan, Eraj	Higher Colleges of Technology, UAE
Legarda-Saenz, Ricardo	Universidad Autónoma de Yucatán, Mexico
López Martínez, José Luis	Universidad Autónoma de Yucatán, Mexico
Malik, Asif	Higher Colleges of Technology, UAE
Manasrah, Ahmed	Higher Colleges of Technology, UAE
Martin-Gonzalez, Anabel	Universidad Autónoma de Yucatán, Mexico
Martínez-Perez, M. Elena	Universidad Nacional Autónoma de México, Mexico
Monroy Borja, Raúl	Tecnológico de Monterrey, Mexico
Navarro Claveria, Carlos	Universidad de Chile, Chile
Omari, Asem	Higher Colleges of Technology, UAE
Ortegón Aguilar, Jaime	Universidad de Quintana Roo, Mexico
Paul, Sujni	Higher Colleges of Technology, UAE
Ramasamy, Lakshmana Kumar	Higher Colleges of Technology, UAE
Safi, Asad	Higher Colleges of Technology, UAE
Silva, Melina	Higher Colleges of Technology, UAE
Siyam, Nur	Higher Colleges of Technology, UAE
Tinkicht, Nassim	Higher Colleges of Technology, UAE
Togher, Madeleine	Higher Colleges of Technology, UAE
Trejo Sánchez, Joel	Centro de Investigación en Matemáticas, Mexico
Ud Din, Shahab	Higher Colleges of Technology, UAE
Vergara, Jorge	Universidad Tecnológica Metropolitana, Chile

Contents

UKRAG: A Unified Knowledge Graph to Enhance Retrieval Augmented Generation Performance

Akram Alkouz[1(✉)], Mohammed I. Al-Saleh[1,2], Abdulsalam Alarabeyyat[1,3], and Majed Bouchahma[1]

[1] Higher Colleges of Technology, Computer Information System, Abu Dhabi, UAE
{aalkouz,malsaleh,aalarabeyyat,mbouchahma}@hct.ac.ae
[2] Computer Science Department, Jordan University of Science and Technology, Irbid, Jordan
[3] Software Engineering Department, Al-Balqa' Applied University, Salt, Jordan

Abstract. Retrieval Augmented Generation models have demonstrated significant potential in enhancing the performance and reducing hallucinations in Large Language Models by incorporating external knowledge sources. However, effectively utilizing both structured and unstructured data in Retrieval-Augmented Generation remains a challenge, as most existing methods retrieve only short, contiguous chunks from a retrieval corpus, limiting the holistic understanding of the overall document context and structure. This paper presents a novel approach to constructing a knowledge graph that seamlessly integrates structured and unstructured data to enhance the performance of Retrieval-Augmented Generation models. Our method involves first converting structured data into a graph model and then merging it with the document context found in unstructured text. This combined data is processed to build a Unified Knowledge graph, providing a rich, interconnected information source for the Retrieval-Augmented Generation model.

To evaluate our approach and proposed model, we conducted extensive experiments on a variety of tasks, including question-answering and complex reasoning. The results demonstrate that our Unified knowledge Graph RAG model significantly outperforms traditional RAG models, achieving higher accuracy and better handling of intricate queries. Notably, on benchmarks such as QuALITY, our model shows substantial improvements in performance metrics. This research underscores the potential of integrating structured and unstructured data into a unified knowledge graph to advance the capabilities of RAG models, offering a promising direction for future developments in Artificial Intelligence and Natural Language Processing.

1 Introduction

Large Language Models (LLMs) like GPT-3 and its successors have demonstrated remarkable capabilities in generating human-like text and performing

A. Safi et al. (Eds.): ISICS 2024, CCIS 2381, pp. 1–19, 2025.
https://doi.org/10.1007/978-3-031-82931-4_1

a variety of Natural Language Processing (NLP) tasks. However, these models have inherent limitations, primarily due to their reliance on the static datasets they were trained on. This static nature means that LLMs can struggle to provide accurate responses when faced with queries about recent events or specialized knowledge domains that were not well-represented in their training data.

1.1 Updating Knowledge in LLMs

Updating the knowledge embedded in LLMs is a challenging and resource-intensive task, especially when considering the vast text corpora these models are trained on [1]. Fine-tuning LLMs involves retraining the model on new data to adjust its parameters and incorporate updated information. This process is inherently complex due to several factors: 1) Scale of Data: LLMs are trained on enormous datasets that encompass diverse and comprehensive information. Adding new data requires integrating it seamlessly with the existing corpus, ensuring that the model retains previously learned knowledge while assimilating the new information. 2) Fine-tuning large models, such as GPT-3, involves extensive computational resources and time. The process can take days or even weeks, depending on the size of the model and the volume of new data. 3) High-performance hardware, such as GPUs or TPUs, is essential for fine-tuning. The cost of these resources can be prohibitive, particularly for organizations with limited budgets. 4) Fine-tuning on a small subset of new data can lead to overfitting, where the model becomes excessively tailored to the new data at the expense of generalizability. Ensuring a balanced integration of old and new information is crucial to maintaining the model's overall performance.

1.2 Retrieval-Augmented Generation (RAG) Models

Instead of fine-tuning, integrating external knowledge sources into large language models (LLMs) has emerged as a powerful technique to enhance their performance and address issues like hallucinations and reliance on outdated data. Retrieval-Augmented Generation (RAG) models represent a significant advancement in this area by leveraging external knowledge retrieval to enhance the capabilities of LLMs [2]. By incorporating information from diverse sources, RAG models excel in complex language understanding and generation tasks, effectively combining the strengths of information retrieval and generative models. This approach allows for the integration of up-to-date, domain-specific knowledge, facilitating easy interpretability and provenance tracking. [3]

1.3 Applications of RAG Models

RAG models have unlocked new potentials for various applications, including: 1) Question Answering: RAG models excel in question-answering tasks by retrieving precise answers from a large corpus and generating coherent, contextually appropriate responses. 2) Information Retrieval: These models enhance traditional information retrieval systems by generating summaries and explanations based on retrieved documents, providing users with more comprehensive insights. 3) Content Generation: In content generation tasks, RAG models can produce more accurate and relevant text by leveraging external knowledge, making them valuable for applications such as automated journalism, report generation, and creative writing. 4) Conversational Agents: For chatbots and virtual assistants, RAG models offer improved response accuracy and contextual awareness, leading to more natural and informative interactions.

Overall, RAG models represent a significant advancement in NLP, providing a framework that enhances the capabilities of LLMs through the strategic integration of external knowledge. This integration not only improves the accuracy and relevance of generated text but also opens new avenues for innovation and application in the field of artificial intelligence and beyond.

1.4 Challenges with Existing RAG Models

Despite their success, RAG models face challenges in effectively utilizing both structured and unstructured data. Most existing methods for external knowledge retrieval in RAG systems are limited to retrieving short, contiguous text segments or chunks from a retrieval corpus. This approach restricts the model's ability to comprehend the broader context and structure of documents, hindering its performance on tasks requiring nuanced understanding. Integrating knowledge from multiple chunks that are semantically related either explicitly or implicitly can enhance the nuanced comprehension of text documents [4–6].

1.5 Our Contribution

To address this limitation, this paper introduces a novel approach to constructing a unified knowledge graph that seamlessly integrates structured and unstructured data from a document. Our method involves converting structured data and its hierarchy into a graph model and merging it with the document context extracted from unstructured text. This combined data is then processed to create a comprehensive knowledge graph. The comprehensive knowledge graph then integrated with RAG to serving as Unified Knowledge Retrieval Augmented Graph (UKRAG) model so that it can effectively and efficiently answer questions at different levels.

1.6 Research Objective

The primary objective of this research is to investigate the effectiveness of integrating structured and unstructured data into a unified knowledge graph to enhance the performance of RAG models. We hypothesize that leveraging a unified knowledge graph will enable the RAG model to access a richer set of information, leading to improved accuracy and better handling of complex queries. Our main contribution is the idea of generating unified knowledge graph of structured and unstructured data extracted from documents in some specific domain.

1.7 Evaluation

To evaluate our approach, we conduct extensive experiments on QA tasks using six Models: GPT-3.5 [7], GPT-4 [8], GPT3.5 with typical RAG models. GPT-4 with typical RAG Model, GPT-3.5 with UKRAG Model, and GPT-4 with UKRAG model. Results showed that our proposed UKRAG model outperforms current retrieval augmentation and gives new state-of-the-art results including question-answering and complex reasoning. The results demonstrate the superiority of our UKRAG model over traditional RAG models, achieving significant improvements in performance metrics across different benchmarks.

By bridging the gap between structured and unstructured data through the integration of a unified knowledge graph, this research contributes to advancing the capabilities of RAG models. Our findings offer valuable insights into the potential of unified knowledge graphs in augmenting language understanding and generation, paving the way for future developments in AI and natural language processing.

1.8 Organization of the Paper

This paper is organized as follows. Background on LLMs and RAG, knowledge graphs, and the technologies and techniques used in this paper is given in Sect. 2. Our Methodology model is presented in Sect. 3. This is followed by Sect. 4 that explains our experimental setup and results. This is followed by discussion and conclusion.

2 Related Work

Traditional language models often fail to effectively utilize long-range context, resulting in decreased performance as the context lengthens, particularly when key information is buried within a lengthy text. Additionally, handling long contexts is both costly and slow in practical applications [9,10]. Therefore, it remains essential to select the most relevant information for knowledge-intensive tasks.

[9,10] have observed that language models often struggle to effectively utilize long-range context, leading to decreased performance as the context lengthens, especially when key information is buried within lengthy text. Handling such long contexts is also costly and slow in practical applications, making it essential to select the most relevant information for knowledge-intensive tasks. Recent studies propose using large language models as retrievers due to their ability to store extensive knowledge [11].

Despite the diversity in methods among LLMs, their retrieval components mainly rely on standard approaches, such as chunking, corpora, and using BERT-based retrievers. While widely adopted, [12] point out a potential drawback: contiguous segmentation may fail to capture the full semantic depth of the text. Extracted snippets from technical or scientific documents might miss crucial context, making them hard to read or even misleading.

RAG models have gained considerable attention in recent years among researchers as a hybrid approach that combines the strengths of retrieval-based methods and generative models. The seminal work by [13] introduced the concept of RAG, demonstrating that augmenting a generative model with retrieved documents from an external corpus can significantly improve performance on tasks such as open-domain question answering. This hybrid approach leverages the precision of retrieval systems and the flexibility of generative models, creating a robust framework for complex language tasks.

The effectiveness of RAG models heavily depends on the quality of the retrieval component. If the retrieved documents are irrelevant or only loosely related to the query, the generative model's output may be inaccurate or misleading. Ensuring high-quality retrieval in diverse and open-domain settings is particularly challenging [13]. The quality of the retrieval components depends heavily on the way it was chunked.

2.1 Knowledge Graph in NLP

Knowledge graphs are structured representations of information that capture relationships between entities. They have been extensively used in various NLP applications to enhance understanding and reasoning capabilities [14]. Traditional knowledge graphs, such as DBpedia [15], and Freebase [16], organize structured data into a graph format, enabling sophisticated querying and inferencing. In recent years, there has been a growing interest in integrating knowledge graphs with unstructured data to enrich the contextual understanding of language models. Notable works include incorporating knowledge graphs into LLMs to improve tasks like entity linking, relation extraction, and commonsense reasoning [17].

2.2 Integration of Structured and Unstructured Data

The integration of structured and unstructured data remains a critical challenge in NLP. Most approaches to date have focused on either structured or unstructured data, with few effectively combining both. Methods such as K-BERT [18] and ERNIE [19] have incorporated structured knowledge into pre-trained language models to enhance their performance on downstream tasks. These models embed knowledge graph triples into the text representation, allowing the model to leverage structured knowledge. However, these approaches often do not fully integrate unstructured data, limiting their ability to provide comprehensive context.

2.3 Limitations of Existing RAG Models

Current RAG models primarily focus on retrieving short, contiguous text segments from a large corpus, which can limit their ability to understand the broader context and structure of documents. This retrieval mechanism often overlooks the hierarchical and relational information inherent in structured data. [1] introduced a novel approach involving the recursive embedding, clustering, and summarizing of text chunks to construct a hierarchical tree with varying levels of summarization from the bottom up. During inference, the model retrieves information from this tree, integrating details across lengthy documents at different levels of abstraction. Controlled experiments demonstrate that retrieval using recursive summaries significantly outperforms traditional retrieval-augmented LLMs on various tasks. In question-answering tasks requiring complex, multi-step reasoning, this model achieved state-of-the-art results; for instance, when paired with GPT-4, it improved the best performance on the QuALITY benchmark by 20% in absolute accuracy. Furthermore, the integration process often overlooks the rich interconnections between different pieces of information, resulting in suboptimal performance on tasks that require deep understanding and reasoning.

2.4 Advances in Unified Knowledge Graphs

Recent advancements in the construction of unified knowledge graphs have shown promise in addressing the limitations of traditional RAG models [20]. Techniques for merging structured data with unstructured text into a cohesive graph structure are emerging. These unified knowledge graphs aim to provide a more holistic view of the information landscape, enabling models to access a richer, interconnected source of knowledge. Approaches such as Turing-NLG [21] and Knowledge Graph-Augmented Models [22] are pioneering this integration, demonstrating the potential for significant improvements in various NLP tasks.

2.5 Our Contribution

Building on these advancements, our research introduces a novel method for constructing a unified knowledge graph that integrates both structured and unstructured data to enhance RAG models. Our approach not only converts structured data into a graph model but also seamlessly merges it with the context derived from unstructured text. This unified knowledge graph serves as a comprehensive information source, enabling the RAG model to perform more accurately and handle complex queries more effectively.

In summary, our work contributes to the growing body of research on RAG models and knowledge graphs by addressing the critical challenge of integrating structured and unstructured data. We demonstrate that this integration can significantly enhance the performance of RAG models, paving the way for future advancements in NLP and AI.

3 Methodology

RAG improves LLMs performance by providing chunked and embedded documents, thereby mitigating the risk of hallucination. This technique is widely used by organizations and enterprises that manage extensive collections of documents, such as books, manuals, tutorials, and technical reports, typically in

PDF format. Building on the idea that long text documents present subtopics and hierarchical structures [23], these PDFs contain structured data, organized into hierarchies like chapters, sections, and subsections, as well as unstructured data represented in the text itself.

Our methodology focuses on constructing a unified knowledge graph that integrates both structured and unstructured data, thereby enhancing the performance of RAG models. Her and after this model is referred as UKRAG. The integration of structured data, such as the hierarchical organization of chapters, sections, and subsections, with unstructured data, such as the text within these sections, creates a comprehensive and coherent dataset.

We propose a method for chunking unstructured data into manageable pieces, guided by hierarchies extracted from the structured data. This hierarchical chunking ensures that each piece of unstructured data retains its explicit and implicit context. Explicit context refers to the clear, straightforward relationships and information within the text, while implicit context involves the underlying, nuanced connections and meanings [24].

By aligning the chunking process with the document's inherent structure, we maintain the logical flow and interconnections between different sections of the text. This is crucial for several reasons:

- Context Preservation Maintaining both explicit and implicit contexts ensures that the information remains coherent and meaningful when retrieved and utilized by the RAG model. It prevents the loss of critical nuances that could affect the interpretation and relevance of the data.
- Enhanced Retrieval Accuracy By structuring the data in a way that mirrors its original hierarchical organization, the RAG model can more accurately retrieve relevant information. This is particularly important for complex queries that require an understanding of the broader context.
- Improved Summarization and Inference The hierarchical chunking facilitates better summarization and inference capabilities. When the model processes the chunks, it can more effectively generate summaries and insights that reflect the document's overall structure and content.
- Scalability and Manageability Chunking large volumes of unstructured data into smaller, manageable pieces makes it easier to process and analyze. This method enhances the scalability of the RAG model, allowing it to handle extensive datasets without compromising performance.

This section outlines the detailed steps involved in our approach, including structured data preprocessing and extraction, unstructured data extraction and chunking, knowledge graph construction, and integration with the RAG model. The preprocessing phases involves extracting and organizing the hierarchical structure from the structured data. Subsequently, unstructured data is chunked according to this hierarchy, and the knowledge graph is constructed to integrate these chunks, maintaining their contextual integrity. Finally, we detail how this integrated knowledge graph is utilized within the RAG model to achieve enhanced performance in information retrieval and generation tasks.

3.1 Structured Data Preprocessing and Extraction

Our methodology entails a multi-step process to extract structured hierarchy from PDF documents contain the table of content, leveraging recent advancements in OpenAI's API capabilities [25]. Below is a detailed explanation of the pipeline implementation used in this process:

- Step 1: Load and Concatenate PDF Content: The process begins by loading the PDF document and concatenating its content into a single string using the PyPDFLoader [26] class. The concatenated content is then saved as a JSON file for subsequent processing.
- Step 2: Define the Prompt Template: Using ChatPromptTemplat functionality from OpenAI API, We engineered the following prompt: "A text book's table of contents will be passed to you. Extract all the chapters, sections and sub-sections, If no information are mentioned that's fine - you don't need to extract any! Just return an empty list. if not explicitly provided do not make up or guess any extra information. Only extract what exactly is in the text". This prompt template is used to instruct the model to extract chapters, sections, and subsections from the PDF's table of contents.
- Step 3: Define Data Models and Schema: LLMs generate non-deterministic outputs in terms of data format and structure, meaning identical inputs can produce different outputs each time. This variability is due to the probabilistic nature of the underlying algorithms, which select from a range of possible responses based on learned patterns rather than fixed rules. As a result, the output format and structure can vary, creating challenges for applications that require consistent response formatting, such as data extraction. To ensure consistency of extracted data using the OpenAI API, we define data models with Pydantic [27] to structure the information. These models ensure the hierarchical organization of chapters, sections, and subsections, accurately reflecting the document's structure as shown in Listing 1. To maintain consistency across different OpenAI API responses, we standardize various schemas and map the data into a common format. This step is critical for integrating generated data from diverse OpenAI API calls into a unified system.
- Step 4: The extracted table of contents is returned as a Pandas DataFrame for further processing. This DataFrame includes three columns: the page reference number, the text representing chapter, section, and subsection titles, and an indexed list indicating sibling chapters. This step ensures that the structured data accurately reflects the document's hierarchy, which is essential for effective retrieval and processing by our RAG models.

```
prompt = ChatPromptTemplate.from_messages([
        ("system", "A text book's table of contents will be passed to you. Extract all the chapters, sections and sub-sections, If no information are mentioned that's fine - you don't need to extract any! Just return an empty list. if not explicitly provided do not make up or guess any extra information. Only extract what exactly is in the text."),
        ("human", "{input}")
        ])


    class SubSection(BaseModel):
        """Information about sub-section"""
        name: str
        pageNo: int

    class Section(BaseModel):
        """Information about section."""
        name: str
        pageNo: int
        subSections: Optional[SubSection]

    class Chapter(BaseModel):
        """Information about the chapter"""
        name: str
        pageNo: int
        sections: List[Section]


    class Chapters(BaseModel):
        """Information about the chapters"""
        chapter: List[Chapter]

    course_extraction_function = [
        convert_pydantic_to_openai_function(Chapters)
    ]
```

Listing 1.1. pydantic function models to ensure the hierarchical organization of chapters sections and subsections

3.2 Unstructured Data Extraction and Chunking

Our goal is to segment the unstructured text in the PDF content based on its topics to facilitate better data organization and retrieval. Here's a detailed look at our approach:

- Reading the PDF into a DataFrame: We start by reading the PDF file and converting its content into a structured format. Each page of the PDF is

represented as a row in a dataframe. The dataframe consists of columns for the page number, the text extracted from that page, and any relevant metadata. This structured approach allows for easy manipulation and analysis of the content.
- Matching Extracted Text with its corresponding tag from the Table of Contents (TOC): Using the page number, we align the extracted text with the entries in the extracted previously TOC. This step is crucial as it allows us to understand which sections or topics are covered on each page.
- Topics Spanning Multiple Pages: One of the challenges we face is that a single topic can extend across multiple pages. To manage this, we developed an algorithm that can detect where a topic ends. The algorithm works by continuously matching the text content of consecutive pages with the corresponding entries in the TOCt. When a match with a new TOC entry is found, it indicates the start of a new topic, thereby marking the end of the previous topic.
- Pages Containing Multiple Topics: Another challenge is the presence of multiple topics within a single page. This can occur in cases where a page transitions from one topic to another. To resolve this, we implemented an algorithm that splits the page content based on the titles from the TOC. The algorithm scans the page for keywords or phrases that match the TOC entries and segments the text accordingly. By doing this, we ensure that each chunk of text is accurately categorized under its respective topic, even if multiple topics are covered on the same page.
- Implementation Details: The algorithms use NLP techniques to analyze the text content and identify topic boundaries. This includes text matching, pattern recognition, and context analysis. We also account for variations in formatting, such as headings, subheadings, and other typographical cues that can indicate the structure of the document.

By implementing these steps, we ensure that the extracted content from the PDF is well-organized, accurately reflecting the document's structure and making it easier to work with when constructing the knowledge graph.

3.3 Knowledge Graph Construction

The next step involves constructing a unified knowledge graph by merging the previously extracted structured and unstructured data. This process organizes the information to highlight semantic relationships and dependencies between topics, facilitating efficient retrieval and processing by an LLM model.

- Graph Model for Structured Data: The first task is to convert structured data into a graph format. In this graph, nodes represent various entities (such as topics, sections, and named entities), and edges represent the relationships between these entities.
- Hierarchical Structuring: To capture the relationships and dependencies between entities, we organize the graph hierarchically. This hierarchical structuring involves several steps:

1. Add Chunked Topics as Nodes: We begin by adding each chunked topic from the PDF as a node in the graph database as shown in Fig. 1. Her and after, these nodes are called Chunked Topic Node (CTN). Each CTN includes detailed properties such as the title, text, and page number of the chunk. This ensures that each segment of the document is represented as a distinct entity within the graph.
2. Create Connections Between consecutive CTNs: To reflect the logical flow of the document, we create edges between consecutive CTNs. These connections labeled as "Semantically followed by" represent the sequential order of topics, ensuring the graph maintains the document's narrative structure as shown in Fig. 1.
3. Construct the graph structure of TOC: Next, we iterate through the TOC and create a node for each entry labeled as (chapter, section, and subsection). Her and after these nodes called Topic Node (TN). TNs are then linked in a hierarchical manner based on the structure provided in the TOC as shown in Fig. 2. This step preserves the organizational framework of the document within the graph.
4. Mapping TN to its corresponding CTN: a CTN might be semantically related to multiple Chapters, Sections, and/or Subsections. Mapping each CTN to its corresponding TN based on the similarity between the title property of the CTN and the label property of TN to extract the explicit semantic relations that can be derived from the TOC as show in Fig. 3. The extraction of implicit semantic relations between CTNs and TN requires further NLP processing using Named Entity Recognition [28].
5. Named Entity Recognition and Disambiguation [29]: Using NLP techniques and LLM models, we identify and disambiguate Named Entities (NEs) within the CTNs. These named entities are added as separate nodes in the graph. We then create edges between each NE node and the CTN from which it was extracted, establishing a clear relationship between entities and their contexts as shown in Fig. 4.
6. Identify Other Semantic Relationships: Finally, we use LLMs to discover implicit semantic relationships between NEs and TNs as shown in Fig. 5. This involves analyzing the text to find connections that might not be immediately obvious. Once these relationships are identified, we create edges between the semantically related nodes, enriching the graph with meaningful connections.

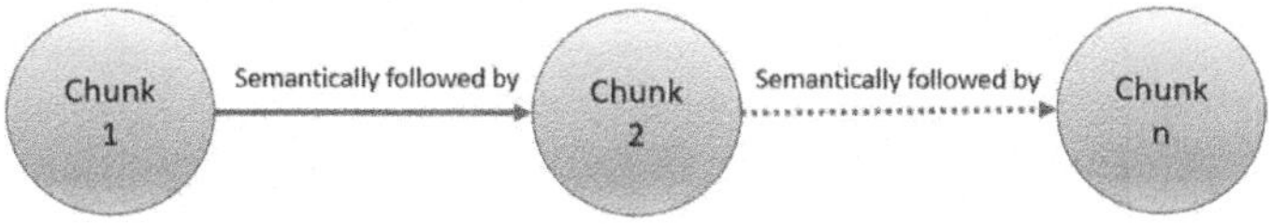

Fig. 1. Chunked topics added as nodes into the graph. The connection between consecutive nodes is labels as "Semantically followed by" to represent the sequential order of topics.

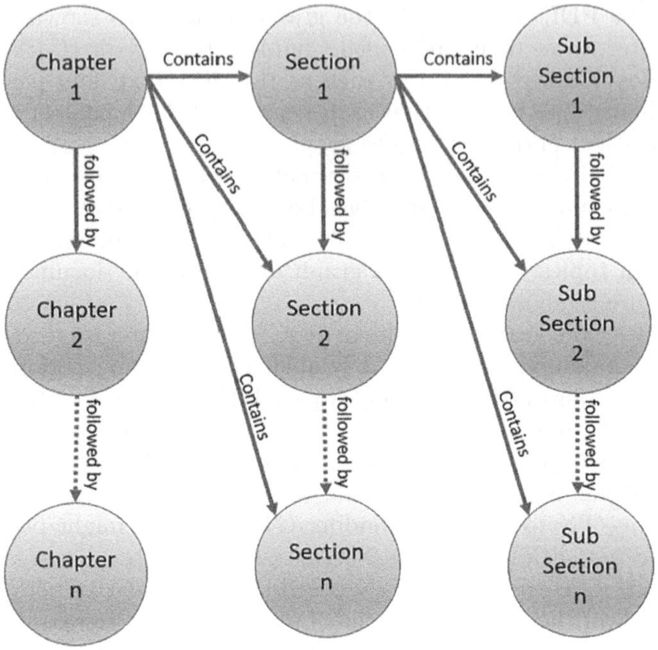

Fig. 2. A node for each entry (chapter, section, and subsection) is added into the graph. These nodes are then linked in a hierarchical manner based on the structure provided in the TOC.

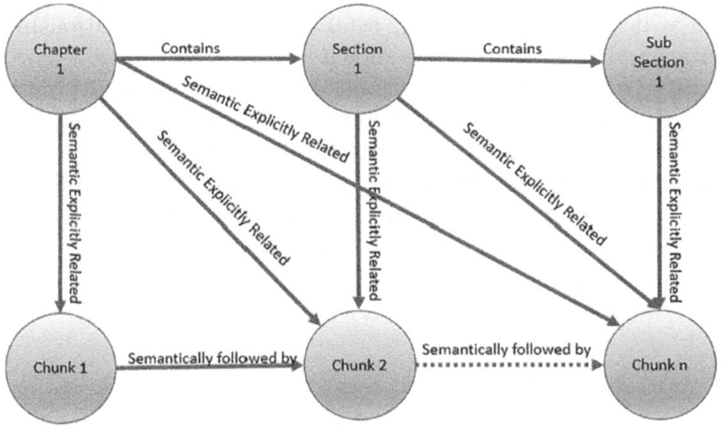

Fig. 3. Mapping each CTN to its corresponding TN based on the similarity between the title property of the CTN and the label property of TN to extract the explicit semantic relations.

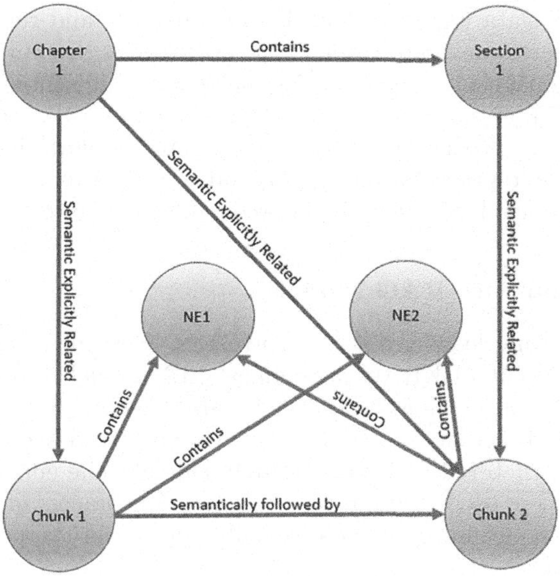

Fig. 4. Named Entities within the CTNs are added as separate nodes in the graph. Edges are created between each NE node and the CTN from which it was extracted.

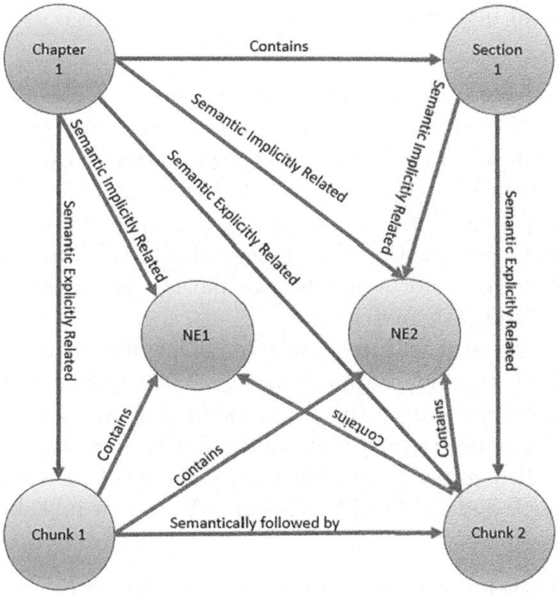

Fig. 5. Representing the implicit semantic relationships between NEs and TNs.

By constructing this unified knowledge graph, we achieve several key advantages: Enhanced Data Organization: The hierarchical and relational structuring makes it easier to navigate through the document's content. Improved Data Retrieval: Relationships between entities enable more efficient and accurate data retrieval. Rich Contextual Understanding: The graph format preserves the context of information, providing deeper insights into the data. Facilitated Analysis: The structured representation supports advanced data analysis and machine learning applications, leveraging the interconnectedness of entities.

3.4 Integration with RAG Models

Once the unified knowledge graph is constructed, it is integrated with the RAG model to from UKRAG. UKRAG can enhance LLM model's performance on various NLP tasks. Incorporating the knowledge graph embeddings into the retrieval mechanism of the RAG model, UKRAG allowing it to retrieve relevant information from both structured and unstructured sources. The enriched information from the UKRAG is used to improve the generation process of LLMs, enabling it to produce more accurate and contextually appropriate responses

4 Experiments

4.1 Evaluation

To evaluate the effectiveness of UKRAG model, we conduct extensive NLP experiments using several benchmark datasets.

Benchmark Datasets. Question Answering: Datasets: We evaluate UKRAG's performance on two question-answering datasets: NarrativeQA and QuALITY.

NarrativeQA consists of question-answer pairs derived from the full texts of books and movie transcripts, totaling 1,572 documents. [30]. The NarrativeQA-Story task requires a deep understanding of the entire narrative to answer the questions accurately, thus testing the model's ability to comprehend longer texts in the literary domain. Performance on this dataset is measured using the standard BLEU-1 and ROUGE metrics.

The QuALITY dataset features multiple-choice questions, each accompanied by context passages averaging approximately 5,000 tokens in length [31]. This dataset requires reasoning over the entire document for QA tasks, enabling us to assess the performance of our retrieval system on medium-length documents. We present controlled comparisons using the GPT-3.5-turbo and GPT-4 models on the NarrativeQA and QuALITY datasets. As shown in Tables 1 and 2.

Performance Metrics. To measure the accuracy of retrieving and generating correct information, we employ two widely-used performance metrics: ROUGE and BLEU-1.

- Recall-Oriented Understudy for Gisting Evaluation (ROUGE) is a set of metrics used to evaluate the quality of summaries by comparing them to reference summaries [32]. Specifically, we use ROUGE to assess the overlap of n-grams, word sequences, and word pairs between the generated answers and the reference answers. The primary ROUGE metrics we focus on are: ROUGE-N: Measures the overlap of n-grams between the generated and reference texts. For example, ROUGE-1 considers unigram overlap, while ROUGE-2 considers bigram overlap. ROUGE-L: Measures the longest common subsequence between the generated and reference texts, capturing the fluency and informativeness of the generated text. ROUGE provides a comprehensive evaluation of how well the model's output matches the expected answers, ensuring that the generated information is both accurate and relevant.
- BLEU-1 (Bilingual Evaluation Understudy) BLEU-1 is a precision-based metric used to evaluate the quality of text which has been machine-translated from one language to another. In the context of question-answering, we use BLEU-1 to measure the overlap of unigrams between the generated and reference answers [33]. BLEU-1 focuses on the precision of the generated text, ensuring that the words used in the answers are correct and relevant to the questions posed.

  By employing both ROUGE and BLEU-1, we obtain a balanced assessment of the model's performance. ROUGE ensures the generated content is comprehensive and fluent, while BLEU-1 ensures it is precise and relevant. These metrics together provide a robust evaluation framework for measuring the accuracy of information retrieval and generation in our experiments.

Comparative Analysis. Baseline Comparison of the performance of UKRAG model with traditional RAG models and other state-of-the-art approaches. We first present controlled comparisons using GPT-3.5-turbo, GPT-4 with and without RAG on toe different datasets NarrativeQA and QuALITY. our results demonstrate that UKRAG, when combined with any retriever, consistently outperforms the respective retriever across both datasets.

- As shown in Tables 1 and 2, the longest common subsequence between the generated answers and the reference answers using Higher ROUGE-L scores indicate that the models are generating answers that are more similar in structure and content to the reference answers. From the results:

  GPT-4 consistently outperforms GPT-3.5-Turbo across all configurations (without RAG, with RAG, and with UKRAG), indicating that UKRAG produces more fluent and informative answers that align closely with the reference answers. GPT-4-UKRAG outperforms GPT-4-RAG by 4% which considered a good enhancement.
- The precision of the generated answers using BLEU-1 scores is similar to ROUGE-L: GPT-4 achieves higher BLEU-1 scores compared to GPT-3.5-Turbo in all configurations. This suggests that UKRAG not only produces more accurate answers but also uses more relevant words that are found in the reference answers.

- Effect of RAG and UKRAG: The addition of RAG techniques and UKRAG generally improves performance across both metrics for both GPT-3.5-Turbo and GPT-4 models on both of the datasets. UKRAG generally shows a higher improvement in ROUGE-L and BLEU-1 scores compared to RAG, suggesting it contributes more significantly to the model's ability to retrieve and generate accurate answers. This enhancement indicates that incorporating mechanisms to retrieve relevant information before generating answers leads to better performance in terms of both fluency (ROUGE-L) and precision (BLEU-1).

Furthermore, the comparative analysis highlighted that integrating UKRAG led to significant enhancements over traditional RAG approaches. Particularly, the synergy of structured data hierarchy and unstructured text chunking within the unified knowledge graph framework proved pivotal in advancing the capabilities of RAG models in handling complex queries and generating contextually appropriate responses. By following this methodology, we aim to demonstrate the effectiveness of integrating structured and unstructured data into UKRAG for enhancing the performance of RAG models. Our approach addresses the limitations of existing methods and paves the way for future advancements in NLP and AI.

Table 1. NarrativeQA Performance With + Without UKRAG: Performance comparison of various retrieval models (GTP-3.5-Turbo, GPT-4, DPR) with and without RAG and UKRAG on the NarrativeQA dataset, UKRAG outperforms baselines of each respective retrieval model.

Model	ROUGE-L	BLEU-1
GPT-3.5-Turbo	40%	24%
GPT-4	72%	32%
GPT-3.5-Turbo-RAG	52%	31%
GPT-4-RAG	85%	43%
GPT-3.5-Turbo-UKRAG	65%	44%
GPT-4-UKRAG	89%	49%

Table 2. QuALITY Performance With + Without UKRAG: Performance comparison of various retrieval models (GTP-3.5-Turbo, GPT-4, DPR) with and without RAG and UKRAG on the QuALITY dataset, UKRAG outperforms baselines of each respective retrieval model.

Model	ROUGE-L	BLEU-1
GPT-3.5-Turbo	42%	25%
GPT-4	73%	34%
GPT-3.5-Turbo-RAG	55%	34%
GPT-4-RAG	87%	45%
GPT-3.5-Turbo-UKRAG	69%	48%
GPT-4-UKRAG	92%	52%

5 Conclusion

In this study, we introduced and evaluated the Unified Knowledge Graph Retrieval-Augmented Generation (UKRAG) model, designed to enhance the performance of Large Language Models (LLMs) in question-answering tasks by integrating structured and unstructured data sources. Our approach leverages the construction of a unified knowledge graph that seamlessly merges hierarchical structured data with unstructured text, providing a cohesive information retrieval and generation framework.

Through extensive experiments on the NarrativeQA and QuALITY datasets, we demonstrated the efficacy of UKRAG compared to traditional RAG models using GPT-3.5-Turbo and GPT-4 as generative engines. The results consistently showed that UKRAG, when combined with any retriever, outperformed its counterparts across various metrics.

Specifically, UKRAG achieved substantial improvements in both ROUGE-L and BLEU-1 scores. The higher ROUGE-L scores indicate that UKRAG generated answers closely aligned with the structure and content of reference answers, demonstrating its ability to maintain context and fluency. Concurrently, the elevated BLEU-1 scores underscored UKRAG's precision in selecting relevant words that are crucial for accurate responses.

In conclusion, our study underscores the potential of integrating structured and unstructured data into a unified knowledge graph to propel the evolution of Retrieval-Augmented Generation models. The findings not only validate the effectiveness of UKRAG in enhancing information retrieval and generation tasks but also pave the way for future advancements in Artificial Intelligence and Natural Language Processing research.

References

1. Sarthi, P., Abdullah, S., Tuli, A., Khanna, S., Goldie, A., Manning, C.D.: Raptor: recursive abstractive processing for tree-organized retrieval (2024)
2. Chen, D., Fisch, A., Weston, J., Bordes, A.: Reading Wikipedia to answer open-domain questions. In: Proceedings of the 55th Annual Meeting of the Association for Computational Linguistics (Volume 1: Long Papers), pp. 1870–1879. Association for Computational Linguistics (2017)
3. Akyurek, E., et al.: Towards tracing knowledge in language models back to the training data. In: Findings of the Association for Computational Linguistics: EMNLP, pp. 2429–2446. Association for Computational Linguistics (2022)
4. Al-kouz, A., Awajan, A., Jeet, M., Al-Zaqqa, A.: Extracting Arabic semantic graph from aljazeera.net. In: 2013 IEEE Jordan Conference on Applied Electrical Engineering and Computing Technologies (AEECT), pp. 1–6 (2013)
5. Biltawi, S.T.M., Awajan, A., Al-Kouz, A.: Exploiting multilingual Wikipedia to improve Arabic named entity resources. Int. Arab J. Inf. Technol. **14**(4A), 598–607 (2017)
6. Akram, A.-K.: An interests discovery approach in social networks based on a semantically enriched Bayesian network model. In: International Conference on Knowledge Discovery and Information Retrieval (KDIR-2012), pp. 300–305 (2012)

7. Brown, T.B.: Language models are few-shot learners (2020)
8. Achiam, J., et al.: GPT-4 technical report (2024)
9. Liu, N.F.: Lost in the middle: how language models use long contexts (2023)
10. Sun, S., Krishna, K., Mattarella-Micke, A., Iyyer, M.: Do long-range language models actually use long-range context? In: Moens, M.-F., Huang, X., Specia, L., Yih, S.W. (eds.) Proceedings of the 2021 Conference on Empirical Methods in Natural Language Processing, Online and Punta Cana, Dominican Republic, pp. 807–822. Association for Computational Linguistics (2021). https://aclanthology.org/2021.emnlp-main.62
11. Yu, W., et al.: Generate rather than retrieve: large language models are strong context generators (2023)
12. Nair, I., et al.: A neural CRF-based hierarchical approach for linear text segmentation. In: Vlachos, A., Augenstein, I. (eds.) Findings of the Association for Computational Linguistics: EACL 2023, Dubrovnik, Croatia, pp. 883–893. Association for Computational Linguistics (2023). https://aclanthology.org/2023.findings-eacl.65
13. Lewis, P.: Retrieval-augmented generation for knowledge-intensive NLP tasks (2020)
14. Ji, S., Pan, S., Cambria, E., Marttinen, P., Yu, P.S.: A survey on knowledge graphs: representation, acquisition, and applications. IEEE Trans. Neural Netw. Learn. Syst. **33**(2), 494–514 (2022). https://doi.org/10.1109/TNNLS.2021.3070843
15. Auer, S., Bizer, C., Kobilarov, G., Lehmann, J., Cyganiak, R., Ives, Z.: DBpedia: a nucleus for a web of open data. In: Aberer, K. (eds.) The Semantic Web, pp. 722–735. Springer, Heidelberg (2007)
16. Tanon, T.P., Vrandečić, D., Schaffert, S., Steiner, T., Pintscher, L.: From freebase to wikidata: the great migration. In: World Wide Web Conference (2016)
17. Pan, S., Luo, L., Wang, Y., Chen, C., Wang, J., Wu, X.: Unifying large language models and knowledge graphs: a roadmap. arXiv preprint arXiv:2306.08302 (2023)
18. Liu, W., et al.: K-BERT: enabling language representation with knowledge graph (2019)
19. Sun, Y., et al.: Ernie: enhanced representation through knowledge integration (2019)
20. Soman, K., et al.: Biomedical knowledge graph-optimized prompt generation for large language models (2024)
21. Smith, S., et al.: Using deepspeed and megatron to train megatron-turing NLG 530b, a large-scale generative language model (2022)
22. Sen, P., Mavadia, S., Saffari, A.: Knowledge graph-augmented language models for complex question answering. In: Dalvi Mishra, B., Durrett, G., Jansen, P., Neves Ribeiro, D., Wei, J. (eds.) Proceedings of the 1st Workshop on Natural Language Reasoning and Structured Explanations (NLRSE), Toronto, Canada, pp. 1–8. Association for Computational Linguistics (2023). https://aclanthology.org/2023.nlrse-1.1
23. Cao, S., Wang, L.: Hibrids: attention with hierarchical biases for structure-aware long document summarization (2022)
24. Sang, Z.: A relevance theory perspective on translating the implicit information in literary texts (2006). https://api.semanticscholar.org/CorpusID:8891885
25. OpenAI API. https://platform.openai.com/docs/api-reference/introduction. Accessed 12 June 2024
26. pypdf. https://pypi.org/project/pypdf/. Accessed 07 Mar 2024
27. pydantic. https://docs.pydantic.dev/latest/concepts/models/. Accessed 15 June 2024

28. m. . . p. . . t. . I. d. . . M Biltawi, A Awajan, S Tedmori, Al-Kouz Akram, year = 2017
29. Marwah Alian, A.A.-K., Awajan, A.: Arabic word sense disambiguation-survey. In: 2017 International Conference on New Trends in Computing Sciences (ICTCS), pp. 236–240 (2017)
30. Kočiský, T., et al.: The narrativeqa reading comprehension challenge (2017)
31. Pang, R.Y., et al.: QuALITY: question answering with long input texts, yes!. In: Carpuat, M., de Marneffe, M.-C., Meza Ruiz, I.V. (eds.) Proceedings of the 2022 Conference of the North American Chapter of the Association for Computational Linguistics: Human Language Technologies, Seattle, United States, pp. 5336–5358. Association for Computational Linguistics (2022). https://aclanthology.org/2022.naacl-main.391
32. Lin, C.-Y.: ROUGE: a package for automatic evaluation of summaries. In: Text Summarization Branches Out. Barcelona, Spain, pp. 74–81. Association for Computational Linguistics (2004) https://aclanthology.org/W04-1013
33. Papineni, K., Roukos, S., Ward, T., Zhu, W.J.: Bleu: a method for automatic evaluation of machine translation (2002)

Heart Disease Analysis and Prediction with Machine Learning Techniques Using Cleveland Dataset

Kishore Govindaraju[1] and Govindaraju Kalimuthu[2](✉)

[1] Vellore Institute of Technology, Chennai, India
[2] Higher Colleges of Technology, Fujairah, United Arab Emirates
grajukm@gmail.com

Abstract. For the past two decades, heart diseases have been the major cause of deaths worldwide. Various risk factors along with aging population, and evolving lifestyles have been major contributors for their prevalence. The World Health Organization has made various efforts to emphasize the need to address the ongoing challenge of cardiovascular diseases on a global scale. Adopting Machine Learning (ML) algorithms can be utilized by health care officials to study and analyze the risk of various medical conditions and furthermore, come up with better diagnostic tools to treat the same. The Machine Learning tools study the datasets provided to them, analyse them for patterns and scan the factors for relationships among them gaining knowledge on how every factor affects the final outcome. The primary focus of this research is based on the implementation of advanced machine learning techniques to predict and prevent heart diseases using the Cleveland dataset. Careful preprocessing which includes outlier removal, missing data imputation and feature scaling has been applied on the dataset. Exploratory data analysis has been conducted to understand the relationships between various factors contributing to heart diseases. Amongst the various ML techniques used, XGBoost has shown impressive accuracies of up to 95%. In addition to that, the ROC curve analysis exhibits an exceptional under the curve area of 0.99 emphasizing on the model's ability to differentiate between positive and negative outcomes efficiently. Findings from this study underscore the efficacy of employing ML techniques. The results obtained help contribute to the ongoing efforts of leveraging data driven methods to enhance the prediction and prevention of cardiovascular diseases.

Keywords: Heart disease · Cleveland Data set · Machine Learning Techniques · XG Boost's · ROC Curve Analysis

1 Introduction

Heart diseases remain to be a leading global cause of death [1] According to the World Health Organization (WHO), cardiovascular diseases (CVDs) have accounted for nearly 17.9 million deaths in 2019, representing nearly one-third of all global deaths. Their existence varies acrossnumerous regions taking a specific individual's lifestyle, risk factors,

A. Safi et al. (Eds.): ISICS 2024, CCIS 2381, pp. 20–43, 2025.
https://doi.org/10.1007/978-3-031-82931-4_2

genetics and many more into account [2]. Machine Learning techniques have evolutionized the field of medical science by providing innovative and advanced solutions on a global scale. The techniques implemented by ML algorithms have played a crucial role in the prediction of various diseases by leveraging vast datasets and analyzing complex relationships to study patterns between important factors of the dataset [5]. The range of services that can be done by ML models seem to be endless [6]. Continued collaboration between healthcare providers and data scientists plays a vital role in maximizing the health benefits that can be provided to fellow individuals. Various studies have explored the effectiveness of ML models in analyzing the Cleveland heart disease dataset to predict heart diseases with varying accuracies for different models. Employing Machine Learning techniques in preventing heart disease, particularly using the Cleveland Heart Disease Dataset has been a subject of extensive research. This dataset comprises of various factors leading to heart diseases while also offering a rich resource for the development for ML models [7]. Ensemble methods, like Random Forests show great promise by leveraging multiple decision trees to enhance capability thus providing greater accuracies. Support Vector Machines (SVMs) have also shown success in capturing non-linear relationships which contribute to the improved classification performance. Logistic regression has been deployed most frequently due to its success in capturing the relationships that lead to heart diseases. Studies such as Logistic regression technique for prediction of cardiovascular disease Ambrish et al. [8] has explored the use of Logistic Regression models. These models, characterized by their interpretability, effectively capture the relationships between various risk factors and the likelihood of heart disease occurrence with an average accuracy of 87.10%. Research by Madhumita Pal et al. on Risk prediction of cardiovascular disease using machine learning classifiers [9] have taken an experimental approach using two reliable machine learning techniques, MLP and KNN with an accuracy of 82.47% and an area under the curve value of 86.41% whereas studies by Chandrasekhar et al. on the topic Enhancing Heart Disease Prediction Accuracy through Machine Learning Techniques and Optimization show an accuracy of 93.44% on the Cleveland dataset which was achieved by a soft voting ensemble classifier containing all six algorithms [10]. Karthick et al. [11] investigated the efficacy of Support Vector Machines in heart disease prediction which obtained the highest accuracy of 80.32% from their journal Implementation of a Heart Disease Risk Prediction Model Using Machine Learning SVM, known for its capability to identify complex patterns in data, demonstrated promising results in capturing nuanced relationships within the Cleveland dataset. Taking the study proposed by Ibomoiye Domor Mienye, Yanxia Sun (Professor), Zenghui Wang (Professor) on the topic an improved ensemble learning approach for the prediction of heart disease risk an [12] as an example, they have proposed a new technique using CART and classifier ensemble WAE to boost the accuracy of their ML model with reference to the cleveland dataset. An ensemble method based multilayer dynamic system to predict cardiovascular disease using machine learning approach by Uddin and Halder [13] have deployed an intelligent agent designed to predict cardiovascular diseases, a layer to layer prediction system is employed that is capable of increasing its knowledge at each level. New studies show a hybrid model seems to show high accuracy in predicting if an individual is affected with heart diseases or not. A hybrid model is a mix of Random forest and Decision trees, the journal Heart Disease Prediction using Hybrid machine Learning Model by Kavitha et al. [15] seem to have used a hybrid model to attain accuracies close to 88.7%. The literature on ML techniques applied to predict heart diseases using the Cleveland dataset holds great promise for the risk assessment of cardiovascular diseases enhancing early detection and personalized intervention strategies. So, in this Research, the Cleveland dataset related to heart diseases has been studied and machine learning models were built to predict the occurrence of heart related diseases. Appropriate pre-process and cleaning of data was done to the dataset before building the models. A maximum accuracy of 96% was achieved using XGBoost, which can further be increased with the help of deep learning techniques. Various metric such as accuracy, sensitivity, specificity, precision and area under the Receiver Operating Characteristic (ROC) curve have also been utilized to compare the performance of our ML models [9].

2 Machine Learning Models

2.1 Logistic Regression

This is one of the most popular ML algorithms that's comes under the category of supervised Learning technique. We choose this particular algorithm for the Cleveland heart disease dataset, as the Cleveland dataset usually consists of a binary outcome which indicates if a person has a heart disease or not. Also since there is a linear relationship among data, therefore using Logistic regression can be advantageous as it simplifies the creation of the model.

$$P(Y = 1) = \frac{1}{1 + e^{-(\beta_0 + \beta_1 x_1 + \beta_2 x_2 + \cdots + \beta_n x_n)}} \tag{1}$$

2.2 Random Forest

Random Forest is a popular ensemble learning technique that is used for both classification and regression tasks, here we will be using Random Forest classification technique for our model. We use Random Forest as it tends to give us high accuracies and it can also capture complex and non-linear relationships between data present in the dataset. One another important advantage is it is less prone to overfitting which is a robust choice for datasets with relatively small number of samples.

2.3 Support Vector Machines (SVMs)

SVMs are another popular machine learning algorithm which us used for classification tasks. It works by creating a hyperplane that separates data into different classes with its aim to maximize the margin between the classes. They are effective in high-Dimensional spaces which makes them suitable for datasets with a large number of features, they are also robust to overfitting and can handle non-linear relationships.

$$(x) = sign(w \cdot x + b) \tag{2}$$

2.4 XGBoost

Extreme Gradient Boosting is a powerful and popular ML algorithm that is also used for both classification and regression tasks. Due to its high performance and flexibility, we use this algorithm. XGboost uses gradient boosting which helps reduce a loss function by iteratively adding weak learners. This way, complex relationships between the data is captured. It also employs a technique called tree pruning which prunces the branches of the trees that contribute less to the reduction of the loss function thus avoiding overfitting.

$$Y_{XGBoost}(X) = \sum_{i=0}^{T} f_i(X) \quad (3)$$

2.5 K-Nearest Neighbors (KNN)

KNN is yet another simple yet effective ML algorithm that is used commonly for classification tasks. It doesn't make assumptions about the distribution of the data but instead relies on the proximity of instances in feature space. KNN is very adaptive to different type of datasets including the ones with non-linear decision boundaries.

$$Y = mode(\{Y_1, Y_2, \ldots\ldots Y_k\}) \quad (4)$$

3 Materials Methodology

This paper's primary goal is to showcase the findings and present the accuracies of various ML models (Logistic regression, Random Forest, Support Vector Machines (SVMs), XGBoost and K-Nearest Neighbors (KNN)) employed to predict the certainty of heart diseases. References were taken from a couple of previous published journals on the same topic from renowned research websites such as Springer, Elsevier and IEEE. Google Collab notebook was used to write the codes for the proposed model. The code was written in Python language.

3.1 Dataset Description

The Cleveland Heart Disease dataset is a widely recognized collection of data originating from the Cleveland Clinic Foundation, extensively employed in machine learning and cardiovascular research. It consists of 14 attributes containing crucial clinical and demographic information such as age, sex, chest pain type, blood pressure, cholesterol levels, and electrocardiographic results [16]. The certainty of getting affected by a heart disease is represented in binary where (1) stands for a positive outcome and (0) stands for a negative outcome. Numerous researchers utilize this dataset to build ML models and predict the outcome of their models to understand the effectiveness of their model in predicting the occurrence of heart diseases.

3.2 Dataset Depiction

The Cleveland dataset comprising of 14 attributes along with their respective explanation is attached in Table 1 [17].

Table 2 is a sample of how the dataset would look like, only a few rows are printed for reference:

Table 1. Cleveland heart disease dataset

Features	Description
Age	Years of age
Sex	Sex (male = 1; female = 0)
Cp	Type of chest pain Standard angina is value 1, Atypical angina is value 2, Non-anginal pain, value 3, Value 4 indicates asymptomatic
Trestbps	Blood pressure at rest at the time of hospital admission (in mm Hg).
Chol	Per deciliter, the amount of serum cholesterol.
Fbs	Above 120 mg/dl of fasting blood sugar is present (1 is true; 0 is false).
Restecg	Findings of resting electrocardiography Value 0: regular, Value 1 indicates that the ST-T wave is aberrant (T wave inversions, ST elevation, or ST depression of greater than 0.05 mV), Value 2: demonstrating potential or actual left ventricular hypertrophy according to Estes' criteria.
Thalach	Maximal heart rate reached
Exang	Exercise-induced angina (1 = yes; 0 = no)
Oldpeak	Compared to rest, exercise promotes ST depression.
Slope	The incline of the ST segment of the summit exercise Value 1 slopes upward, Value 2 is level, and Value 3 is sliding downward.
Ca	Main vessels colored by fluoroscopy in number (0–3) (for calcification of vessels)
Thal	Results of the nuclear stress test (normal: 3, fixed: 6, and reversible: 7)
Num	Target variable (angiographic disease status) showing the presence of heart disease in any major vessel Value 0: A diameter reduction of 50%. Value 1: More than 50% diameter narrowing

Table 2. Sample of Cleveland Data set

age	sex	cp	trtbps	chol	fbs	restecg	thalachh	exng	oldpeak	slp	caa	thall	output
63	1	3	145	233	1	0	150	0	2.3	0	0	1	1
37	1	2	130	250	0	1	187	0	3.5	0	0	2	1
41	0	1	130	204	0	0	172	0	1.4	2	0	2	1
56	1	1	120	236	0	1	178	0	0.8	2	0	2	1
57	0	0	120	354	0	1	163	1	0.6	2	0	2	1
57	1	0	140	192	0	1	148	0	0.4	1	0	1	1
56	0	1	140	294	0	0	153	0	1.3	1	0	2	1
44	1	1	120	263	0	1	173	0	0	2	0	3	1
52	1	2	172	199	1	1	162	0	0.5	2	0	3	1
57	1	2	150	168	0	1	174	0	1.6	2	0	2	1

Show 10 per page 1 2 10 30 31

3.3 Sequential Order of Building of the ML Model

Necessary functions from Python library were imported to the ML model. After importing the dataset and visualizing the values, missing values are checked for:

```
[ ] #checking for missing values
    df.isnull().sum()

    age         0
    sex         0
    cp          0
    trtbps      0
    chol        0
    fbs         0
    restecg     0
    thalachh    0
    exng        0
    oldpeak     0
    slp         0
    caa         0
    thall       0
    output      0
    dtype: int64
```

Since there are no missing values, duplicate values are looked for and dropped:

```
[ ] #looking for duplicate values
    df.duplicated().sum()

    1

[ ] #display duplicated data
    df[df.duplicated()]
```

	age	sex	cp	trtbps	chol	fbs	restecg	thalachh	exng	oldpeak	slp	caa	thall	output
164	38	1	2	138	175	0	1	173	0	0.0	2	4	2	1

Once this is done, duplicated values are checked again just to be sure. Next, Fig. 1 below shows the correlation between the data present in the dataset:

Correlation

```
[ ] plt.figure(figsize=(16,8))
    sns.heatmap(df.corr(),annot=True,cmap='Reds')
```

```
<Axes: >
```

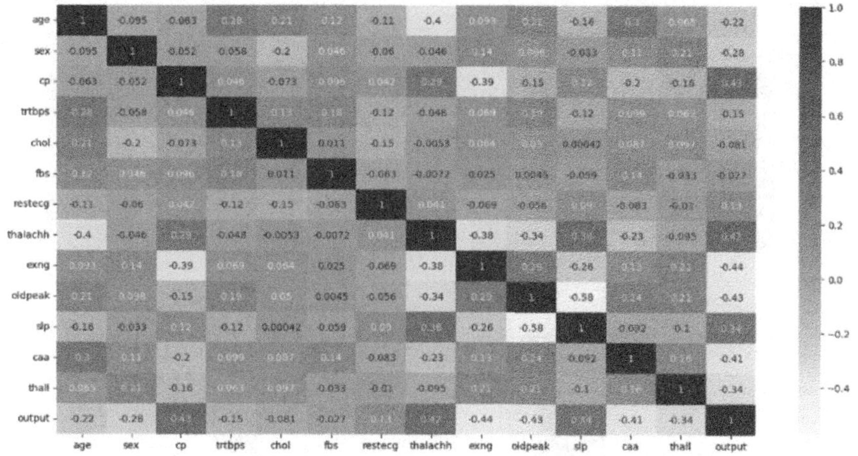

Fig. 1. Correlation between the data present in the dataset

Similarly, an examination is done on how every variable in the dataset is related to the output using the following code snippet:

```
[ ] correlation_matrix = df.corr()
    correlation_matrix["output"]
```

```
age        -0.221476
sex        -0.283609
cp          0.432080
trtbps     -0.146269
chol       -0.081437
fbs        -0.026826
restecg     0.134874
thalachh    0.419955
exng       -0.435601
oldpeak    -0.429146
slp         0.343940
caa        -0.408992
thall      -0.343101
output      1.000000
Name: output, dtype: float64
```

The datasets are visualized to gain a deeper insight on how every variable present in the dataset is related to one another and to the final output with the help of various plots and graphs, the plot Fig. 2 shows the prevalence of heart attack caused by various factors with respect to the output (Possibility of heart attack), where 0 represents lower probability and 1 represents higher probability of heart attack.

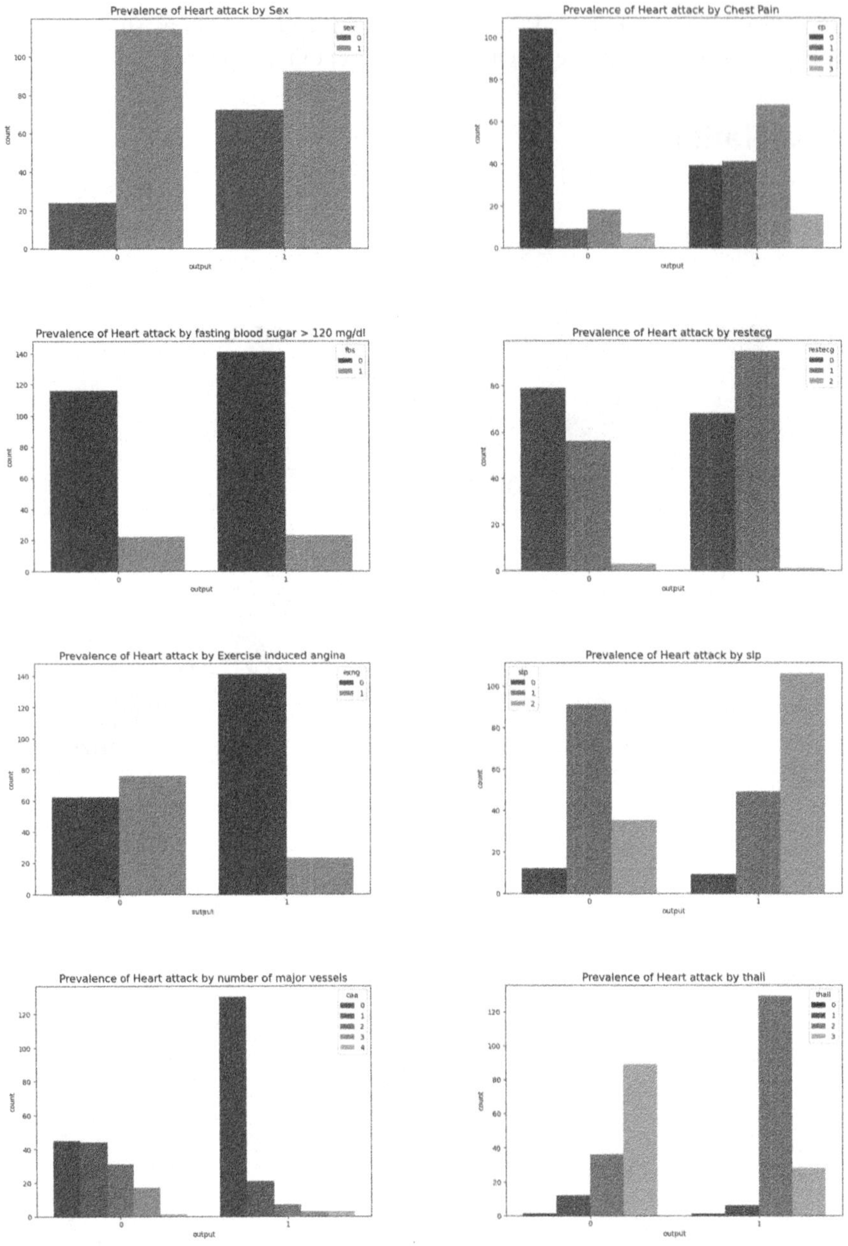

Fig. 2. Bar plot of factors leading to heart attack

The plot (Fig. 3) below depicts a scatter plot to visualize the relationship between the variables ‘age’ and ‘cholesterol’ with different levels of chest pain that is color-coded by the ‘output’ variable:

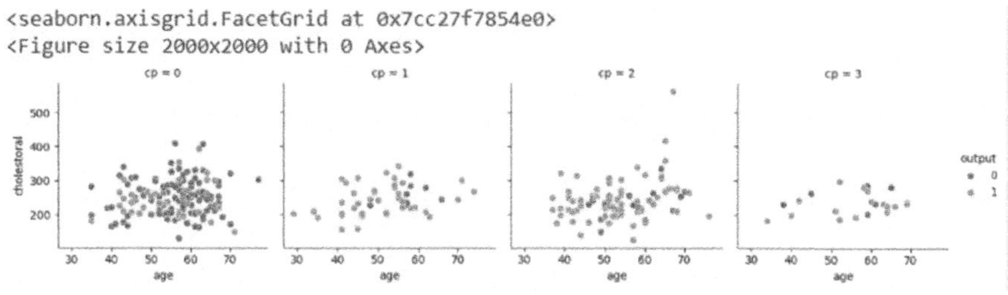

Fig. 3. Cholesterol vs age scatter plot

Figure 4 below generates a bar plot of the variables 'thalach' against 'slp'(Slope) with the bars colored by the 'output' and Fig. 5 generates a box plot of 'age' against 'restecg' with boxes colored by 'output':

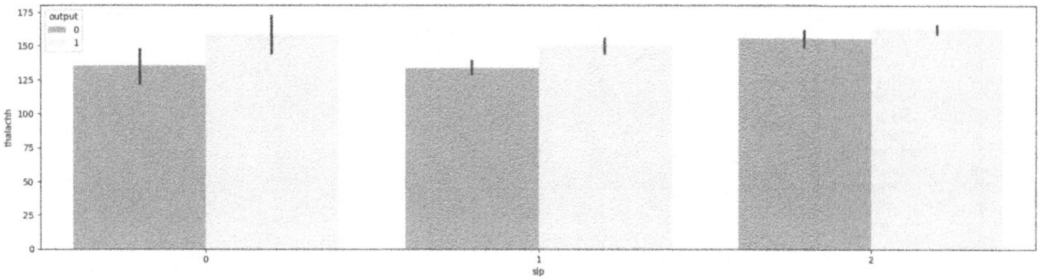

Fig. 4. Bar plot of thalach vs slp

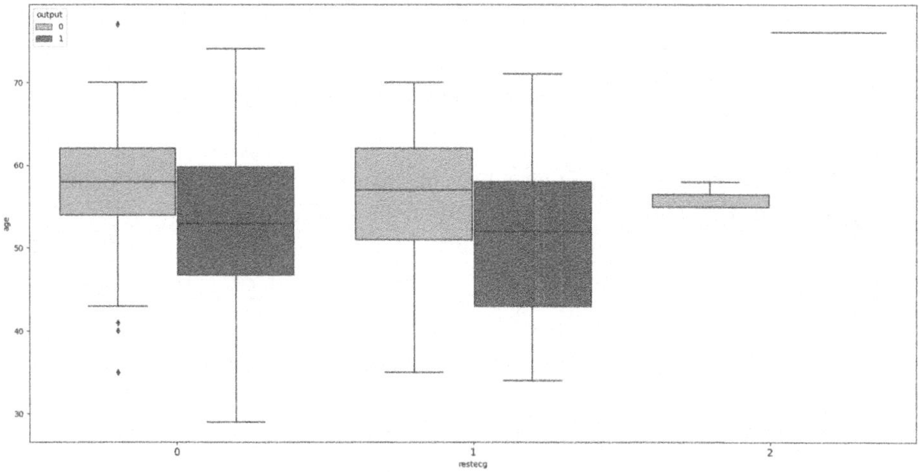

Fig. 5. Box plot of Age vs rectecg

The swarm plot Fig. 6 below visualizes the distribution of ages for each category of the variable 'ca' based on the 'output' variable:

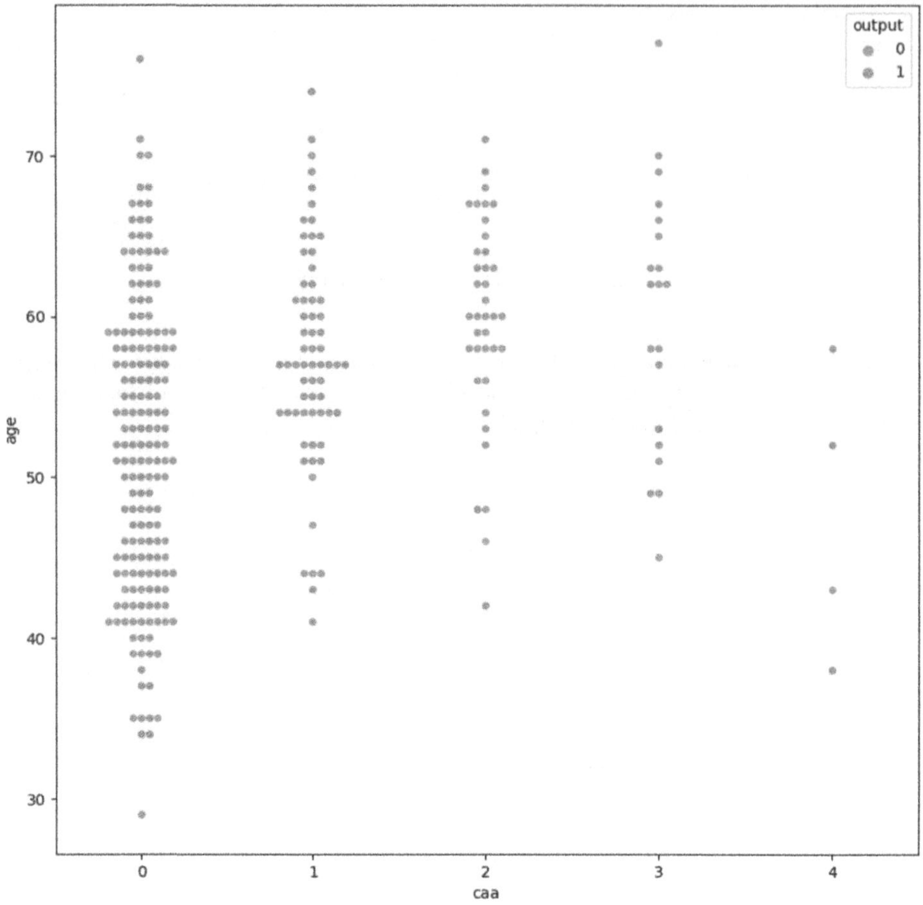

Fig. 6. Swarm plot of Age against ca

Finally, a violin plot Fig. 7 that visualizes the distribution of ages for different levels of Thallium and the violins are colored based on the 'output' variable:

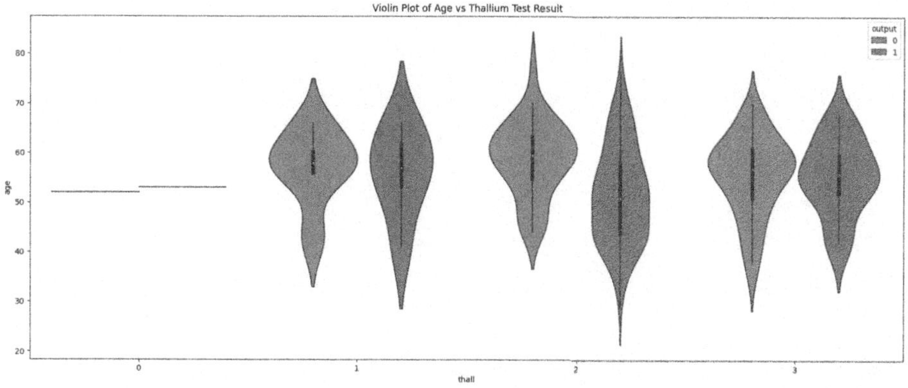

Fig. 7. Violin plot of age vs thall

Outliers are checked for in the dataset and removed accordingly:

```
Column age outliers = 0.0 => 0.00%
Column trtbps outliers = 13.0 => 4.30%
Column chol outliers = 5.0 => 1.66%
Column thalachh outliers = 1.0 => 0.33%
Column oldpeak outliers = 8.0 => 2.65%
```

Outliers are present at the following positions, visualization has been done with the help of boxplots (Fig. 8);

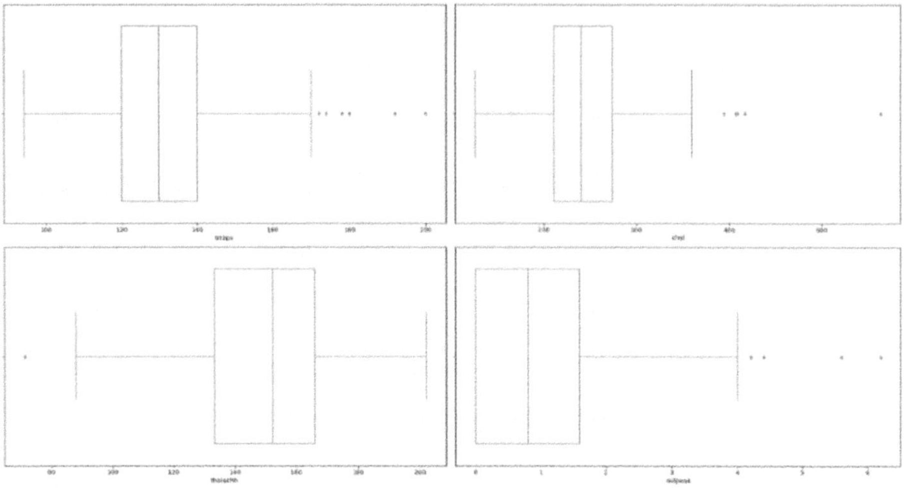

```
Outliers Present at position:

trtbps: (array([  8, 101, 110, 152, 194, 202, 222, 227, 240, 247, 259, 265, 291]),)
chol: (array([ 28,  85,  96, 219, 245]),)
thalachh: (array([271]),)
oldpeak: (array([101, 203, 220, 249, 290]),)
```

Fig. 8. Position of Outliers present

Therefore to treat the outliers, log transforms have been performed to minimize the values of the outliers, here are the changes to the outliers after the log transformation was done;

```
---Log Transform performed---
Column age outliers = 1 => 0.33%
Column trtbps outliers = 9 => 2.98%
Column chol outliers = 6 => 1.99%
Column thalachh outliers = 4 => 1.32%
Column oldpeak outliers = 8 => 2.65%
```

On an additional note, research related to removing outliers have also been performed similarly using the DBSCAN algorithm [13]. Next, the dataset is split into the Training set and the Test set to X_train, Y_train, X_test, Y_test with the test size set to 0.18:

```
from sklearn.model_selection import train_test_split
X=df.iloc[:, :-1].values
Y=df.iloc[:, -1].values
X_train, X_test, Y_train, Y_test = train_test_split(X, Y, test_size = 0.18, random_state = 9)
```

'X' consists of all the values in the dataset except the final output whereas 'Y' contains only the output row. After the splitting of the dataset, feature scaling is also done to the training set and the test set by using the StandardScaler() function.

4 Results Obtained and Visualization of Results:

4.1 Logistic Regression

Firstly, in order to maximize the accuracy of the LR model, the best random state is to be found. Iteratively testing different random states and evaluating the accuracies of the LR model for each random state and plot them (Fig. 9.)

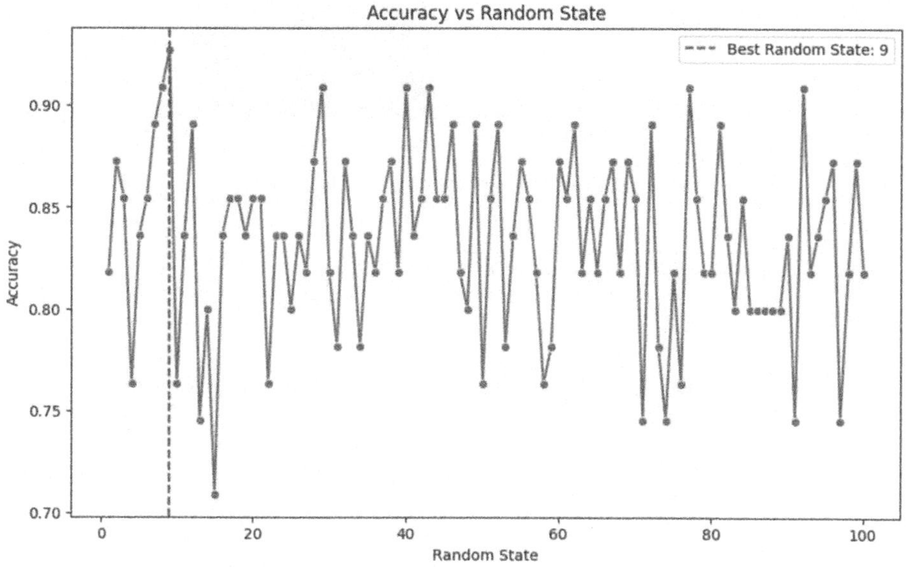

Fig. 9. Accuracy vs Random State

After plotting them against the graph, the graph shows the best random state to be 9. The logistic regression function with solver 'lbfgs' has been implemented to get the best accuracy with the best random state taken. The corresponding accuracy for the random state (best random state) turns out to be 92.73%. Here is the corresponding confusion matrix for the same (Fig. 10):

- True positive: 22 instances were predicted correctly as positive.
- False positive: 1 instance was incorrectly predicted as positive.
- False Negative: 3 instances were incorrectly predicted as negative.
- True Negative: 29 instances were correctly predicted as negative.

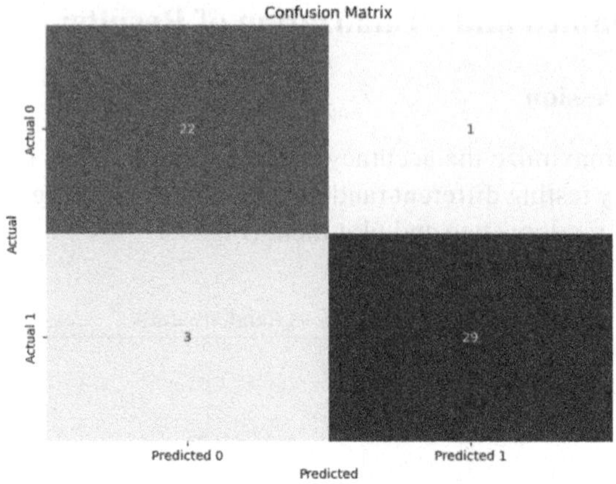

Fig. 10. Confusion Matrix for LR model

The corresponding classification report is as follows:

```
Classification Report:
              precision    recall  f1-score   support

           0       0.88      0.96      0.92        23
           1       0.97      0.91      0.94        32

    accuracy                           0.93        55
   macro avg       0.92      0.93      0.93        55
weighted avg       0.93      0.93      0.93        55
```

Here is how the variables in the classification report is calculated:

$$Accuracy = \frac{Number\ of\ Correct\ Preditions}{Total\ Number\ of\ Predictions} \times 100 \tag{5}$$

$$Precision = \frac{True\ Positive\ (TP)}{True\ Positive(TP) + False\ Positive\ (FP)} \tag{6}$$

$$Recall = \frac{True\ Positive\ (TP)}{True\ Positive(TP) + False\ Negative\ (FN)} \tag{7}$$

$$F1\ Score = 2 \times \frac{Precision \times Recall}{Precision + Recall} \tag{8}$$

Receiver Operating Characteristic (Roc) Curve of the LR Model is as follows (Fig. 11):

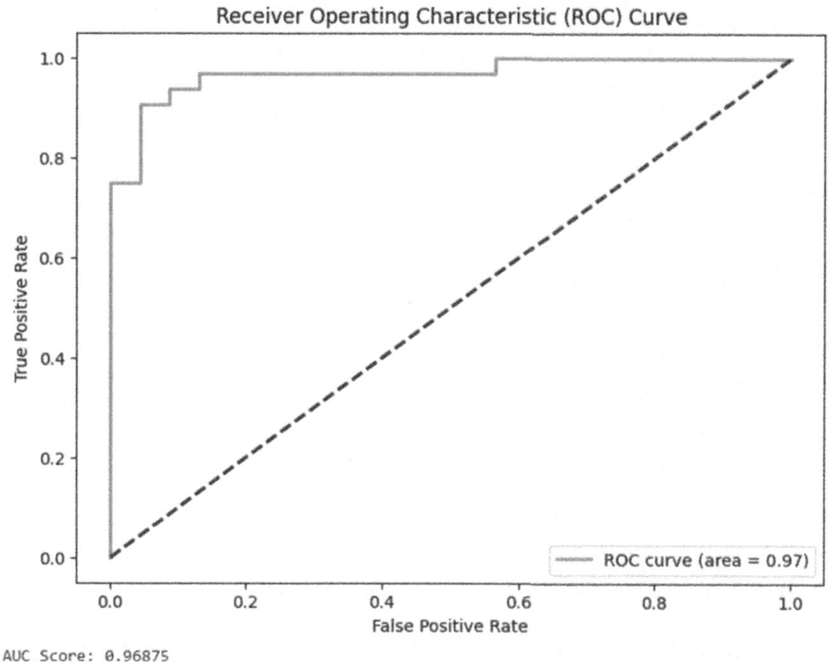

Fig. 11. Roc Curve of the LR Model

Here, the AUC Score and the Roc Curve Area almost score a perfect values of 1, which means the model that was chosen handles this dataset quite well.

4.2 Random Forest

Firstly, the best hyperparameters for the Random Forest model are to be found, in order to do so a Grid Search is performed with cross-validation to find the optimal values for estimators, random state and max depth, 'gini' criterion is used. The code snippet below shows how the grid search has been done to find the best hyper-parameters:

```
from sklearn.model_selection import GridSearchCV

# Define the parameter grid
param_grid = {
    'n_estimators': [100, 200, 300],
    'max_depth': [None, 10, 20, 30],
    'random_state': [5, 10, 15]
}

# Create the Random Forest model
rf_model = RandomForestClassifier()

# Use GridSearchCV to find the best hyperparameters
grid_search = GridSearchCV(estimator=rf_model, param_grid=param_grid, cv=5, scoring='accuracy')
grid_search.fit(X_train, Y_train)

# Get the best parameters
best_params = grid_search.best_params_

# Build the final model using the best parameters
final_model = RandomForestClassifier(**best_params)
final_model.fit(X_train, Y_train)
Y_pred_final = final_model.predict(X_test)

# Print the best parameters
print("Best Hyperparameters:", best_params)

# Print execution time and accuracy for the final model
final_model_time = time.time() - start
final_model_accuracy = round(accuracy_score(Y_test, Y_pred_final), 4) * 100  # Accuracy
print(f"Execution time of final model: {round(final_model_time, 5)} seconds")
print(f"Accuracy of final model: {final_model_accuracy}%")

# Plot and compute metrics for the final model
compute(Y_pred_final, Y_test)
```

The hyper-parameters obtained as per the Grid Search are as follows:

```
Best Hyperparameters: {'max_depth': 10, 'n_estimators': 200, 'random_state': 5}
```

The accuracy obtained for the following model is 91.80% The corresponding confusion matrix is as follows (Fig. 12):

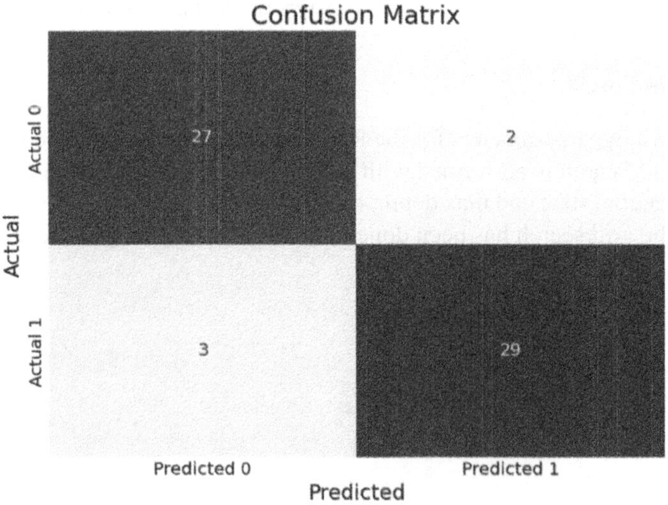

Fig. 12. Confusion matrix for Random Forest Model

The classification report is provided as well:

Classification Report:

	precision	recall	f1-score	support
0	0.90	0.93	0.92	29
1	0.94	0.91	0.92	32
accuracy			0.92	61
macro avg	0.92	0.92	0.92	61
weighted avg	0.92	0.92	0.92	61

The description of the parameters have already been provided when discussed about the LR Model, it applies to every other model as well. The ROC curve is as follows (Fig. 13):

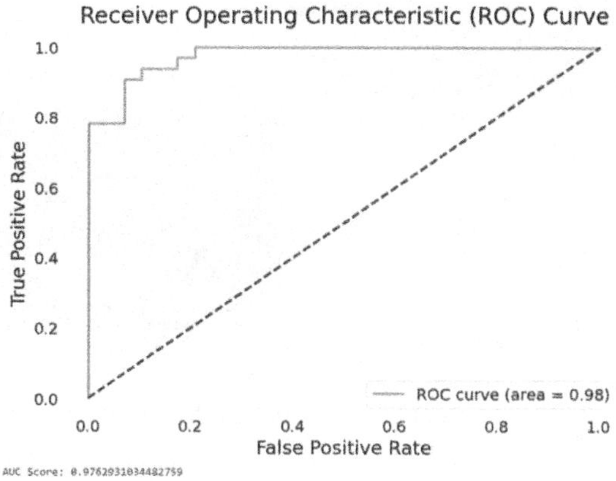

Fig. 13. Roc Curve of the Random Forest Model

The ROC curve area and the AUC score is also almost 1, it's a near perfect model for our dataset.

4.3 Support Vector Machines (SVMs)

The SVM model is created with the help of a radial basis function (RBF) kernel as this is commonly used for a variety of datasets. The confusion matrix is provided below (Fig. 14):

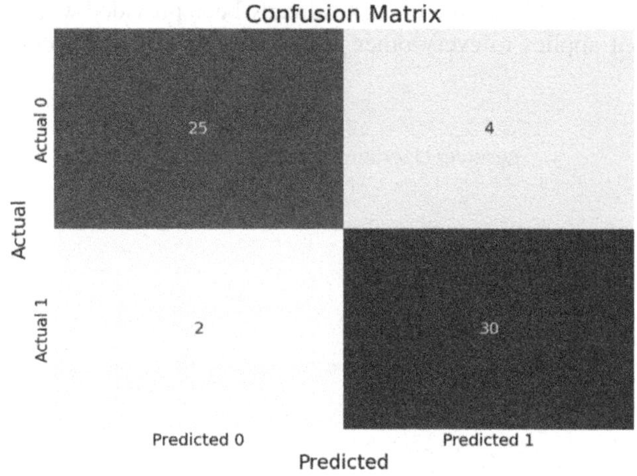

Fig. 14. Confusion matrix for SVM Model

The accuracy of the specific model turns out to be 90.16%. The classification report for the same is provided below:

Classification Report:

	precision	recall	f1-score	support
0	0.93	0.86	0.89	29
1	0.88	0.94	0.91	32
accuracy			0.90	61
macro avg	0.90	0.90	0.90	61
weighted avg	0.90	0.90	0.90	61

The ROC curve is provided below for the specific model (Fig. 15):

From the graph obtained its evident that the high score doesn't complement with the low accuracy obtained relatively, this is not uncommon when dealing in scenarios with imbalanced classes which happens to be so in this case.

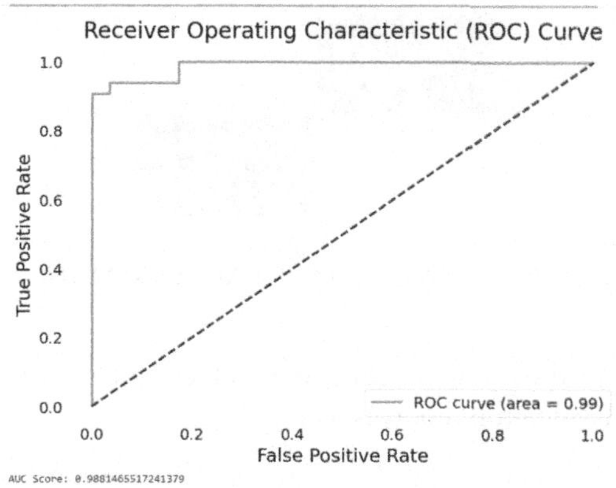

Fig. 15. Roc Curve of the SVM Model

4.4 XGBoost

Again, to find the best hyper-parameters for our XGBoost model Grid Search technique is implemented with cross-validation to find the optimal values for 'n_estimators', 'colsample_bytree', 'learning_rate' and 'max_depth'. Binary: logistic is used as this is a binary classification-based problem. The below code snippet shows the best hyper-parameters obtained:

```
from sklearn.model_selection import GridSearchCV
from xgboost import XGBClassifier

# Define the parameter grid
param_grid = {
    'n_estimators': [50, 100, 150],
    'colsample_bytree': [0.5, 0.7, 1.0],
    'learning_rate': [0.1, 0.01, 0.001],
    'max_depth': [1, 3, 5]
}

# Create the XGBoost model
xgb_model = XGBClassifier(objective='binary:logistic')

# Use GridSearchCV to find the best hyperparameters
grid_search = GridSearchCV(estimator=xgb_model, param_grid=param_grid, cv=5, scoring='accuracy')
grid_search.fit(X_train, Y_train)

# Get the best parameters
best_params = grid_search.best_params_

# Build the final model using the best parameters
final_model_xgb = XGBClassifier(objective='binary:logistic', **best_params)
final_model_xgb.fit(X_train, Y_train)
Y_pred_final_xgb = final_model_xgb.predict(X_test)

# Print the best parameters
print("Best Hyperparameters:", best_params)

# Print execution time and accuracy for the final model
final_model_xgb_time = time.time() - start
final_model_xgb_accuracy = round(accuracy_score(Y_test, Y_pred_final_xgb), 4) * 100  # Accuracy
print(f"Execution time of final XGBoost model: {round(final_model_xgb_time, 5)} seconds")
print(f"Accuracy of final XGBoost model: {final_model_xgb_accuracy}%")

# Plot and compute metrics for the final XGBoost model
compute(Y_pred_final_xgb, Y_test)
```

The best Hyperparameters are as follows:

```
Best Hyperparameters: {'colsample_bytree': 0.5, 'learning_rate': 0.1, 'max_depth': 1, 'n_estimators': 100}
```

Here is the corresponding confusion matrix (Fig. 16):

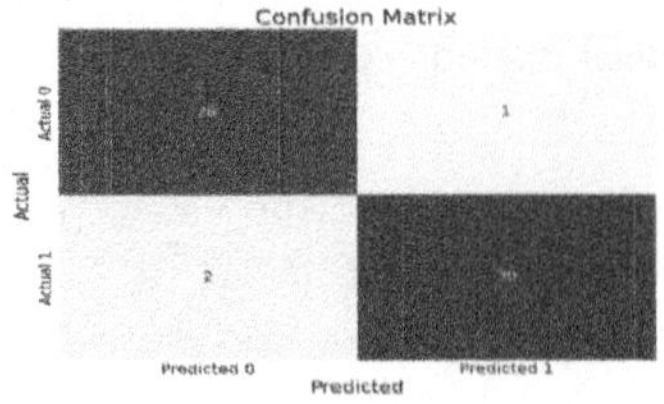

Fig. 16. Confusion matrix for XG Boost Model

The accuracy obtained for this model and also the highest turns out to be 95.08%. The corresponding classification report is as follows:

```
Classification Report:
              precision    recall  f1-score   support

           0       0.93      0.97      0.95        29
           1       0.97      0.94      0.95        32

    accuracy                           0.95        61
   macro avg       0.95      0.95      0.95        61
weighted avg       0.95      0.95      0.95        61
```

The ROC curve is attached below (Fig. 17):

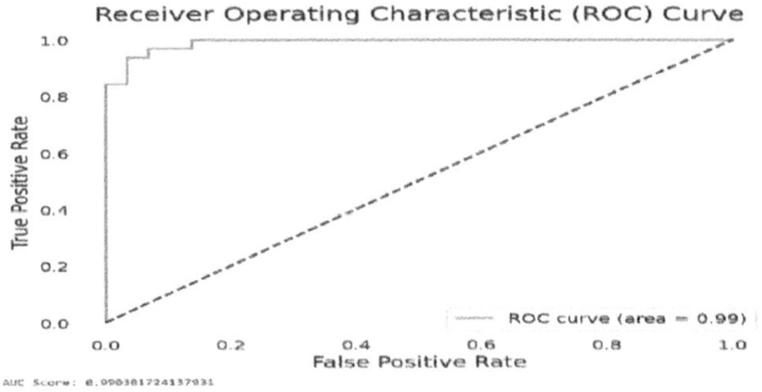

Fig. 17. Roc Curve of the XGBoost Model

The obtained value of the area under the ROC curve and the AUC score is 0.99, therefore this is the highest value seen in terms of AUC score and in terms of accuracy as well, therefore it is safe to say XGBoost outperforms the various other models that were used before.

4.5 K-Nearest Neighbors (KNN)

Grid Search is performed again to find the best hyperparameter which is n_neighbors. Here is the code snippet for the same:

```python
from sklearn.model_selection import GridSearchCV
from sklearn.neighbors import KNeighborsClassifier

# Define the parameter grid
param_grid = {
    'n_neighbors': [5, 10, 15, 20],  # Adjust the values based on your requirements
}

# Create the KNN model
knn_model = KNeighborsClassifier()

# Use GridSearchCV to find the best hyperparameters
grid_search = GridSearchCV(estimator=knn_model, param_grid=param_grid, cv=5, scoring='accuracy')
grid_search.fit(X_train, Y_train)

# Get the best parameters
best_params = grid_search.best_params_

# Build the final model using the best parameters
final_model_knn = KNeighborsClassifier(**best_params)
final_model_knn.fit(X_train, Y_train)
Y_pred_final_knn = final_model_knn.predict(X_test)

# Print the best parameters
print("Best Hyperparameters:", best_params)

# Print execution time and accuracy for the final model
final_model_knn_time = time.time() - start
final_model_knn_accuracy = round(accuracy_score(Y_test, Y_pred_final_knn), 4) * 100  # Accuracy
print(f"Execution time of final KNN model: {round(final_model_knn_time, 5)} seconds")
print(f"Accuracy of final KNN model: {final_model_knn_accuracy}%")

# Plot and compute metrics for the final KNN model
compute(Y_pred_final_knn, Y_test)
```

The best n_neighbors turns out to be 20: Here is the corresponding confusion matrix (Fig. 18):

```
Best Hyperparameters: {'n_neighbors': 20}
```

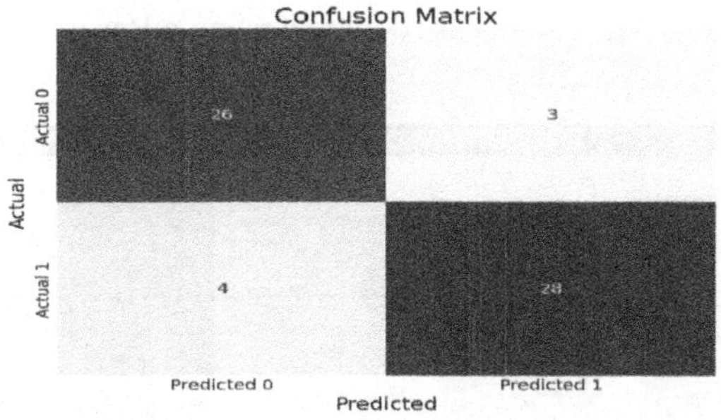

Fig. 18. Confusion matrix for KNN Model

The accuracy for the specific model turns out to be 88.52%. Here is the classification report for the same:

Classification Report:

	precision	recall	f1-score	support
0	0.87	0.90	0.88	29
1	0.90	0.88	0.89	32
accuracy			0.89	61
macro avg	0.88	0.89	0.89	61
weighted avg	0.89	0.89	0.89	61

The ROC curve graph is as follows (Fig. 19):

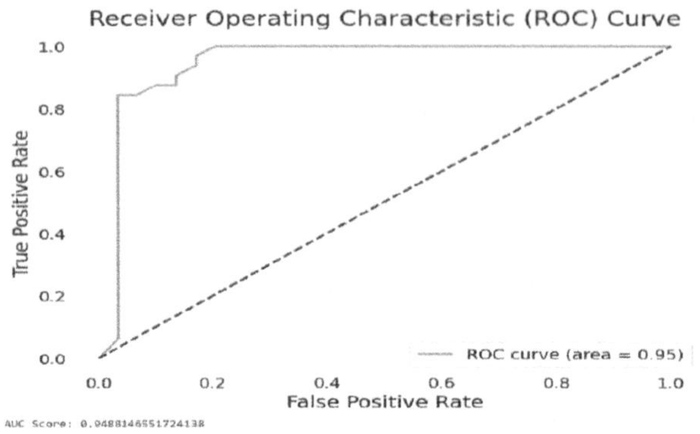

Fig. 19. Roc Curve of the KNN Model

Here the ROC curve area and AUC score is almost 1 as well, which means this is also a suitable model for the dataset.

4.6 Comparison of Different Models

From the results obtained by employing the five models in this research, a comparison of accuracies of various ML models are depicted using a Bar plot in Fig. 20.

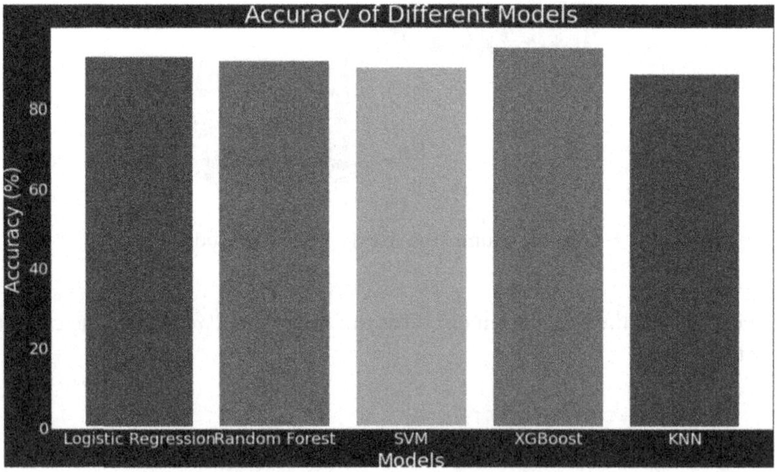

Fig. 20. Comparison of all models

Conclusion and Findings:

After employing various Machine Learning models on the Cleveland Heart Disease Dataset, the machine learning models used in this research perform outstandingly well in predicting the susceptibility of heart diseases. With an accuracy of 95% (highest), it is safe to say that employing Machine Learning models in the field of medical science would do wonders in predicting various outcomes of a given medical scenario with near perfect accuracies. In developing a machine learning model with 95% accuracy using the Cleveland Heart Disease dataset, several innovative steps were undertaken to ensure the robustness and precision of the predictions. The key aspects of the novelty in our approach are detailed below:

1. Use of Log Transforms to Remove Outliers

Outliers can significantly distort the performance of machine learning models, particularly with algorithms like XGBoost that are sensitive to the scale and distribution of data. To address this, log transformations were applied to features exhibiting skewed distributions. This process helped stabilize the variance and make the data more normally distributed. By mitigating the influence of outliers, the log transformations enhanced the model's performance, leading to more accurate and reliable predictions.

2. Hyperparameter Tuning and Comparison

A systematic approach to hyperparameter tuning was essential in optimizing the model's performance. A combination of grid search and random search techniques were used to explore a wide range of hyperparameter values. This comprehensive search allowed me to identify the optimal configuration that maximized the model's accuracy. The process involved:

- Comparing different hyperparameter values.
- Evaluating their impact on model performance.
- Iteratively refining the parameters to achieve the best results.

This meticulous tuning process was crucial in achieving the high accuracy of 95%.

3. Visual Data Analysis

Visualizing the dataset played a pivotal role in understanding the relationships between features. Various visualization techniques were utilized, including scatter plots and correlation heatmaps, to gain insights into the data. These visualizations revealed important patterns and correlations that informed the feature engineering and model- building process. By studying the dataset as a whole, the following were done:

- Identify and address potential issues.
- Make informed decisions about feature selection and transformation.
- Enhance the overall effectiveness of the model.

4. Correlation Analysis

A thorough correlation analysis was conducted to study the relationships between features and the target variable. By examining correlation graphs, the most relevant features that had a significant impact on predicting heart disease were identified. This analysis guided the feature selection process, ensuring that only the most informative features were included in the model. Examples of strong and weak correlations were carefully considered, and appropriate measures were taken to enhance the model's performance.

5. Comparative Analysis

To highlight the effectiveness of my approach, A comparative analysis were conducted with other models and previous results. By benchmarking the model against baseline models and existing methods, improvements made were demonstrated. The combination of log transformations, systematic hyperparameter tuning, and comprehensive visual and statistical analysis resulted in superior performance, with an accuracy of 95%.

6. Novelty and Contribution

The unique aspects of my methodology lie in the integration of several advanced techniques:

- Applying log transformations to address outliers.
- Conducting a thorough and systematic hyperparameter tuning process.
- Utilizing visual data analysis to inform feature engineering decisions.
- Performing detailed correlation analysis to select the most relevant features.

These combined methods led to a highly accurate and robust model. The challenges encountered during the process were addressed through iterative refinement and continuous evaluation, ensuring the model's reliability and precision. In summary, the novelty of this approach lies in the careful and innovative application of these techniques, which collectively contributed to achieving an exceptional accuracy of 95% in predicting heart disease using the Cleveland Heart Disease dataset.

In addition to machine learning models, deep learning has also been employed in recent years, especially neural networks such as Convolutional Neural Networks (CNNs) and Recurrent Neural Networks (RNNs) to study intricate patterns from a raw collection of data [18]. They have been known to handle thee structured and sequential factors of the Cleveland dataset, providing promising results.

Therefore, it is safe to conclude with the findings of ML models on a successful note highlighting the impact they have caused in the field of medical science, taking the Cleveland Heart Disease Dataset as an example.

Disclosure Statement. On behalf of all authors, the corresponding author states that there is no conflict of interest. Funding: This work was supported by the Higher Colleges of Technology, United Arab Emirates [grant Type &No: Interdisciplinary _212318; Fund Code: 113170].

References

1. AHA: Heart disease remains leading cause of death worldwide; trends discouraging. Accessed 14 Dec 2023 [Online]. Available: https://www.healio.com/news/cardiology/20210127/aha-heart-disease-remains-leading-cause-of-death-worldwide-trends-discouraging
2. Cardiovascular diseases. Accessed 14 Dec 2023 [Online]. Available: https://www.who.int/health-topics/cardiovascular-diseases#tab=tab_1
3. Heart Disease and Stroke | CDC. Accessed 14 Dec 2023 [Online]. Available: https://www.cdc.gov/chronicdisease/resources/publications/factsheets/heart-disease-stroke.htm
4. Kyker, K.A., Limacher, M.C.: Gender differences in the presentation and symptoms of coronary artery disease. Curr. Women's Health Rep. **2**(2), 115 (2002)

5. Javaid, M., Haleem, A., Pratap Singh, R., Suman, R., Rab, S.: Significance of machine learning in healthcare: features, pillars and applications. Int. J. Intell. Netw. **3**, 58 (2022). https://doi.org/10.1016/j.ijin.2022.05.002
6. Dara, S., Dhamercherla, S., Jadav, S.S., Babu, C.M., Ahsan, M.J.: Machine learning in drug discovery: a review. Artif. Intell. Rev. **55**(3), 1947 (2022). https://doi.org/10.1007/s10462-021-10058-4
7. Nagavelli, U., Samanta, D., Chakraborty, P.: Machine learning technology-based heart disease detection models. J. Healthc. Eng. **2022**, 1 (2022). https://doi.org/10.1155/2022/7351061
8. Ambrish, G., Ganesh, B., Ganesh, A., Srinivas, C., Dhanraj, K., Mensinkal, K.: Logistic regression technique for prediction of cardiovascular disease. Glob. Trans. Proc. **3**(1), 127 (2022). https://doi.org/10.1016/j.gltp.2022.04.008
9. Pal, M., Parija, S., Panda, G., Dhama, K., Mohapatra, R.K.: Risk prediction of cardiovascular disease using machine learning classifiers. Open Med. (Poland) **17**(1), 1100 (2022). https://doi.org/10.1515/med-2022-0508
10. Chandrasekhar, N., Peddakrishna, S.: Enhancing heart disease prediction accuracy through machine learning techniques and optimization. Processes **11**(4), 1210 (2023). https://doi.org/10.3390/pr11041210
11. Karthick, K., Aruna, S.K., Samikannu, R., Kuppusamy, R., Teekaraman, Y., Thelkar, A.R.: Implementation of a heart disease risk prediction model using machine learning. Comput. Math. Methods Med. **2022**, 1 (2022). https://doi.org/10.1155/2022/6517716
12. Mienye, D., Sun, Y., Wang, Z.: An improved ensemble learning approach for the prediction of heart disease risk. Inform. Med. Unlocked **20**, 100402 (2020). https://doi.org/10.1016/j.imu.2020.100402
13. Uddin, M.N., Halder, R.K.: An ensemble method based multilayer dynamic system to predict cardiovascular disease using machine learning approach. Inform. Med. Unlocked **24**, 100584 (2021). https://doi.org/10.1016/j.imu.2021.100584
14. Arooj, S., ur Rehman, S., Imran, A., Almuhaimeed, A., Alzahrani, A.K., Alzahrani, A.: A deep convolutional neural network for the early detection of heart disease. Biomedicines **10**(11), 2796 (2022). https://doi.org/10.3390/biomedicines10112796
15. Kavitha, M., Gnaneswar, G., Dinesh, R., Sai, Y.R., Suraj, R.S.: Heart disease prediction using hybrid machine learning model. In: Proceedings of the 6th international conference on inventive computation technologies, ICICT 2021 (2021). https://doi.org/10.1109/ICICT50816.2021.9358597
16. Heart Disease - UCI Machine Learning Repository. Accessed 14 Dec 2023 [Online]. Available: https://archive.ics.uci.edu/dataset/45/heart+disease
17. Cleveland Clinic Heart Disease Dataset. Accessed 14 Dec 2023. [Online]. Available: https://www.kaggle.com/datasets/aavigan/cleveland-clinic-heart-disease-dataset
18. Yamashita, R., Nishio, M., Do, R.K.G., Togashi, K.: Convolutional neural networks: an overview and application in radiology. Insights Imaging **9**(4), 611 (2018). https://doi.org/10.1007/s13244-018-0639-9

Using LLMs to Enhance Research Output Tracking in Weakly Categorized Research Areas: A Case Study to Classify Publications in Islamic Economics, Finance, Banking and Business

Asem Kasem[1](✉), Imran Alvi[2], and Elie Fares[1]

[1] Higher Colleges of Technology, Sharjah, United Arab Emirates
{akasem,efares}@hct.ac.ae
[2] Oxford Intellect, Oxford, Oxfordshire OX1 3HJ, England
imran@oxfordintellect.co.uk

Abstract. This paper investigates the application of Machine Learning techniques and use of Large Language Models (LLMs) to categorize research output in weakly classified academic fields, specifically focusing on classifying publications in Islamic Economics, Finance, Banking, and Business (IEFBB). Using a dataset of about 3,958 Scopus-indexed publications, we employed text classification techniques as a scalable enabler to analyze research trends and collaborations within this niche area. Initial experiments using traditional machine learning methods, among which Neural Network model provided the highest cross-validated accuracy of 85%, and 75% test set accuracy. This provided a benchmark that we then used to explore LLM-based approaches, leveraging GPT-4o-mini model with prompt engineering and fine-tuning. Our results demonstrate that zero-shot prompt approach achieved 82% and 71% accuracy on validation and test sets, respectively. While iterative prompt engineering attempts after error analysis improved classification accuracy to 86% and 73% accuracy on validation and test sets; fine-tuning GPT-4o-mini with a tailored prompt significantly improved classification accuracy, achieving up to 86% on validation and 83% on the test sets. These findings underscore the potential of LLMs in automating the categorization of research output in specialized fields that lack established categorization systems.

Keywords: Text Classification · Large Language Models · Neural Networks · Finetuning LLMs · Prompt Engineering

1 Introduction

Accurate categorization of research publications is essential for analyzing research trends and impact, tracking the evolution of specific subfields, identifying key contributors, and fostering collaborations. The rapid growth of academic publications in weakly categorized fields poses challenges for researchers seeking to navigate and analyze the

A. Safi et al. (Eds.): ISICS 2024, CCIS 2381, pp. 44–53, 2025.
https://doi.org/10.1007/978-3-031-82931-4_3

landscape of scholarly work. In particular, research in some niche areas such as Islamic Economics, Finance, Banking, and Business (IEFBB) lack well-defined categorization systems, making it difficult to track where researchers are investing their efforts and how the intellectual capital is being distributed.

Our study addresses this challenge by leveraging Artificial Intelligence (AI) and Large Language Models (LLMs) to classify research output in IEFBB field. The primary objective is to develop a robust system that can spontaneously categorize published works, and thus enable analysis that provides insights into the growth and evolution of research in this field over time. To automatically classify published works into categories of interest, we utilize AI methods to perform text classification based on textual markers of those published papers. We explore the use of traditional Machine Learning (ML) techniques to develop and evaluate the accuracy of multiple classification models, in addition to the use and evaluation of LLM's ability to perform the same classification task.

Previous work has shown that traditional ML models, such as Neural Networks [1], SVM [2], and XGBoost [3], can achieve reasonable classification performance [4–6]. However, recent advancements in LLMs [7] offer the potential for significant improvements. In this paper, we compare the performance of traditional models with that of LLMs. Specifically, we utilize GPT-4o-mini, a variant of GPT-4 family of models [8], to perform the required classification task with focus on improving the accuracy in two ways: one with iterative refinement of the used prompts, and the other via fine-tuning the used LLM. We analyze the obtained experimental results, and eventually highlight the benefits of using LLMs for complex text classification tasks in weakly categorized research areas.

2 Background

2.1 Existing Categorization Systems

A significant hurdle is categorizing the research works according to a standard system. When established categorization standards exist, it will be straightforward to perform a required analysis that looks directly into those categories. On such system is the JEL classification system in the field of Economics, developed for use in the Journal of Economic Literature [9], which provides an extensive list of categories from which authors self-classify their work. These codes then enable a measurement of research activity in different sub-fields of economics.

The JEL codes were not written with the sub-branches of IEFBB in mind. Thus, even when the authors of a publication are working in an area of IEFBB, and they have defined a JEL code for their work, the code is not helpful in identifying a sub-category of IEFBB.

The King Abdulaziz University Journal of Islamic Economics (KAUJIE) categorization system [10] provides a framework specifically designed for classifying research in IEFBB. It offers a structured approach to categorizing papers based on key themes and topics relevant to the field. While the use of the KAUJIE categorization is mandatory for certain journals, it is fair to say that it has not received the same level of prominence in usage as the JEL codes. It cannot therefore act as a substitute for the JEL codes in identifying trends in IEFBB research categories over time.

2.2 Weakly Categorized Research Areas

Based on the above discussion, we identify scholarly work in areas similar to IEFBB as weakly categorized research areas. Such areas often suffer from a lack of standardized classification systems, leading to difficulties in tracking and analyzing their scholarly investment and output. Traditional categorization methods rely heavily on manual curation, which is time-consuming and prone to inconsistencies, and therefore cannot be used at scale. Automated approaches using ML and Natural Language Processing (NLP) have been proposed to address these challenges [11, 12], but their effectiveness in specialized fields remains limited.

2.3 Large Language Models in Text Classification

LLMs, such as GPT-3 and GPT-4 -based models, have demonstrated exceptional capabilities in understanding and generating human-like text. These models can be adapted for specific tasks, including text classification, through prompt engineering and fine-tuning. The ability of LLMs to capture complex linguistic patterns makes them well-suited for categorizing research publications in specialized fields, where traditional models may struggle with the nuances of domain-specific language.

3 Methodology

3.1 Text Classification Task

This study focuses on predicting one of the three top-level categories of the KAUJIE categorization system identified below:

- **Islamic Economics**: including sub-categories for Maqasid Al-Shariah and Economics, Islamic Jurisprudence and Economics, History of Islamic Economic Thought, Comparative Economic Systems, Islamic Economics Theoretical Development, or Islamic Economics in Practice.
- **Islamic Finance and Banking**: including sub-categories for Maqasid Al-Shariah in Finance and Banking, Islamic Jurisprudence and Finance and Banking, History of Islamic Finance and Banking, Comparative Financial and Banking Systems, Islamic Finance and Banking Theoretical Development, or Islamic Finance and Banking in Practice.
- **Islamic Business Administration and Management**: including sub-categories for Maqasid Al-Shariah in Business Administration and Management, Islamic Jurisprudence and Business Administration and Management, History of Islamic Business Administration and Management, Comparative Business Administration and Management Systems, Islamic Business Administration and Management theoretical development, or Islamic Business Administration and Management in Practice.

It is not rare to have a paper with possible assignment to more than one single category. For example, a publication analyzing what drives economic growth in a country with its banking development, may be assigned as Economics related, and Finance and Banking related. In such cases, the aim of the publication and most dominant work can be utilized to assign only a single category.

3.2 Data Collection and Preprocessing

We limit our attention to Scopus indexed research outputs. This gives a minimal check on the quality of published work and is in line with previous literature interested in research trends in the general field of Economics. Using the Scopus search engine, we conducted a wild card search on Title, Keywords and Abstracts available. This resulted in over four thousand documents being found.

We omitted documents that were not in English, removed non-English texts where dual languages used, and identified duplicates. For example, when two publications have the same title and abstract (or very close abstract), same year and authors, one of them was considered redundant. A rare single paper in year 1955 was also omitted, since the immediate next paper found was in 1980.

This resulted in a final dataset used in this study which consists of 3,958 publications related to IEFBB. Each publication includes the title, abstract, keywords, in addition to many metadata information such as publication type and year, number of authors, country of origin, etc. which are useful for any post-classification analysis. For categorization purposes, we focused only on the textual elements of the data, namely the title, abstract, keywords.

Table 1 below shows our data by decade and type of publication, with groupings of related document types being made to form Articles (include: Article, Article-in-Press, and Business Article), Conferences (include: Conference Paper and Conference Review), Books (include: Book and Book Chapter), and Others (include: Data Paper, Editorial, Erratum, Letter, Note, Review, and Short Survey):

Table 1. Summary of grouped document types over the years.

Year	Articles	Conferences	Books	Others	**Total**
1980–1989	24			5	29
1990–1999	79		1	9	89
2000–2009	219	14	49	33	315
2010~	2884	173	305	163	3525

A subset of 307 papers was randomly selected and manually labeled by experts in the IEFBB field, providing a high-quality labeled dataset. This subset was split further into training (100 papers), validation (100 papers), and test (107 papers) sets. The assigned categories were reviewed and refined by a co-author with expertise in IEFBB, ensuring the accuracy and reliability of the labeled data.

3.3 Traditional Machine Learning Models

We initially employed traditional machine learning models, including Neural Networks, Naïve Bayes, Support Vector Machines (SVMs), and XGBoost trees, to classify the papers. Term Frequency-Inverse Document Frequency (TF-IDF) was used to preprocess the textual elements. All algorithms to generate the model have been run using implementations from RapidMiner Studio 10.3 [13], with some form of hyper-parameter tuning to optimize models' parameters.

The models were trained using the training dataset (100 papers), and any hyper-parameter tuning of the algorithms to optimize performance was conducted on the validation dataset (100 papers). Accuracy metric was judged sufficient to evaluate the performance of the text classification tasks. Eventually, the best performing algorithm was selected and re-evaluated using 10-fold cross-validation applied to the combined training and validation datasets (200 papers) to serve an estimated performance of the best traditional ML model. Performance evaluation on the test dataset (107 papers) was conducted at the end when no more model development work continued, and the test set results would serve as the basis for comparison with the other classification approach using LLMs.

3.4 LLM Implementation

For the LLM-based approach, we experimented with several OpenAI models to evaluate the ability of performing the required papers classification task.

We developed a zero-shot prompt based on the KAUJIE categorization system, and conducted initial experiments with iterative prompt engineering to obtain a classification label for each paper. The KAUJIE system served as the foundation for the prompts used in our LLM experiments, ensuring that the model's classifications were aligned with established domain knowledge.

We selected GPT-4o-mini model due to its comparable performance to the full GPT-4o model on the training set, and for its computational and economic advantages, and we used OpenAI APIs to conduct several experiments as outlined below.

Prompt Engineering. Two main prompts were developed through iterative refinement using the training and validation datasets. The process can be summarized as follows:

- **Initial Attempts:** After the zero-shot prompt was created, it was refined by continuous evaluation on the training dataset to obtain the best performing prompt, which we named "Prompt-1". After that, the performance on both validation and test datasets was recorded and labeled as "**GPT-4o-mini with Prompt-1**".
- **Prompting with Error Analysis in Mind:** We conducted Error Analysis on the papers from training dataset that were misclassified when we used "Prompt-1". Improved prompts were introduced to capture the logic for countering potential reasons of misclassifications, as identified by the error analysis. These prompts were refined by continuous evaluation on the training dataset to pick the best prompt, "Prompt-2", and its performance on the validation and test datasets was recorded and labeled as "**GPT-4o-mini with Prompt-2**".

Fine-Tuning. We used OpenAI's finetuning capabilities to optimize GPT-4o-mini performance further. We created training and validation datasets, with "System", "User", and "Assistant" messages formatted to align with the two prompts above and the desired response from the LLM model. The process in this approach can be summarized as follows:

- **Fine-Tuning with Prompt-1:** We utilized the training and validation datasets created for "Prompt-1" to run multiple finetuning experiments. The number of epochs tried were 3 (default), 10, and 15 epochs. The learning rates were 1.8 (default) and 0.6. It turned out that for our task and validation dataset, the different tuning parameters did not make a noticeable difference. The best performance on the validation dataset, and in parallel on the test dataset, was recorded and labeled as **"Finetuned GPT-4o-mini with Prompt-1"**.
- **Fine-Tuning with Prompt-2:** We utilized the training and validation datasets created for "Prompt-2" to run two finetuning jobs (epochs 3 and 10), and the performance on the validation dataset, and in parallel on the test dataset, was recorded and labeled as **"Finetuned GPT-4o-mini with Prompt-2"**.

Evaluation Comparisons: We use the accuracy metric obtained from the LLM experiments above, and from the traditional ML methods, on training, validation, and test datasets, to discuss the outcome of proposed approaches and to draw conclusions on which one to use for the objective of the study. Once the best model/approach is determined, it can be then used to categorize all the ~ 4k publications in our dataset, or any other research works that may be produced in future. Of course, any analysis needs to consider that the models may not be 100% accurate, and thus make any conclusions with an expected margin of error. The production of such analysis is outside the scope of this paper, and would be left for related future works in the field of IEFBB.

4 Results and Discussion

In this section, we present the results of our experiments, comparing the performance of traditional machine learning models and LLM-based approaches on the classification of IEFBB research papers. We include quantitative results for accuracy across training, validation, and test sets, as well as a discussion of the implications and insights derived from these findings.

4.1 Performance of Traditional Machine Learning Models

Table 2 below summarizes the classification accuracy results obtained by the best variation of each ML model, evaluated on the training and validation datasets combined, and on the test set.

The Neural Network model outperformed other traditional models with an average training accuracy of $85.37\% \pm 6.21\%$. However, the overall performance on the test set was still modest, suggesting the need for more sophisticated models capable of handling the nuanced nature of the IEFBB domain.

Table 2. Classification accuracy results obtained by ML methods.

Model	Accuracy (%) on combined Training & Validation Sets - 10-Fold Cross-Validation	Accuracy (%) on Test Set
Neural Network	**85.0** ± 6.24	**75.8**
SVM	80.5 ± 5.5	74.7
XGBoost	71.0 ± 8.43	67.29
Naïve Bayes	67.5 ± 7.55	62.6

4.2 Performance of LLM with Prompt Engineering

Table 3 summarizes the classification accuracy results obtained by "Prompt-1" and "Prompt-2", after evaluation of GPT-4o-mini on training, validation, and test datasets.

Table 3. LLM accuracy results obtained by GPT-4o-mini.

LLM Attempt	Training Accuracy (%)	Validation Accuracy (%)	Test Accuracy (%)
GPT-4o-mini with Prompt-1	84.0	82.0	71.03
GPT-4o-mini with Prompt-2	**91.0**	**86.0**	**73.83**

The results above show that "Prompt-2", refined through error analysis, outperformed "Prompt-1" across all datasets, achieving 91% accuracy on the training set, 86% on validation, and 74% on the test set. The improvement highlights the effectiveness of prompt refinement and expert feedback in enhancing LLM performance.

However, the relatively large gap between validation and test results indicates that some overfitting has happened when trying to embed a lot of the correction logic into "Prompt-2" to account for the misclassified instances identified in error analysis.

4.3 Performance of Finetuned LLMs

Table 4 summarizes the classification accuracy results obtained using each of "Prompt-1" and "Prompt-2" with its corresponding finetuned GPT-4o-mini model, and again evaluated on training, validation, and test datasets.

The results above show that Fine-tuning GPT-4o-mini with "Prompt-1" resulted in a significant increase in training accuracy to 98%, and an improvement on the test set to 83%. These results are significantly higher than the initial zero-shot performance with the same prompt, and the one with the prompt refined via error analysis (the two entries in Table 3).

Conversely, fine-tuning with "Prompt-2" led to a notable decline in performance, particularly on the test set, which achieved only 57% accuracy. This contrast underscores

Table 4. Accuracy of finetuned GPT-4o-mini models.

Finetuned LLM Model	Training Accuracy (%)	Validation Accuracy (%)	Test Accuracy (%)
Finetuned GPT-4o-mini with Prompt-1	**98.0**	**86.0**	**83.18**
Finetuned GPT-4o-mini with Prompt-2	71.0	65.0	57.01

the importance of prompt selection and the potential pitfalls of overfitting during fine-tuning when prompts are overly specialized or not aligned with the validation and test distributions.

4.4 Comparative Analysis and Discussion

Comparative Performance Analysis

- **Traditional Models vs. GPT-4o-mini:** While traditional models like Neural Networks provided a baseline for performance, the LLM approaches with GPT-4o-mini demonstrated superior accuracy. In particular, the finetuned model seems to be better at handling the text nuances within IEFBB publications.
- **Prompt Engineering Impact:** The transition from "Prompt-1" to "Prompt-2" showed how expert-driven prompt refinement could lead to substantial performance gains. Prompt-2's iterative improvements led to increased accuracy on the training and validation sets, reflecting the value of domain expertise in guiding the LLM application.
- **Fine-Tuning Advantages:** Fine-tuning GPT-4o-mini with "Prompt-1" yielded the highest test set accuracy of 83%, marking it as the best overall performer. This approach capitalized on the model's adaptability to learn from domain-specific data while maintaining generalizability across unseen examples.
- **Challenges with Fine-Tuning Prompt-2:** The performance drop with fine-tuned "Prompt-2" on validation and test sets highlights the risks associated with overfitting and the need for careful prompt selection as part of a rigor data preparation strategy. These results suggest that finetuning with overly specific or misaligned prompts can detract from model's robustness.

Implications for IEFBB Research Classification

- The success of LLMs in this study suggests that they are well-suited for categorizing research in weakly defined fields, where traditional classification methods may struggle. This capability can greatly enhance the ability to track research trends, identify key contributors, and analyze co-authorship networks within specialized domains like IEFBB.

- Our findings emphasize the importance of prompt design and fine-tuning strategies in maximizing the performance of LLMs, particularly in fields where precise categorization is critical for downstream analysis.

5 Conclusion

This study explored the use of large language models (LLMs), specifically GPT-4o-mini, to classify research papers in the weakly categorized field of Islamic Economics, Finance, Banking, and Business (IEFBB). By leveraging text classification techniques, we aimed to enable a scalable approach that can be applied to provide insights into the growth and evolution of academic research within this niche domain. Our approach involved the application of traditional machine learning models, prompt engineering with LLMs, and fine-tuning to improve classification accuracy of research papers.

The results demonstrated that LLMs, particularly when fine-tuned properly, significantly outperformed traditional machine learning models. The application of LLMs in this context offers a significant step forward in the automated analysis of academic research, which can be particularly beneficial for other similar fields that lack well-defined categorizations.

Further Directions

To build on the findings of this study, several future directions are recommended.

- Refine Fine-Tuning Strategies: Future research should focus on optimizing fine-tuning methodologies, including exploring prompt-agnostic fine-tuning approaches, to mitigate overfitting and improve the generalizability of the models across diverse datasets.
- Investigate Prompt Optimization Techniques: Systematic exploration of prompt optimization techniques, such as reinforcement learning for prompt selection or automated prompt generation, could yield further enhancements in classification accuracy and model reliability.
- Extend to Other Weakly Categorized Fields: Applying the approach to other fields with similar categorization challenges could validate the generalizability of the methodology and contribute to the broader adoption of LLMs in academic research classification.

By addressing these future directions, the potential of LLMs for classifying research in weakly categorized fields can be fully realized, ultimately supporting a deeper understanding of research landscapes and facilitating more strategic investment in intellectual capital across diverse academic disciplines.

References

1. Goodfellow, I., Bengio, Y., Courville, A.: Deep Learning. MIT Press (2016)
2. Cortes, C., Vapnik, V.: Support-vector networks. Mach. Learn. **20**, 273–297 (1995). https://doi.org/10.1007/BF00994018

3. Chen, T., Guestrin, C.: XGBoost: a scalable tree boosting system. In: Proceedings of the 22nd ACM SIGKDD international conference on knowledge discovery and data mining, pp. 785–794. ACM, New York (2016)
4. Aggarwal, C.C., Zhai, C.: A survey of text classification algorithms. In: Mining text data, pp. 163–222. Springer, Boston, MA (2012)
5. Kim, Y.: Convolutional neural networks for sentence classification. In: Proceedings of the 2014 conference on empirical methods in natural language processing (EMNLP), pp. 1746–1751. Association for Computational Linguistics, Doha, Qatar (2014)
6. Joachims, T.: Text categorization with support vector machines: learning with many relevant features. In: Proceedings of the 10th European conference on machine learning, pp. 137–142. Springer, Berlin, Heidelberg (1998)
7. Brown, T.B., et al.: Language models are few-shot learners. Adv. Neural. Inf. Process. Syst. **33**, 1877–1901 (2020)
8. OpenAI: GPT-4 Technical Report. Available at: https://openai.com/research/gpt-4. Accessed August 2024
9. Journal of Economic Literature (JEL): Classification System. Available at: https://www.aeaweb.org/econlit/jelCodes.php. Accessed August 2024
10. King Abdulaziz University Journal of Islamic Economics (KAUJIE): Categorization Guidelines. King Abdulaziz University, Jeddah (2014). Available at: https://iei.kau.edu.sa/Files/121/Files/155285_TasnifEnglish.pdf . Accessed August 2024
11. Kandimalla, B., Rohatgi, S., Wu, J., Giles, C.L.: Large scale subject category classification of scholarly papers with deep attentive neural networks (2020). arXiv preprint arXiv:2007.13826
12. Ech-Chouyyekh, M., Omara, H., Lazaar, M.: Scientific paper classification using convolutional neural networks. In: Proceedings of the 4th international conference on big data and Internet of Things, pp.1–6 (2019). https://doi.org/10.1145/3372938.3372951
13. RapidMiner Studio 10.3: Machine Learning Workflow and Data Analysis Software. Altair Engineering Inc. Available at: https://docs.rapidminer.com/latest/studio/. Accessed August 2024

Evaluating AI-Generated Video Quality: A Novel Assessment Model

M. Izani(✉), A. Assad, A. Kaleel, L. Wong, D. Abdulla, and A. Hamdan

Applied Media Department, Abu Dhabi, UAE
izainal@hct.ac.ae

Abstract. The rapid development of AI video generation has proliferated AI-generated videos through almost every segment of entertainment, education, and marketing. Despite such huge potential, this segment always stands out facing inconsistent video quality as one of the most critical challenges. It therefore follows that it sets up an integrated model with which to assess the quality of AI-generated videos in terms of fidelity, realism, consistency, accuracy, relevance, creativity, seamlessness, coherence, engagement, innovation, resolution and detail, color accuracy, frame rate and smoothness, AI artifacts and limitations, the uncanny valley effect, bias, and continuity. The study has critically analyzed the videos obtained from leading AI platforms to pinpoint key quality indicators and develop a robust benchmarking model capable of adapting to the changing standards of AI technology. A few of the key strengths seen for current AI tools (realism and resolution) were also clear weaknesses found (handling AI artifacts, continuity). This model offers an organized system that can be utilized to assess AI-generated videos (while identifying areas of enhancement) and also gives specific recommendations for moving forward with machine learning video generation. The research helps to create new benchmarks for AI powered media, drives innovation and improves the standard of AI driven video outputs in line with a rapidly expanding market demand for superior digital content.

Keywords: Artificial Intelligence · Generative AI · Video quality metrics

1 Introduction

The advent of artificial intelligence (AI) has revolutionized the creation of digital content, leading to the emergence of AI-generated videos. These videos, produced by sophisticated algorithms, are increasingly used in various domains such as entertainment, education, marketing, and social media. Companies like Sora, Kling, RunwayML, and LumaLabs are at the forefront of this technological innovation, offering tools that enable the generation of high-quality videos with minimal human intervention [1]. Despite the growing popularity and application of AI-generated videos, there remains a critical need to evaluate their quality comprehensively. Assessing the quality of these videos is essential to ensure they meet the desired standards of realism, coherence, and engagement, which are crucial for their effectiveness and acceptance by audiences [2]. Existing

A. Safi et al. (Eds.): ISICS 2024, CCIS 2381, pp. 54–66, 2025.
https://doi.org/10.1007/978-3-031-82931-4_4

research on video quality assessment has primarily focused on traditional video content, with metrics designed to evaluate aspects such as resolution, frame rate, and color accuracy [3–5]. However, AI-generated videos present unique challenges that traditional metrics may not adequately address [6, 7]. Recent studies have begun to explore the specific needs of AI-generated content. For instance, a novel deep blind quality assessment model for user-generated videos has been proposed, which considers content variety and temporal memory effects [7, 8]. Another study introduces a spatiotemporal interactive VQA model that integrates spatial characteristics and temporal motion to infer video distortion [9]. These efforts underscore the necessity for specialized evaluation criteria tailored to the nuances of AI-generated videos [10]. While there has been progress in developing evaluation methods for AI-generated content, a comprehensive model that addresses all critical aspects of video quality remains lacking. Current approaches often focus on specific elements, such as action quality or visual realism, without providing a holistic assessment framework [10]. This gap highlights the need for a robust model that can evaluate AI-generated videos across multiple dimensions, ensuring a thorough and reliable quality assessment.

The primary objective of this research is to evaluate existing AI-generated videos using a set of specific metrics and to develop a comprehensive quality assessment model. By analyzing videos from leading AI content creators such as Sora, Kling, RunwayML, PikaLabs and LumaLabs, we aim to identify key quality indicators and establish a standardized approach for evaluating AI-generated videos. This model will incorporate criteria such as fidelity, realism, consistency, accuracy, relevance, creativity, seamlessness, coherence, engagement, innovation, resolution and detail, color accuracy, frame rate and smoothness, AI artifacts and limitations, uncanny valley effect, bias, and continuity. The significance of this research lies in its potential to set a benchmark for the quality assessment of AI-generated videos. By providing a standardized evaluation model, this study will contribute to the development of more reliable and effective AI-generated content. The findings will offer valuable insights for content creators, researchers, and developers, facilitating the improvement of AI algorithms and enhancing the overall quality of AI-generated videos. The goal of this study is to assess the strengths and limitations of AI-generated videos, offering recommendations for future development with a particular focus on video quality criteria, promoting higher standards and greater acceptance of AI-generated videos in various applications.

2 Methodology

The primary objective of this methodology section is to outline the systematic approach employed in developing a robust and comprehensive model for benchmarking the quality of AI-generated videos. This model aims to evaluate video outputs based on a set of well-defined criteria, ensuring a thorough and accurate assessment that can guide future advancements in AI video generation.

2.1 Criteria Selection

The criteria for evaluating video quality were carefully selected to capture the most critical aspects of AI-generated content (Fig. 1). These videos were selected based on the original videos created for promotional purposes by each developer.

Fig. 1. The figures show selected videos used for this evaluation: (A) Sora, (B) KlingAI, (C) RunwayML, (D) Pikalabs & (E) Lumalab, All images are the property of their respective creators, as indicated.

The following criteria in Table 1 were chosen based on their relevance to both technical and perceptual video quality:

These criteria were selected based on their critical importance in both industry standards and academic literature, ensuring that the evaluation captures a holistic view of video quality.

Table 1. Criteria list for assessing Ai generated video

Criteria	Description
Fidelity	Measures how accurately the video represents the intended content, free from artifacts, distortions, or discrepancies from the source material
Realism	Evaluates the degree to which the video appears lifelike and convincing to the viewer
Consistency	Assesses the uniformity of video quality across all frames, focusing on smooth transitions and coherent motion
Accuracy	Evaluates the precision of visual elements, ensuring that representations align with the intended reality or artistic vision
Relevance	Determines how well the content aligns with its intended purpose or target audience
Creativity	Assesses the originality and innovation in the video, particularly in how AI is utilized to enhance or create new forms of visual expression
Seamlessness	Looks at how smoothly different elements integrate, such as CGI with real footage, creating a cohesive and immersive experience
Coherence	Measures the logical flow and connectivity between scenes and elements, ensuring a clear and understandable narrative or visual sequence
Engagement	Evaluates the video's ability to capture and retain viewer attention, reflecting the emotional and cognitive impact
Innovation	Assesses the degree of newness or groundbreaking use of AI in video production, pushing the boundaries of traditional methods
Resolution and Detail	Examines the sharpness and clarity of the video, especially in preserving fine details and textures in high-definition content
Color Accuracy	Checks the fidelity of colors, ensuring they are true-to-life and consistent with real-world scenarios or the intended artistic palette
Frame Rate and Smoothness	Evaluates the smoothness of motion, ensuring that the frame rate supports fluid and natural movement without jitter or lag
AI Artifacts and Limitations	Identifies any technical flaws or limitations in AI-generated content, such as glitches, unnatural elements, or other artifacts
Uncanny Valley Effect	Assesses whether the video causes discomfort due to overly realistic yet slightly off-putting representations, often in near-human characters

(*continued*)

Table 1. *(continued)*

Criteria	Description
Bias	Evaluates the presence of unintended bias in the content, ensuring fairness and impartiality across different contexts and demographics
Continuity	Measures the logical and visual consistency over time, ensuring scenes follow naturally without disruptive jumps or inconsistencies

2.2 Data Collection

The AI-generated videos were sourced from a diverse array of platforms known for their advanced video generation capabilities, including Sora, Kling, RunwayML, and LumaLabs. Each platform represents a key player in the field, offering unique approaches to AI-driven content creation. A total of five videos were selected, ensuring a balanced representation of different types of content, including animations and generative AI videos that render like live-action footage. The selection process was guided by the need to include a variety of challenges in video generation, ensuring the model's broad applicability.

2.3 Evaluation Process

Critique of the AI-generated videos was performed by a panel of experts-very highly selected for their great insight into and knowledge of the film and animation world. The three well-known professionals each had at least 20 years in various fields, representing a huge span of responsibilities in the realms of story development, special effects, animation process, and artistic expression. Deep-rooted in film principles and all the subtleties that come with visually appealing storytelling, they were in a great position to judge the quality and impact of the AI-generated content.

To ensure strength and reliability in the assessment without biases, the Group Consensus Method was adopted. The process started with the individual rating of experts against each video on a 1 to 5 rating scale. Following this introduction, the Delphi Method provided a method for structured discussion, where the group arrived at consensus on the final ratings. This iterative process minimized individual biases and balanced informed judgments, enhancing the consistency and accuracy of video quality evaluations by leveraging the collective expertise of the panel. They provided a wider insight into how well these videos met established industry norms and audience engagement, with many of their insights informing ongoing development and refinement related to AI video generation technology.

2.4 Statistical Analysis

Following the consensus ratings, statistical analysis was conducted to develop the benchmarking model. Since the ratings were derived from a consensus, the focus was on understanding the predictive power of each criterion in determining overall video quality. A multiple regression analysis was performed to identify the relative importance of each criterion. This analysis provided the coefficients needed to assign weighted scores to each criterion, forming the basis of the benchmarking model. The model was further refined through iterative testing, ensuring that it accurately reflects the quality standards across different types of AI-generated videos.

2.5 Development of the Model

The benchmarking model, developed from multiple regression analysis, assigns weighted scores to each criterion based on its impact on overall video quality. Designed for flexibility and adaptability, the model evolves with AI advancements and video standards. Testing across diverse video genres and computational resources confirmed its effectiveness, offering reliable benchmarks for developers and researchers in AI video generation.

3 Results

3.1 Regression Results

In this section, we present the key findings from the multiple regression analysis performed on the dataset. The regression coefficients obtained from the analysis provide insights into the relative importance of each criterion (e.g., Fidelity, Realism, Consistency, Accuracy, Relevance) in determining the overall quality of the videos evaluated (Video A to Video E) as shown in Fig. 2. The regression coefficients reflect the magnitude and direction of the impact each criterion has on the dependent variable, which

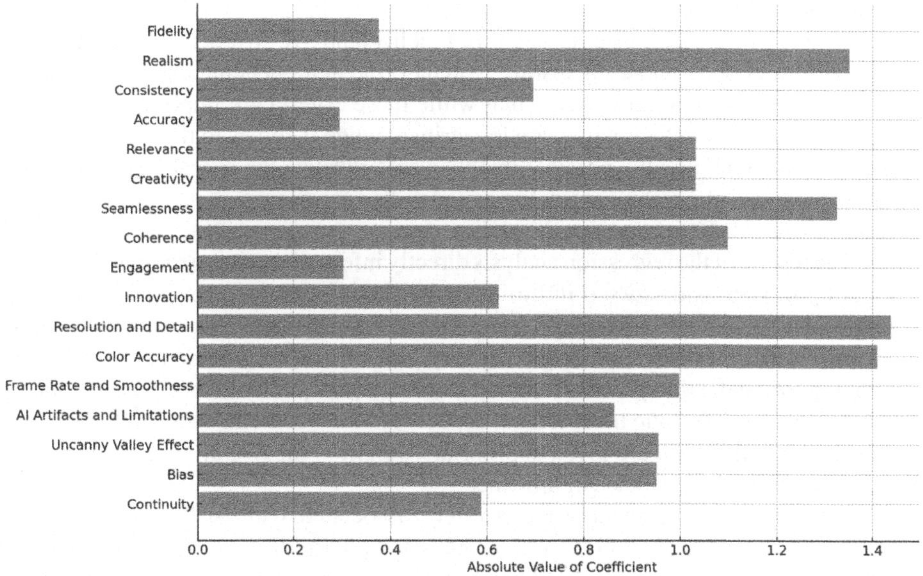

Fig. 2. Importance of each criterion based on regression coefficient

in this context could be a measure of overall video performance or quality. The significance levels associated with these coefficients were assessed to determine whether the observed relationships were statistically meaningful.

The bar chart presented in Fig. 2 illustrates the relative importance of each criterion as determined by the regression coefficients. Each bar represents the absolute value of the coefficient for a specific criterion, highlighting the impact that criterion has on the overall quality assessment.

3.2 The Analysis Reveals Several Key Insights

1. High-Impact Criteria:

   Criteria such as Realism and Resolution and Detail exhibit the highest coefficients, indicating their significant influence on the quality scores. This suggests that improvements in these areas could have a substantial effect on the perceived quality of the videos. For instance, Realism is a critical factor, likely due to its direct impact on the viewer's immersion and engagement with the content. Similarly, Resolution and Detail are essential for maintaining visual fidelity and enhancing the overall viewing experience.
2. Moderate-Impact Criteria:

   A number of criteria, including Seamlessness and Continuity, show moderate levels of influence. While these factors are still important, their impact is less pronounced compared to the high-impact criteria. These criteria might reflect aspects of the content that contribute to user engagement or satisfaction but do not drastically alter the overall quality. For example, Seamlessness ensures smooth transitions and flow in video content, which is important but may be secondary to the clarity and realism of the visuals.
3. Low-Impact Criteria:

   On the other hand, criteria such as Fidelity and AI Artifacts and Limitations exhibit lower coefficients, suggesting a smaller role in influencing the overall quality.

   These findings might indicate that while these criteria are important for certain aspects of content delivery, they are less critical when it comes to the holistic assessment of video quality. It's possible that viewers prioritize the overall experience and immersion over the technical fidelity of individual frames.
4. Implications for Benchmarking Model:

   The results of the regression analysis directly inform the construction of the benchmarking model, as discussed in this section. The relative weights derived from the regression coefficients will be applied in the model to evaluate video quality comprehensively. The model will place greater emphasis on criteria with higher coefficients, aligning the evaluation process with the key drivers of quality identified in the analysis. This ensures that the most critical aspects of video content, such as Realism and Resolution and Detail, are given appropriate weight in the overall assessment.
5. Consideration of Statistical Significance:

   It is also essential to note the p-values associated with each criterion, which indicate the statistical significance of the results. Criteria with lower p-values are considered to have a more reliable and consistent impact across the dataset, which should be factored into the interpretation of the results. While the chart primarily highlights the importance based on coefficient size, the accompanying regression table should be consulted to understand which findings are statistically robust.

This analysis provides a clear understanding of how each criterion contributes to the overall quality of AI-generated video content. By identifying and quantifying these contributions, we can better target improvements and refine the tools used in content generation to meet the highest standards of quality and user satisfaction.

3.3 Comprehensive Criteria Analysis

To fully understand the performance of each video across a wide range of quality metrics, all relevant criteria were analyzed. These criteria encompass critical aspects of video content, including Fidelity, Realism, Consistency, Accuracy, Relevance, Creativity, Seamlessness, Coherence, Engagement, Innovation, Resolution and Detail, Color Accuracy, Frame Rate and Smoothness, AI Artifacts and Limitations, Uncanny Valley Effect, Bias, and Continuity. The analysis aimed to identify not only the strengths but also the areas where the videos might be lacking, providing a comprehensive assessment of video quality.

3.4 Heatmap Analysis

The heatmap in Fig. 3 visualizes the performance of each video across all the criteria listed above. Each cell in the heatmap represents the performance score of a video on a specific criterion, with color gradients indicating the level of performance—darker shades for better performance and lighter shades for poorer performance.

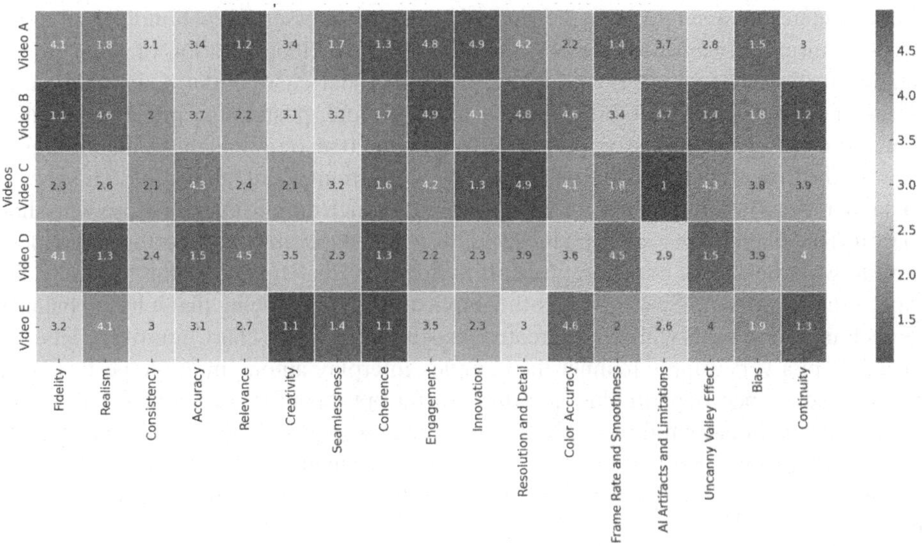

Fig. 3. Heatmap of performance on all criteria across video

3.5 Implications

The comprehensive criteria analysis through the heatmap highlights several key areas for improvement:

Balancing Realism and Creativity: While some videos excel in delivering realistic content, they may lack in creativity, which is essential for engaging and retaining viewers. Efforts should be made to enhance creativity without compromising realism.
Balancing Realism and Creativity: While some videos excel in delivering realistic content, they may lack in creativity, which is essential for engaging and retaining viewers. Efforts should be made to enhance creativity without compromising realism.
Addressing AI Limitations: Videos that suffer from high levels of AI Artifacts and Uncanny Valley Effect indicate a need for improved algorithms that can generate more natural and lifelike content, reducing viewer discomfort.
Enhancing Engagement and Innovation: Videos that score low in Engagement and Innovation suggest a need for more dynamic and novel content that can capture and maintain the audience's interest.
Improving Technical Consistency: Criteria such as Frame Rate and Smoothness, Continuity, and Color Accuracy are crucial for delivering a polished final product. Videos scoring low in these areas should focus on technical enhancements to meet industry standards.

The gaps in the representations on the radar chart (Fig. 4) allow for fine-tuning of the video generation tools, supporting technical and creative standards for better viewer satisfaction and overall engagement. The radar chart helps to indicate how each AI-generated video scores on the wide range of criteria, all the way from Realism, Creativity, and Consistency to effective visualization. This chart is particularly advantageous as it consolidates on a single page the strengths and weaknesses of each individual video across multiple dimensions, thereby facilitating a rapid identification of areas necessitating further refinement. For example, from the radar chart, Video C is excellent in terms of creativity and resolution and details; therefore, postulating great possibilities concerning visually impressive and creative outputs. It also reveals that Video E lags in most of the important areas, including creativity, continuity, and innovation. This means that much work is still required for this to impress in such dimensions for those who shall view it. The graph helps zero in on those points where the even strong-performing videos have to work upon. For example, Video B is strong in Realism and Color Accuracy, but lags in Innovation and Seamlessness-the implication thereby being that it has to balance its technical precision with more creative execution. A radar chart intuitively lets one visualize in a very simple manner the complex interplay among multiple performance criteria and to specify particular opportunities for optimization. Performed in this way, the visual benchmark intuitively gives a guide on how one could go about improving AI video generation technologies by turning developer attention to weak areas-like Innovation and Seamlessness-without losing strengths which videos like Video C already possess.

Fig. 4. Performance radar with weighted importance

3.6 Summary Description

This analysis of AI-generated videos is, at best, a mixed bag of some remarkable strengths and grave concerns across key evaluation criteria (Fig. 5). The base visual quality is strong, with realism, resolution, and color accuracy. However, significant challenges persist in creativity, coherence, engagement, and the presence of AI-related artifacts-all features that most greatly impact viewer experience and believability. Most prominently, the limitations of the uncanny valley effect and continuity in the generated content point to key areas that require more development and refinement in terms of the AI algorithms.

Strong Criteria: The videos generally excel in *Realism*, *Resolution and Detail*, and *Color Accuracy*, indicating a high level of visual fidelity and consistency in color rendering. These are strengths that should be maintained and further optimized.
Middle Criteria: Areas like *Creativity*, *Coherence*, and *Engagement* show varied performance across the videos. While some videos excel, others lag behind, suggesting a need for more consistent approaches in these aspects.
Weakest Criteria: The most critical weaknesses lie in *AI Artifacts and Limitations*, *Uncanny Valley Effect*, and *Continuity*. These areas are where the videos are most deficient, indicating significant room for improvement in the algorithms used to generate content.

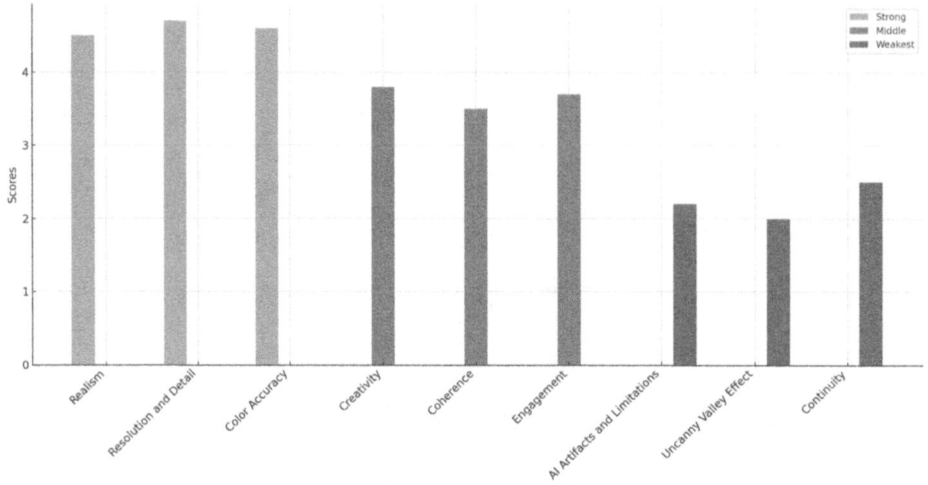

Fig. 5. Grouped bar chart of criteria performance across video

The grouped bar chart below visually represents the performance of various criteria across different categories (Strong, Middle, Weakest). Each bar group shows how each criterion performs relative to others in its category, providing a clear picture of strengths and weaknesses across the videos. This chart helps to highlight the areas that require more attention and improvement, ensuring that the development of video generation tools can be more targeted and effective. By focusing on the weak and middle-performing criteria, developers can make significant strides in enhancing the overall quality and user experience of generated videos.

4 Discussion

The findings from this study reveal that while AI-generated videos excel in *Realism, Resolution and Detail*, and *Color Accuracy*, significant challenges persist in addressing *AI Artifacts, Uncanny Valley Effect*, and *Continuity*. These weaker criteria diminish the overall quality, suggesting that despite impressive visual fidelity, critical areas still require focused improvement. Unlike traditional video quality assessments, which often emphasize limited metrics such as resolution and frame rate, this study offers a comprehensive evaluation of AI-generated content by considering a broader range of criteria. This approach uncovers deficiencies that are essential to the success of AI-driven video production, providing a more detailed and actionable understanding of where current tools are lacking. The strength of this study lies in its holistic approach, capturing the complexity of AI-generated videos through a diverse set of quality metrics. However, the illustrative nature of the data and the reliance on averages may obscure individual variations, which could be explored further in future research.

To elevate the quality of AI-generated videos, the focus should be on:

- **Mitigating AI Artifacts and Uncanny Valley Effects**: Enhance the algorithms to produce smoother, more natural content.

- **Improving Continuity and Engagement**: Develop more robust solutions for seamless transitions and content flow, while also boosting creativity and viewer engagement.

The main contribution of this paper is identifying the critical weaknesses in AI-generated video quality and providing clear pathways for improvement. Future research should aim to refine these weaker and mid-level criteria, establishing standardized benchmarks that can guide the evolution of AI video tools towards producing consistently high-quality content.

5 Conclusions

The key findings of this study indicate that while AI-generated videos demonstrate significant strengths in areas such as Realism, Resolution and Detail, and Color Accuracy [11, 12], they are notably deficient in handling AI Artifacts, Uncanny Valley Effect, and Continuity. These weaknesses highlight the limitations of current AI video generation tools, where high visual fidelity is often achieved at the expense of smooth and natural content delivery. The comprehensive approach taken in this study, which evaluates a wide range of criteria beyond traditional metrics, provides a more nuanced understanding of video quality. This method not only identifies the existing strengths but also pinpoints critical areas that require further development. The impact of this research on the field of AI-generated video quality assessment is significant. By broadening the scope of evaluation criteria, this study contributes to a more holistic understanding of what constitutes high-quality AI-generated content. The identification of specific areas where current tools fall short offers clear directions for improvement, which can guide future advancements in AI video generation technology. These insights are crucial for developers aiming to create more robust and reliable video generation tools that meet the growing demands for high-quality AI-driven content. In conclusion, this study provides a detailed analysis of the strengths and weaknesses of AI-generated videos, offering valuable recommendations for future development. The findings underscore the need for continued research and innovation in AI video generation, particularly in addressing the identified deficiencies. As AI technology continues to evolve, there is significant potential for future developments to overcome these challenges, leading to the creation of more seamless, engaging, and visually stunning AI-generated content.

References

1. Kancharla, P., Channappayya, S.S.: Completely blind quality assessment of user generated video content. IEEE Trans. Image Process. **31**, 263–274 (2022)
2. Wu, H., et al.: Towards explainable in-the-wild video quality assessment: a database and a language-prompted approach. In: Proceedings of the 31st acm international conference on multimedia, pp. 1045–1054 (Year)
3. Aafaq, N., Mian, A., Liu, W., Gilani, S.Z., Shah, M.: Video description: a survey of methods, datasets, and evaluation metrics. ACM Comput. Surv. **52**, 115 (2019)
4. Bandi, A., Adapa, P.V.S.R., Kuchi, Y.E.V.P.K.: The power of generative AI: a review of requirements, models, input-output formats, evaluation metrics, and challenges. Future Internet **15**, 260 (2023)

5. Zhou, P., Wang, L., Liu, Z., Hao, Y., Hui, P., Tarkoma, S., Kangasharju, J.: A survey on generative AI and LLM for video generation, understanding, and streaming (2024). arXiv preprint arXiv:2404.16038
6. Liu, C., Yu, H.: AI-empowered persuasive video generation: a survey. ACM Comput. Surv. **55**, 285 (2023)
7. Conde, M.V., et al.: AIS 2024 challenge on video quality assessment of user-generated content: methods and results. In: Proceedings of the IEEE/CVF conference on computer vision and pattern recognition, pp. 5826–5837 (Year)
8. Kancharla, P., Channappayya, S.S.: Completely blind quality assessment of user generated video content. IEEE Trans. Image Process. **31**, 263–274 (2021)
9. Zhu, H., Chen, B., Zhu, L., Wang, S.: Learning spatiotemporal interactions for user-generated video quality assessment. IEEE Trans. Circuits Syst. Video Technol. **33**, 1031–1042 (2022)
10. Liu, Y., Wu, J., Li, L., Dong, W., Zhang, J., Shi, G.: Spatiotemporal representation learning for blind video quality assessment. IEEE Trans. Circuits Syst. Video Technol. **32**, 3500–3513 (2022)
11. Aziz, M., Rahman, U., Safi, S.A., Abbasi, A.Z.: Visual verity in AI-generated imagery: computational metrics and human-centric analysis (2024). arXiv preprint arXiv:2408.12762
12. Roşca, C.M., Gortoescu, I.A., Tănase, M.R.: Artificial intelligence–powered video content generation tools

A Non-blind Audio Watermarking in 3D Mesh Models Using Daubechies Wavelet Technique

G. Julie Sharine[1], S. D. Aditya Sai[1], L. Jani Anbarasi[1(✉)], and Benson Edwin Raj[2]

[1] School of Computer Science and Engineering, Vellore Institute of Technology, Chennai, India
{juliesharine.g2021,adityasai.sd2021}@vitstudent.ac.in,
janianbarasi.l@vit.ac.in

[2] Department of Computer Information Sciences, Higher Colleges of Technology, Fujairah, UAE
braj@hct.ac.ae

Abstract. Digital watermarking is a copyright protection technique that helps to identify the ownership of the data through a process of hiding digital data. Watermarking in 3D mesh models includes challenges like robustness against attacks and imperceptibility. Embedding Audio in 3D mesh model is used for protecting intellectual property rights and adhering the authenticity of the 3D models. A watermarking process using audio in 3D mesh models is proposed which embeds imperceptible audio watermarks into the mesh while protecting the visual quality of the model. 3D mesh models are pre-processed using Principal Component Analysis to attain normalized model vertices which helps in standardizing the data and improving the efficiency of subsequent watermark embedding. This pre-processed 3D mesh model is transformed into the discrete wavelet transform using Daubechies wavelets and an audio watermark is embedded into the transformed vertices of the 3D mesh model. The watermark is extracted from the watermarked model by performing the Inverse DWT and reconstruction of the audio file is performed to enhance the authentication process thus reducing the risk of false positives or negatives. The extracted watermark and original watermark are compared to assess the effectiveness of the proposed work by evaluating the robustness and imperceptibility. The proposed audio watermarking scheme was evaluated using metrics like PSNR and Hausdorff distance yielding approximately 43 dB and 3.75 $\times$ 10^{-5} respectively.

Keywords: 3D Watermarking · 3D mesh models · Audio signal · Imperceptibility

1 Introduction

In recent years, there has been a significant advancement in Information Technology advancements. With rapid progress in technology and data visualization techniques, the creation and dissemination of 3D models have become increasingly common and in high demand. However, along with this rise comes a multitude of concerns, including

A. Safi et al. (Eds.): ISICS 2024, CCIS 2381, pp. 67–79, 2025.
https://doi.org/10.1007/978-3-031-82931-4_5

copyright infringements, ownership verification, and integrity assurance for 3D models. Addressing these issues has become paramount, particularly in light of concerns surrounding the illegal reproduction of media content. 3D model theft or model duplication leads to copyright protection development and Digital Rights Management (DRM) of multimedia data. Digital Watermarking is one such method that helps in support of multimedia content protection.

The need for owner authentication stems from the challenge of establishing the intellectual property rights of the 3D model creator, which can lead to ownership disputes if not addressed effectively. Watermarking 3D models offers a distinctive solution by embedding a secret code within the mesh structure without altering its appearance. This process involves inserting various types of content, such as messages, audio, video, text, or logos, into the host 3D mesh model. Watermarking techniques can be broadly classified into visible and invisible watermarking.

The Watermarking scheme that is unrecognizable by the human vision is called invisible watermarking and some types of watermarking that are intentionally recognizable are called visible Watermarking Cox et al. [1]. In mesh models, objects are defined by vertices, edges, and faces, forming the basic structure. Various attacks are attempted to destroy or remove the watermarks. Attacks involve the process of cropping, rotation, translation, simplification, and smoothing. Ai et al. [2] observed that complex geometric operations can decrease the visual quality and utility of the model. Araghi et al. [3] proposed that watermarking is performed either in the spatial or spectral domain, with data embedded in the spectral domain exhibiting good imperceptibility and high robustness against attacks compared to the spatial domain.

The contributions of the proposed work are given as follows:

- 3D mesh models are pre-processed using principal component analysis (PCA) that enhances the 3D model vertices, resulting in a structure that is independent and uncorrelated.
- Selection for the.ogg audio file format for watermarking offers advantages in terms of compatibility and efficiency.
- Daubechies 8 wavelet with a 3-level decomposition is employed in the discrete wavelet domain (DWT) enabling high embedding capacity for the watermark embedding and extraction of the audio file through inverse discrete wavelet transform (IDWT).
- Performance is evaluated using metrics such as peak signal-to-noise ratio (PSNR) and Hausdorff distance, ensuring robustness and fidelity.

The proposed paper includes: Sect. 2 discusses the related work about 3D watermarking in the spectral domain along with the limitations of various techniques. The proposed embedding of audio data in 3D model along with the architecture is presented in Sect. 3. Section 4 states the performance evaluation and Sect. 5 present the results obtained by the proposed watermarking technique. Finally, the future scope and conclusion are presented in Sect. 6

2 Related Work

3D mesh models are commonly used in computer graphics, virtual reality, gaming and other fields to represent the geometry and structure of objects or scenes in a 3D space. Audio embedding in 3D mesh watermarking involves integrating audio information into a 3D mesh model. Watermarking in 3D meshes typically involves embedding audio data within vertices, edges, or faces without compromising the visual integrity of the model. Mohammad et al. [4] proposed semi blind scheme, where image and logo is processed and transformed into the DWT domain as watermark for a single pass where LL band undergoes transformation into Singular Value Decomposition (SVD) values. The cover image is processed by two-level decomposition and watermark bits are embedded using the Zigzag technique and the results showed better performance using zigzag embedding. Ikbel Sahayi et al. [5] proposed an innovative technique for enhancing security in 3D models by embedding grayscale images using a hybrid approach. This method leverages both the wavelet domain and spherical harmonics of 3D multiresolution meshes, resulting in improved security measures with high embedding rate and high robustness against various attacks.

Jin Jian et al. [6] proposed watermarking on 3D mesh based on spherical wavelet transform to improve the data embedding capacity. In this method the decomposition of the mesh is done using spherical wavelet transform along with three methods like global parameterization, spherical uniform sampling and spherical wavelet forward transform. Resampling of the data was performed for recovering the topological connectivity to effectively extract the embedded data. Mallika et al. [7] introduced a method for copyright protection of 3D meshes using a multi-resolution domain approach applied in multi-wavelet transforms. This technique involves dual insertion in various types of wavelet transforms, with the first iteration in Haar wavelet transform and the second in Schauder wavelet transform. The watermark embedding includes both mesh description and source mesh signature. O.H.Kalil et al. [8] proposed an blind watermarking technique to embed one pixel of the grey-scale image in each of three vertices that attained better visual quality on watermarked object and the extracted image.

Muna Lathaf [9] examined the low-frequency domain of the host 3D multiresolution mesh and applied wavelet transform to select the coarsest level for data embedding. The embedding process was based on various strength factors, demonstrating improved imperceptibility and robustness against geometric attacks. The correlation factor was utilized to gauge the distortion level in the watermark. Wajdi Elhamzi et al. [10] introduced a novel approach for embedding a high capacity of data using crypto-watermarking in the 3D multiresolution mesh via Clifford multiwavelet transform. This transformation involved two iterations, with the LSB technique applied for watermark insertion. Turboencoder was employed to encode all data generated from SHA512 and RSA algorithms. Despite high data embedding capacity, the proposed method achieved good mesh quality, and extraction remained accurate even after various attacks were applied.

Abdallah [11, 12] partitioned the 3D mesh models into sub-meshes, and embedded the watermark into the spectral coefficients of the partitioned sub-meshes, achieving effective watermark retrieval. This approach demonstrated robustness against various attacks such as scaling and transformation attacks, but required high computational speed. The MeTiS software was utilized to create non-overlapping sub-meshes from the larger mesh, where watermarks were embedded into these sub-meshes. These spectral coefficients were shifted to represent different frequency components, leading to high robustness against smoothing and compression techniques. Mun and Jang [13] introduced a watermarking technique that preserves the printing orientation, ensuring synchronization between the printed and scanned versions and the original orientation. This method involves embedding a binary watermark of any length into a spread spectrum signal by synthesizing a sinusoidal signal in the frequency domain post pre-processing and axis alignment.

3 Proposed Methodology

The proposed work preprocessing the host 3D model using Principal Component Analysis (PCA) to attain normalized model vertices which helps in standardizing the data and improving the efficiency of subsequent watermark embedding. The audio file is chosen as the watermark and is embedded in the discrete wavelet domain of the preprocessed 3D model that allows better imperceptibility and robustness against various attacks, ensuring the integrity of the ownership information. The embedding of audio files into a host 3D mesh was performed at Daubechies 8 wavelet 3-level domain offers a balance between embedding capacity thus maintaining the visual quality of the 3D model. The watermark is extracted from the watermarked model by performing the Inverse DWT and reconstruction of the audio file is performed for enhancing the authentication process thus reducing the risk of false positives or negatives. Figure 1 shows the watermarking technique proposed in this work.

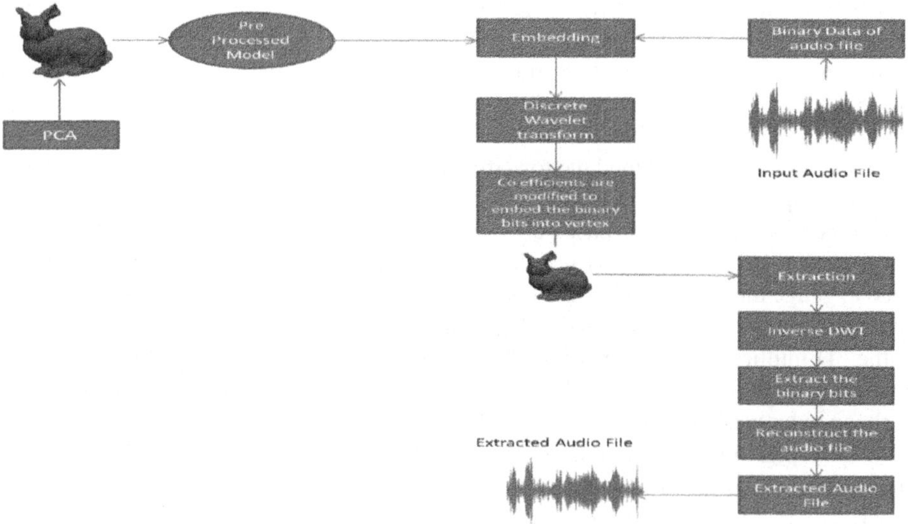

Fig. 1. Overall Architecture of the Proposed 3D Mesh Watermarking

3.1 Pre-processing the 3D Mesh Model Using PCA

The 3D mesh model undergoes preprocessing using PCA [14], which reduces the dimensionality of the 3D model to obtain a normalized representation for the embedding process. PCA, a widely used dimensionality reduction technique, aims to identify the principal directions (eigenvectors) that capture the maximum variance in a high-dimensional dataset. Mathematically, PCA involves computing the eigenvectors and eigenvalues of the covariance matrix of the dataset, where the eigenvectors represent the principal components and the eigenvalues indicate the amount of variance explained by each component. By projecting the data onto these principal components, PCA effectively reduces the dimensionality while retaining much of the original information. This technique offers various advantages, including simplified analysis, improved interpretability, and enhanced computational efficiency, making it effective in data preprocessing tasks. Additionally, PCA helps to mitigate the curse of dimensionality and reduces noise and redundancy in the dataset, thereby facilitating better data visualization and feature selection. The covariance matrix (Cov_M for the data points M_i, mean vector the 3D mesh model $\overline{M}$ and number of vertices in 3D models V is given as Eq. 1.

$$Cov_M = \frac{1}{V}\sum_{i=1}^{V}(M_i - \overline{M})(M_i - \overline{M})^T \tag{1}$$

The eigen value decomposition where e refers to the eigen vector and ρ corresponds to the eogen value as shown in Eq. 2. The projected 3D data matrix P' is obtained from the original 3D mesh model M_i, and matrix of principal component W as given in Eq. 3.

$$Cov_M e = \rho e \tag{2}$$

$$P = M_i W \tag{3}$$

Explained variance (E_V) that quantifies how much of the original information in the data is captured by each principal component is given in Eq. 4 where p is the number of principle components.

$$E_V = \frac{\rho_i}{\sum_{i=1}^{P}\rho_i} \times 100\% \tag{4}$$

This is performed iteratively to compute the principal component that efficiently reduced the dimensionality of the 3D mesh model while effectively retaining the variance to enhance the model perceptibility.

3.2 Daubechies Discrete Wavelet Domain of 3D Mesh Model

Wavelet transforms are mathematical transformations widely used across various fields due to their exceptional ability for energy compression [15, 16]. Transform domain techniques, including Discrete Cosine Transform (DCT), Singular Value Decomposition (SVD), Discrete Fourier Transform (DFT), and Discrete Wavelet Transform (DWT), are employed in various applications. Watermarking in the transform domain ensures high robustness and fidelity. The Daubechies wavelets, named after Ingrid Daubechies, constitute a family of orthogonal wavelets that define a discrete wavelet transform, characterized by a maximum number of vanishing moments for a given support. These wavelets generate an orthogonal multiresolution analysis for each wavelet type using scaling functions. Similar to the Haar wavelet transform, Daubechies wavelets compute running averages and differences using additional signal data.

DaubJ wavelet strand can be extended to multiple levels as many times and length of signal is divided by 2. If a signal referred as F has even number of 'N' values, then the 1-level Daub J transform mapping is mapped as given in Eq. 5.

$$\mathrm{F} \xrightarrow{D_1} \left(a^1/d^1\right) \tag{5}$$

The signal F and its sub signal a^1 where the first fluctuation is referred as sub signal a^1. Each value a_m of ($a^1 = a_1 \ldots\ldots a_{N/2}$) is equal to the scalar product as shown in Eq. 6.

$$a_m = f \cdot V_m^1 \tag{6}$$

where f which is a 1-level signal and its scaling signals is referred to as V_m^1. Likewise, each value applied in d_m in of $d = (d1 \ldots\ldots d_{N/2})$ is equal to the scalar product represented as Eq. 7.

$$d_m = f \cdot w_m^1 \tag{7}$$

where f which is a 1-level wavelet w_m. In Daubechies wavelet transform, a pair of linear filters is employed, with each filter accompanied by a quadrature mirror filter. The coefficients of the linear filter, denoted as αi, are determined using the quadrature mirror filter to compute coefficient values of order 4. The scaling coefficients $\alpha_1, \alpha_2, \alpha_3, \alpha_4$ can be expressed as Eq. 8.

$$\alpha_1 = \frac{1+\sqrt{3}}{4\sqrt{2}}, \alpha_2 = \frac{3+\sqrt{3}}{4\sqrt{2}}, \alpha_3 = \frac{3-\sqrt{3}}{4\sqrt{2}}, \alpha_4 = \frac{1-\sqrt{3}}{4\sqrt{2}} \tag{8}$$

The Daubechies wavelet transforms can be included with DaubJ transforms for $J = 4, 8, 10 \ldots .20$ values and the scaling numbers as $\alpha_1 \ldots\ldots\ldots \alpha_{ij}$ if it satisfies $\alpha_1^2 + \alpha_2^2 \ldots\ldots\ldots + \alpha_j^2 = 1$ and $\alpha_1 + \alpha_2 + \ldots\cdots + \alpha_j = \sqrt{2}$ condition. The DaubJ wavelets generates a smooth and oscillatory signal for audio embedding due to their efficient representation of both low and high frequency localization, computational efficiency, and robustness against signal distortions.

3.3 Audio Embedding in 3D Mesh Model

In the proposed method watermark is chosen as an audio file where.ogg audio file format is considered. The .ogg file is converted into binary bits. The audio file is converted to binary bits and each binary bit is embedded into the wavelet domain. To analyze imperceptibility, an embedding strength factor denoted as α is applied, with values ranging from 0.0001 to 0.99. These different strength factor values are utilized to assess the imperceptibility of the resulting watermarked 3D model.

3.4 Watermark Extraction

The process of 3D watermark extraction is essential for computer graphics and digital media security. It entails recovering or erasing covert watermarks inserted into 3D models, textures, or animations. DWT decomposition is performed on the flattened vertices of a mesh to extract the watermark from the specified co-efficient of the highest frequency sub band. Inverse DWT is performed on the extracted wavelet co-efficient in order to reconstruct to the original signal.

4 Results and Discussions

This section provides details on the dataset utilized and the tests carried out on the watermark embedding and extraction process. The imperceptibility comparison between the various types of watermarks like text, binary image and grayscale image is compared with the audio watermark embedded in the DWT domain.

4.1 Experimental Setup

The proposed technique was performed using python software. The processing is done using the OpenCV libraries. Intel ® CORE ™i5-4200U CPV@1.60 GHzMhz,2 CORE(S),4 Logical Processor, 4 GB Memory Size, and 1 TB Hard-Disk are the basic system configuration. Python Libraries trimesh 3.21.6, Pywavelsts 1.4.1, Pandas-1.4.4, Numpy 1.23.3 are used for processing, and Matplotlib-3.6.0 is used for plotting.

4.2 Dataset Description

This section details the dataset description about the 3D model and the audio files used in this proposed work.

3D Mesh Models

A 3D mesh is a very basic geometric representation that is depicted as a collection of vertices and edges put together in 3D space to form polygons [17–19]. Polygons of the same type make up a regular mesh, where the frequently used is a triangular mesh, which is made completely of triangles. Each of the object models has three sets: edges, vertices, and faces. A correlated 3D point and a collection of edges that come together at that point define a vertex. If an edge is not a straight line, it has a starting point, an ending point, a face to its left and right, and an arc that defines its shape. A face is made up of a surface that defines its shape and a number of borders, such as its outer boundaries and whole boundaries. A boundary has a face and a set of edges that go along with it. A polygonal mesh is defined as $[V, E, F]$ with vertices $V = [V_1, V_2 \ldots\ldots V_m]$, set of edges $E = \{e_{ij}\}, 1 \leq i, j \leq m$, and '$n$' faces $F = \{f_1, f_2, \ldots\ldots f_m\}$. Every vertex $V_i = (x_i, y_i, z_i)$ consists of 3 values representing the position in 3D space. The pair of connected vertices V_i and V_j is represented as an edge e_{ij} as shown in Eq. 9. Sample 3D models used for analysis in the proposed work is shown in Fig. 2.

$$V = \begin{bmatrix} V_1 \\ V_2 \\ \vdots \\ V_m \end{bmatrix} F = \begin{bmatrix} f_1 \\ f_2 \\ \vdots \\ f_m \end{bmatrix} = \begin{bmatrix} V_{i1} & V_{j1} & \cdots & V_{k1} \\ V_{I2} & V_{j2} & \cdots & V_{k2} \\ \vdots & \vdots & \ldots & \vdots \\ V_{im} & V_{jm} & \cdots & V_{k3} \end{bmatrix} \tag{9}$$

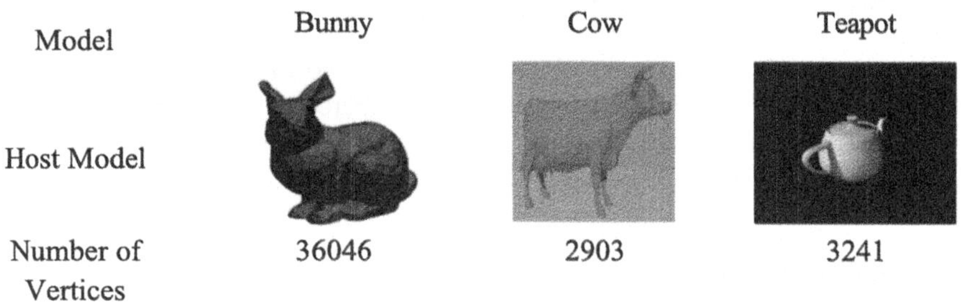

Fig. 2. Sample 3D models along with its Vertices Count

Opus audio File

Opus is created by the Xiph.Org Foundation [20]. It is an open source loss audio coding format and is usually used in internet based communication platforms. In this paper OPUS files are chosen for their relatively small size and flexible bitrates. We could also go with mp3 or wav file extensions, but Opus was chosen for its efficient compression rate. The file bell.opus was chosen for the embedding process. The file is first run through for reducing the file size to 4.5 KB from 8.24 KB. For the embedding process db8 wavelet with level 3 is chosen. In the proposed work 1000 vertices are used for embedding with a bit rate of 16 bits. Table 1 shows some sample audio file types along with its uses.

Table 1. Audio File types and Uses:

File Name	File Type	Uses
MP3/MP4	Common File Type	Used in Internet
AAC	Lossy Compressed format	Used in iPod and Apple Devices
Ogg Vorbis	Open Source, Lossy Compressed	Free and editable
FLAC	Lossless Compressed file format	Used in all devices
WAV/AIFF	Lossless Uncompressed Audio	Used in PC and Apple Devices

Watermark Embedding in Wavelet Domain of a 3D model

DWT decomposition is performed using Daubechies-8 wavelet and an audio file format of.ogg file is used as watermark in the 3D mesh model. The highest frequency sub band is chosen for embedding the watermark. Watermark embedding is performed for different strength factors α and Table 2 illustrates the various host models and watermarked models generated for different embedding strength factors.

Table 2. Host 3D model and Watermarked 3D model for different strength factor α:

Host Model	*α =0.00001*	*α =0.01*	*α =0.5*	*α =0.99*
	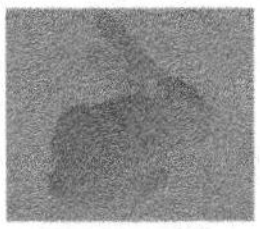	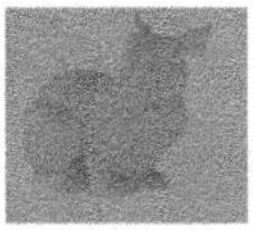		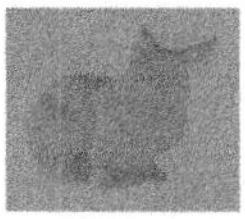
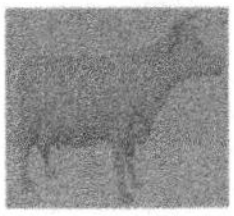	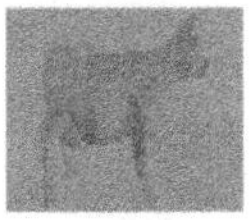	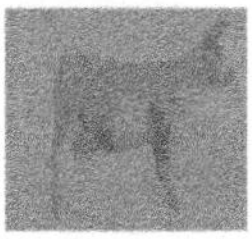	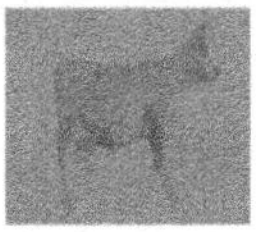	
	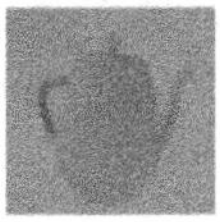		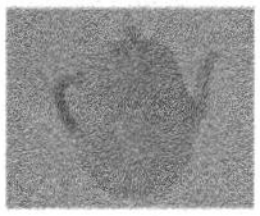	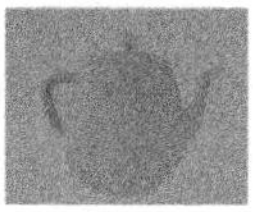

Watermark Extraction from the 3D Watermarked Model

DWT decomposition on the flattened vertices of a mesh is performed and extraction is done for a specified number of co-efficient in the highest frequency sub band. Inverse DWT is performed on wavelet co-efficient and reconstruction of the original signal is obtained. Table 3 shows the embedded audio for different host models and the audios the extracted audios from the models.

Table 3. Extraction of watermarked Audio from the Host Model:

Strength Factors	α =0.00001	α =0.01	α =0.5	α =0.99
Original Audio	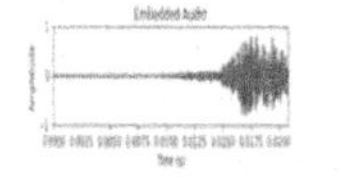	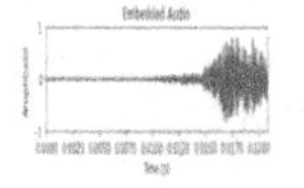	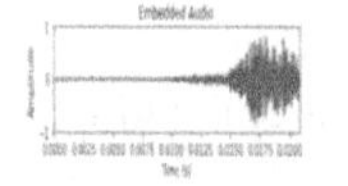	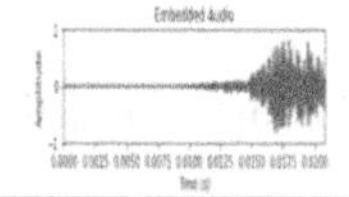
Extracted Audio For Bunny Model	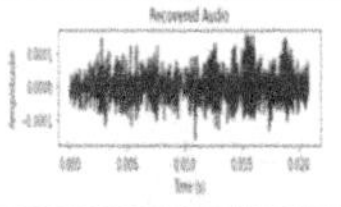	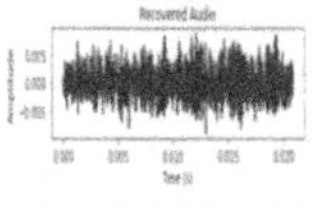	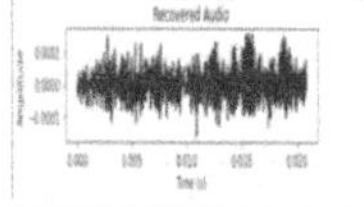	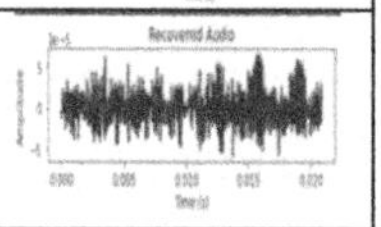
Extracted Audio for Cow Model	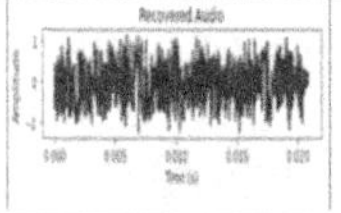	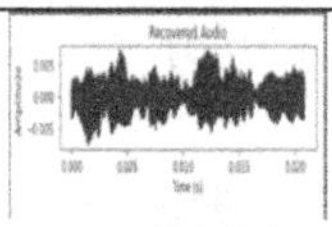	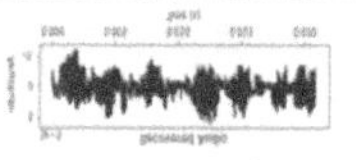	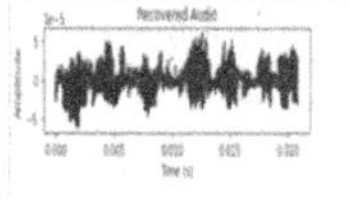
Extracted Audio for Tea Pot	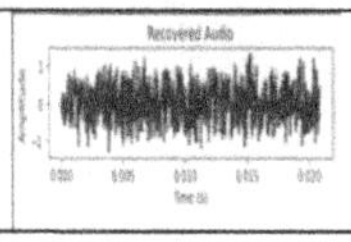	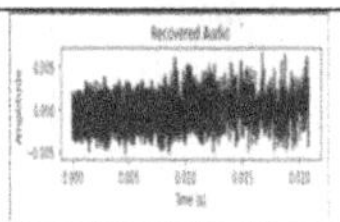	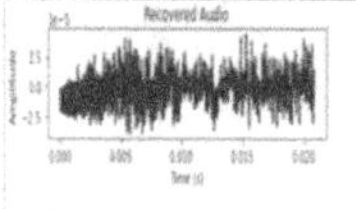	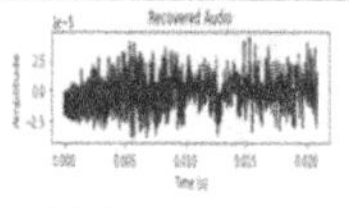

5 Performance Evaluation

Imperceptibility is the major factor to be considered for evaluating the performance of the watermark embedding and extraction process. In the proposed method, the quality of the extracted audio file is measured by the peak signal to noise ratio. The visual quality of the watermarked model is analysed by the Hausdorff distance.

5.1 Peak Signal to Noise Ratio (PSNR)

The other metric used to assess the geometrical distortion between the host and watermarked model is signal-to-noise ratio (SNR), as given in Eqs. 10, and 11 where max refers to the highest value present in the vertices, v_{ix}, v_{iy} *and* v_{iy} shows the original signal and v'_{ix}, v'_{iy} *and* v'_{iz} represents the watermarked signal. The PSNR value obtained is 43.5 dB.

$$\mathrm{SNR} = 20\log_{10}\frac{\sum_{i=1}^{N}(v_{ix}^2 + v_{iy}^2 + v_{iz}^2)}{\sum_{i=1}^{N_v}\left(v'_{ix} - v_{ix}\right)^2 + \left(v'_{iy} - v_{iy}\right)^2 + \left(v'_{iz} - v_{iz}\right)^2} \tag{10}$$

$$PSNR = 20\ log_{10}(Max) + \mathrm{SNR} \tag{11}$$

5.2 Hausdorff Distance

The Hausdorff distance is a metric that measures the degree of resemblance between two sets of points. The metric is used in 3D watermarking for analysing the visual quality of the watermarked model with the original model. It is calculated by finding the minimum distance between each point in one set and the closest point in the other set. This distance can be used to estimate the degree of resemblance between each vertex v of the host model M and the watermarked model M′ as shown in Eq. 12.

$$D(\mathrm{M}, \mathrm{M}') = \max(d_H(\mathrm{M}, \mathrm{M}'), d_H(\mathrm{M}', \mathrm{M})) \tag{12}$$

Hausdorff distance is calculated for models like the Bunny, Cow and Teapot by embedding the binary bits in the Wavelet domain of the mesh model. Hausdorff distance obtained for the various models ranged from 2.75×10^{-5} to 3.76×10^{-5}.

5.3 Effectiveness of the Proposed Work

Audio embedding in 3D models was executed in Python and analysed for a variety of 3D models. The 3D models like Bunny, Cow and Teapot are used in experiments are pre-processed by PCA. The .ogg audio file type is used for embedding in the DWT domain of 3D model. The audio file is converted into binary bits and embedded in the DWT domain. The analysis of the experiments shows the use of wavelet domain to embed audio in to 3D model shows excellence. The experimental evaluation of the proposed watermarking scheme was analysed with respect to imperceptibility (PSNR) and Hausdorff distance to identify the level of distortion and visual quality. The Table 4 shows the PSNR and Hausdorff distance for the watermarked models.

Table 4. PSNR and Hausdorff Distance of the watermarked model

Model name	Strength Factor	$\alpha = 0.\,00001$	$\alpha = 0.01$	$\alpha = 0.5$	$\alpha = 0.99$
	PSNR	−49.00 dB	34.05 dB	43.501 dB	43.507 dB
	Hausdorff	3.31×10^{-5}	3.31×10^{-5}	3.31×10^{-5}	3.31×10^{-5}
	PSNR	−49.00 dB	34.05 dB	43.501 dB	43.507 dB
	Hausdorff	3.31×10^{-5}	3.31×10^{-5}	3.31×10^{-5}	3.31×10^{-5}
	PSNR	−49.002 dB	36.72 dB	43.504 dB	43.507 dB
	Hausdorff	2.75×10^{-5}	2.75×10^{-5}	2.75×10^{-5}	2.75×10^{-5}

5.4 Comparison with Existing Watermarks

A comparison is conducted between the proposed audio watermarking method and existing watermarking techniques embedded in the wavelet domain. The visual quality of the watermarked model is evaluated against the original model, using different types of watermarks such as text and grayscale images. Table 5 presents the comparison of these different watermark types with audio embedding. Our proposed method demonstrates enhanced PSNR and Hausdorff values compared to other watermark types, indicating improved performance.

Table 5. Comparison with the State of Art research works

Ref	Types of Watermarks	PSNR dB	Hausdorff
Laftah [9]	Text	40.12	0.00002
Khalil et al. [8]	Gray scale Image	22.59	–
Proposed Method	Audio	43.5	0.00003

6 Conclusion and Future Work

In conclusion, this proposed watermarking technique embedded audio files in the wavelet domain for 3D mesh models. By choosing.ogg audio files and converting them into binary bits, the method effectively embeds the watermark into the wavelet domain of the pre-processed 3D model. The embedding strength factor α was varied to analyze imperceptibility, and the method achieved promising results with respect to imperceptibility and robustness, as evidenced by high PSNR values and Hausdorff distances. Comparisons with existing watermarking techniques, including text and grayscale image watermarks, revealed superior performance of the proposed audio watermarking method in terms of PSNR values. Overall, this study demonstrates the effectiveness and potential applicability of audio watermarking in enhancing the security and integrity of 3D mesh models. Future research work could explore the resilience of these techniques against diverse model attacks.

References

1. Cox, I.J., et al.: Digital watermarking and steganography. Morgan Kaufmann Publishers, Amsterdam/Boston (2008)
2. Ai, Q.S., Liu, Q., Zhou, Z.D., Yang, L., Xie, S.Q.: A new digital watermarking scheme for 3D triangular mesh models. Signal Process. **89**(11), 2159–2170 (2009)
3. Araghi, T.K., et al.: A survey on digital image watermarking techniques in spatial and transform domains. Int. J. Adv. Image Process. Tech. **3**(1), 6–10 (2016)
4. Mohammed, A.A., et al.: An imperceptible semi-blind image watermarking scheme in DWT-SVD domain using a zigzag embedding technique. Multimed. Tools Appl. **79**(43), 32095–32118 (2020)

5. Sayahi, I., et al.: Robust hybrid watermarking approach for 3D multiresolution meshes based on spherical harmonics and wavelet transform. Multimed. Tools Appl. **82**, 1–26 (2023)
6. Jian-qiu, J., et al.: Watermarking on 3D mesh based on spherical wavelet transform. J. Zhejiang Univ. Sci. A **5**(3), 251–258 (2004)
7. Jallouli M, et al.: Robust watermarking approach for 3D multiresolution meshes based on multi-wavelet transform, SHA512 and turbocodes. In: Computer analysis of images and patterns: 19th international conference, CAIP 2021, virtual event, September 28–30, 2021, proceedings, part II 19. Springer International Publishing (2021)
8. Khalil, O.H., Elhadad, A., Ghareeb, A.J.T.I.S.J.: A blind proposed 3D mesh watermarking technique for copyright protection. Imaging Sci. J. **68**(2), 90–99 (2020)
9. Laftah, M.M.: 3D model watermarking based on wavelet transform. Iraqi J. Sci. **62**, 4999–5007 (2021)
10. Wajdi, E., Jallouli, M., Bouteraa, Y.: High efficiency crypto-watermarking system based on clifford-multiwavelet for 3D meshes security. Comput. Mater. Continua **73**(2), 4329 (2022)
11. Abdallah, E.E., Hamza, A.B., Bhattacharya, P.: Spectral graph-theoretic approach to 3D mesh watermarking. In: Proceedings of graphics interface 2007, pp. 327–334 (2007)
12. Abdallah, E.E., Hamza, A.B., Bhattacharya, P.: Watermarking 3d models using spectral mesh compression. SIViP **3**(4), 375 (2009)
13. Mun, S.-M., Jang, H.-U., Kim, D.-G., Choi, S., Lee, H.-K.: A robust 3d mesh watermarking scheme against cropping. In: 2015 International conference on 3D imaging (IC3D), pp. 1–6. IEEE (2015)
14. Maćkiewicz, A., Ratajczak, W.: Principal components analysis (PCA). Comput. Geosci. **19**(3), 303–342 (1993)
15. Singh, A.K., et al.: Wavelet based image watermarking: futuristic concepts in information security. Proc. Natl. Acad. Sci., India, Sect. A **84**, 345–359 (2014)
16. Ali, M., Ahn, C.W.: An optimized watermarking technique based on self-adaptive DE in DWT–SVD transform domain. Signal Process. **94**, 545–556 (2014)
17. https://graphics.stanford.edu/data/3Dscanrep/
18. https://www.adobe.com/in/creativecloud/video/discover/best-audio-format.html
19. https://www.xiph.org
20. https://www.canto.com/blog/audio-file-types

Assessing the Impact of Data Augmentation Techniques on YOLO's Performance in PV Anomaly Detection

Zakwan Skaf(✉), Imad Zyout, Mansoor Albanna, Abdulla Alshareif, and Abulla Al Ali

Higher Colleges of Technology, Sharjah Campuses, Sharjah, UAE
zskaf@hct.ac.ae

Abstract. Solar energy has become of specific interest since it is more affordable than any other energy source, causing less environmental hazard. With improved analytics and monitoring, anomalies in solar energy systems will be detected and resolved with speed, enhancing the overall prevention of failures, lengthening the periods of effective maintenance, and ensuring system dependability and efficiency. According to recent research, You Only Look Once (YOLO), one of the most advanced target detection algorithms available for multiple defects in solar panels, depends heavily on the training dataset for the best accuracy results. Therefore, its performance will be poor if the number of samples with defects is low. Using data augmentation to raise the quantity of training samples is a practical way to improve YOLO performance. This paper assesses the impact of various data augmentation techniques on the performance of the YOLOv5 model using precision, recall, and mAP50. The results reveal that the mAP50 of the YOLOv5 algorithm with the scaling data augmentation technique improves by 2.9% over that obtained with the original dataset. The combined YOLOv5 and scale data augmentation method gives precisions, recalls, and mAP50 scores attained for PV panel defect detection as 88.3%, 89.2%, and 89.9%, respectively.

Keywords: PV Panels · YOLO · Data Augmentation · Anomaly Detection

1 Introduction

The UAE has revised its 2050 energy strategy in view of developments in energy generation and reduction in emissions technologies. Among the major goals is the three-fold increase in the contribution of renewable energy sources in the energy mix by 2030. This will involve more investments in clean power to manage the increasing electricity demand while ensuring that zero carbon emissions are attained by the year 2050. In essence, this places the UAE at the top of those countries that, within the MENA region, have taken the initiative to do so, showing a fierce commitment to emission-free targets. Important to note is that renewable energy is a plethora of this strategy obtained from natural processes, which are sustainable. These solar, wind, hydro, and biomass types can help avert greenhouse gas emissions and add diversity to the nation's energy mix.

A. Safi et al. (Eds.): ISICS 2024, CCIS 2381, pp. 80–94, 2025.
https://doi.org/10.1007/978-3-031-82931-4_6

In fact, among all these sources of renewable energy, prominence has been accorded to harnessing sunlight as the prime mover of electricity generation via solar panels. This will be in conjunction with the UAE's environmental protection and energy requirements, which is set to embrace PV systems capable of effectively transforming sunlight into clean electric power. For PV systems to generate maximum power and efficiency, their high performance should be maintained. One major way to maintain performance is through prompt fault detection in PV components and scheduling maintenance tasks in advance to prevent drastic efficiency drops. Researchers have thus been evolving many image acquisition methods and deep machine learning framework approaches to anomaly detection and classification of anomalies on PV panels [1–6].

To improve detection accuracy, the YOLO series was developed. YOLO (you only look once) is an object detection algorithm that gained popularity over recent years. Released in 2015, what we now call YOLO V1 unifies target classification and localization into a regression problem. It is faster than CNN, less likely to predict false positives on backgrounds, and is very good at generalization. However, it still falls short in some respects. Mainly regarding its bounding box, which makes it hard to differentiate smaller objects [7, 8]. A year later, in 2016, YOLO V2 was released. It outperforms other algorithms like Faster RCNN. It has been improved compared with YOLO V1 with batch normalization and High-Resolution Classifier and anchor boxes. YOLO V3 came out in 2018. It uses bounding boxes that come in different scales. It is better at identifying small objects but struggles with medium and large ones than the previous versions [9].In 2020, YOLO V4 has been released. It utilises a new cross-stage partial network architecture and training techniques, such as a bag of freebies and a bag of specials. YOLO V4 not only outshines its predecessor in terms of speed and accuracy but also beats state-of-the-art alternatives [10]. In the same year, YOLO V5 was developed. YOLO V5 uses the PyTorch user-friendly framework, which is easy-to-read code. Along with its lightweight size, YOLO V5 is great if you need to train, patch, and release quickly, making it popular with application developers [7]. Then, in 2022, YOLO V6 was released with a focus on optimizing both model performance and inference speed. YOLOv6 incorporates new design elements like the EfficientRep Backbone and techniques like knowledge distillation to enhance its performance further, making it good for real-time applications [11]. Also, in the same year, YOLO V7 was released, revealing several innovations like E-ELAN (Extended Efficient Layer Aggregation Networks) for improving feature representation and dynamic label assignment and maximizing the trade-off between accuracy and efficiency. It improved the performance while maintaining a high inference speed [12]. Finally, YOLO V8 was launched in 2023. By comparing its performance with older YOLO versions like YOLO V5, it concluded that while YOLO V5 has the upper hand in efficiency, YOLO V8 has better visual detection for complex scenarios like fires and smoke [13]. February 2024 saw the introduction of YOLOv9 as its most recent mainstream variant [14]. Two critical inventions in YOLOv9 are the Generalized Efficient Layer Aggregation Network and the Programmable Gradient Information architecture. Building on the innovative momentum of the YOLO series, another major milestone was the release of YOLOv10 in 2024. This improves upon the prior by solving the problems that make real-time object detection tasks of a great number of applications necessary, including auto-navigation and agricultural monitoring [15]. The timeline for YOLO algorithm development is shown in Fig. 1.

YOLOv5, one of the most sophisticated target detection algorithms available, is largely dependent on the training dataset for optimal performance. The model will not be able to fully finish training if the number of defect fault images that can be acquired is low, lowering defect detection accuracy. Improving the YOLO algorithm's generalization ability is one of the most difficult challenges when implemented for anomaly detection of PV panels. Challenges such as model overfitting and small datasets lead to models with poor generalizability. Data Augmentation is one technique that has been developed to reduce model overfitting and deal with YOLO applications on small datasets. As a result, anomaly detection of PV panels through data augmentation remains a potential solution to this issue. Section 2 presents a brief overview of data augmentation techniques.

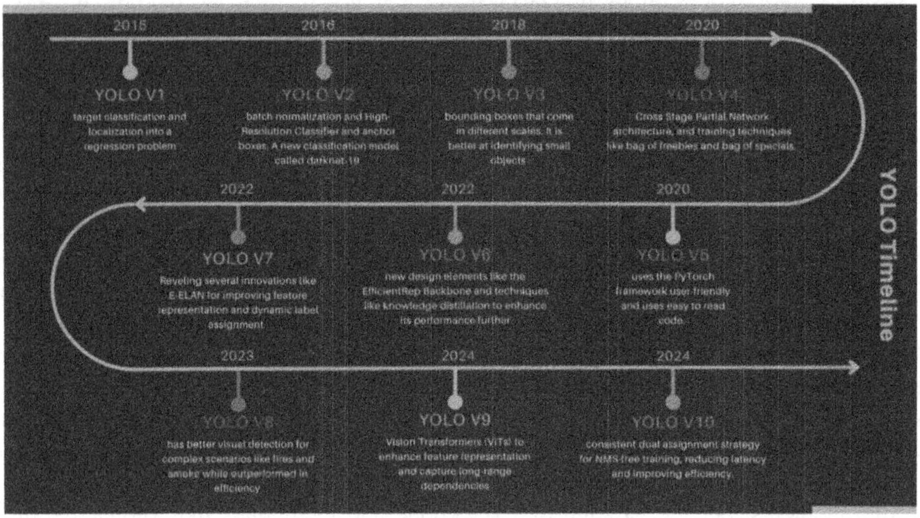

Fig. 1. YOLO Timeline

2 Data Augmentation

Data augmentation is essential in deep learning, which aims to work with limited data [16]. Different techniques help artificially increase the size and improve the quality of training datasets so that more intricate models may be learned in the process known as deep learning [17]. Data augmentation can be described as taking an image and applying various operations to it to create one or more new images while keeping the original label unaltered [18]. Data augmentation has many benefits. It reduces overfitting by expanding the training data to increase the amount of directly derived training data from the original dataset [19]. Moreover, it has been useful for migrating from computer models to physical tasks in general. On the other side, data augmentation satisfied the two core concerns of researchers: producing more data out of a small amount of data and suppressing over-fitting [17, 19]. Nonetheless, data augmentation has its drawbacks. The augmented data will keep the biases that were in the initial dataset. For example, when a set is skewed or unbalanced, its augmented version also reflects these biases, and the skewed or unbalanced data set may contain the same bias levels as the supplemented [17]. Moreover, data augmentation can't correct every bias in a small dataset. If we have a dataset for a dog breed classification task and it doesn't contain even one instance of a golden retriever, then no matter what kind of augmentation is applied, it won't be able to create the representational dataset for golden retriever [16].

Image data augmentation can be broadly categorized into traditional transformations and deep learning transformations [16]This paper will focus on traditional approaches only. Figure 2 shows the main categories of conventional data augmentation techniques.

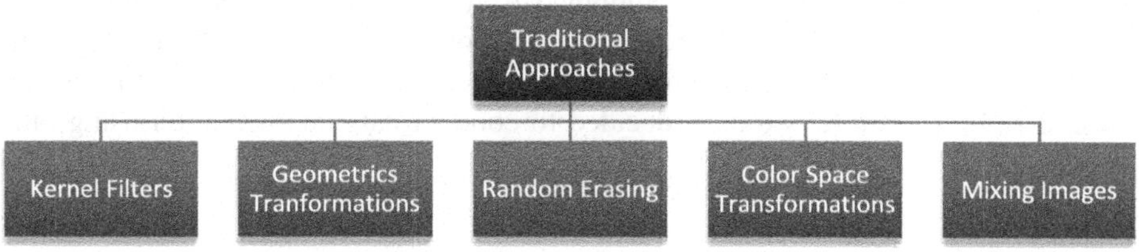

Fig. 2. Traditional Data Augmentation Techniques

The traditional data augmentation approaches include the following techniques:

Kernel Filters: Images can be blurred or sharpened using kernel filters. These specific filters move a matrix of n x n over an image, using a Gaussian blur filter to give a blurred one or high-contrast vertical and horizontal edge filters to make it sharper along the edges [16].

Geometric Transformation: These methods can be termed the most straightforward to apply and, if correctly done, very effective. These are some of the reasons why this technique will be used in carrying out data augmentation for this study [16, 20]. Some of the techniques for this group include:

- Scaling: This involves increasing or decreasing the size of the photos. This can be done by either expanding the image to increase its size or cropping it to decrease the size.
- Rotation: As the term shows, this method performs a rotation in an image by a certain degree from 0° to 360°. One can also define the centre of rotation manually.
- Translation: This routine only shifts the X and Y directions.
- Shearing: This method distorts images at the X and Y axes based on coordinates.
- Flipping: As the term describes, flipping is the act of flipping an image's pixels in either a horizontal or vertical direction.

Random Erasing: As the name indicates, the random erasing method consists of randomly removing parts of the original image.[21] This simple technique is very useful to avoid overfitting since it forces the model to focus on the whole image and not just one of its features This technique has not been used in this work due to the intention to preserve essential info in case the faults are partially corrected.

Color Space Transformation: Digital picture data is usually represented as a tensor of dimension, which encompasses the height, width, and color channels [22]. Hence, one of the simplest color augmentations will be extracting one color channel, for example, R, G, or B. Extracting one matrix and concatenating two zero matrices from the other color channels readily maps an image to its representation in one color channel. Adjusting the brightness of the image is also fairly easy, as this only requires manipulation of the RGB values through some matrix operations.

Mixing Images: Several photos are combined to create a new one. Although this method may seem strange to the human eye, it has been proven to perform well in many of the most famous datasets. There are, however, very few cases when concatenating images is useful [23]. Therefore, we have decided to conduct data augmentation using other methods.

3 Yolo Algorithm

In this paper, the YOLOV5 model is adopted as the baseline model for PV anomaly detection, and its architecture is described in detail in Fig. 3.

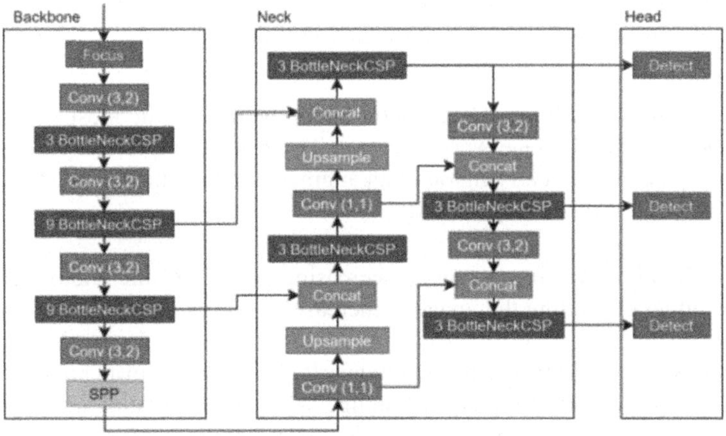

Fig. 3. YOLO V5 Structure [16]

YOLOV5 is one of the most lightweight models. It is designed to be relatively small and run quickly, with comparatively modest computing requirements compared to other similar models of its type. YOLOV5 architecture is made up of three distinct components: the backbone, the neck, and the output head. The main functionality of the backbone part in a given network is to identify the feature of an input image. The fundamental concept implemented in the YOLO v5 model is the CSP (Cross Stage Partial Networks), which essentially serves as the backbone to extract as many features as possible from a given image. The neck part is largely exploited to build feature pyramids. Feature pyramids are beneficial to models in the sense that they help in the generalization and scaling of objects. It helps recognize shapes of different sizes and dimensions. To enhance model performance, feature pyramids are employed, where PANET is incorporated into the YOLOV5 model. The head is used mainly in the final detection phase. It focuses on the last stage of the detection process. It generates final output vectors with class probability and bounding box coordinates which have been subjected to anchors.

4 Performance Evaluation Metrics

Recall, precision, mAP, and the F1 score represent the four key metrics frequently utilized for evaluating and comparing models [24]; our selection was to assess the performance of the proposed models. It is important to note that higher values in mAP, precision, recall, and F1 scores signify improved outcomes.

The recall metric is the ratio between the correctly classified positives (true positive) and the total number of positives (true positive and false negative). The equation for calculating the recall is.

$$\text{Recall} = \frac{TP}{TP + FN} \tag{1}$$

Precision is a metric calculated as the ratio between true positives and the total number of positives (true positives and false positives). The equation for calculating the precision is

$$\text{Precision} = \frac{TP}{TP + FP} \tag{2}$$

where True Positive (TP), True Negative (TN), False Positive (FP), and False Negative (FN).

The F1 score is a comprehensive evaluation metric which takes the harmonic mean of recall and precision. The equation for calculating the F1 score is.

$$\text{F1 score} = 2 \times \frac{Precision \times Recall}{Precision + Recall} \tag{3}$$

Average Precision (AP) computes the area under the precision-recall curve, providing a single value that encapsulates the model's precision and recall performance.

$$AP = \int_0^1 P(R)dR \tag{4}$$

Mean Average Precision (mAP extends the concept of AP by calculating the average AP values across multiple object classes. This is useful in multi-class object detection scenarios to comprehensively evaluate the model's performance.

$$mAP = \frac{\sum_{j=0}^{n} AP(j)}{n} \tag{5}$$

mAP50 represents mean average precision which is calculated at an intersection over union (IoU) threshold of 0.50.

5 Data Description

In this research paper, the PVEL-AD dataset was provided by Hebei University of Technology and Beihang University [24]. It contains EL-scanned images of PV cells. These images include both defect-free images and twelve different types of defective panels. The defective images are categorized based on the type of defect, such as cracks, broken grids, black cores, unaligned, thick lines, etc. Due to variations in sample counts across defect types, this study excludes types with fewer than 500 samples. Furthermore, the dataset encompasses both high and low-resolution images, as illustrated in Fig. 4. Approximately 6.91% of the dataset consists of low-resolution images removed entirely from the dataset. As a result, we used only the following four categories of defects in our paper, namely black core (D1), crack (D2), finger (D3), and horizontal dislocation (D4). Figure 3 presents examples from each defect category.

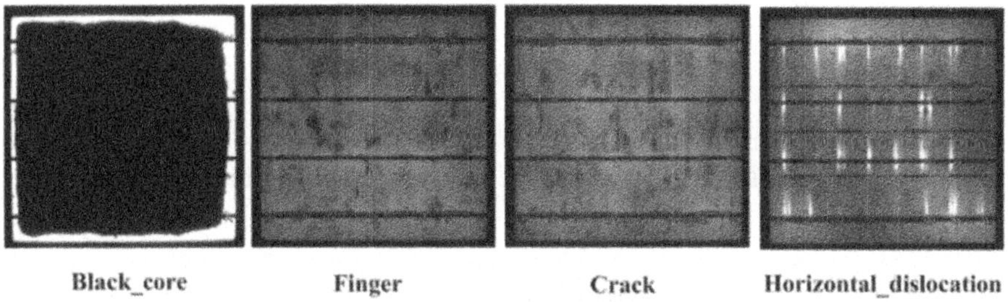

Fig. 4. Type of Defects

6 Results and Discussion

In our paper, we trained the YOLOv5 model using the PVEL-AD dataset as input. The goal of YOLOV5 implementation is to evaluate the algorithm's performance in identifying defective PV panels with various flaws. In the YOLO series model, the main evaluation metrics are precision (P), recall (R), and mean average accuracy (mAP), which can easily be read from this graphical presentation because they come directly from the training process using the PVEL-AD dataset. The experimental dataset was divided into three subsets based on random selection: testing, validation, and training. The present method also allows the possibility of cross-validation and early stopping in order to prevent a model from overfitting. The subsets were 85% for training, 10% for assessment, and 5% for testing. Training was carried out on all models for 100 epochs and 16 batches. The data augmentation methods tested in this study include image rotation, image translation, random scaling, shear, image flipping, blurring, brightness, mosaic, Mixup, copy-paste, etc. The results of the YOLO performance metrics with these data augmentation techniques are shown in Table 1 and Fig. 5.

Table 1. Comparison of detection across different augmentation methods

Data Augmentation Method	Class	Precision	Recall	mAP50
No Augmentation	all	0.887	0.866	0.874
BLUR	all	0.887	0.866	0.874
Brightness	all	0.902	0.839	0.88
Copy-paste	all	0.887	0.866	0.874
Flip	all	0.904	0.877	0.894
Gaussian	all	0.887	0.866	0.874
MixingUp	all	0.887	0.866	0.874
Mosaic	all	0.873	0.897	0.894
Scale	all	0.883	0.892	0.899
Shear	all	0.872	0.881	0.875

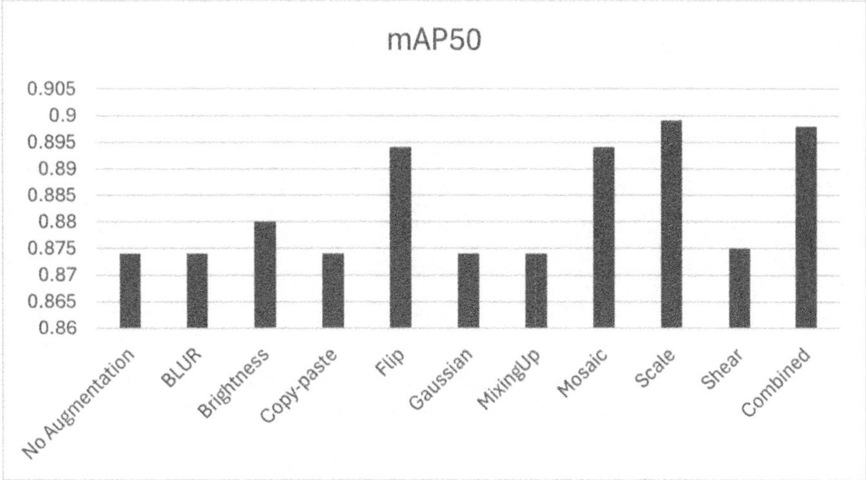

Fig. 5. Comparison mAP50 of detection across different augmentation methods

These metrics show precision, recall, and mAP50 scores in different augmentation methods applied to all classes in a dataset. Each method causes a little bit of change in these metrics of performance. Some of these methods resulted in more noticeable changes, like brightness and gamma, while some, like BLUR, remained very consistent in the scores. Both the No Augmentation and BLUR methods have the same precision, recall, and mAP50: 0.887, 0.866, and 0.874, respectively. As such, applying a simple Blur technique in this case does not seem to significantly change the model's performance metrics compared to when the model is implemented without data augmentation. Some methods exhibit more radical tradeoffs between precision and recall, while others, like Flip, Mosaic, and Scale, mostly improve or balance out the metrics in general. It means that the choice of augmentation method makes a huge difference in precision, recall, and mAP50 scores. Figure 5 shows that the image scaling method has the best detection result with a mAP50 of 0.899 which is higher than the results of no data augmentation by 2.9%. Therefore, more analysis of the YOLO V5 model combined with the scale data augmentation technique will be presented in this paper.

Figure 6 provides a thorough visual representation of the outcomes, including the numerous parameters and metrics acquired after finishing the training phase. YOLOv5 model loss components, box loss, objectness loss, and classification loss comprise the first three columns of Fig. 6. The leftmost row is used for training, while the second row is used for validation. Three measures of an algorithm's object prediction performance, box loss, objectiveness loss, and classification loss, are shown in Fig. 6. These findings indicate that the four PV panel defects we employ for detection throughout the training phase are correctly identified.

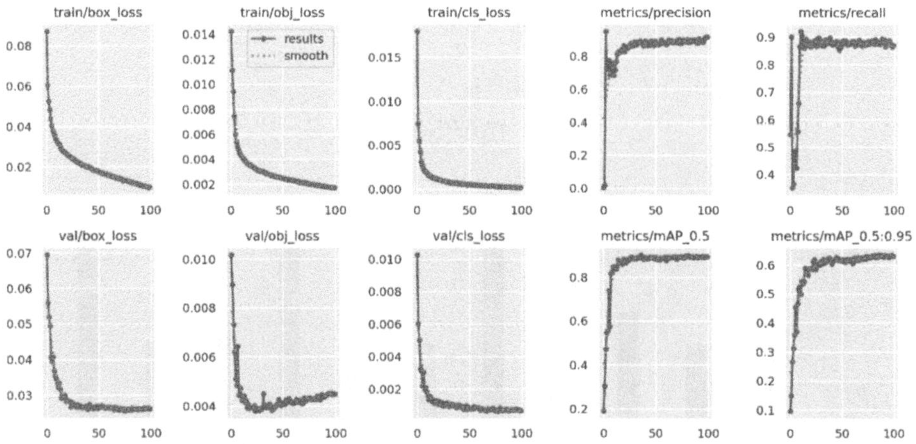

Fig. 6. Plotting of the loss box, object loss, categorized loss, precision, recall, and mean average precision (map) over the training epochs for the training and validation set

Figures 7, 8, 9, 10, 11, 12 and 13 illustrate our model's overall performance and effectiveness for the testing phase. Figure 7 represents an image classification example as output from the YOLOV5 model with data augmentation.

Fig. 7. Example of image classifications as output from the YOLOV5 model with data augmentation

Figure 8 shows the F1-score versus confidence of 89% with a confidence of 0.326. Basically, the confidence value gives an idea about how confident the model is with the defect detection; values close to 1 are completely confident in the positive detection of the correct defect. Figure 9 represents the precision versus confidence of 100% with 0.928 confidence. Figure 10 displays the recall versus confidence of 95% with 0 confidence. Figure 11 shows the precision versus recall. The mAP for all defects is high at 89.9%, with a threshold of 0.5.

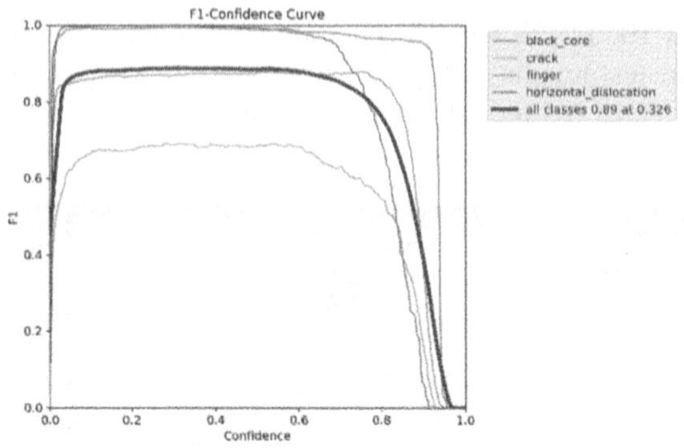

Fig. 8. Plotting of F1-score vs. confidence

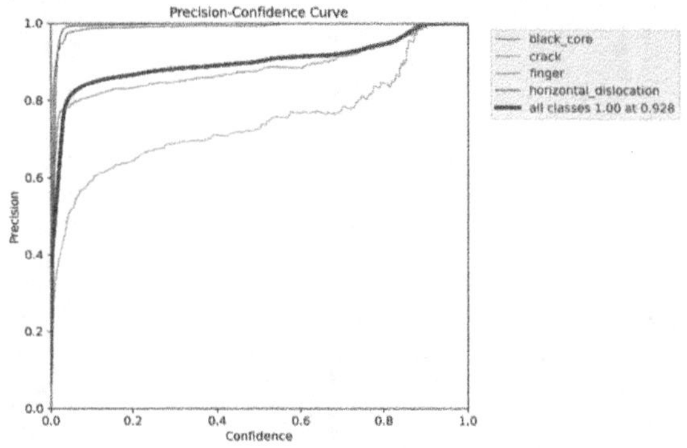

Fig. 9. Plotting of Precision vs. confidence

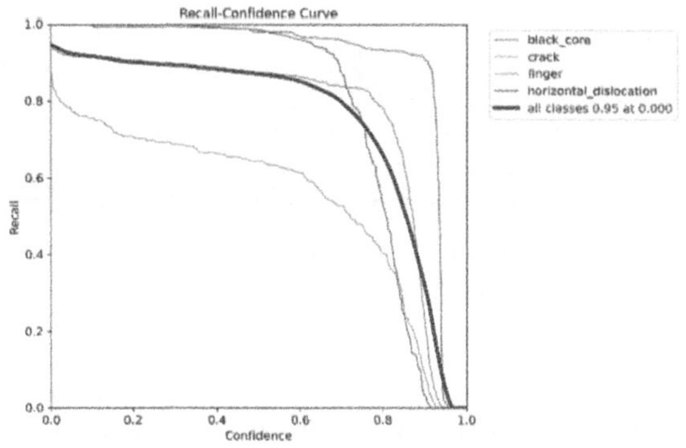

Fig. 10. Plotting of Recall vs. Confidence

As can be seen from the mAP50 plot of Fig. 12, as the number of epochs increases, the accuracy increases rapidly during the training phase. Analysing the mAP50 graph in Fig. 12 reveals that the YOLOV5 algorithm's convergence stabilized at the 70th iteration,

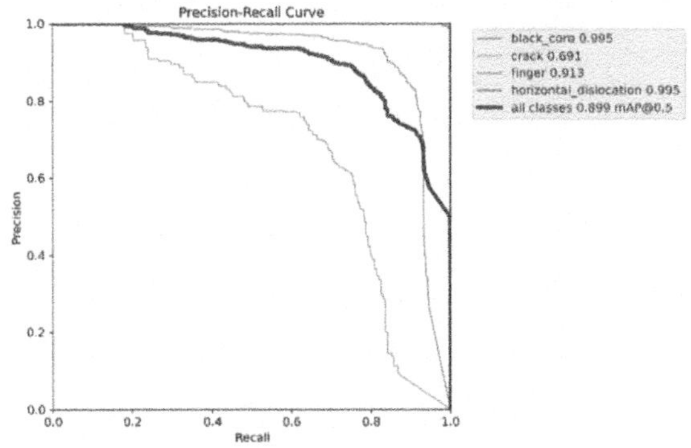

Fig. 11. Plotting of Precision vs. Recall

achieving high defect detection accuracy. Figure 13 represents the loss curve during the training phase. The loss value decreases smoothly with increased epochs, reflecting the model's gradual stability.

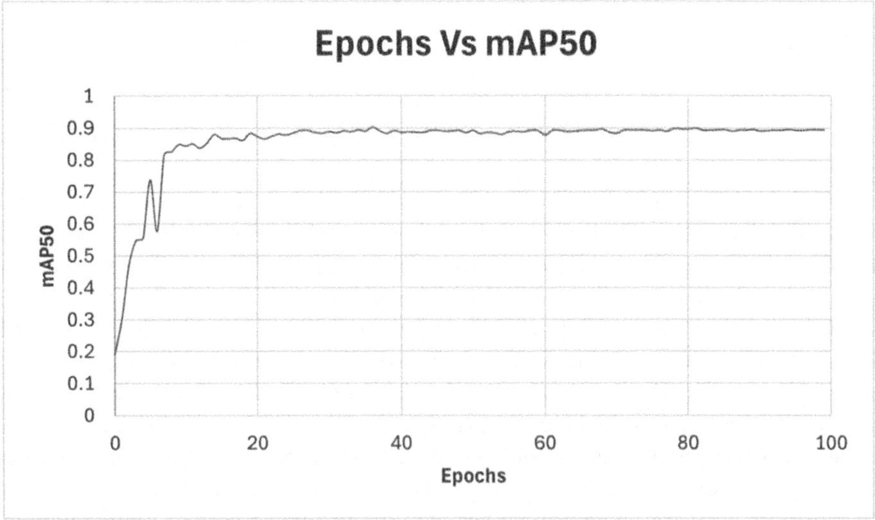

Fig. 12. Plotting of Epochs vs mAP50

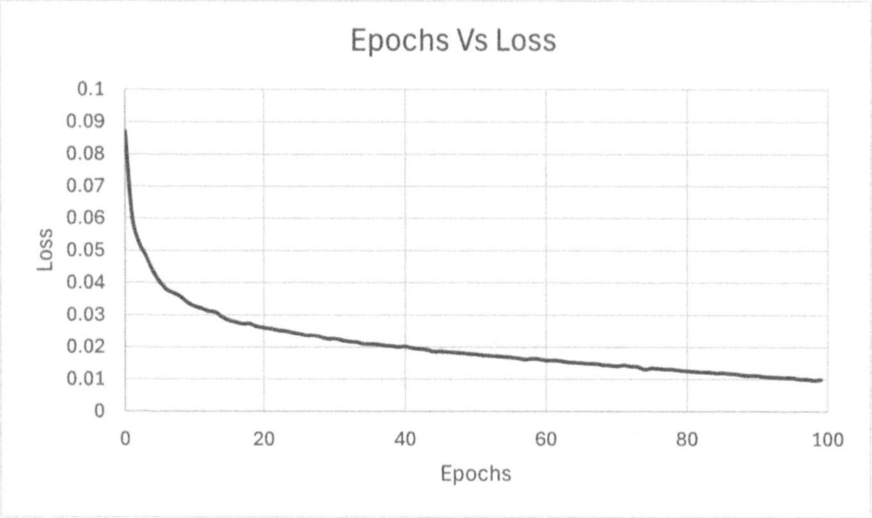

Fig. 13. Plotting of Epochs vs Loss

7 Conclusion

Compared to other sources of energy sources, solar energy is the cheapest with the least environmental mutation. With advanced monitoring and superior analytics, anomalies in solar energy will instantly be detected and resolved, making it very reliable and efficient and, therefore, having the least risk of breakdowns and less frequent maintenance. This paper has studied a combination of YOLOv5 with different data augmentation for PV panel defect detection techniques. The framework has been evaluated by EL-scanned images of PV cells. Those images are of defect-free panels and four other different types of defective panels: black core, crack, finger, and horizontal dislocation. Model training was done for 100 epochs and 16 batches. After training, validating, and testing the model, the results show that the image scaling method has the best detection result with a mAP50 of 0.899, which is higher than the results of no data augmentation by 2.9%. The combined YOLOV5 and scale method gives precisions, recalls, and mAP50 scores attained for PV panel defect detection as 88.3%, 89.2%, and 89.9%, respectively. Also, it shows that both mPA50 increased with the number of epochs, while the value of loss decreased with an increase in the number of epochs. This result indicates that our model effectively predicts PV panel defects.

Acknowledgements. This work was supported by the HCT Applied Research Grant (Fund # 113510).

References

1. Manno, D., Cipriani, G., Ciulla, G., Di Dio, V., Guarino, S., Lo Brano, V.: Deep learning strategies for automatic fault diagnosis in photovoltaic systems by thermographic images. Energ. Convers. Manag. **241**, 114315 (2021). https://doi.org/10.1016/j.enconman.2021.114315
2. Le, M., Van, S.L., Dang, K.N., Dao, V.D., Ngoc, H.V., Hong, H.T.V.: Remote anomaly detection and classification of solar photovoltaic modules based on deep neural network. Sustain. Energ. Technol. Assess. **48**, 101545 (2021). https://doi.org/10.1016/J.SETA.2021.101545
3. Balzategui, J., Eciolaza, L., Maestro-Watson, D.: Anomaly detection and automatic labeling for solar cell quality inspection based on generative adversarial network. Sensors **21**(13), 4361 (2021). https://doi.org/10.3390/s21134361
4. Yin, W., Jingyong, Z., Gang, X., Zhicheng, Z., Xiao, H.: PA-YOLO-Based multifault defect detection algorithm for PV panels. Int. J. Photoenergy **2024**(1) (2024). https://doi.org/10.1155/2024/6113260
5. Skaf, Z., Albanna, M., Alshareif, A., AlAli, A., Abdulmouti, H., Zyout I.: YOLOv5 and data augmentation: a dual approach to enhancing PV anomaly. In: World Conference on Science Engineering and Technology (WCSET) International Conference proceedings, pp. 14–23, Institute for Technology and Research (ITRESEARCH), Al Ain, UAE (2024)
6. Skaf, Z., Albanna, M., Alshareif, A., AlAli, A., Abdulmouti, H.: A comparative study of anomaly detection algorithms for solar photovoltaic defects. In: World Conference on Science Engineering and Technology (WCSET) International Conference proceedings, pp. 24–30, Institute for Technology and Research (ITRESEARCH), Al Ain, UAE (2024)
7. Jiang, P., Ergu, D., Liu, F., Cai, Y., Ma, B.: A review of yolo algorithm developments. Procedia Comput. Sci. **199**, 1066–1073 (2022). https://doi.org/10.1016/j.procs.2022.01.135
8. Redmon, J., Divvala, S., Girshick, R., Farhadi, A.: You only look once: unified, real-time object detection. In: Proceedings of IEEE Conference on Computer Vision and Pattern Recognition, IEEE, Las Vegas, USA, pp. 779–788 (2016). https://doi.org/10.1109/CVPR.2016.91
9. Redmon, J., Farhadi, A.: YOLOv3: An Incremental Improvement. arXiv preprint arXiv:1804.02767 (2018)
10. Bochkovskiy, A., Wang, C.Y., Liao, H.Y.M.: YOLOv4: optimal speed and accuracy of object detection (2020). http://arxiv.org/abs/2004.10934
11. Li, C., et al.:YOLOv6: A Single-Stage Object Detection Framework for Industrial Applications (2022). http://arxiv.org/abs/2209.02976
12. Wang, C.Y., Bochkovskiy, A., Liao, H.Y.M.: YOLOv7: Trainable bag-of-freebies sets new state-of-the-art for real-time object detectors (2022). https://doi.org/10.48550/arXiv.2207.02696
13. Casas, E., Ramos, L., Bendek, E., Rivas-Echeverria, F.: YOLOv5 vs. YOLOv8: performance benchmarking in wildfire and smoke detection scenarios. J. Image Graph. **12**(2), 127–136 (2024). https://doi.org/10.18178/joig.12.2.127-136
14. Wang, C.Y., Yeh, I.H., Liao, H.Y. M.: YOLOv9: Learning What You Want to Learn Using Programmable Gradient Information (2024). http://arxiv.org/abs/2402.13616
15. Wang, A., et al.: YOLOv10: Real-Time End-to-End Object Detection (2024). https://doi.org/10.48550/arXiv.2405.14458
16. Maharana, K., Mondal, S., Nemade, B.: A review: data pre-processing and data augmentation techniques. Global Transit. Proc. **3**(1), 91–99 (2022). https://doi.org/10.1016/j.gltp.2022.04.020
17. Shorten, C., Khoshgoftaar, T.M.: A survey on image data augmentation for deep learning. J. Big Data (2019). https://doi.org/10.1186/s40537-019-0197-0
18. Zhang, J., Yu, K., Wen, Z., Qi, X., Paul, A.K.: 3D Reconstruction for motion blurred images using deep learning-based intelligent systems. Comput. Mater. Continua **66**(2), 2087–2104 (2020). https://doi.org/10.32604/cmc.2020.014220

19. Perez, L., Wang, J.: The Effectiveness of Data Augmentation in Image Classification using Deep Learning (2017). http://arxiv.org/abs/1712.04621
20. Francisco, L.R., José, L.G.-S., Robert, S.R., Rafael, M., Antonio, F.C.: Geometric transformation-based data augmentation on defect classification of segmented images of semiconductor materials using a ResNet50 convolutional neural network. Expert Syst Appl (2022). https://doi.org/10.1016/j.eswa.2022.117731
21. Zhong, Z., Zheng, L., Kang, G., Li, S., Yang, Y.: Random Erasing Data Augmentation (2017). http://arxiv.org/abs/1708.04896
22. Luo, J., Long, H., Sheng, W., Hui, H., Li, R., Yan, T.: Residential solar panel object detection based on multi-combination data augmentation and YOLOv5. In: 2023 IEEE 6th International Electrical and Energy Conference, CIEEC 2023, Institute of Electrical and Electronics Engineers Inc., pp. 2117–2122 (2023). https://doi.org/10.1109/CIEEC58067.2023.10166986
23. Naveed, H., Anwar, S., Hayat, M., Javed, K., Mian, A.: Survey: image mixing and deleting for data augmentation (2021). http://arxiv.org/abs/2106.07085
24. Chen, A., Li, X., Jing, H., Hong, C., Li, M.: Anomaly detection algorithm for photovoltaic cells based on lightweight multi-channel spatial attention mechanism. Energies **16**(4), 1619 (2023). https://doi.org/10.3390/en16041619

Studying Factors Affecting Attitudes on Artificial Intelligence Voice Assistants in the United Arab Emirates

Eslam Badran[1(✉)] and Huseyin Seker[2]

[1] Computer Information Science, Higher Colleges of Technology, Abu Dhabi, UAE
ebadran@hct.ac.ae

[2] College of Computing and Informatics, The University of Sharjah, Sharjah, UAE
hseker@sharjah.ac.ae

Abstract. Artificial intelligence (AI) is an entangling force impacting the scope of businesses in areas such as health, finance, education, and even consumer technology. Against this background, we sought to explore the influence of demographic factors on attitudes towards AI among Arabic speakers. A total of 210 participants were selected from the Arab speaking community in the United Arab Emirates, followed by a hypothesis testing using an independent t-test of the data collected through the survey that contained 30 questions divided into five different categories including demographics, voice assistant usage, specific aspect of AI voice assistants, challenges of AI voice assistants and IT specific field of AI voice assistants. Results demonstrated that the variable of gender shows a significant influence on the perceived importance of AI, where females think AI to be more important than males. There was a significant difference: that is, those who did not perceive cultural barriers rated AI as more important than those who did. This outcome indicates that the cognitive representation of AI depends on the cultural context. Likewise, no significant difference was found across the question of whether technical knowledge is perceived to be a barrier, or not. This might imply that technical knowledge may raise awareness, though not necessarily related to being translated to a higher perceived importance of AI. The study sheds light on how demographic factors interact with each other in a complex way and puts emphasis on the importance of demographic-specific approaches in implementing AI technology to boost integration and acceptance effectively.

Keywords: Artificial Intelligence · Demographic Factors · Gender Differences · Cultural Impact · Technical knowledge

1 Introduction

In each sector including healthcare, finance, education, and consumer tech, AI is making a significant difference in almost all industries [8]. Nevertheless, its general acceptance relies mainly on public opinion which demonstrates a dynamic variable among different segments of the society. These differences exist and they matter, because what is essentially AI-friendly changes the (social) development of such technologies at large [19].

A. Safi et al. (Eds.): ISICS 2024, CCIS 2381, pp. 95–106, 2025.
https://doi.org/10.1007/978-3-031-82931-4_7

Some researchers suggest that gender, cultural background and technical expertise are all important demographic factors with moderate to strong effects on how individuals understand AI [5]. This holds particularly for gender difference where women express opinions about AI ethics and dangers, whereas, males are concerned with technological efficiency and technological capacity of AI. This underlines the necessity of applying gender-sensitivity of AI and implementation of solutions to account for diverse expectations of all groups [6].

Moreover, cultural influences also determine the acceptance level of AI [11]. Regions with more developed technology generally have a higher acceptance level and benefit from the potentials of AI. In contrast, in areas that have had reduced technological intertwining into their society there can be strong hesitations and distrusts where cultural narratives of technology are historical markers on perceived ill effects [19]. These observations emphasise the importance of AI applications being culturally sensitive, where they respect and reflect local values as well as norms so that it will work properly and provide a reliable function to people [10].

In addition, an individual's level of technical knowledge has a great effect on the acceptance and understanding of AI [14]. People with deeper technical understanding may better appreciate both the potential and caveats of AI which enables a more rounded view. This capability not only impacts personal adoption but also dictates public endorsement alongside wider societal embracement of AI technologies [4]. Therefore, the role of educational programs that aim to increase AI literacy is vital in alleviating concerns and constructing a comprehensive public trust ecosystem for AI technologies [13].

Similar to most countries, artificial intelligence is gradually being taken up in the United Arab Emirates. The country intends to be among the top in AI, and to achieve this, it has launched a blueprint known as the Artificial Intelligence Strategy 2031. Fields where AI integration will be implemented include the health sector, education sector, and even the transportation sector [9]. Nevertheless, the integration of AI in the Arab world is challenging as observed by some culture, economical, and infrastructure barriers. People's concern arises from privacy problems, moral issues and the stress of being replaced by the AI technology. All these challenges are compounded by the fact that people's technical literacy is rather diverse [1]. Furthermore, the fact that the Arab nations do not have the same level of access to the physical and informational structures of AI illustrates why it is necessary for development and enhancement initiatives to ensure that everyone can take benefit from AI technology in the same way [16]. To address these problems, it is important to create AI incentives that are sensitive to culture and context.

With this background, the current study attempts to empirically understand the influence of these demographic realities on AI perceptions by leveraging data from an inclusive sample. The outcomes have significant implications for AI important, policy makers and educators who seek to design technologies that are accessible and responsible in a global context [9]. A clear understanding of these demographic influences may help overcome barriers to AI adoption and build an inclusive future with AI.

2 Literature Review

The section intends to review studies concerning the impact of demographic factors on attitudes toward AI. It was reported that men emphasize technological benefits and security, while women are more pessimistic about privacy or ethical concerns [15]. Further research on other demographic factors including gender, age, and education in influencing attitudes towards AI in the Arab world is required. Privacy in AI and bias problems are uniquely viewed across various cultures [20], so an understanding of the unique perspective of the Arab community would be important in that respect.

A factor that really has an influence on the acceptance of AI by people is their cultural background. Relating to the cultural dimension, Chi et al. [3] stated that cultures that have a higher rate of uncertainty avoidance are least likely to adopt AI technologies. On the other hand, while having a reduced ability for AI in daily ritualization of practices specifically high in individualism, cultures are more likely to incorporate AI [7]. These findings, are therefore, emphasis how important the AI systems should be flexible enough to fit different cultural practices, therefore helping them to deploy globally. Moreover, another influential factor is the level of technical knowledge such that participants with more technical information have a stronger perception of the potential of AI [2].

Moreover, Kaya et al. [11] also showed a higher acceptability and tolerance level of younger people towards AI than older people. This is so because the young generation is more conversant with computers and emerging technology. Due to the difference in awareness level, individuals from previous generations may have least acceptance to AI in contrast to the current generations.

Literature further indicates that a person's social status significantly influences their perception of AI. Those who belong to the high classes of society are more capable of affording technology and are usually more accepting of new advancements in AI. Thus, the differences in the socioeconomic status can be reduced by promoting educational incentives concerning the adoption and effectiveness of AI. Ideally, attainments of these projects should be to make the AI technology accessible to all and impact the society in a positive way [13].

There are interesting dynamics at play in the utilization of AI voice assistants, especially within non-English contexts. A similar dilemma faces Arabic speaking communities where the design has to be culturally exact for AI acceptance [18]. Negotiating these cultural differences and local needs will be crucial for the responsible development and deployment of AI systems within the Arab world [17]. Together, these studies underscore the myriad factors that can shape AI perceptions and acceptance. They point to an urgent requirement for AI systems that are not only competent in technology, but also culturally and linguistically customized as per different user desires [12]. Therefore, given the rapid advancements in AI technology and its increasing integration into different spheres of life, it is important to examine how demographic influences shape attitudes towards these innovations within the Arab world.

2.1 Research Hypotheses

The hypotheses were structured to align with the relationships between the independent variables (IVs) and dependent variables (DVs) depicted in the diagram (see Fig. 1).

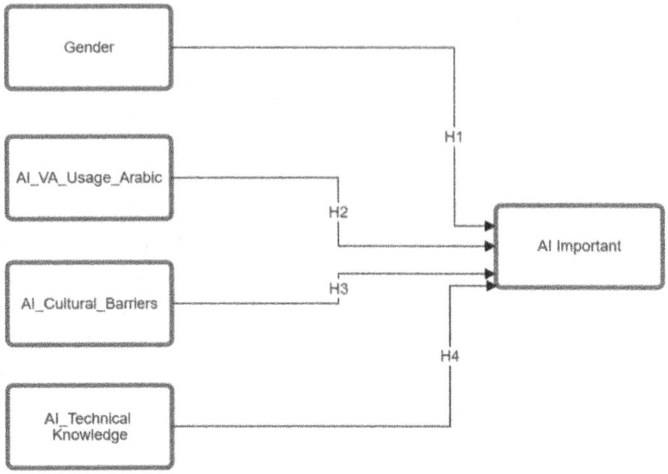

Fig. 1. Conceptual Hypothesis.

H1: There is a significant difference in AI importance between genders.

H2: There is a significant difference in AI Importance between groups based on AI_VA_Usage_Arabic.

H3: There is a significant difference in AI Importance between groups based on AI_Cultural_Barriers_Arabic.

H4: There is a significant difference in AI Importance between groups based on AI_Technical_Knowledge.

3 Methodology

The study utilized a structured questionnaire to capture data about independent and dependent variables related to AI perceptions. For dependent variables, the Likert scale was used to measure the perceived importance of AI to the participants. Whereas categorical level was used for independent variables. Data collection involved the development of one online questionnaire on Google Forms and distribution to participants from various demographics. The questionnaire was made available for a three-month period to allow for an adequate time frame and get a larger number of responses. The final sample size consisted of 210 participants, representing a range of genders and age groups.

4 Results

4.1 Demographics of Respondents

Summary statistics of each variable including Frequencies, Percentages, Mean and Standard deviation are presented. Table 1 identifies the gender composition of the sample of respondents. There were 210 participants, and a significant case of gender imbalance was seen, with 118 males, accounting for 56.2% of the total, and 92 females, accounting for 43.8% of the total sample. This gender breakdown is important in knowing the demographic makeup of subjects under study. Accounting for the responses based on gender can help in spotting variations in the way different genders may view the relative importance of AI and its developers, adding a finer degree of resolution to the understanding of demographic influences on AI acceptance.

People are also classified by their age showing the distribution of the population in concerns to the perception of AI. Among them, most of the respondents are young-25 to 54 years of age accounting for 81% of the total sample. From this concentration, it can be deduced that the study encompasses view mostly from early career to mid-career individuals which may affect perceptions on the importance of AI and its users. Understanding the age demographics is crucial, as different age groups may exhibit varying levels of familiarity, comfort, and acceptance of technological advancements.

Table 1. Descriptive summary of demographic variables.

Variables		Frequency	Percent	Valid Percent	Cumulative Percent
Gender	Female	92	43.8	43.8	43.8
	Male	118	56.2	56.2	100.0
	Total	210	100.0	100.0	
Age	18–24	29	13.8	13.8	13.8
	25–34	42	20.0	20.0	33.8
	35–44	67	31.9	31.9	65.7
	45–54	62	29.5	29.5	95.2
	55 and above	10	4.8	4.8	100.0
	Total	210	100.0	100.0	

The Table 2 provides summary statistics of independent variables. Concerning the usage of AI Voice assistants in Arabic, the data highlights whether individuals currently use AI Voice assistants in Arabic, illuminating an important aspect of technological adoption within the sample population. The higher usage rate (59.5%) indicates a significant inclination towards adopting these technologies, suggesting a general openness or a necessity driven by the linguistic and functional preferences in AI interactions within Arabic-speaking contexts. Understanding this usage pattern is crucial, as it reflects not only the technological engagement of the respondents, but also the potential cultural acceptance of AI solutions tailored to meet specific linguistic needs. The predominance of users over non-users in this category could influence how AI technologies are further developed, marketed, and deployed in regions with significant Arabic-speaking populations.

Furthermore, the summary of participants' perceptions regarding cultural barriers to AI usage in Arabic indicated a substantial occurrence of cultural barriers among the majority (79.5%) of the sample. Such a significant proportion suggests deep-rooted cultural concerns or challenges that may hinder the broader acceptance and effectiveness of AI technologies tailored for Arabic-speaking users.

Moreover, the data concerning the variable AI_Technical_Knowledge illustrated that a majority of the respondents, 59.0%, reported having technical knowledge about AI-based systems. This is indicative of a relatively high level of awareness or familiarity with AI technologies within the sampled population, which could potentially influence their perceptions of AI's importance and its users. The higher percentage of participants with technical knowledge might be reflective of a technologically inclined sample or a demographic that is generally more engaged with or interested in technological developments. This demographic characteristic can significantly impact how AI technologies are perceived, especially concerning their capabilities and limitations.

Table 2. Descriptive summary of independent variables.

Variables		Frequency	Percent	Valid Percent	Cumulative Percent
AI_VA_Usage_Arabic	No	85	40.5	40.5	40.5
	Yes	125	59.5	59.5	100.0
	Total	210	100.0	100.0	
AI_Cultural_Barriers_Arabic	No	43	20.5	20.5	20.5
	Yes	167	79.5	79.5	100.0
	Total	210	100.0	100.0	
AI_Technical_Knowledge	No	86	41.0	41.0	41.0
	Yes	124	59.0	59.0	100.0
	Total	210	100.0	100.0	

4.2 Hypotheses Testing

H1: There is a significant difference in AI importance between genders.

An independent-samples t-test was conducted (see summary in Table 3) to compare the importance of AI between genders. For the AI Importance variable, Levene's Test (see summary in Table 4) for Equality of Variances indicated that the variances were not equal ($F = 21.114$, $p < 0.001$), so the second line of the t-test output (Equal variances not assumed) was used for interpretation.

The results showed that there is a significant difference in AI Importance between genders ($t\ (162.421) = 2.178$, $p = 0.031$). Females ($M = 1.45$, $SD = 0.830$) rated the importance of AI higher as compared to males ($M = 1.22$, $SD = 0.615$). The mean difference was 0.225 with a standard error difference of 0.103. The 95% confidence interval of the difference ranged from 0.021 to 0.430, which does not include zero, indicating a significant difference.

Therefore, we conclude that females perceive AI as more important than males.

H2: There is a significant difference in ai importance between groups based on AI_VA_Usage_Arabic.

An independent-samples t-test was conducted (see summary in Table 3) to compare the importance of AI between those who use Arabic voice assistants (Yes) and those who do not (No). For the AI Importance variable, Levene's Test (see summary in Table 4) for Equality of Variances indicated that the variances were not equal ($F = 6.549$, $p = 0.011$), so the second line of the t-test output (Equal variances not assumed) was used for interpretation.

The results show no significant difference in AI Importance between those who use Arabic voice assistants and those who do not ($t\,(160.994) = 1.298$, $p = 0.196$). The mean difference was 0.136 with a standard error difference of 0.105. The 95% confidence interval of the difference ranged from -0.071 to 0.343, which includes zero, indicating no significant difference.

H3: There is a significant difference in AI Importance between groups based on AI_Cultural_Barriers_Arabic.

An independent-samples t-test was conducted (see summary in Table 3) to compare the importance of AI between those who perceive cultural barriers in Arabic (Yes) and those who do not (No). For the AI Importance variable, Levene's Test (see summary in Table 4) for Equality of Variances indicated that the variances were not equal ($F = 29.411$, $p < 0.001$), so the second line of the t-test output (Equal variances not assumed) was used for interpretation.

The results show a significant difference in AI Importance between those who perceive cultural barriers in Arabic and those who do not ($t(52.825) = 2.593$, $p = 0.012$). Those who do not perceive cultural barriers ($M = 1.63$, $SD = 0.926$) rated the importance of AI higher compared to those who do perceive cultural barriers ($M = 1.24$, $SD = 0.642$). The mean difference was 0.388 with a standard error difference of 0.150. The 95% confidence interval of the difference ranged from 0.088 to 0.689, which does not include zero, indicating a significant difference.

H4: There is a significant difference in AI Importance between groups based on AI_Technical_Knowledge

An independent-samples t-test was conducted to compare the importance of AI between those who perceive technical knowledge as a barrier (Yes) and those who do not (No). For the AI Importance variable, Levene's Test (see summary in Table 4) for Equality of Variances indicated that the variances were not equal ($F = 8.199$, $p = 0.005$), so the second line of the t-test output (Equal variances not assumed) was used for interpretation.

The results showed no significant difference in AI Importance between those who perceive technical knowledge as a barrier and those who do not ($t\,(200.771) = -1.492$, $p = 0.137$). The mean difference was -0.146 with a standard error difference of 0.098. The 95% confidence interval of the difference ranged from -0.340 to 0.047, which includes zero, indicating no significant difference.

Table 3. Descriptive statistics.

Independent variables	Dependent Variables	Groups	N	Mean	Std. Deviation	Std. Error Mean
Gender	AI_Important	Female	92	1.45	0.830	0.087
		Male	118	1.22	0.615	0.057
AI_VA_Usage_ Arabic	AI_Important	No	85	1.40	0.790	0.086
		Yes	125	1.26	0.674	0.060
AI_Cultural_Barriers_Arabic	AI_Important	No	43	1.63	0.926	0.141
		Yes	167	1.24	0.642	0.050
AI_Technical_Knowledge	AI_Important	No	86	1.23	0.645	0.070
		Yes	124	1.38	0.771	0.069

Table 4. Two independent Sample t test.

		Levene's Test for Equality of Variances						Mean Difference	Std. Error Difference	95% Confidence Interval of the Difference	
Independent variables	Dependent Variables		F	Sig	t	df	Sig. (2-tailed)			Lower	Upper
Gender	H1 AI_Important	Equal variances assumed	21.114	0.000	2.259	208.000	0.025	0.225	0.100	0.029	0.422
		Equal variances not assumed			2.178	162.421	0.031	0.225	0.103	0.021	0.430
AI_VA_Usage_ Arabic	H2 AI_Important	Equal variances assumed	6.549	0.011	1.338	208.000	0.182	0.136	0.102	−0.064	0.336
		Equal variances not assumed			1.298	160.994	0.196	0.136	0.105	−0.071	0.343
AI_Cultural_Barriers_Arabic	H3 AI_Important	Equal variances assumed	29.411	0.000	3.205	208.000	0.002	0.388	0.121	0.149	0.627
		Equal variances not assumed			2.593	52.825	0.012	0.388	0.150	0.088	0.689
AI_Technical_Knowledge	H4 AI_Important	Equal variances assumed	8.199	0.005	−1.445	208.000	0.150	−0.146	0.101	−0.346	0.053
		Equal variances not assumed			−1.492	200.771	0.137	−0.146	0.098	−0.340	0.047

5 Discussion

Such a validated study is an important resource to understand the demographics of artificial intelligence and perceptions in an Arabic-speaking community. There was a significant difference in the gender perception of the importance of AI, with women rating it much more important than men. This is consistent with previous findings that indicated gendered differences in technology acceptance and adoption [15]. Gender-sensitive RP requires AI-makers and policymakers to understand the specific views and worries of both men and women in designing/deploying new AI technologies.

Table 4 explores the influence of the independent variable AI_VA_Usage_Arabic on a dependent variable, AI Important. The Levene's Test for Equality of Variances reveals a significant result for AI_Important which indicates that the assumption of equal variances is violated. Consequently, both the equal variances assumed and not assumed conditions are considered. The t-test for Equality of Means shows a non-significant difference in means, suggesting that perceptions of AI Importance do not significantly differ based on AI usage in Arabic contexts. The mean difference, a standard error and the 95% confidence interval ranges encompassing zero and further supporting the non-significant results.

Moreover, Table 4 delves into the independent variable AI_Cultural_Barriers_Arabic and its impact on the same dependent variable. As for the Levene's Test for AI_Important, the result obtained is significant, which means the test should be performed under both variance assumptions. The t-test for equality of means show certainty at .05 when variances are equal and gave similar result of significance when the variances were not equal. This means that cultural factors play a major role in determining the perceived relevance of AI. Table 4 also shows the essential detail regarding demographic factors that have assumed the perception of AI in the UAE in connection with the application of AI and cultural issues in the Arabic context.

The visibility of these cultural boundaries contributed to different perceptions around how fundamental AI was, and attitudes towards those making the technology. Those who perceived cultural challenges were less likely to rate AI as important and had more negative feelings toward developers. The importance of developing culturally sensitive AI systems that reflect and adhere to local values, norms, and languages (for Arabic contexts) which has been supported by this study. Taking local cultural considerations into account is crucial for increasing the uptake and take-up of AI technologies.

5.1 Limitations of Study and Avenues for Future Research

While this study offers valuable information about the role of demographics in AI perception, several limitations are essential to acknowledge. Though the sample was diverse, it is primarily derived from one geographical location, thus restricting the generalizability of results to other countries and regions. Secondly, self-reported measures of AI perceptions and technical knowledge of participants may lead to biases, such as social desirability or response. Furthermore, the depth and breadth (i.e., technical knowledge was self-assessed, not assessed by a 3rd party rendering it subjective) may have resulted in giving an inaccurate estimate on domain expertise or understanding AI.

Future research may potentially implement longitudinal studies to track how perceptions of AI technology evolve over time and provide insights into the dynamic nature of its acceptance with increasing familiarity or emerging developments. Generalisability of the results may be enhanced by including participants from international regions. It may reveal how differences in culture across a wider stretch of the globe, influence AI perception. Moreover, more objective methods of measuring technical knowledge should be implemented (e.g., using standardized tests or practical tasks) to obtain a better indicator that an individual indeed understands AI.

Using qualitative methods such as interviews or focus groups could further explain the reasons why people with certain demographics and experience's view AI in a particular way. This approach would result in a more detailed exploration of the reasons for attitudes and beliefs. Finally, the implementation of experimental designs could help in establishing causal relationships between demographic factors and AI perceptions. For instance, randomizing different subpopulations to the AI intervention under controlled circumstances might simultaneously measure program performance and individual-level effects towards AI acceptance.

6 Conclusion

The study focused on the impact of demographic factors such as gender, culture/background and technical skills for sector-specific employment influence AI perception. The results demonstrated a striking difference in the way different age, gender and national groups perceive AI important. Women are, on average, significantly more likely to view AI as important than men -- suggesting that we need to think carefully about gender considerations in the development and deployment of AI. The view of cultural barriers defines whether we consider AI is really needed and how people perceive designers (especially in Arabic-speaking contexts). It is clear that we need AI systems to be culturally intelligent, i.e., follow and respect local values and norms.

Those with more in-depth familiarity have a higher-rated view of how vital AI is and have a better rating for the perception on creators working for Artificial Intelligence. This outcome suggests that educational programmes to increase AI literacy have a role in reducing fears and increasing the public trust which is essential for accepting AI technologies. Policymakers, educators and AI Users can benefit from these insights because they indicate that different exercises need to be done to promote the acceptance and integration of AI technologies. In summary, given the increasing prevalence of AI and its everyday life applications, it is critical for developers, as well as policymakers to consider a range of demographic groups in their design process. This would help in making AI more effective and also their ethical integration into society which will lead to better acceptance of this technology around the globe.

Acknowledgments. For those who have responded to the survey.

References

1. Armutat, S., Wattenberg, M., Mauritz, N.: Artificial intelligence – gender-specific differences in perception, understanding, and training interest. Int. Conf. Gender Res. **7**(1), 36–43 (2024). https://doi.org/10.34190/icgr.7.1.2163
2. Bedué, P., Fritzsche, A.: Can we trust AI? an empirical investigation of trust requirements and guide to successful AI adoption. J. Enterp. Inf. Manag. **35**(2), 530–549 (2022). https://doi.org/10.1108/JEIM-06-2020-0233

3. Chi, O.H., Chi, C.G., Gursoy, D., Nunkoo, R.: Customers' acceptance of artificially intelligent service robots: The influence of trust and culture. Int. J. Inf. Manage. **70**, 102623 (2023). https://doi.org/10.1016/j.ijinfomgt.2023.102623
4. Dwivedi, Y.K., et al.: Artificial Intelligence (AI): multidisciplinary perspectives on emerging challenges, opportunities, and agenda for research, practice and policy. Int. J. Inf. Manage. **57**, 101994 (2021). https://doi.org/10.1016/j.ijinfomgt.2019.08.002
5. Gerlich, M.: Perceptions and acceptance of artificial intelligence: a multi-dimensional study. Soc. Sci. **12**(9), 502 (2023). https://doi.org/10.3390/socsci12090502
6. Ghotbi, N., Ho, M.T.: Moral awareness of college students regarding artificial intelligence. Asian Bioeth. Rev. **13**(4), 421–433 (2021). https://doi.org/10.1007/s41649-021-00182-2
7. Hasija, A., Esper, T.L.: In artificial intelligence (AI) we trust: a qualitative investigation of AI technology acceptance. J. Bus. Logist. **43**(3), 388–412 (2022). https://doi.org/10.1111/jbl.12301
8. How, M.-L., Cheah, S.-M.: Forging the future: strategic approaches to quantum AI integration for industry transformation. AI **5**(1), 290–323 (2024). https://doi.org/10.3390/ai5010015
9. Islam, M.M.: Utilizing AI for social good: tackling global issues and fostering inclusive solutions. J. Artific. Intell. General Sci. **3**(1), 341–362 (2024). https://doi.org/10.60087/jaigs.v3i1.124
10. Kashyap, R., Samuel, Y., Friedman, L.W., Samuel, J.: Artificial intelligence education & governance-human enhancive, culturally sensitive and personally adaptive HAI. Front. Artif. Intell. **7**, 1443386 (2024). https://doi.org/10.3389/frai.2024.1443386
11. Kaya, F., Aydin, F., Schepman, A., Rodway, P., Yetişensoy, O., Demir Kaya, M.: The roles of personality traits, AI anxiety, and demographic factors in attitudes toward artificial intelligence. Int. J. Hum.-Comput. Interact. **40**(2), 497–514 (2024). https://doi.org/10.1080/10447318.2022.2151730
12. Lainjo, B.: The implications of Artificial Intelligence on international development management. J. Autonom. Intell. **7**(5), 1258 (2024). https://doi.org/10.32629/jai.v7i5.1258
13. Laupichler, M.C., Aster, A., Schirch, J., Raupach, T.: Artificial intelligence literacy in higher and adult education: a scoping literature review. Comput. Educ.: Artific. Intell. **3**, 100101 (2022). https://doi.org/10.1016/j.caeai.2022.100101
14. Lu, V.N., et al.: Service robots, customers and service employees: what can we learn from the academic literature and where are the gaps? J. Serv. Theory Pract. **30**(3), 361–391 (2020). https://doi.org/10.1108/JSTP-04-2019-0088
15. Ofosu-Ampong, K.: Gender differences in perception of artificial intelligence-based tools. J. Digit. Art Human. **4**(2), 52–56 (2023). https://ssrn.com/abstract=4667448
16. Sampene, A.K.: Artificial intelligence as a path way to Africa's transformations. Artific. Intell. **9**(1) (2020). https://www.researchgate.net/profile/Agyemang-Sampene/publication/358440753_Artificial_Intelligence_as_a_Path_Way_to_Africa's_TransformationS/links/620a060bcf7c2349ca124bb1/Artificial-Intelligence-as-a-Path-Way-to-Africas-TransformationS.pdf
17. Seymour, W., Zhan, X., Cote, M., Such, J.: A systematic review of ethical concerns with voice assistants. In: Proceedings of the 2023 AAAI/ACM Conference on AI, Ethics, and Society, pp. 131–145 (2023). https://doi.org/10.1145/3600211.3604679
18. Shafeeg, A., Shazhaev, I., Mihaylov, D., Tularov, A., Shazhaev, I.: Voice assistant integrated with chat GPT. Indonesian J. Comput. Sci. **12**(1) (2023). http://3.8.6.95/ijcs/index.php/ijcs/article/view/3146

19. Vu, H.T., Lim, J.: Effects of country and individual factors on public acceptance of artificial intelligence and robotics technologies: a multilevel SEM analysis of 28-country survey data. Behav. Inform. Technol. **41**(7), 1515–1528 (2022). https://doi.org/10.1080/0144929X.2021.1884288
20. Wei, M., Zhou, Z.: Ai ethics issues in real world: Evidence from AI incident database (2022). arXiv preprint arXiv:2206.07635

Conceptualizing a Generative AI-Based Solution for Emotional Intelligence Interventions: Application to Education and Training

Faouzi Bouslama(✉)

CIS Department, Dubai Academic City Campus, Higher Colleges of Technology, Dubai, UAE
fbouslama@hct.ac.ae

Abstract. In the past years, generative artificial intelligence (AI) models have shown significant potential in augmenting human capabilities across various domains such as business and finance, creative arts and media, and education and training. This paper explores the development of a generative AI-based solution designed specifically to generate text for emotional intelligence (EI) interventions. Emotional intelligence, the ability to recognize, understand, and manage emotions, plays a critical role in personal and professional success. Despite the growing importance of EI, interventions aimed at enhancing these skills often face challenges due to the subjective nature of emotional experiences, and the complexity of human emotions and some of EI assessment tools. This paper proposes an innovative conceptual approach that proposes to leverage generative AI techniques to create personalized and contextually relevant text for EI training and development. The domain of interest is the education and training with a focus on students' EI skills, academic success, and future career development. The AI model can be trained on a diverse corpus of emotionally rich content, allowing it to generate nuanced and empathetic responses tailored to individual students' needs. Two approaches are considered. Fine-tuning existing models and prompt engineering using GPT-4 are considered. Application to generating prompts for the EI interventions is demonstrated. By integrating generative AI technologies, the proposed conceptual solution aims to enhance the effectiveness of EI interventions, making them more accessible, engaging, and impactful.

Keywords: Artificial intelligence (AI) · Emotional intelligence (EI) · Generative AI · EI interventions · Conceptualization · Prompt engineering

1 Introduction

In the rapidly advancing and complex business landscape of today, emotional intelligence (EI) has emerged as a critical competency for personal and professional success. Emotional intelligence, which encompasses the ability to recognize, understand, manage, and influence one's own and others' emotions is integral to adaptability, resilience, effective communication, decision-making, leadership, and relationship-building. Despite its importance, many individuals, such employees and managers, as well as organizations struggle to self-assess, train, develop and sustain these skills, often due to the lack of assessment strategies and effective training and interventions.

A. Safi et al. (Eds.): ISICS 2024, CCIS 2381, pp. 107–121, 2025.
https://doi.org/10.1007/978-3-031-82931-4_8

The concept of emotional intelligence (EI) has gathered significant attention since it was popularized by Daniel Goleman in the mid-1990s [1]. EI is broadly understood as the ability to perceive, use, understand, and manage emotions in oneself and others. Research has consistently shown that advanced skills of EI are associated with better attitude and mindset, adaptability, enhanced interpersonal relationships, resilience, and improved job performance. In education and training, for example, the educational institutions have a considerable interest in identifying links between personality traits and academic success. The learning rarely occurs in isolation, and so the ability to accurately perceive how others feel or react may also be an indicator, or at least a contributor, to educational success [2].

To improve EI skills, various training and interventions are used. Traditional EI interventions typically involve in-person training, workshops, or the use of self-help materials, focusing on strategies such as self-awareness, emotion regulation, empathy development, leadership, and social skills training. However, these methods often face limitations, including self-pace customized training, meaningful feedback, high costs, scalability issues, and a lack of personalization. In [3], the authors discuss the limitations of existing EI assessment tools and interventions, including the challenges in measurement, the variability in training outcomes, and the lack of consistency in the methods used to enhance EI. In [4], the authors explore the effectiveness of EI interventions and highlights the individual differences that can impact the success of these programs, and discuss the limitations related to the one-size-fits-all approach in EI training and the need for more personalized interventions.

The advent of artificial intelligence (AI), and more specifically, generative AI models like GPT (Generative Pre-trained Transformer), has opened new avenues for enhancing EI interventions. In [5], the authors developed a foundational text in the field of AI, particularly focusing on deep learning, which is the backbone of many generative AI models covering key concepts, techniques, and applications of AI, including generative models like GANs (Generative Adversarial Networks). In fact, generative AI models are capable of producing human-like text based on vast amounts of training data, making them suitable for creating personalized and contextually relevant content. Research in this area has shown that AI can be effectively used to process natural language and provide useful feedback on emotional expressions and generate tailored content that can enhance EI. In [6], the authors introduced GPT-3, one of the most advanced generative AI models to date. They discussed the architecture, capabilities, and applications of large language models, highlighting the transformative potential of generative AI in natural language processing.

Several studies have explored the use of AI in education and training, and emotional well-being. For example, in [7], the authors applied GPT-3 in generating textual summaries and insights from survey data in the field of educational research. The proposed approach is used as a complementary-supportive tool to assist and enhance higher education (traditional) pedagogical practices, without replacing human educators. In fact, ChatGPT was used as a useful research assistant tool to aid educators and students in the research process. The study demonstrated how GPT-3 can be leveraged to automate the process of interpreting and presenting survey results, enhancing the efficiency and consistency of data analysis. Therefore, highlighting how AI can be utilized in various ways to enhance pedagogical practices in higher education, and AI tools such as ChatGPT can aid the generation of content and ideas for further investigation. Furthermore, the study reported on the ethical usage of such a tool, its limitations, risks, misuses, and concerns, where appropriate training is expected to facilitate thoughtful implementation of such approaches and answer any concerns.

Despite the growing body of research on AI in various domains such as Gaming and Virtual Reality [8], Arts & Media [9], Business & Finance [10], and Marketing & Advertising [11], the specific application of generative AI for EI interventions remains underexplored. Existing studies have primarily focused on AI's role in identifying emotional states through sentiment analysis and natural language processing (NLP). In [12], the study provides a comprehensive review of advancements in NLP, particularly focusing on sentiment analysis as a tool for identifying emotional states in text. It explores various techniques used in NLP to detect and classify emotions, highlighting the role of AI in processing and understanding human emotions. In [13], the survey paper covers the application of deep learning techniques in sentiment analysis, a key aspect of identifying emotional states in text. It discusses how AI models, particularly those based on deep learning, have significantly advanced the ability to analyze and interpret sentiments expressed in various forms of text, contributing to better emotion recognition. While these approaches provide valuable insights into emotional dynamics, they do not fully leverage AI's potential to actively enhance emotional intelligence through personalized content generation.

This paper explores the conceptualization of a generative AI-based solution designed to generate text for emotional intelligence interventions. The focus is on the use of AI in education and training focusing on emotional intelligence and well-being of students, faculty, and staff. An EI assessment tool and interventions developed in [14, 15], and [16] are used in this study. The purpose is to suggest using a tool such as GPT-4 to generate from the collected EI survey data meaningful textual summaries and insights for effective EI interventions. The proposed approach can be used as a complementary-supportive tool to assist and enhance conventional EI assessments and interventions used in higher education and pedagogical practices, without replacing human educators, counselors, and career development professionals. The remainder of the paper presents a review of the approaches to building EI-compatible GPT models, and how to create a custom model tailored to users' needs in academia.

2 Approaches to Building EI-Compatible GPT Models

There is no specific Generative Pre-training Transformer-GPT [17] model publicly available that is pre-trained on assessment results of Emotional Intelligence (EI) surveys to directly reflect the core dimensions of EI, such as the ones used in this study, namely self-awareness, self-management, social awareness, relationship management, adaptability, and general mood, and maps them into appropriate interventions. However, there are several approaches and resources that can be utilized to create or adapt a GPT model to better understand and generate emotionally intelligent summary and responses.

2.1 Steps to Follow to Create a Custom EI-Focused GPT Model

The below flowchart outlines the sequential steps needed to develop a custom GPT model focused on Emotional Intelligence, including data collection, preparation, fine-tuning, testing, deployment, and continuous improvement (Fig. 1).

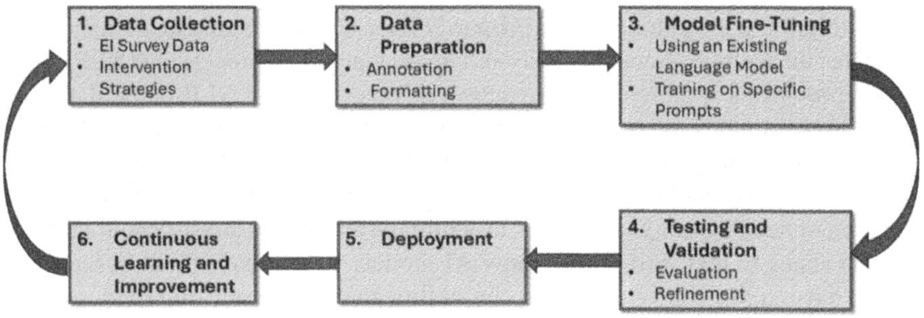

Fig. 1. The six steps to follow to develop a custom GPT model focused on Emotional Intelligence.

Data Collection: While there is no pre-built GPT model specifically tailored for EI assessment and intervention, it is possible to fine-tune existing models using a well-prepared dataset to create a custom solution that meets user's needs. This approach allows to leverage the powerful language capabilities of GPT models while tailoring them to specific EI-related use case.

- **EI Survey Data**: Gather datasets from EI assessments that measure the core dimensions. Ensure that the data is comprehensive and represents diverse scenarios and responses.
- **Intervention Strategies**: Collect data on various EI interventions that have been effective in enhancing each EI dimension. These are usually drawn from psychological studies, therapeutic practices, and educational programs.

Data Preparation

- **Annotation**: Annotate the dataset to align responses and assessment results with appropriate EI dimensions and possible interventions. For example, responses indicating low self-awareness might be paired with the Learning to name emotions accurately as part of the ABCs of emotions to increase a person's vocabulary.
- **Formatting**: Format the data into a structure suitable for fine-tuning a language model. This usually involves converting the data into a question-answer format or using prompts that simulate user inputs followed by desired outputs.

Model Fine-Tuning

- Use an existing language model like GPT-3 or GPT-4 [17] as a base. These models can be fine-tuned using the annotated dataset. Fine-tuning involves training the model on the specific dataset, so it learns to generate outputs that align with the data's patterns and insights.
- Consider training on specific intervention-related prompts, such as "What is a suitable intervention for someone with low self-management skills?" and providing model responses based on the used data.

Testing and Validation

- **Evaluation**: Test the model with unseen EI assessment results to evaluate its ability to generate appropriate and effective EI interventions. This can involve both qualitative assessments (expert reviews) and quantitative metrics (accuracy, relevance).
- **Refinement**: Use feedback to refine the model, adjusting the training data or fine-tuning parameters to improve performance.

Deployment: Once the model meets the accuracy and relevance criteria, deploy it within the intended application. This could be a chatbot, educational tool, or a thera-peutic assistant.

Continuous Learning and Improvement: Implement a mechanism for continuous feedback and learning. As the model interacts with users, collect data on its performance and periodically retrain the model to improve its accuracy and relevance.

2.2 Alternative Approaches

If building a custom model from scratch is too resource-intensive, then consider:

- **Prompt Engineering**: Use existing GPT-4 [17] capabilities to design prompts that extract EI-related insights. For example, carefully crafted prompts can help elicit interventions related to different EI dimensions.
- **Combining Models**: Use a hybrid approach by integrating GPT with rule-based systems that apply specific interventions based on assessment results.

3 Creating a Custom EI-Focused GPT Model for HCT Students

It is possible to create a custom model tailored to users' needs in academia, such as in the ones encountered in the domain of education and training, using the previously detailed approach:

3.1 Data Collection

There are several measurement tools available for E.I., with varying levels of complexity, expertise and cost required for proper administration. The focus in this study in on the work done by researchers in [14–16]. In [15], the authors developed a series of localized bilingual surveys to assess the students' and faculty's E.I. skills. The skills in E.I. are crucially necessary to know how to interpret our emotions to effectively communicate with all stakeholders (other educators and students). The EI assessment tool is a localized six-quadrant model of EI which features Self-awareness at the center of the model as shown in Fig. 2.

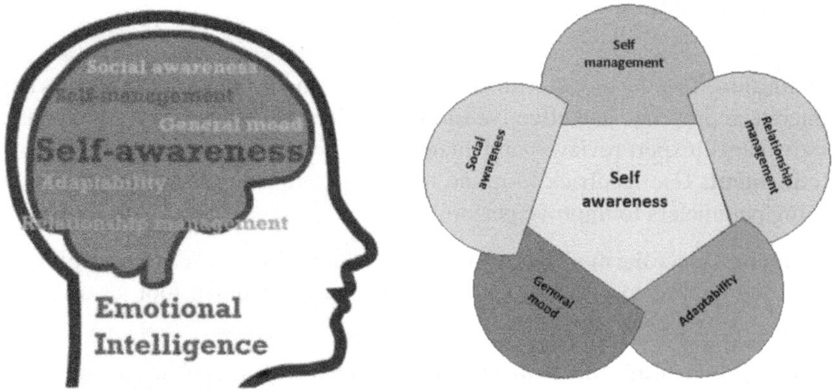

Fig. 2. The six-dimensional E.I. Model [15].

The entire six questionnaire survey consisted of 47 Likert scale items in total. Students were presented with an item in both English and Arabic and asked to assess their EI skills using a five-response option scale with 1 being 'very low' and 5 'very high' [15]. Table 1 shows a summary of the dimensions and their respective total scores.

Table 1. Number of Questions and Total Score Competency

Core Competency	*# of Questions*	*Total score*
Self-awareness	7	35
Self-management	7	35
Social awareness	7	35
Relationship management	9	45
Adaptability	10	50
General Mood	7	35

The below tables depict the localized and bilingual questions used in surveys for only the first two dimensions of the EI assessment framework. In total 300 students took part in the survey administration (Tables 2 and 3).

Table 2. Self-awareness survey questions.

Q. #.	Question in English	Question in Arabic	Gr.1-5
1	I understand and know myself	أفهم نفسي وأعرفها جيدا	
2	I know my values and beliefs	أنا مدرك لقيمي ومبادئي	
3	I have self-confidence in all situations	ثقتي بنفسي عالية في المواقف جميعها	
4	I consider myself an honest person	أعتبر نفسي إنسانًا صادقا	
5	I understand my own personal power and its effect on others	أعرف قوتي الشخصية وتأثيرها على الآخرين	
6	I am comfortable with myself	أجد الراحة و السلام الداخلي مع نفسي	
7	I know exactly what motivates me	أعرف بالضبط ما الذي يحفزني	

Table 3. Self- management survey questions.

Q. #	Question in English	Question in Arabic	Gr.1-5
1	I understand and use self-coaching techniques	أفهم تقنيات التدريب الذاتي وأستخدمها	
2	I have high self-esteem	لدي تقدير عالٍ لذاتي	
3	I can become an effective role model	أنا قادر على أن أصبح نموذجًا يحتذى به	
4	I can manage personal change effectively	يمكنني إدارة التغيير الشخصي بفعالية	
5	I set personal goals and take actions towards them	أضع أهدافًا شخصية وأتخذ إجراءات تجاهها	
6	I practice positive thinking	أمارس التفكير الإيجابي	
7	I trust my intuition	أثق بحدسي وتوقعاتي	

The sample of participants included 75 Foundations students, and 225 Bachelor students at the Higher Colleges of Technology [18], Dubai Colleges. The Bachelor common year students who were chosen to participate in the project had in common a General Studies course on Life and Study Skills (LSS 1003).

3.2 Intervention Strategies

Findings from research in a range of areas have consistently shown that people can improve their emotional competencies through systematic training [19]. EI can be developed through focused intervention strategies which would typically involve developing specific skills and competencies related to emotional intelligence. These interventions can be done individually, through coaching or therapy, or in a group setting through workshops or classes. The key is to find an approach that works best for the individual and to be consistent and committed to practicing and developing emotional intelligence skills over time. These interventions have been grouped as package activities [17] are divided into three parts:

- **Part I** is about knowing yourself and includes self-awareness and self-management dimensions.
- **Part II** is about knowing others and includes social awareness and relationship management.
- **Part III** is on positivity and well-being and includes the dimensions of adaptability and general mood (Fig. 3)

These interventions can be tailored to the individual's specific challenges and preferences, helping a trainee develop and improve their emotional intelligence skills.

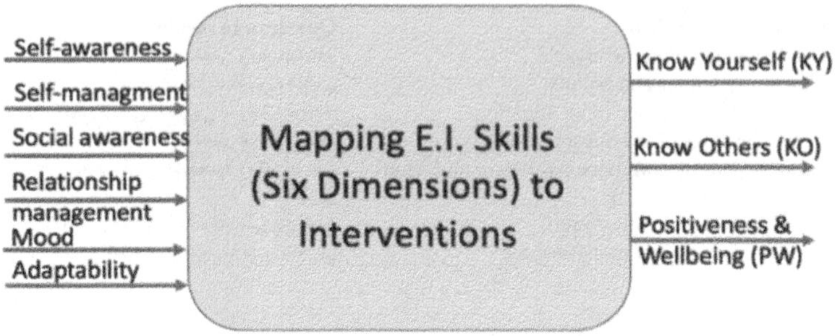

Fig. 3. E.I. skills mapping into interventions.

3.3 Data Preparation (Part 1)

Annotate the dataset to align responses and assessment results with appropriate EI dimensions and possible interventions [16].

Dimension 1: Self-awareness:

- Responses indicating low self-awareness (in the range of [1–15] of the self-awareness assessment scale) might be paired with:
  - ABCs emotions-increase your vocabulary, or
  - Plutchik's Wheel of Emotion
  - The Emotoscope feeling Chart
- Responses indicating medium [16–21], [22–25] self-awareness might be paired with:
  - The trainee can pick-up an action from a list and experiment with it for a week seeing if this new action creates positive outcomes in his or her life.
  - The trainee can watch a selected YouTube clip or a movie about 2 or more people having real-life conversation, and they have to pick up 5 different emotions that they can see in their facial expressions.
- Responses indicating high [26–35] self-awareness might be paired with:
  - I am aware activity. The trainees must stop themselves two times a day for 5 days to become aware of their emotions. They have to pick times when their feelings of emotions have shifted due to a thought, feeling, and/or a situation that has risen. Then, they need to write down their thoughts why they are feeling this way, etc.

Dimension 2: self-management:

- Responses indicating low self-management (in the range of [1–15] of the self-management assessment scale) might be paired with:

  - Mood check: This exercise is designed to help a trainee understands his or her moods and identify the moods of others in a working team for example.

- Responses indicating medium self-management (in the range of [16–25] of the self-management assessment scale) might be paired with:

  - Watch a video on YouTube on Let's talk self-management. Then reflect on possible answers to a series of questions such as What did they find interesting about self-management skill examples in the video, etc.

- Responses indicating high self-management (in the range of [26–35] of the self-management assessment scale) might be paired with:

  - Trainees are requested to copy and paste the YouTube video, watch it and then provide answers to a series of questions that further clarifies and reinforces the meaning of self-management.

The annotation for the remaining four dimensions of the EI framework to align responses and assessment results with appropriate EI dimensions and possible interventions are developed.

3.4 Data Preparation (Part 2)

Formatting data for fine-tuning a language model, such as GPT, involves structuring it in a way that the model can learn to generate the desired outputs based on specific inputs. To convert the EI data into a suitable structure, it is possible to use a **question-answer format** or **prompt-based format** to simulate user interactions and the corresponding responses as detailed hereafter:

Question-answer (QA) Format for EI Data:

In the QA format, each data point is structured as a question followed by an answer. This format is effective when a developer wants the model to provide concise responses to specific questions. Example for the case of EI data:

- **Input**: "What is an appropriate intervention for someone with low self-awareness?"

  - **Output**: "Practicing in ABCs emotions-increase your vocabulary and reflective journaling can help increase self-awareness."

- **Input**: "How can one improve relationship management in a team setting?"

  - **Output**: "Engaging in actives to discover more about your communication style and the people around you while listening and seeking feedback from team members are effective strategies for improving relationship management."

- **Input**: "What strategies can enhance general mood?"

- **Output**: "Check the 42 scientifically proven ways to improve a person's general mood while connecting to others."

Based on the six EI dimensions (self-awareness, self-management, social awareness, relationship management, adaptability, general mood), all the questions which are relevant to each dimension can be identified. Then, clear and answers for each question that reflect the interventions or insights related to EI are written (such as the examples shown above). Finally, it is important to ensure that each question is paired with its answer in a structured dataset, like a CSV or JSON file, ready for fine-tuning.

Prompt-Based Format for EI Data:

As an alternative to a Q/A structure, it is possible to use a prompt-based format. In this format, prompts that simulate user inputs followed by desired outputs are created. This method is more flexible and allows for various types of interactions, such as advice, explanations, or scenario-based recommendations. Here are some examples of prompt-based input:

- **Prompt**: "User: I feel overwhelmed at work and often react impulsively. What can I do to improve my emotional control?"
  - **Completion**: "To improve emotional control, you could try practicing deep breathing exercises, taking short breaks to reset your mindset, and developing a habit of pausing before reacting."
- **Prompt**: "User: How can I better understand the emotions of my colleagues?"
  - **Completion**: "To better understand the emotions of your colleagues, try observing their body language, listening actively to their concerns, and asking open-ended questions to encourage them to share more."

Based on the six EI dimensions (self-awareness, self-management, social awareness, relationship management, adaptability, general mood), all prompts and model responses are created. First, prompts that reflect typical user questions or statements related to EI are created. Second, the ideal model response or completion for each prompt is written. Finally, the prompts and their corresponding completions are organized in a structured dataset. Here also, data can be organized into a structure such as CSV, JSON, or plain text files.

3.5 Model Fine-Tuning, Deployment, and Continuous Improvement

To fine-tune an existing language model like GPT-3 or GPT-4 using the developed Emotional Intelligence (EI) annotated dataset, there is a need to follow a structured process that involves preparing the concerned data, setting up the environment for training, and then fine-tuning the model.

First, the EI annotated dataset must be prepared. This includes cleaning the EI data, structuring and annotating it, and choosing a platform for fine-tuning. Depending on the resource available, a platform such as OpenAI API for models like GPT-3 can be chosen. Then, the environment is set up where the necessary libraries like transformers, datasets, and torch, and to ensure Python are installed. If using OpenAI's GPT-3, it is necessary to ensure the access to their API and API keys. The dataset is converted to the required format and the model is fine-tuned.

The model's performance is evaluated using a qualitative method for example where the model outputs of interventions recommendations is reviewed for a variety of prompts to ensure its accuracy and appropriateness, and finally deployed which can be integrated as part of a larger EI assessment and intervention system. For continuous improvement, there is a need to implement a mechanism to monitor the model performance over time and collect user's feedback. This data can be used to further fine-tune and improve the model iteratively.

3.6 Prompt Engineering of EI Interventions Using GPT-4

The GPT-4 capabilities are used to design prompts that extract EI-related insights. First of all, the model is fine-tuned using the results of the research in [17] where the paper has been uploaded to GPT-4 as depicted in Fig. 4.

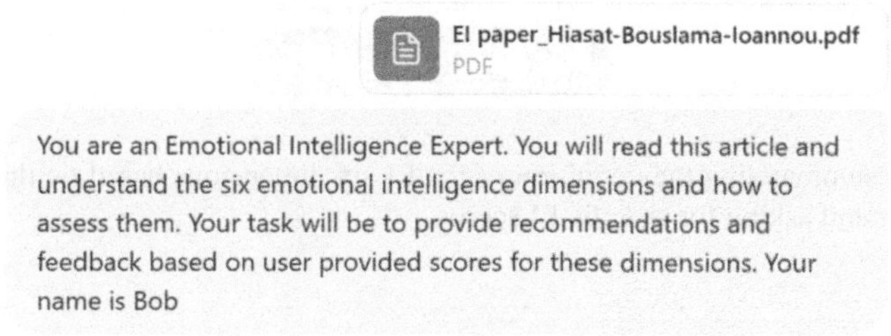

Fig. 4. Using prompt engineering to design prompts that extract EI-related insights.

Then, carefully crafted prompts can help elicit interventions related to the different EI dimensions of the author's framework [15, 16] as shown in the following screenshots extracted from GPT-4 (Figs. 5, 6, 7 and 8).

In summary, GPT-4 summarizes that the user shows strong capabilities in dimensions 4 and 5 but highlights that the use needs more focus on improving Dimensions 1, 2, and 6. The findings suggest that AI-driven interventions, particularly those leveraging advanced language models like GPT-4, can play a significant role in educational settings by not only supporting academic learning but also nurturing essential soft skills that are critical for long-term success in the workplace. Future research should explore the scalability of this approach across different educational contexts and its long-term impact on students' career trajectories [20].

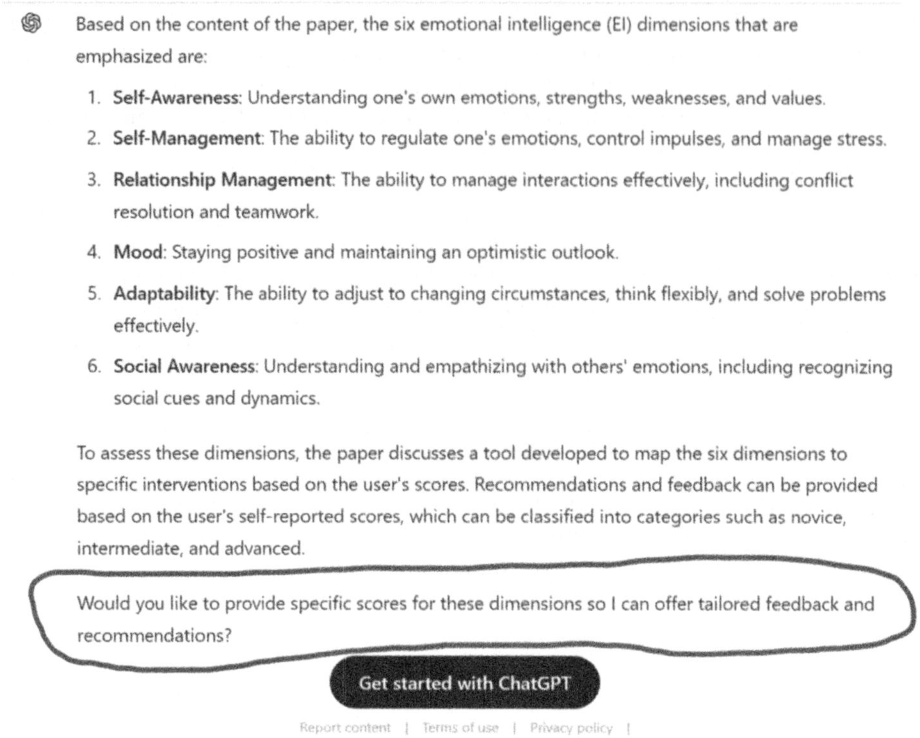

Fig. 5. GPT-4 summarizing the definition of the EI six dimensions based on the content of the uploaded paper and asking for specific EI scores.

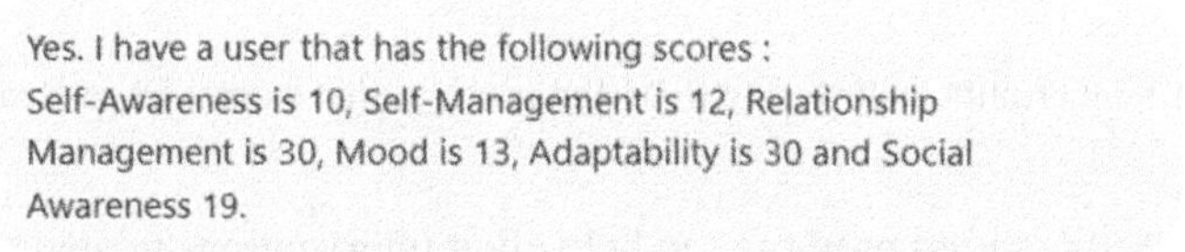

Fig. 6. A scenario where a sample set of EI assessment scores is used as a prompt.

In prompt engineering the model, it is crucial to address ethical considerations. The model must ensure that the assessments and interventions are delivered in a way that respects the data privacy and user's confidentiality, avoids causing emotional harm, provides learners with informed consent before any assessment takes place, and finally provides appropriate disclaimers when dealing with sensitive issues. The model should also be of a larger system [21] and include mechanisms to detect and prevent the reinforcement of negative patterns or any unintentional biases in emotional responses that may lead to an unfair assessment.

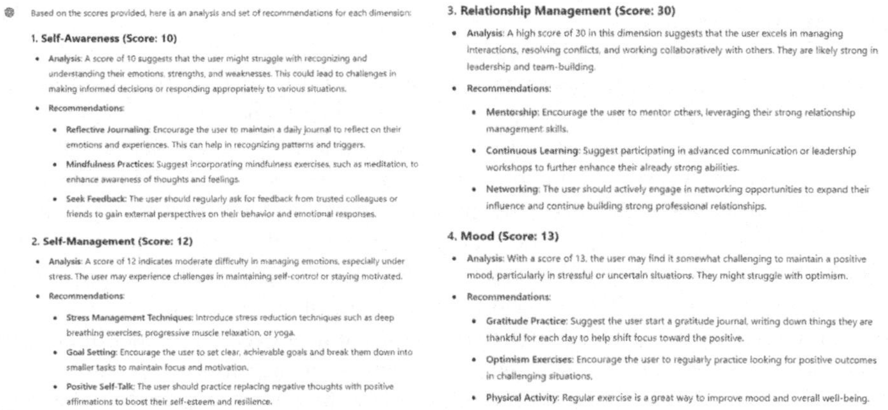

Based on the scores provided, here is an analysis and set of recommendations for each dimension:

1. **Self-Awareness (Score: 10)**
   - **Analysis**: A score of 10 suggests that the user might struggle with recognizing and understanding their emotions, strengths, and weaknesses. This could lead to challenges in making informed decisions or responding appropriately to various situations.
   - **Recommendations**:
     - **Reflective Journaling**: Encourage the user to maintain a daily journal to reflect on their emotions and experiences. This can help in recognizing patterns and triggers.
     - **Mindfulness Practices**: Suggest incorporating mindfulness exercises, such as meditation, to enhance awareness of thoughts and feelings.
     - **Seek Feedback**: The user should regularly ask for feedback from trusted colleagues or friends to gain external perspectives on their behavior and emotional responses.
2. **Self-Management (Score: 12)**
   - **Analysis**: A score of 12 indicates moderate difficulty in managing emotions, especially under stress. The user may experience challenges in maintaining self-control or staying motivated.
   - **Recommendations**:
     - **Stress Management Techniques**: Introduce stress reduction techniques such as deep breathing exercises, progressive muscle relaxation, or yoga.
     - **Goal Setting**: Encourage the user to set clear, achievable goals and break them down into smaller tasks to maintain focus and motivation.
     - **Positive Self-Talk**: The user should practice replacing negative thoughts with positive affirmations to boost their self-esteem and resilience.
3. **Relationship Management (Score: 30)**
   - **Analysis**: A high score of 30 in this dimension suggests that the user excels in managing interactions, resolving conflicts, and working collaboratively with others. They are likely strong in leadership and team-building.
   - **Recommendations**:
     - **Mentorship**: Encourage the user to mentor others, leveraging their strong relationship management skills.
     - **Continuous Learning**: Suggest participating in advanced communication or leadership workshops to further enhance their already strong abilities.
     - **Networking**: The user should actively engage in networking opportunities to expand their influence and continue building strong professional relationships.
4. **Mood (Score: 13)**
   - **Analysis**: With a score of 13, the user may find it somewhat challenging to maintain a positive mood, particularly in stressful or uncertain situations. They might struggle with optimism.
   - **Recommendations**:
     - **Gratitude Practice**: Suggest the user start a gratitude journal, writing down things they are thankful for each day to help shift focus toward the positive.
     - **Optimism Exercises**: Encourage the user to regularly practice looking for positive outcomes in challenging situations.
     - **Physical Activity**: Regular exercise is a great way to improve mood and overall well-being.

Fig. 7. The GPT-4 analysis and set of recommendations for self-awareness, self-management, relationship management and mood.

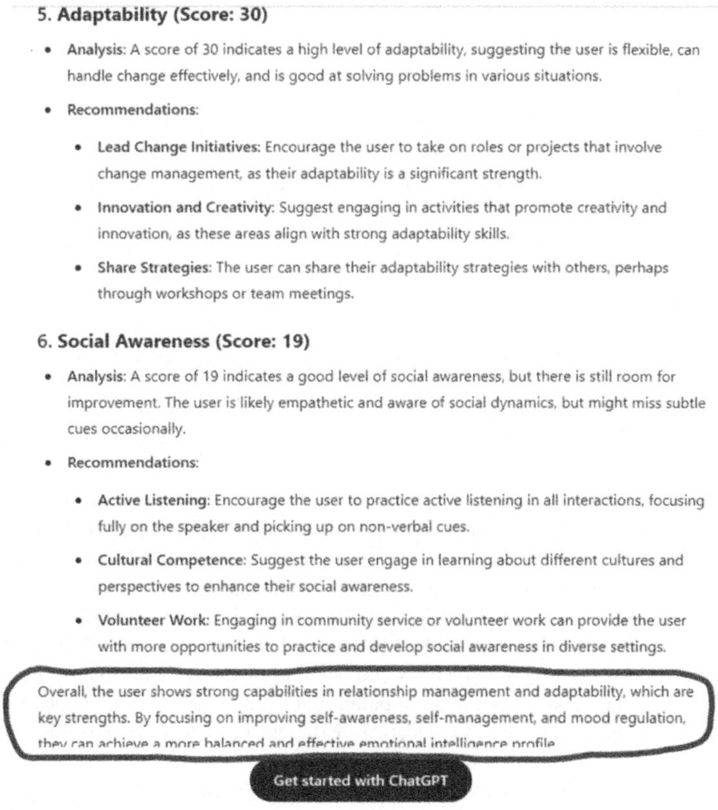

5. **Adaptability (Score: 30)**
   - **Analysis**: A score of 30 indicates a high level of adaptability, suggesting the user is flexible, can handle change effectively, and is good at solving problems in various situations.
   - **Recommendations**:
     - **Lead Change Initiatives**: Encourage the user to take on roles or projects that involve change management, as their adaptability is a significant strength.
     - **Innovation and Creativity**: Suggest engaging in activities that promote creativity and innovation, as these areas align with strong adaptability skills.
     - **Share Strategies**: The user can share their adaptability strategies with others, perhaps through workshops or team meetings.
6. **Social Awareness (Score: 19)**
   - **Analysis**: A score of 19 indicates a good level of social awareness, but there is still room for improvement. The user is likely empathetic and aware of social dynamics, but might miss subtle cues occasionally.
   - **Recommendations**:
     - **Active Listening**: Encourage the user to practice active listening in all interactions, focusing fully on the speaker and picking up on non-verbal cues.
     - **Cultural Competence**: Suggest the user engage in learning about different cultures and perspectives to enhance their social awareness.
     - **Volunteer Work**: Engaging in community service or volunteer work can provide the user with more opportunities to practice and develop social awareness in diverse settings.

Overall, the user shows strong capabilities in relationship management and adaptability, which are key strengths. By focusing on improving self-awareness, self-management, and mood regulation, they can achieve a more balanced and effective emotional intelligence profile

Get started with ChatGPT

Fig. 8. The GPT-4 analysis and set of recommendations for adaptability and social awareness.

4 Conclusions

In conclusion, the use of prompt engineering and GPT-4 for conceptualizing a solution for generating text-based interventions on emotional intelligence (EI) has shown promising results to enhance students' EI skills within an academic setting. Through carefully crafted prompt engineering, tailored content that addressed specific EI competencies, such as self-awareness, self-management, adaptability, and general mood skills were produced. These effective interventions are expected not only to help students develop a better understanding of their emotional responses but also provided practical strategies for managing emotions effectively and work in teams in harmony. As a result, students and young professionals will be able to demonstrate improved emotional intelligence, which is decisive for their personal and professional growth. Furthermore, the enhanced EI skills fostered through these interventions have the potential to increase students' employability and career success. Finally, continuous improvement of the model will be achieved through feedback loops where users can evaluate the relevance and effectiveness of the interventions. This feedback helps refine the model's recommendations and ensures that the interventions remain aligned with best practices in emotional intelligence development and ethical considerations.

References

1. Goleman, D.: Emotional Intelligence: Why It Can Matter More than IQ. Bantam Books, New York, NY (1995)
2. Duckworth, A.: Grit: The Power of Passion and Perseverance. Scribner/Simon & Schuster, New York, NY (2016)
3. Matthews, G., Roberts, R.D., Zeidner, M.: Emotional Intelligence: Science and Myth. MIT Press (2004)
4. McEnrue, M.P., Groves, K.S., Shen, W.: Emotional intelligence development: leveraging individual characteristics. J. Manage. Dev. **28**(2), 150–174 (2009)
5. Goodfellow, I., Bengio, Y., Courville, A.: Deep Learning. MIT Press (2009)
6. Brown, T.B., et al.: Language models are few-shot learners. Adv. Neural Inform. Process. Syst. **33**, 1877–1901 (2020)
7. Zhang, Y., Lin, H., Meishar-Tal, H., Wang, W., Zhang, H.: Automated text generation from survey data: a GPT-3 application in educational research. Int. J. Educ. Technol. High. Educ. **18**(1), 1–16 (2021)
8. Thompson, B., Blake, J.: AI in gaming: creating dynamic and immersive experiences through procedural content generation. J. Game Des. Dev. Educ. **5**(2), 25–40 (2021)
9. Elgammal, A., Liu, B., Elhoseiny, M., Mazzone, M.: CAN: creative adversarial networks, generating "art" by learning about styles and deviating from style norms. In: Proceedings of the 8th International Conference on Computational Creativity (ICCC), pp. 96–103 (2017)
10. Mikolov, T., Chen, K., Corrado, G., Dean, J.: Efficient Estimation of Word Representations in Vector Space. arXiv preprint arXiv:1301.3781 (2013)
11. Radford, A., Wu, J., Child, R., Luan, D., Amodei, D., Sutskever, I.: Language Models are Unsupervised Multitask Learners. OpenAI Blog (2019)
12. Cambria, E., White, B.: Jumping NLP curves: a review of natural language processing research. IEEE Comput. Intell. Mag. **9**(2), 48–57 (2014)
13. Zhang, L., Wang, S., Liu, B.: Deep learning for sentiment analysis: a survey. Wiley Interdisc. Rev.: Data Min. Knowl. Discovery **8**(4), e1253 (2018)

14. Bouslama, F., Housley, M., Steele, A.: Using a fuzzy logic-based emotional intelligence framework for testing emotional literacy of students in an outcomes-based educational system. J. Netw. Innov. Comput. **3**, 105–114 (2015)
15. Bouslama, F., Hiasat, L, Medina, C, Coombe, C., Manser, R.: Designing localized bilingual surveys for emotional literacy and intelligence assessment. In: Proceedings of the International Academic Conference on Education and Teaching (WEI-ET-Montreal 2019), pp. 11–27. Canada, 28–30 Oct 2019
16. Hiasat, L., Bouslama, F., Ioannou, S.: User-friendly automated evaluation tool for assessment of emotional intelligence. In: Kurosu, M., Hashizume, A. (eds.) Human-Computer Interaction: Thematic Area, HCI 2023, Held as Part of the 25th HCI International Conference, HCII 2023, Copenhagen, Denmark, July 23–28, 2023, Proceedings, Part II, pp. 196–214. Springer Nature Switzerland, Cham (2023). https://doi.org/10.1007/978-3-031-35599-8_13
17. OpenAI: *ChatGPT* (GPT-4). OpenAI. https://openai.com/ (2023)
18. The Higher Colleges of Technology https://www.hct.ac.ae (2024)
19. Brackett, M.A., Geher, G.: Measuring emotional intelligence: Paradigmatic shifts and common ground. In: Ciarrochi, J., Forgas, J.P., Mayer, J.D. (eds.) Emotional intelligence and everyday life, pp. 27–50. Psychology Press, New York, USA (2006)
20. Bouslama, F., Hiasat, L., Coombe, C.: Rethinking Career Development Post COVID-19: The Career Profile of the Future Framework (CPFF), an E.I.-Based Human Skill Approach, Future Trends in Education Post COVID-19, Springer (2023), https://doi.org/10.1007/978-981-99-1927-7
21. Bouslama, F., Hiasat, L., Mellouli, S., Dragovic Andersen, T.: Architecturing the future Citizen Competencies (FCC) System: Use of ISO/IEC/IEEE 42010 International Standards as Ontology, presented at the Twentieth International Conference on Technology, Knowledge, and Society, Universitat Politècnica de València, Spain, 7–8 Mar 2024

Dental Caries Segmentation from Orthopantomograms Using Optimized DeepLabV3+

R. Neeraja[1], L. Jani Anbarasi[1](✉), S. Geetha[1], Gadhamsetty Revanth[1], Prudhvi Prasad[1], Benson Edwin Raj[2], and Geetha Mohan[3]

[1] School of Computer Science and Engineering, Vellore Institute of Technology, Chennai, India
{neeraja.r2020,gadhamsety.revanth2021, sikharamprudhvi.prasad2021}@vitstudent.ac.in, {janianbarasi.l, geetha.s}@vit.ac.in

[2] Department of Computer Information Sciences, Higher Colleges of Technology, Fujairah, UAE
braj@hct.ac.ae

[3] Computer Science, Institute of Applied Technology, Abu Dhabi, UAE

Abstract. Orthopantomograms are essential tools for dentists in analyzing dental conditions like dental caries. Typically, dentists diagnose cavities by manually examining these images. However, manual detection can sometimes miss cavities due to factors such as negligence from excessive workloads and lack of expertise. Hence, the demand arises for computer-based smart vision technologies that employ machine learning, image processing approaches and artificial intelligence techniques to tackle these challenges. This study leverages an advanced deep CNN based DeepLabV3+ techniques such as atrous convolutions and encoder-decoder architectures to capture rich contextual information and fine-grained spatial details from orthopantomograms (OPGs). The encoder-decoder architecture enhances the ability to capture minute details in the segmentation of tooth caries, by capturing multi-scale context with multiple parallel filters employing different atrous rates, enabling the model to consider features at various scales simultaneously. The OPGs were obtained from the Nanded Rural Dental College & Research Centre in Maharashtra. A total of 153 OPGs selected and processed by an experienced dentist to identify the caries regions in the original images. The mask dataset is generated by extracting the caries region for the segmentation process. Various augmentation approaches such as zooming, rotation, horizontal and vertical flipping were applied to expand the dataset and achieved improved segmentation results. The results indicate that the model is highly effective in diagnosing dental caries, achieving an accuracy score of 99.2%, IoU score as 99.3% and Dice coefficient as 99.68%, respectively.

Keywords: Orthopantomograms · Tooth Caries · DeepLabV3+ · Segmentation

A. Safi et al. (Eds.): ISICS 2024, CCIS 2381, pp. 122–136, 2025.
https://doi.org/10.1007/978-3-031-82931-4_9

1 Introduction

Dental caries are a prevalent oral health concern that impacts persons across all age groups. The American Dental Association has classified dental caries into various categories according to the distribution and severity of lesions, which include severe, moderate, initial and normal [1]. Diagnosing early posterior proximal caries using standard clinical tests is highly challenging in clinical practice. To overcome these limitations, orthopantomograms (OPG_S) are used as a primary method for detecting dental caries. While dental radiography aids human experts in identifying caries and other anomalies, diagnosing early proximal caries in posterior teeth remains difficult. However, finding an effective solution for this issue can prevent invasive treatments and significantly reduce healthcare costs.

Most of the research studies employed conventional Machine Learning (ML) based techniques [2–4] for identifying dental cavities through feature extraction. In recent years, advancements in Artificial Intelligence (AI) and Deep Learning (DL) [5–7] have opened new opportunities for automating the detection and segmentation of dental caries. Semantic segmentation [8], a subfield of computer vision, involves classifying each pixel in an image into a specific category. In the context of dental caries, semantic segmentation aims to delineate caries regions from healthy dental structures with high precision. Convolutional neural networks (CNNs), a type of deep learning models, have shown exceptional ability in identifying dental caries [9]. This study leverages an advanced deep CNN based DeepLabV3+ techniques such as atrous convolutions and encoder-decoder architectures to capture rich contextual information and fine-grained spatial details from OPG_S. By integrating these sophisticated methods, DeepLabV3+ can effectively segment dental caries, providing a valuable tool for dental professionals. This approach not only enhances the accuracy and efficiency of caries detection but also facilitates better monitoring and treatment outcomes. The Incorporation of AI-based segmentation tools into dental practice represents a significant advancement in utilizing technology to enhance oral health care.

The primary contributions of the proposed work are as follows:

- Performed a thorough evaluation of the DeepLabV3+ model to determine its effectiveness in segmenting tooth caries from orthopantomograms (OPGs).
- Generated a dataset of 153 OPG images collected from Nanded Rural Dental College & Research Center in Maharashtra and identified the caries regions along with their corresponding masks using the expertise of an experienced dentist.
- Performed various augmentations to increase the dataset count to enhance the segmentation performance.
- DeepLabV3+ model is highly effective in segmenting dental caries, achieving an impressive accuracy score of 99.2%, IoU score as 99.3% and Dice coefficient as 99.68%, respectively.

2 Related Works

Qayyum et al. [10] proposed a self-supervised learning strategy based on a student-teacher paradigm for dental caries identification, which utilizes both unlabelled images and labelled images. The centroid cropping approach is employed to extract the caries region dynamically from dental X-ray images. The dental caries detection dataset (DCD^2) comprised of 229 dental X-rays with 88 unlabelled and 141 labelled images for caries identification. An average accuracy of 99.43% was achieved using the Deeplab-v3 model with a ResNet-101 backbone. Imak et al. [11] introduced an innovative method for automatically diagnosing dental caries using periapical images with a deep CNN based ensemble called MI-DCNNE. This method used a score-based ensemble scheme to enhance performance, processing both unprocessed and modified periapical images. Evaluated on a dataset of 340 images, the model achieved a precision rate of 99.13%, demonstrating high effectiveness in diagnosing dental caries. Alharbi et al. [12] employed various U-Net models to identify caries lesions in dental panoramic X-ray images, utilizing DNS dataset (Detection, Numbering, and Segmentation) Panoramic Images. The main goal is to enhance the dataset by creating binary ground truth images that highlight voids in the X-rays, serving as benchmarks for model evaluation. These image masks are reviewed by dentists to ensure accuracy. The augmented dataset is applied to variations of U-Net models to improve the boundary of cavities. U-Net3+ outperformed the other models, achieving a testing accuracy of 95%. Mahran et al. [13] demonstrated the feasibility of using the Attention U-Net design for the purpose of segmenting teeth. The paper highlights the exceptional efficacy of this network in precisely segmenting caries utilising a recently accessible public dataset known as Tufts Dental X-Ray. The model was trained and tested using a 10-fold cross-validation technique, achieving an IoU and accuracy score of 90.6% and 98.82%. And an average Dice coefficient of 95.01%,

Park et al. [14] assessed the effectiveness of a deep learning system for caries detection by precisely identifying and segmenting tooth surfaces in images. A total of 2348 intraoral images from 445 participants were collected and randomly divided into 1638 training images, 410 validation images and 300 test images. The CNN based architectures such as faster R-CNN, ResNet-18 and U-Net were used for the segmentation of tooth surface, caries classification, and localization attaining 0.813 and 0.837 as accuracy and area under curve. Saini et al. [15] identified dental cavities in preliminary stages using digital colour images, enhancing treatment efficiency, and facilitating tele-dentistry. Various transfer learning models including Inception-V3, VGG16, ResNet50, and VGG19 were trained on a binary dataset with and without dental caries. Inception-V3 obtained the highest training and validation accuracy score of 99.89% and 98.95% compared to the other models. A U-Net based architecture was developed by Lee et al. [16] to detect caries from dental radiographs, aiming to enhance clinician performance. A total of 304 radiographs were utilised for training the model, while an additional 50 radiographs were reserved for evaluation purposes, all in accordance with ethical norms. The architecture attained 63.29% precision, 65.02% recall and 64.14% F1-score on test dataset, demonstrating a notable degree of accuracy. A diagnostic algorithm incorporating adaptive thresholding, laplacian filtering and neural network architecture was developed by

Geetha et al. [17] to identify dental cavities in digital radiography. Using 105 radiographs annotated by a dentist, the model was trained with 10-fold cross-validation. The algorithm achieved an accuracy score 97.1%, 0.987 ROC (Receiver Operating Characteristic) area, False Positive (FP) rate of 2.8% and 0.987 PRC (Precision Recall Curve) area.

Muthu Lakshmi et al. [18] combines Sobel edge detection with deep Convolutional Neural Networks (CNN) to accurately detect early-stage cavities. Preprocessing involves histogram equalization, contrast enhancement, and feature selection. The approach is evaluated using several CNN-generated segmentation algorithms, including Otsu's thresholding and Watershed segmentation. Sobel edge detection identifies edges in dental images by calculating pixel intensity gradients in the Gx and Gy directions. This method proves highly efficient, achieving an accuracy rate of 96.08%. Geetha et al. [19] introduced a dental caries diagnosis technique with Support Vector Machine (SVM) classifier, laplacian filtering, texture analysis and adaptive thresholding. Adaptive thresholding outperformed Otsu thresholding, watershed segmentation, and active contouring, achieving a higher level of performance with an accuracy score and precision rate of 96.9% and 96.1%. Thanh et al. [20] aimed to diagnose various stages of smooth surface caries using smartphone images. The training dataset consisted of 1902 images of dental enamel surfaces from 695 participants. Faster R-CNN, RetinaNet, YOLOv3 and SSD (Single-Shot Multi-Box Detector) architectures were evaluated. YOLOv3 and faster R-CNN architectures demonstrated the highest sensitivity for cavitated caries at 87.4% and 71.4%, respectively, but lower sensitivity for non-cavitated cases at 36.9% and 26%. All models had over 86% specificity for cavitated caries and over 71% for non-cavitated cases. The findings indicate that YOLOv3 and Faster Region based CNN show great potential for identifying dental caries from smartphone images in clinical settings. Khan et al. [21] utilized dataset from Khyber College of Dentistry and Hospital to assess several deep learning algorithms, evaluating their performance using Precision, Recall, Accuracy, and F1-score metrics. Among LeNet, CNN, and AlexNet, transfer learning model VGG16 performed the best, achieving 98.99% accuracy, 0.95 precision, 0.96 F1-score of 0.96, and 0.97 recall. Duong et al. [22] developed a computational method to automatically identify caries on tooth occlusal surfaces. A total of 620 unrestored molars and premolars were photographed and categorized into 3 groups, (a) No Surface Change, (b) Visually Non-Cavitated and (c) Cavitated where a two-phase detection strategy was applied that attained 92.37% accuracy, 88.1% sensitivity, and 96.6% specificity.

3 Proposed Methodology

This study investigated the use of a customised DeepLabV3+ architecture for segmenting dental caries images. The overall structure of the proposed methodology is illustrated in Fig. 1.

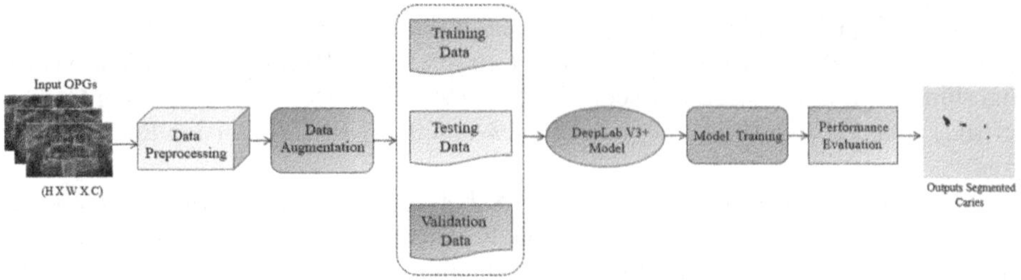

Fig. 1. The overall structure of the proposed methodology.

3.1 DeepLabV3+ Architecture

DeepLabV3+ is an enhanced semantic segmentation model that builds upon DeepLabV3 by integrating atrous convolutions with an encoder-decoder architecture, capturing rich contextual information and fine-grained spatial details to refine high-resolution image segmentation results. DeepLabV3+ utilizes atrous (dilated) convolutions to control the receptive field and feature map resolutions without increasing the number of parameters. Another key feature is the Atrous Spatial Pyramid Pooling (ASPP) to effectively extracts multi-scale features essential for segmentation. This enables the network to capture dense feature maps with rich, long-range information, allowing for accurate image segmentation. The methodology employed an Xception network pre-trained on ImageNet as the backbone to process the input dental caries images and extract multi-scale features through its deep convolutional layers. DeepLabV3+ utilizes atrous convolutions to efficiently capture multi-scale contextual features, further enhanced by spatial pyramid pooling and an encoder-decoder structure for precise localization. Xception is a deep neural network that extracts complex patterns and features for dental caries segmentation. The implementation of depthwise separable convolutions decreases processing while allowing the model to concentrate on key features without unnecessary complexity. The DeepLabV3+ architecture is shown in Fig. 2.

3.2 Atrous Convolution

Atrous convolution [23] is a modification of standard convolution that incorporates a dilation rate parameter. This technique generates gaps within the convolutional kernel, effectively expanding its receptive field without adding more parameters or computational cost. Atrous convolution alters the standard convolution by inserting spaces between the kernel elements, which is regulated by the dilation rate. For 2-D input images, atrous convolution is applied to the input feature map i at each location l on the output O and using a filter f as in Eq. (1).

$$O[l] = \sum_{kl} i[l + r_a * kl]f[kl] \quad (1)$$

where atrous or dilation rate 'r_a' determines how the input image is sampled, where larger values correspond to a greater stride. This is achieved by convolving the input i with upsampled filters, which are generated by inserting $r_a - 1$ zeros between consecutive filter values along each spatial dimension. The standard convolution occurs when r_a equals 1. Atrous convolution allows for flexible adjustment of the filter's receptive field by varying the dilation rate.

3.3 Atrous Spatial Pyramid Pooling (*ASSP*)

Atrous Spatial Pyramid Pooling [24] uses atrous (dilated) convolutions with different dilation rates for capturing multi-scale information. The *ASSP* module employs atrous convolutions, as described in Eq. (2), utilizing different dilation rates $'r_a'$. This approach captures information across multiple scales and incorporates global context through a global average pooling layer. *ASSP* is structured with several parallel branches to enhance feature extraction in semantic segmentation tasks. It includes branches with 1×1 convolutions and multiple 3×3 convolutions, each utilizing different dilation rates ($r_{a_1} = 6$, $r_{a_2} = 12$, $r_{a_3} = 18$) for output stride 16 and all with filter size of 256. These variations in dilation rates allow the module to capture contextual information at different scales, which is crucial for accurately delineating caries of varying sizes in images.

$$F_{ASSP} = Conv_{1\times1} \oplus Conv_{3\times3}\left(r_{a_1} = 6\right) \oplus Conv_{3\times3}\left(r_{a_2} = 12\right) \oplus Conv_{3\times3}\left(r_{a_3} = 18\right) \tag{2}$$

Additionally, *ASSP* incorporates image-level feature pooling followed by a 1×1 convolution, enabling the model to gather global context information efficiently. This comprehensive approach within *ASSP* ensures that the network can effectively analyse complex visual data and produce precise segmentation results.

3.4 Up Sampling

The features extracted by the *ASSP* module is concatenated F_{Concat} to form a rich, multi-scale feature representation. This concatenated output is then unsampled $F_{ASSP_{up}}$ as in Eq. (3) and combined with a lower-level feature map F_{Low} from the backbone network, as described in Eq. (4). The lower-level feature map has been processed through another 1×1 convolution and upsampled to match the spatial resolution of the *ASSP* output.

$$F_{ASSP_{up}} = upsample(F_{ASSP}, scalefactor = 4) \tag{3}$$

$$F_{Concat} = F_{ASSP_{up}} \oplus F_{Low} \tag{4}$$

This fusion of high-level and low-level features integrates both global context and detailed spatial information. The combined feature map is further refined through additional convolutional layers, batch normalization, and ReLU activation to enhance feature quality. Finally, the refined feature map $F_{Refined}$ as in Eq. (5) is upsampled to the original input resolution to form the final upsampling output as in Eq. (6).

$$F_{Refined} = Conv_{3\times3}(Conv_{3\times3}(F_{Concat}(F_{ASSP_{up}}, F_{Low}) \oplus Conv_{1\times1}))) \tag{5}$$

$$F_{Upsampling\_output} = upsample\left(F_{Refined}, scalefactor = 4\right) \tag{6}$$

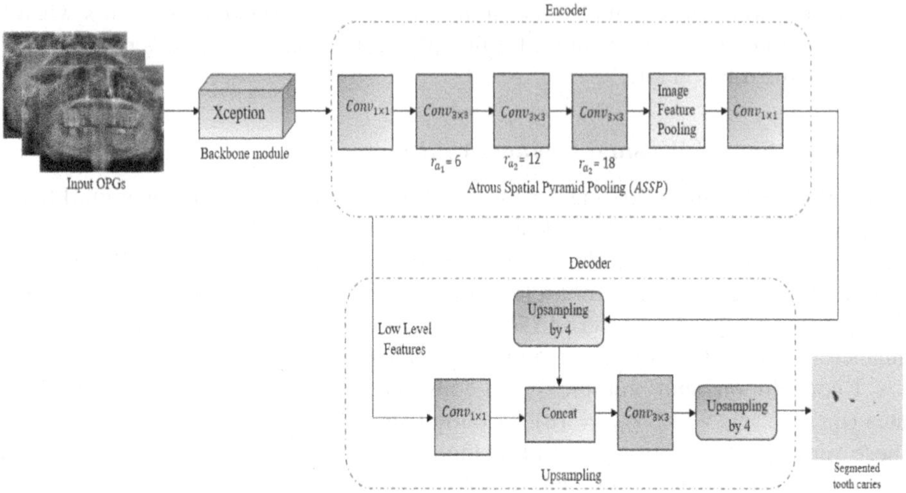

Fig. 2. The DeepLabV3+ Architecture.

3.5 Output Layer

The segmentation mask is produced by the final output layer F_{Output} as in Eq. (7), which comprised of a 1×1 convolution followed by a sigmoid activation for dental caries segmentation.

$$F_{Output} = Sigmoid(Conv_{1\times1}(F_{Refined})) \tag{7}$$

4 Results and Discussion

This paper analyzes orthopantomographs (OPGs) of teeth to detect caries using advanced deep learning model DeepLabV3+. This section includes an in-depth review of data acquiring, hyperparameter tuning, model training and validation, and the efficacy of the DeepLabV3+ architecture in precisely detecting the caries in OPGs. Additionally, it involves a comprehensive evaluation of the stated methodology in contrast to prior research attempts.

4.1 Data Set Collection and Preprocessing

The X-ray radiographs were acquired from the Nanded Rural Dental College & Research Center in Maharashtra. 153 OPGs (Orthopantomograms) were selected and processed by a dentist to identify the caries region in the original images. The identified regions of interest (ROI) were used to create masks for effective segmentation of the caries. The cavities in these images were carefully outlined using Adobe Photoshop, a powerful tool for image annotation. This annotation procedure was facilitated by a dental doctor, ensuring precise detection and segmentation of cavities in the OPGs. The thorough annotation process aims to support accurate analysis and training of models, thereby enhancing the overall effectiveness of cavity investigation. Figure 3 displays a panoramic OPGs image along with its corresponding ground truth. The highlighted area denotes the precise position of the cavity on the radiograph, with the segmented cavity indicated by the white section.

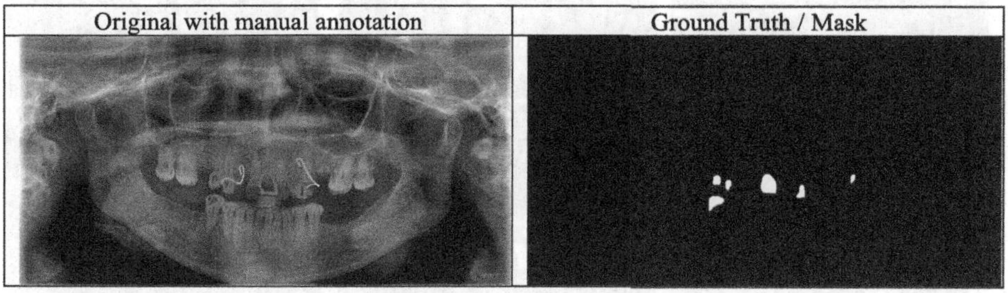

Fig. 3. Sample panoramic X-ray image with their ground truth

4.2 Data Augmentation

To enhance the dataset and improve the applicability of the models, augmentation techniques were employed to achieve better performance. The initial dataset consisted of 153 X-ray images of teeth and their corresponding masks indicating the presence of tooth caries. To increase the dataset size and variability, Albumentations library a Python library for image augmentation was utilized. Augmentation techniques included flipping (both horizontal and vertical) and rotating the images at random angles, as shown in Eqs. 8. This approach aimed to improve the model's robustness and generalization by exposing it to a wider variety of image transformations. Horizontal flipping is an image augmentation technique where the image is mirrored along its vertical axis. This means that the left side of the image becomes the right side and vice versa. Let the original image be $O_{DC}(m, n)$ with coordinate m, n along with the width 'w' then the image can be horizontally flipped resulting as $O'_{DC}(m', n')$ as shown in Eq. 8.

$$O'_{DC}(m', n') = w - 1 - O_{DC}(m, n) \tag{8}$$

Vertical flipping, flips the image around its horizontal axis, such that the top row becomes the bottom row, the second row from the top becomes the second row from the bottom, and so on.

Let the original image be $O_{DC}(m, n)$ with coordinate m, n along with the height 'h' then the image can be horizontally flipped resulting as $O'_{DC}(m', n')$ as shown in Eq. 9.

$$O'_{VF}(m', n') = h - 1 - O_{DC}(m, n) \tag{9}$$

Random rotation rotates an image by a random angle. This technique helps to increase the diversity of the training dataset, making the model more robust to variations in the orientation of objects in the images. Sample augmented images are shown in Fig. 4.

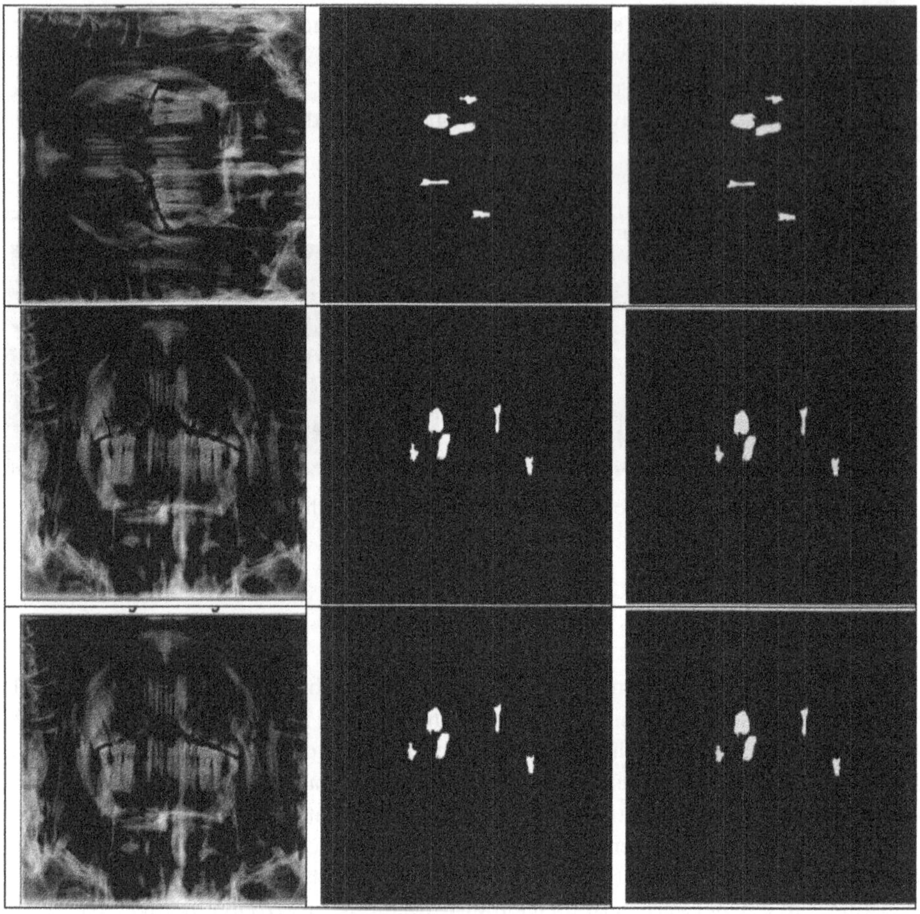

Fig. 4. Sample augmented images along with the ground truth images.

4.3 Training and Validation Analysis

The model was trained on the generated dataset using a training and validation split of 20%. Each model underwent training for 200 epochs with a batch size of 16, utilizing a step size of 13. Training was conducted using the PyTorch framework, leveraging GPU acceleration to expedite the process. Throughout the training process, accuracy and loss metrics were monitored at each epoch of training and validation. Evaluation metrics such as IoU scores (Intersection over Union) were computed to quantify segmentation performance. Additionally, ROC curves were plotted to analyze model discriminative capabilities between tooth regions and areas affected by caries.

The ROC curve for Deeplabv3+ shows a significant ability to distinguish between tooth regions and caries areas, with an area under the curve (AUC) of 0.51. Throughout training, the loss consistently decreases, indicating effective learning, while the validation loss shows a stable trend, reflecting strong generalization capabilities. The Deeplabv3+ model achieved an accuracy of 99.2% in segmenting tooth structures and

Table 1. Learning curve of the model, IoU score and DICE score

	Accuracy	Loss
Model	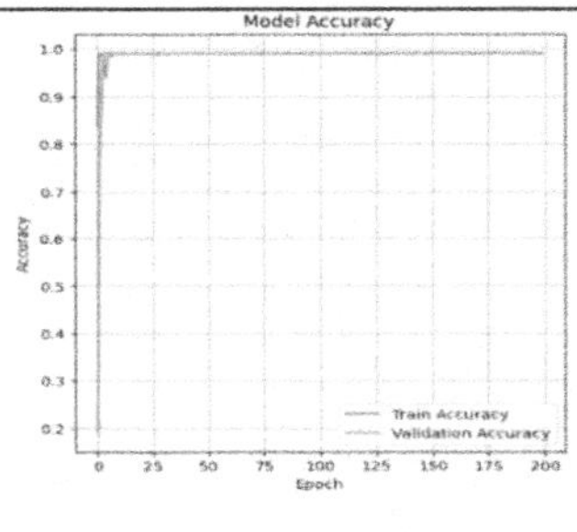	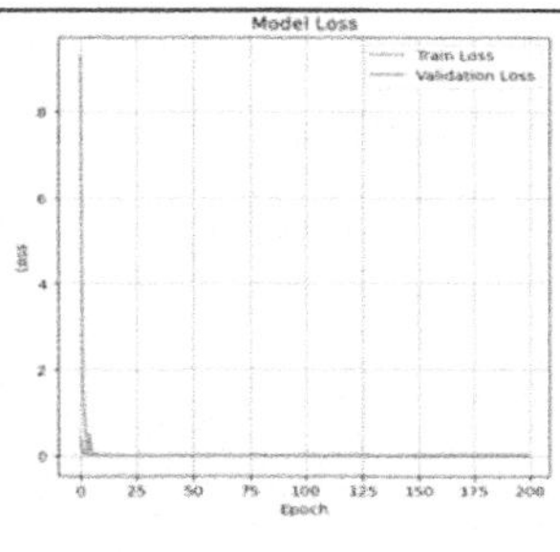
IoU Score	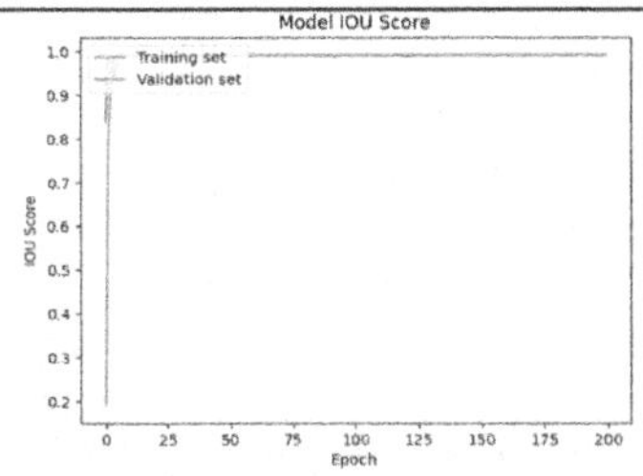	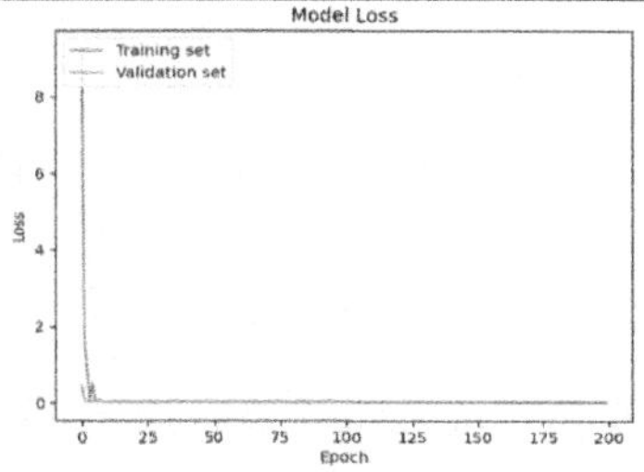
Dice Score	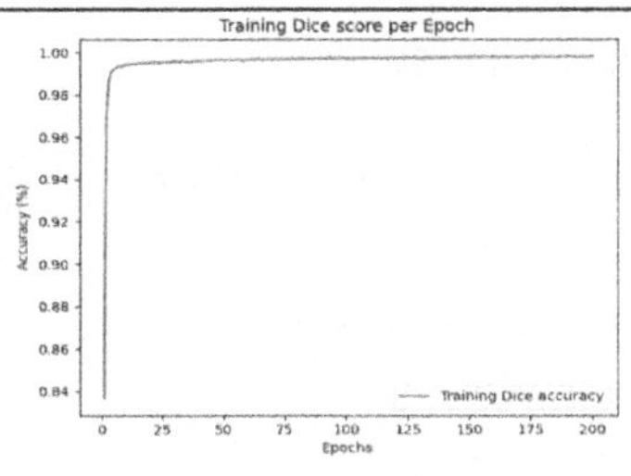	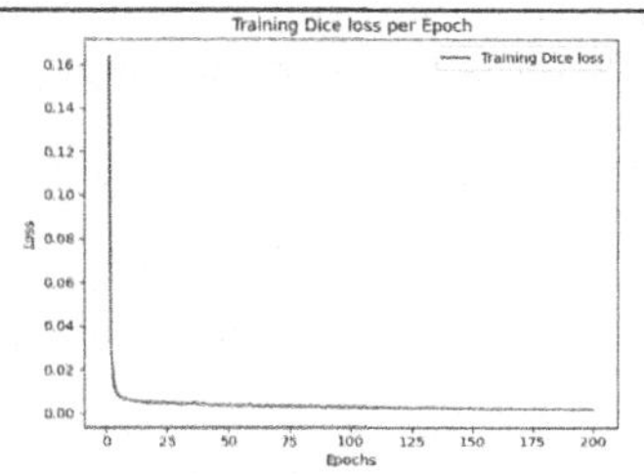

accurately identifying areas affected by caries. The time taken to execute each step is 487 ms/step. Figure 5 represents the ROC representing the performance of the tooth caries detection process. Table 1 visually represents the model's training progress with an accuracy curve and loss plot of the model, IoU and DICE score, highlighting its performance metrics across epochs. The model trained a total of 38,434,601 (146.62 MB) parameters where 38,375,465 (146.39 MB) are trainable parameters and 59,136 (231.00 KB) are Non-trainable parameters. Experimental results underscore the superior effectiveness of the Deeplabv3+ architecture in capturing both spatial and semantic features critical to accurate tooth X-ray image segmentation, demonstrating significant improvements over conventional CNN models in accuracy and robustness.

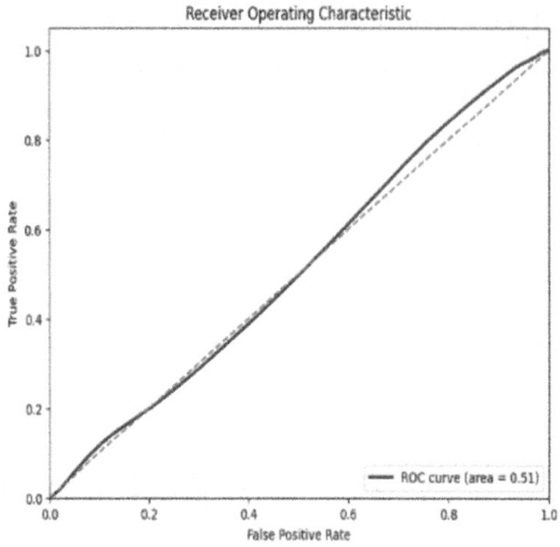

Fig. 5. ROC plot of the tooth caries detection

4.4 Evaluation Metrics

Evaluation metrics are important for evaluating the performance of deep learning models in tooth caries segmentation, ensuring the accurate identification of carious regions while minimizing false predictions. The evaluation metrics used to analyze the segmentation of tooth caries are provided in Eqs. (10) through (15):

$$\text{Accuracy } Acc_{tc} = (\text{TP}_{tc} + \text{TN}_{tc})/(\text{TP}_{tc} + \text{TN}_{tc} + \text{FP}_{tc} + \text{FN}_{tc}) \tag{10}$$

$$\text{Precision } Pre_{tc} = \text{TP}_{tc}/(\text{TP}_{tc} + \text{FP}_{tc}) \tag{11}$$

$$\text{IoU Score} = \text{TP}_{tc}/(\text{TP}_{tc} + \text{FP}_{tc} + \text{FN}_{tc}) \tag{12}$$

$$\text{Dice Score} = (2{*}\text{TP}_{tc})/(2{*}\text{TP}_{tc} + \text{FP}_{tc} + \text{FN}_{tc}) \tag{13}$$

$$\text{Sensitivity} = \text{TP}_{tc}/(\text{TP}_{tc} + \text{FN}_{tc}) \tag{14}$$

$$\text{Specificity} = \text{TP}_{tc}/(\text{TN}_{tc} + \text{FP}_{tc}) \tag{15}$$

Table 2. Evaluation metrics of the segmentation of the tooth caries

Model	Accuracy	IoU	Dice Coefficient	Precision	Sensitivity	Specificity
DeepLabV3+	99.23	0.993	0.9968	0.0031	0.995	0.9993

where TP_{tc} is the True Positive rate showing the number of caries regions identified accurately as caries by the system. TN_{tc} is the True Negative rate indicating the number of healthy regions correctly identified as healthy by the system. FP_{tc} is the False Positive rate showing the number of healthy regions identified incorrectly as caries by the system. FN_{tc} is the False Negative rate indicating the number of caries regions identified incorrectly as healthy by the system. The Intersection over Union (IoU) measures the amount of overlap that exists between the predicted segmentation region and the ground truth by computing the ratio of the region of intersection to the union area. The Dice Score evaluates the similarities between the predicted and the ground truth mask. The results obtained for the evaluation metrics are shown in Table 2.

Table 3. Sample OPGs segmented using DeepLabV3+

Original Image	Mask	Segmeneted ROI
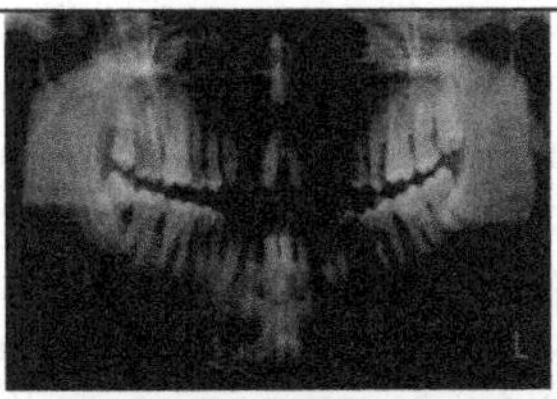	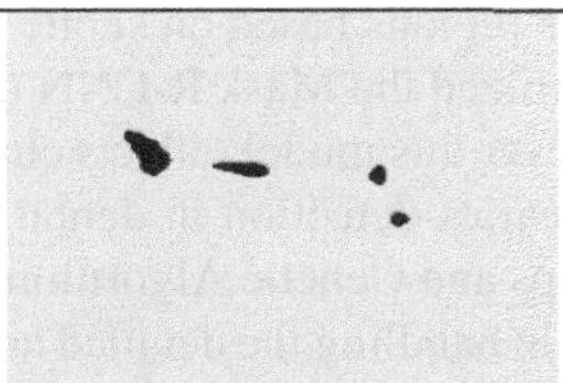	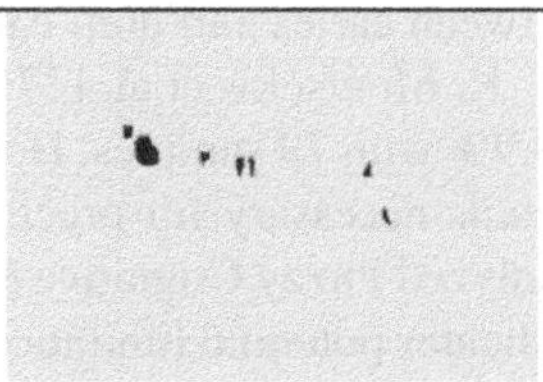
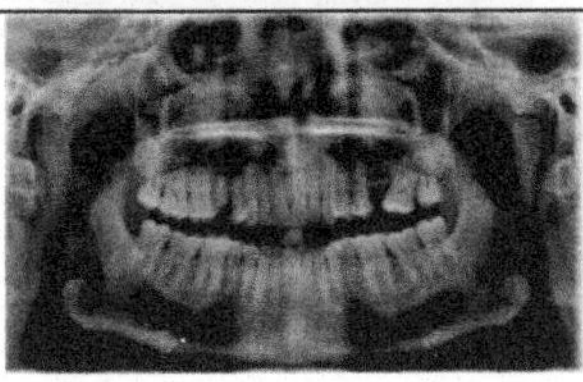	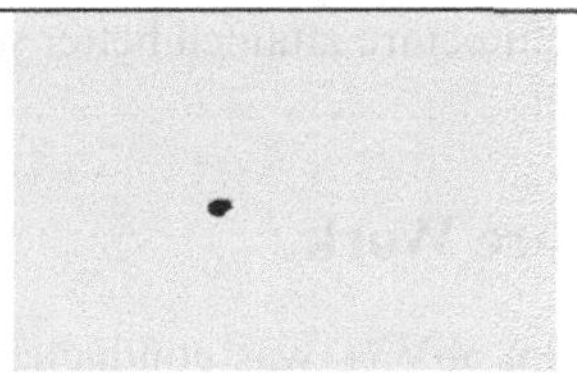	

The segmented images are displayed in Table 3, detailing the predicted edges for segmentation using DeepLabV3. This model effectively learns the caries regions of interest (ROI) with the highest semantic similarity by continuously acquiring new information about complementary caries regions.

4.5 Comparison of Proposed Framework with Existing Architectures

Table 4 compares the outcomes of the proposed network with those of other approaches evaluated on various datasets in recent years. Choudhary et al. [25] employed the VGG19 model, achieving an accuracy of 95% on a dataset of 150 samples containing both caries and normal tooth images. VGG19's deep architecture, with its 19 layers, is effective in feature extraction and classification, making it suitable for complex image recognition tasks. V.R et al. [26] used a Novel HLS (Hue, Lightness, and Saturation) method and attained an accuracy of 97.221% on a smaller dataset with 86 samples. This method

Table 4. Comparison with the existing research work

Ref.	Network Architecture/Algorithm	Accuracy	Image size
[25]	Convolutional neural networks - VGG19	95%	150 samples of caries and normal images
[26]	Novel HLS	97.221%	86 samples
[27]	Mask R-CNN	88.9%	79 samples
[28]	Fuzzy Cognitive Maps and Genetic Algorithm	75.61%	
DeepLabV3+	Deep Residual Network	99.2%	153 samples

leverages color information to enhance segmentation, allowing the model to distinguish between caries and non- caries regions based on subtle variations in hue and lightness.

K. Moutselos et al. [27] utilized the Mask R-CNN model, achieving an accuracy of 88.9% with 79 samples. However this model reflects challenges in capturing the minute details necessary for precise caries detection in dental images. Haghanifar et al. [28], analyzed Fuzzy Cognitive Maps and Genetic Algorithms achieving accuracy of 75.61% indicates potential limitations in handling the detailed and variable nature of tooth X-ray images, due to the generalized and less precise nature of fuzzy cognitive maps in this context. The DeepLabV3+ architecture attained better segmentation accuracy of 99.2% in the generated private dataset.

5 Conclusion and Future Work

An extensive analysis of DeepLabV3+ was conducted in this study to determine its effectiveness in segmenting tooth caries from OPGs. A dataset of 153 OPG images, including both caries and corresponding masks, was used to evaluate the performance of the proposed method. The encoder-decoder architecture enhances the ability to capture delicate details in the segmentation of tooth caries, crucial for medical imaging applications like dental caries detection, by capturing multi-scale context with multiple parallel filters employing different atrous rates, enabling the model to consider features at various scales simultaneously. The results indicate that the model is highly effective in diagnosing dental caries, achieving an accuracy score of 99.2%. The DeepLabV3+ architectures, when evaluated on the OPG caries dataset, exhibited outstanding performance. There was no apparent variation in performance when assessed using metrics such as the Dice coefficient, Intersection over Union (IoU), accuracy, and sensitivity. In future experiments, it is recommended to include a wider range of datasets to evaluate the capacity of the suggested models to perform well and remain consistent across various OPG caries datasets. This should consider differences in demographics and imaging conditions to ensure the models' generalizability and reliability. As technology advances, dental imaging tools are constantly developing, greatly strengthening the professional abilities of dentists. In recent years, artificial intelligence methods have been combined with dental imaging equipment to create decision assistance systems for dentists.

Acknowledgement. The authors express their sincere gratitude to Dr. Narendra R.M., M.D.S, Periodontics, Dept of Periodontics, Nanded Rural Dental College & Research Center for providing the clinical private dataset and Dr. M. Noveen Rexi, Consultant Dentist, Anand Skin and Dental Care, Nagercoil for their valuable support.

Ethics Statement. This study was approved by the Institutional Ethical Committee for studies on Human Subjects (IECH) at the Vellore Institute of Technology, Chennai.

References

1. Young, D.A., et al.: The american dental association caries classification system for clinical practice: a report of the american dental association council on scientific affairs. J. Am. Dent. Assoc. **146**, 79–86 (2015)
2. Singh, P., Sehgal, P.: Automated caries detection based on radon transformation and DCT. In: Proc. 8th Int. Conf. Comput., Com-mun. Netw. Technol. (ICCCNT), pp. 1–6 (2017). https://doi.org/10.1109/ICCCNT.2017.8204030
3. Naam, J., Harlan, J., Madenda, S., Wibowo, E.P.: 'Identification of the proximal caries of dental X-ray image with multiple morphology gradient method. Int. J. Adv. Sci. Eng. Inf. Technol. **6**(3), 343–346 (2016)
4. Son, L.H., Fujita, H., Dey, N., Ashour, A.S., Ngoc, V.T.N., Chu, D.T.: Dental diagnosis from X-ray images: An expert system based on fuzzy computing. Biomed. Signal Process. Control **39C**, 64–73 (2018). https://doi.org/10.1016/j.bspc.2017.07.005
5. Cantu, A.G., et al.: Detecting caries lesions of different radiographic extension on bitewings using deep learning. J. Dentistry **100**, Art. no. 103425 (2020). https://doi.org/10.1016/j.jdent.2020.103425
6. Lakshmi, M.M., Chitra, P.: 'Tooth decay prediction and classification from X-ray images using deep CNN. In: Proc. Int. Conf. Commun. Signal Process. (ICCSP), pp. 1349–1355 (2020). https://doi.org/10.1109/ICCSP48568.2020.9182141
7. Casalegno, F., et al.: Caries detection with near infrared transillumination using deep learning. J. Dental Res. **98**(11), 1227–1233 (2019). https://doi.org/10.1177/0022034519871884
8. Ronneberger, O., Fischer, P., Brox, T.: Dental X-ray image segmentation using a U-shaped Deep Convolutional network. In: Proceedings of the International Symposium on Biomedical Imaging, Volume 1, p. 3. New York, NY, USA (2015)
9. Lee, J.-H., Kim, D.-H., Jeong, S.-N., Choi, S.-H.: Detection and diagnosis of dental caries using a deep learning-based convolutional neural network algorithm. J. Dent. **77**, 106111 (2018). https://doi.org/10.1016/j.jdent.2018.07.015
10. Qayyum, A., Tahir, A., Butt, M.A., et al.: Dental caries detection using a semi-supervised learning approach. Sci. Rep. **13**, 749 (2023). https://doi.org/10.1038/s41598-023-27808-9
11. Imak, A., Celebi, A., Siddique, K., Turkoglu, M., Sengur, A., Salam, I.: Dental Caries Detection Using Score-Based Multi-Input Deep Convolutional Neural Network. IEEE Access **10**, 18320–18329 (2022). https://doi.org/10.1109/ACCESS.2022.3150358
12. Alharbi, S.S., AlRugaibah, A.A., Alhasson, H.F., Khan, R.U.: Detection of Cavities from Dental Panoramic X-ray Images Using Nested U-Net Models. Appl. Sci. **13**, 12771 (2023). https://doi.org/10.3390/app132312771
13. Helmi Mahran, A.M., Hussein, W., Saber, S.E.D.M.: Automatic Teeth Segmentation Using Attention U-Net. Preprints, 2023061468 (2023). https://doi.org/10.20944/preprints202306.1468.v1

14. Park, E.Y., Cho, H., Kang, S., et al.: Caries detection with tooth surface segmentation on intraoral photographic images using deep learning. BMC Oral Health **22**, 573 (2022). https://doi.org/10.1186/s12903-022-02589-1
15. Saini, D., Jain, R., Thakur, A.: Dental caries early detection using convolutional neural network for tele dentistry. 2021 7th International Conference on Advanced Computing and Communication Systems (ICACCS), pp. 958–963. Coimbatore, India (2021). https://doi.org/10.1109/ICACCS51430.2021.9442001
16. Lee, S., Oh, Si., Jo, J.: et al.: Deep learning for early dental caries detection in bitewing radiographs. Sci. Rep. **11**, 16807 (2021). https://doi.org/10.1038/s41598-021-96368-7
17. Geetha, V., Aprameya, K.S., Hinduja, D.M.: Dental caries diagnosis in digital radiographs using back-propagation neural network. Health information science and systems **8**(1), 8 (2020). https://doi.org/10.1007/s13755-019-0096-y
18. Lakshmi, M.M., Chitra, P.: Classification of Dental Cavities from X-ray images using Deep CNN algorithm. 2020 4th International Conference on Trends in Electronics and Informatics (ICOEI)(48184), pp. 774–779. Tirunelveli, India (2020). https://doi.org/10.1109/ICOEI48184.2020.9143013
19. Geetha, V., Aprameya, K.: Analysis of Image Segmentation Techniques for Diagnosis of Dental Caries in X-ray Images. World Academy of Science, Engineering and Technology, Open Science Index 146, International Journal of Computer and Information Engineering **13**(2), 30–33 (2019)
20. Thanh, M.T.G., Van Toan, N., Ngoc, V.T.N., Tra, N.T., Giap, C.N., Nguyen, D.M.: Deep learning application in dental caries detection using intraoral photos taken by smartphones. Appl. Sci. **12**, 5504 (2022). https://doi.org/10.3390/app12115504
21. Khan, F., et al.: Dental caries and non caries detection using deep learning. Int. J. Health Sci. **7**(S1), 790–804 (2023). https://doi.org/10.53730/ijhs.v7nS1.14277
22. Duong, D.L., Kabir, M.H., Kuo, R.F.: Automated caries detection with smartphone color photography using machine learning. Health Informatics J. **27**(2), 14604582211007530 (2021). https://doi.org/10.1177/14604582211007530
23. Chen, L.-C., Papandreou, G., Kokkinos, I., Murphy, K., Yuille, A.L.: Deeplab: Semantic image segmentation with deep convolutional nets, atrous convolution, and fully connected crfs. arXiv:1606.00915 (2016)
24. Chen, L., Papandreou, G., Schroff, F., Adam, H.: Rethinking Atrous Convolution for Semantic Image Segmentation. ArXiv, abs/1706.05587 (2017)
25. Choudhary, A., et al.: An Effective Approach for Classification of Dental Caries using Convolutional Neural Networks. 2021 10th International Conference on System Modeling & Advancement in Research Trends (SMART), pp. 204–209. MORADABAD, India (2021). https://doi.org/10.1109/SMART52563.2021.9676250
26. R. Vijay, Rajkumar, G.: Dental Caries Detection in X-Ray Images Using Hybrid Learning System in Comparison of Accuracy with K-Nearest Neighbors. 2023 Third International Conference on Ubiquitous Computing and Intelligent Information Systems (ICUIS), pp. 207–211. Gobichettipalayam, India (2023). https://doi.org/10.1109/ICUIS60567.2023.00043
27. Moutselos, K., Berdouses, E., Oulis, C., Maglogiannis, I.: Recognizing occlusal caries in dental intraoral images using deep learning. 2019 41st Annual International Conference of the IEEE Engineering in Medicine and Biology Society (EMBC), pp. 1617–1620. Berlin, Germany (2019). https://doi.org/10.1109/EMBC.2019.8856553
28. Haghanifar, A., Amirkhani, A., Mosavi, M.R.: Dental caries degree detection based on fuzzy cognitive maps and genetic algorithm. Electrical Engineering (ICEE), Iranian Conference on, pp. 976–981. Mashhad, Iran (2018). https://doi.org/10.1109/ICEE.2018.8472687

Convolutional Neural Networks for the Classification of Comet Assay Cells

Ismel Rizo-Blanco[1], Anabel Martin-Gonzalez[1(✉)], Carlos Brito-Loeza[1], Ricardo Legarda-Saenz[1], Arturo Espinosa-Romero[1], and Laura Lafon-Hughes[2]

[1] Computational Learning and Imaging Research, Facultad de Matemáticas, Universidad Autónoma de Yucatán, 97119 Merida, Mexico
{amarting,carlos.brito,rlegarda,eromero}@correo.uady.mx
[2] Centro Universitario Regional Litoral Norte (CENUR), Universidad de la República, Salto, Uruguay
https://clir-lab.org/

Abstract. The comet assay is a versatile method used to determine the DNA damage in individual cells. The cells processed by this technique preserve the stable genetic material in the head of the comet and the unstable portion of DNA in the tail. The analysis of the resulting microscopic images from this test must be carried out by an expert, who must precisely determine the extent of DNA liberated from the head of the comet, since it is related to the level of damage. Since this is a time-consuming and very specialized task, the objective of this research is to develop a computational system, based on the use of a convolutional neural network, for the automatic classification of cells processed by comet assay according to the level of DNA damage they present.

Keywords: Comet Assay · Convolutional Neural Network · Cell Classification · Deep Learning

1 Introduction

In the field of genetics, the evaluation of DNA damage has been the subject of great interest and relevance. The comet assay, also known as single cell gel electrophoresis assay, is a technique introduced by Ostling and Johanson as a revolutionary method to determine the DNA damage in individual cells [13]. This method identifies and evaluates the degree of DNA damage caused by different reasons, such as impairments in some repair system caused by metabolic or endogenous damage, radiation, chemicals and other environmental factors [19]. This versatile technique is based on the microscopic visualization of images of DNA after the cells are suspended in a thin agarose gel, lysed, electrophoresed and stained with a fluorescent dye. An expert must analyse the extent of damage with respect to the migration of DNA molecules, where fragmented genetic material is displaced towards the positive pole (tail of comet), while the portion of DNA with the least damage will remain in its initial position (head of comet). The resulting structure is similar to that of a comet from space (see Fig. 1).

A. Safi et al. (Eds.): ISICS 2024, CCIS 2381, pp. 137–145, 2025.
https://doi.org/10.1007/978-3-031-82931-4_10

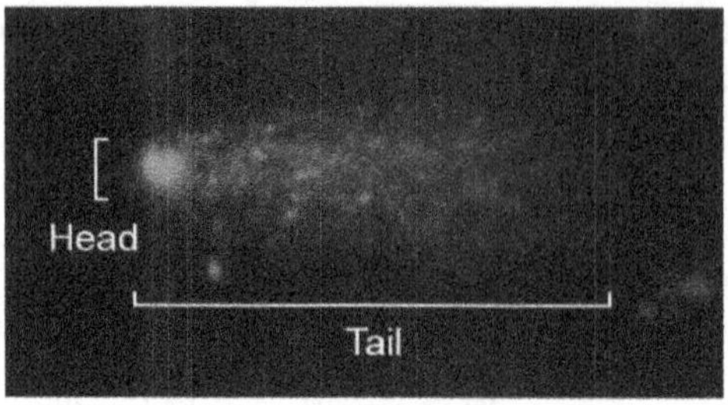

Fig. 1. Cell processed by the Comet Assay technique.

The comet assay is mainly used as a tool in genotoxicity testing, and as part of the process of regulating new chemicals and mixtures [17]. This technique allows scientists to measure cellular damage and has several practical applications. Furthermore, the use of this method allows to obtain parameters that are useful in the study of degenerative diseases such as cancer and diabetes. In recent years, several computer systems have been developed to facilitate the collection, analysis and visualization of comet assay results. In 2007, CometScore [1] was developed as a free software tool, for Windows systems only, created to score comets obtained from the single cell gel electrophoresis process. In 2014, OpenComet [5] was introduced as a free software tool to work along with the ImageJ program, and it was developed to automatically analyze comet assay images. In 2018, HiComet was proposed as a computational tool to facilitate the analysis of comet assay images. Given a noisy image with several arbitrarily placed comets, the tool can recognize normal and damaged comets in a fully automated manner [10]. In 2020, Deep Comet was the first method with deep learning techniques for comet segmentation [7]. Based on the Mask R-CNN [6] model, Deep Comet was implemented by Facebook AI Research using Pytorch. In 2021, Namuduri et al. [12], presented a new approach to quantify the degree of DNA damage, combining deep learning with a rigorous and comprehensive method to optimize hyperparameters by means of statistical tests. The neural network presented involves a novel use of the VGG19 architecture [16] and Multi Task Learning (MTL) [21] to calculate confidence intervals. This architecture presents a challenge in accurately segmenting the individual cells from this assay; variability in the appearance of comets, as well as the presence of noise and other artifacts, can affect its accuracy of segmentation and consequently influence subsequent measurements. In 2022, Afiahayati et al. [2] proposed a web-based buccal mucosa comet assay detection and classification tool using Faster R-CNN model providing satisfactory results on comet assay images from buccal mucosa samples.

Although state-of-the-art work analyzes comet assay cells, none classify the cells according to the level of DNA damage. The extent of DNA damage can be visually categorized into five classes based on the comet's tail size and shape. Cells may exhibit an undamaged nucleus (Class 1) that appears as a tailless circular shape or, a nucleus that suffers severe damage (Class 5), identifiable by a small head and long tail (see Fig. 2).

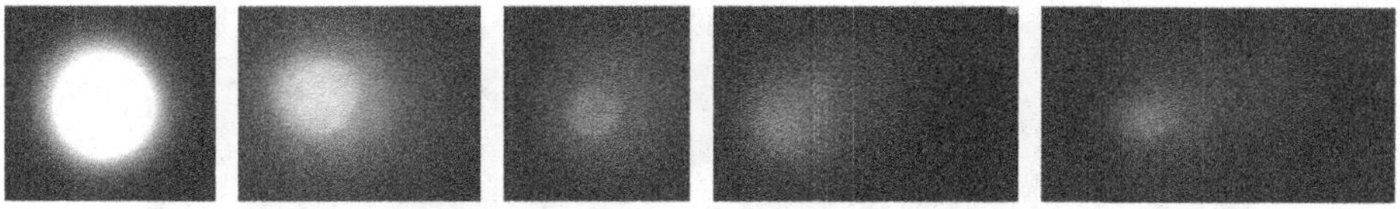

(a) Class 1 (b) Class 2 (c) Class 3 (d) Class 4 (e) Class 5

Fig. 2. Comet assay individual cell classes.

Since the cell information collected consists of 2D images, we propose the implementation of a computational system which relies on convolutional neural networks to detect comet assay individual cells and classify them according to the five different classes mentioned before.

2 Methods

2.1 Dataset

Our database consists of 185 images containing individual cells processed by the comet assay. These images were provided by the Biophysicochemistry Group, CENUR LN, at the Universidad de la República, Salto, Uruguay. Figure 3 shows sample images from our dataset. These images have a resolution of 728 $\times$ 960 pixels in gray scale format. Our dataset is divided into three subsets: training (144 images), validation (19 images) and testing (22 images), containing 78%, 10% and 12%, images from the overall dataset, respectively. Table 1 shows the distribution of comets per class in every subset of the database. In order to train the models, it is necessary to label each comet according to its class. This process was carried out by a comet assay expert using the software tool LabelImg [18].

2.2 Proposed Method

The proposed system for the detection and classification of cells in images processed by the comet assay is made up of three modules, each one is in charge of performing an specific task. The input to the system can be a grayscale image or an RGB image, and the output is the same input image, but with added contours that outline the comets and classify them according to the class to which they belong. In Fig. 4, you can see a representative diagram of the developed system.

The convolutional neural network (CNN) used for this system is the You Only Look Once (Yolo) model which is focused on object detection and classification [14]. Several versions of this model were tested. Such versions were Yolov4 [4], Yolov5 [9], Yolov6 [11] and Yolov7 [20]. To perform detection and classification tasks, many current detection systems work by sliding several windows of different dimensions throughout the image until an object is found and then inserted into a classifier. This process can be very cumbersome and with high computational complexity. Yolo proposes a new approach to perform these

(a) Class 1 samples (b) Class 2 samples (c) Class 3 samples

Fig. 3. Sample images from database.

Table 1. Comets' distribution per class in dataset

Class	Training	Validation	Test	Total
Class 1	64	11	13	88
Class 2	150	20	34	204
Class 3	104	29	21	154
Class 4	14	3	3	20
Class 5	3	1	1	5
Total	335	64	72	471

tasks since it handles them as a simple regression problem, that is, directly from the pixels of the image and using a series of convolutions, it predicts the coordinates of the bounding boxes and the probabilities of the classes. Therefore, it does not have a high computational cost and the performance of the network for the detection and classification of objects is optimized.

The operation of each Yolo module is as follows: 1) The **backbone** is the initial part of the CNN and is responsible for extracting features from the input image. The backbone is usually composed of several convolutional layers, such as 2D convolutions, spatial separable convolutions, among others. 2) **Neck**: Its main function is to merge and combine the features extracted by the backbone module. It is usually made up of additional convolutional layers that help reduce

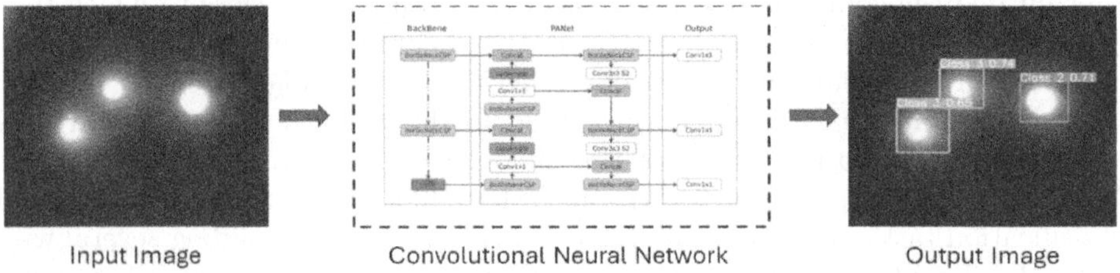

Fig. 4. Comet assay system scheme.

dimensionality and extract more abstract and high-level features. 3) The **head** processes the aggregated features and predicts the bounding boxes, objectness scores, and classification scores.

2.3 Performance Metrics

One of the metrics used to evaluate detection models is the so-called Intersection over Union (IoU) [15]. This metric is used to know the intersection between two bounding boxes, and based on the result, you may eliminate a bounding box or consider it a false detection. After calculating this metric, the Non-maximum Suppression algorithm (NMS) [8] is used to eliminate redundancy of boxes detecting the same object.

Next metric that the model uses is the mean average precision (mAP) metric [3], which analyzes the model's performance for object detection in a set of test images. The mAP is the Average Precision (AP) of each class and then averaged over the number of classes (N). The AP score per class is given by the area under the precision-recall curve. Equation 1 shows how to calculate this metric.

$$mAP = \frac{1}{N}\sum_{i=1}^{N} AP_i \tag{1}$$

where AP stands for average precision, and N for the number of classes.

During training epochs, the mAP with an 50% IoU threshold ($mAP50$) was analyzed. If its value does not improve between one epoch and the next one, an adjustment of the model's hyper-parameters was performed. We also compute the Mean Average Precision averaged over IoU thresholds from 50% to 95% ($mAP50-95$) at 5% steps, providing a more comprehensive view of the model's performance across different levels of detection difficulty.

Other metrics used to evaluate the models performance were: precision (P), recall (R), and F1 score (F_1). Equations 2, 3, and 4 show the corresponding formulas for the mentioned metrics:

$$P = \frac{TP}{TP + FP} \tag{2}$$

$$R = \frac{TP}{TP + FN} \tag{3}$$

$$F_1 = 2\frac{PR}{P + R} \tag{4}$$

where TP stands for true positive, FP, for false positive, and FN for false negative.

3 Results and Discussion

The convolutional neural networks were implemented using the Python programming language together with the Pytorch library in a Google Colaboratory virtual machine, with free access to a NVIDIA K80 GPU model.

To train the networks, the aforementioned training database was used. Transfer learning was applied to the neural networks to speed up the training time. A learning rate of 0.01 and linear activation function was used for the output layer; hidden layers used Sigmoid Linear Unit (SiLU) function. The mean square error was used as the loss function to be optimized.

Table 2 presents the results obtained after training for 200 epochs the proposed Yolo models using the test set composed of 72 instances of cells classified in one of the five comet classes previously defined. These results include all evaluation metrics introduced in Sect. 2.3, allowing us to compare and determine which of the models has better performance in the task of detecting and classifying cells in images processed by the comet assay.

Table 2. Models average results on all five classes

Model	Precision	Recall	F1-score	mAP50	mAP50-95
Yolov4	0.222	0.708	0.338	0.614	0.306
Yolov5	0.677	0.730	0.703	**0.847**	**0.537**
Yolov6	**0.689**	**0.855**	**0.763**	0.755	0.335
Yolov7	0.538	0.830	0.653	0.736	0.358

In Figs. 5, 6 and 7 examples of detection and classification results are visualized.

The best performance for all models was on classifying Class 2 comets (see Fig. 5). This situation may be due to the high number of training samples for that class.

The most difficult class to identify was Class 5 since there were few samples to train (only three samples), one sample to validate and one sample to test. Nevertheless, the algorithms were able to perform well on this class (see Fig. 6).

For comet assay images, overlapping comets are very common. In Fig. 7 we can appreciate one example of detection with comets' overlapping scenarios. As we can see, Yolov4 and Yolov5 were not able to detect all comets in the sample. Although, Yolov7 obtained similar performance on detecting bounding boxes as Yolov6, this last one had better precision on identifying classes.

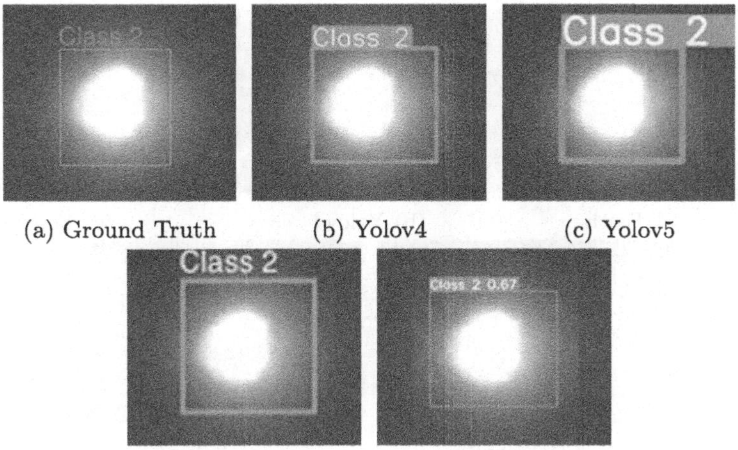

(a) Ground Truth (b) Yolov4 (c) Yolov5

(d) Yolov6 (e) Yolov7

Fig. 5. Qualitative detection and classification results for Class 2

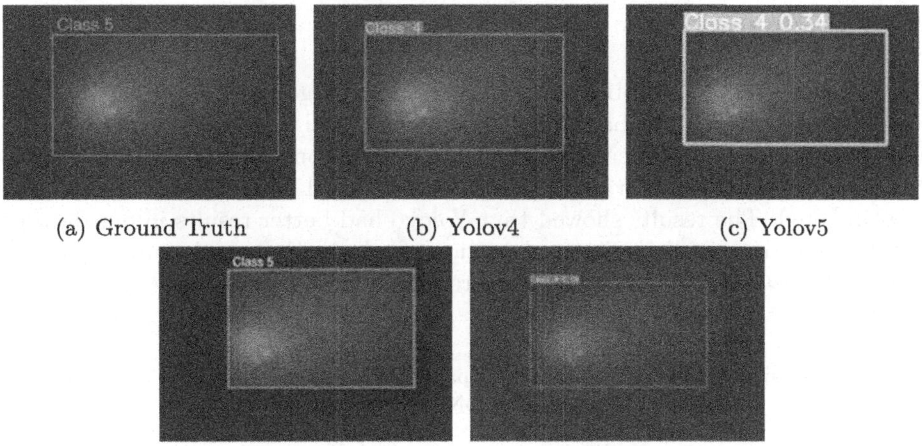

(a) Ground Truth (b) Yolov4 (c) Yolov5

(d) Yolov6 (e) Yolov7

Fig. 6. Qualitative detection and classification results for Class 5

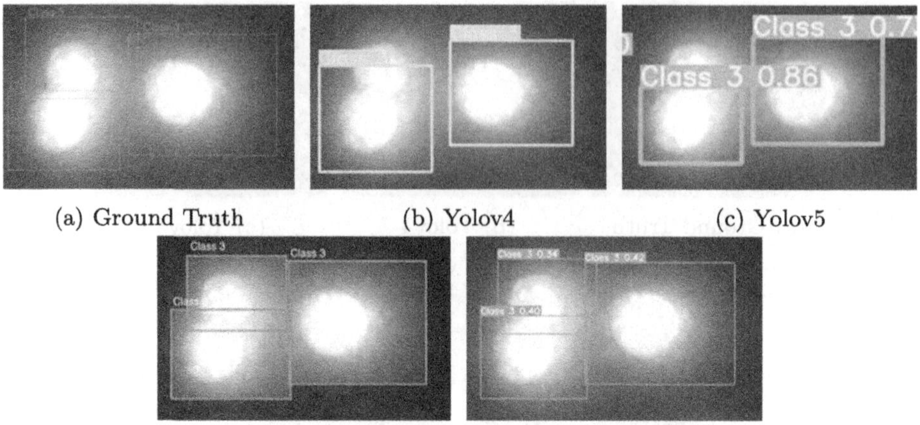

(a) Ground Truth (b) Yolov4 (c) Yolov5

(d) Yolov6 (e) Yolov7

Fig. 7. Qualitative detection and classification results for Class 3

4 Conclusions

The Comet assay is a robust method to measure genotoxicity. In this work, a computational system based on the convolutional neural network Yolo was implemented to automatically detect and classify Comet assay cells. A comprehensive review of the literature was performed, and several Yolo models were implemented. The results showed that Yolov6 had better results in our dataset, achieving greater precision in the detection of cells, with its high value of mAP50 and mAP50-95. The proposed system create a functional method when performing genotoxicity studies.

Acknowledgments. This study was partly funded by Consejo Nacional de Humanidades, Ciencias y Tecnologías (CONAHCYT) from Mexico.

Disclosure of Interests. The authors have no competing interests to declare that are relevant to the content of this article.

References

1. CometScore (2017). http://rexhoover.com/. consultado el 30 de noviembre de 2022
2. Afiahayati, Anarossi, E., Yanuaryska, R.D., Sri, M.: GamaComet: a deep learning-based tool for the detection and classification of DNA damage from buccal mucosa comet assay images. Diagnostics (Basel) **12**(8) (2022). https://doi.org/10.3390/diagnostics12082002
3. Beitzel, S.M., Jensen, E.C., Frieder, O.: MAP, pp. 1691–1692. Springer, Boston (2009). https://doi.org/10.1007/978-0-387-39940-9_492

4. Bochkovskiy, A., Wang, C., Liao, H.M.: YOLOv4: optimal speed and accuracy of object detection. CoRR abs/2004.10934 (2020). https://arxiv.org/abs/2004.10934
5. Gyori, B.M., Venkatachalam, G., Thiagarajan, P., Hsu, D., Clement, M.V.: Opencomet: an automated tool for comet assay image analysis. Redox Biol. **2**, 457–465 (2014). https://doi.org/10.1016/j.redox.2013.12.020
6. He, K., Gkioxari, G., Dollár, P., Girshick, R.B.: Mask R-CNN. In: 2017 IEEE International Conference on Computer Vision (ICCV), pp. 2980–2988 (2017)
7. Hong, Y., et al.: Deep learning method for comet segmentation and comet assay image analysis. Sci. Rep. **10**(1), 18915 (2020). https://doi.org/10.1038/s41598-020-75592-7
8. Hosang, J.H., Benenson, R., Schiele, B.: Learning non-maximum suppression. CoRR abs/1705.02950 (2017). http://arxiv.org/abs/1705.02950
9. Jocher, G., et al.: ultralytics/yolov5: v7.0 - YOLOv5 SOTA Realtime Instance Segmentation. Zenodo (2022). https://doi.org/10.5281/zenodo.7347926
10. Lee, T., et al.: HiComet: a high-throughput comet analysis tool for large-scale DNA damage assessment. BMC Bioinform. **19** (2018). https://doi.org/10.1186/s12859-018-2015-7
11. Li, C., et al.: YOLOv6: a single-stage object detection framework for industrial applications. arXiv abs/2209.02976 (2022). https://api.semanticscholar.org/CorpusID:252110986
12. Namuduri, S., et al.: Faster deep ensemble averaging for quantification of DNA damage from comet assay images with uncertainty estimates (2021)
13. Ostling, O., Johanson, K.J.: Microelectrophoretic study of radiation-induced DNA damages in individual mammalian cells. **123**, 291–298 (1984). https://doi.org/10.1016/0006-291x(84)90411-x
14. Redmon, J., Divvala, S., Girshick, R., Farhadi, A.: You only look once: unified, real-time object detection (2015). https://doi.org/10.48550/ARXIV.1506.02640. https://arxiv.org/abs/1506.02640
15. Rezatofighi, S.H., Tsoi, N., Gwak, J., Sadeghian, A., Reid, I.D., Savarese, S.: Generalized intersection over union: a metric and A loss for bounding box regression. CoRR abs/1902.09630 (2019). http://arxiv.org/abs/1902.09630
16. Simonyan, K., Zisserman, A.: Very deep convolutional networks for large-scale image recognition (2015). https://arxiv.org/abs/1409.1556
17. Tice, R.R., et al.: Single cell gel/comet assay: guidelines for in vitro and in vivo genetic toxicology testing. Environ. Mol. Mutagen. **35**(3), 206–221 (2000). https://doi.org/10.1002/(sici)1098-2280(2000)35:3<206::aid-em8>3.0.co;2-j
18. Tzutalin: Labelimg (Git code, 2015). https://github.com/tzutalin/labelImg
19. Uzen, R., Tomatir, A.G., Cucer, N., Donmez-Altuntas, H.: Comet assay and applications. Int. J. Sci. Technol. Res. (2019). https://api.semanticscholar.org/CorpusID:198270495
20. Wang, C.Y., Bochkovskiy, A., Liao, H.Y.M.: YOLOv7: trainable bag-of-freebies sets new state-of-the-art for real-time object detectors (2022). https://arxiv.org/abs/2207.02696
21. Zhang, Y., Yang, Q.: A survey on multi-task learning. IEEE Trans. Knowl. Data Eng. **34**(12), 5586–5609 (2022). https://doi.org/10.1109/TKDE.2021.3070203

AI Driven Carbon Emission Estimation and Forecasting with Recommended Solution

Micheale H. Tesfai, Milkias Tsegai(✉), Rahel Kiflay, and Ruta Misghina

Higher Colleges of Technology, Fujairah, UAE
h00396244@hct.ac.ae

Abstract. A lot of efforts have been made to prevent potential hazards that could damage our natural resources and spoil our healthy environment. Some of them are preventive actions and policies to reduce carbon emissions. This study will compare different types of forecasting models and discuss the most appropriate ways to forecast carbon emissions in the UAE so that sustainable remedies can be recommended as part of the ongoing endeavor. Currently, artificial intelligence is providing sustainable solutions in almost all areas. Similarly, this tool will be implemented to predict accurate emissions in the next years to take serious actions, which will make the United Arab Emirates an environmentally aware country while providing useful information and implementing preventive policies. Although there are many sources of carbon emissions, this study will use and discuss the total carbon emissions from the transportation sector, but it will also examine methods as well as tools for measuring vehicle emissions. Therefore, the proposed solution will focus on reducing carbon emissions from the transportation sector as well.

Keywords: carbon emission · forecasting · reward

1 Introduction

Humans are always in need of a lot of resources to survive in this world, and most of our day-to-day activities require combustion or the release of carbon dioxide into the atmosphere. Is our planet's environment adversely affected by air pollution? Unarguably yes, and this is mainly due to carbon dioxide emitted when fossil fuels burn. Carbon dioxide allows heat to be absorbed as infrared radiation and acts like a greenhouse pane by preventing heat from escaping and thus raising global temperatures in return.

In time to come, this increase in temperature will lead to more frequent and severe weather events such as hurricanes, heatwaves, heavy rainfall, storms, and droughts as well as increasing sea levels. Furthermore, these changes in the atmosphere also cause climate change that can disturb ecosystems, agriculture, and water resources. The polar ice caps and glaciers melting increase sea levels,

A. Safi et al. (Eds.): ISICS 2024, CCIS 2381, pp. 146–160, 2025.
https://doi.org/10.1007/978-3-031-82931-4_11

consequently swamping coastal areas and displacing populations. Ocean acidification causes marine life, especially coral reefs to suffer terribly while disrupting whole marine ecosystems due to carbon dioxide absorption, which results from it being increased. Terrestrial ecosystems are also damaged by species struggling with changing precipitation and temperature patterns thereby leading to the loss of biodiversity in an area. Heat-borne diseases, the spread of communicable diseases by vectors, and interference with food and water delivery have compromised human health.

Over the long term, if carbon emissions go unchecked, we will eventually see severe weather, a major decline in biodiversity, and drastic changes to our coastlines severely affected by sea level rise. Several everyday activities, such as heating homes, using oil, gas, coal, or natural gas to produce electricity or driving cars that use gasoline, all generate greenhouse gases. These emissions depend on individuals' actions and preferences, such as how frequently or far one drives, their vehicle's fuel efficiency rate, or idling in traffic when driving. Our ultimate target is to reduce or control carbon emission by addressing and working on those causes. We can save the environment and secure a sustainable climate for future generations by embracing cleaner forms of energy.

Energy production is the highest contributor to carbon emissions in the world while transportation comes after it. This includes pollutants from cars, motorcycles, buses, airplanes, and ships that are utilized for both personal moves as well as goods transport. According to US EPA (2024) [2] "Transportation accounts for approximately 28% of total U.S greenhouse gas emissions, making it the largest source, with emissions escalating most rapidly among all sectors between the years from 1990 to 2022". When it comes to the UAE, United Arab Emirates Clean Tech and Environmental Technologies (2023) [1] says that UAE endeavors to be at the forefront globally in addressing climate change by committing to reach net zero carbon emissions by 2050 and invest $163 billion in clean, renewable energy and vital technologies. For instance, in 2017, emissions from transportation were 38.75 million ton as shown in the Fig. 1.

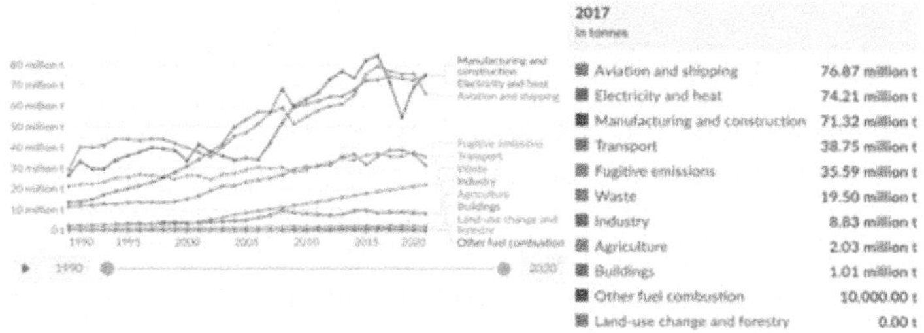

Fig. 1. Emission from transportations in 2017

The UAE has also set goals of sustainable development and environmental responsibility including raising energy efficiency rates, advancing eco-friendly modes of transportation systems, implementing carbon capture technologies, and supporting and participation on international climate agreements and partnerships. This research will be focusing on various forecasting techniques that measure accurate calculations of emissions, especially from automobiles. It aims to identify a reliable method that can effectively quantify and forecast the carbon emissions associated with transportation systems particularly. The objective is to utilize artificial intelligence and advanced data analytics to improve the accuracy of carbon emission estimation for the UAE.

Our research seeks to provide policymakers as well as industries with insights to reduce carbon emissions, improve operational efficiency, and comply with global climate change resolutions by leveraging innovative technologies. We will perform a comprehensive comparison of forecasting methods, which include predictive modeling, data analytics, and machine learning algorithms among others. They will each be evaluated in terms of their ability to provide real-time information on emissions, scalability, and compatibility with existing emission measurement frameworks. What results is a technique that provides concrete steps towards lowering greenhouse gas emissions within transport systems. The recommendations that will be presented will be based on the practical implications of these empirical findings and are meant to guide decision making and policy formulation. We hope to make a major contribution towards lessening the effects of climate change while fostering sustainability, and preserving the environment in the UAE. This move will therefore have a benefit not just to UAE but also contribute positively towards the global low carbon future.

2 Literature Review

The following review provides a helpful insight into the various methods to study emissions forecasting and ways, in which they should be chosen depending on the context and the possible impact on Carbon emission rates. Most of the reviewed models are popular among many researchers to forecast emission and other time series problems.

2.1 Forecasting Models

Traditional Statistical Methods: over the recent years, with the advent of more sophisticated computational techniques, traditional statistical methods used for forecasting carbon dioxide emissions, such as linear regression and time series analysis, could have started to fall by the wayside. However, the specified types of analysis do offer effective and straightforward methods of depicting a trend and illustrating the connections between the analyzed variables. For instance, linear regression can be deemed as one of the most basic types of statistical analysis and the one that allows creating a clear and easily interpretable model of the relationships between variables. For example, Sözen et al.(2007) [14] used the linear regression principle to analyze the carbon emissions and sectoral energy consumption for the purposes of creating a prediction on the greenhouse gas emissions in Turkey. Time series analysis, on the other hand, involves studying datasets that are indexed in time order. Techniques like moving averages, exponential smoothing, and decomposition methods help in understanding the underlying patterns such as trend, seasonality, and cyclic behavior. Sözen et al.(2007) [14] also employed time series analysis to identify long-term trends and seasonal variations in emissions, which is crucial for developing effective mitigation policies.

Neural Network became one of the most frequently used tools for Carbon emissions forecasting due to their ability to model complex non-linear relationships between the data. For instance, Radojevic et al.(2013) [11] used an artificial neural network to make the carbon emissions estimations for Serbia. Hence, the study revealed the significance of ANN for the prediction of environmental indicators which is crucial for sustainable development. Similarly, Liu et al.(2012) [9] used neural networks to predict the CO2 emissions for China. In doing that, the study also illustrated the capacity of this tool to work with various data sets due to its flexibility and accuracy.

ARIMA Models refer to a class of statistical models that are used in the analysis and prediction of time-series data. The model is applied in scenarios where the data exhibits non-stationary properties. Here, the mean, range, or autocorrelation changes with time. The model combines three components: autoregression, differencing, and moving average. ARIMA models have been used effectively in the prediction of carbon emissions. For example, Bhattacharyya and Ghoshal(2010) [6] used an ARIMA model in the prediction of CO2 emissions in India. In fact, this study showed that ARIMA could be used in providing reliable short term predictions. Moreover, it vividly shows that the ARIMA model accounted for linear and non-linear patterns in the data, which means they are more versatile. Equally, Zhang and Wei (2010) [20] used the model to predict carbon emissions in China. The results reflected the country's emission complexity and the changing patterns.

SARIMA Models - Seasonal Auto Regressive Integrated Moving Average models is the extension of ARIMA that models seasonality as a separate factor. Different studies employed the use of SARIMA models for carbon emissions forecasting. For instance, Aydin and Esen (2017) [3] used a SARIMA model to predict Turkey's Carbon emissions, they were able to use both the trend and seasonal fluctuations effectively. Their study demonstrated that SARIMA could model the periodic variations in emissions, providing more accurate & nuanced forecasts compared to non-seasonal ARIMA models when the data has frequent seasonal patterns

Auto ARIMA or Automated ARIMA is used to search for the optimum order p, d and q. Auto Arima uses some algorithm to check for the orders and selects the order that has the least AIC or BIC criteria. Auto ARIMA is being employed by many researchers in the forecasting of carbon emissions. Parsa et al.(2019) [10], for instance, employed auto Arima in the forecasting of carbon emissions in the United States. They found the auto Arima to be selective of the fastest model which made it possible to select the optimum orders and make more accurate predictions with minimal manual effort.

Prophet is a Facebook-developed prediction algorithm that can be used to predict time series data with a strong seasonality effect and many seasons of historical data. Today, many researchers apply Prophet for forecasting CO2 emissions because this tool is user-friendly and versatile. Thus, for example, Tang and Lei(2018) [15] used Prophet to predict CO2 emissions in the industrial sector of China. The authors stated that the model was able to account for the seasonal and holiday effects, which play a significant role in the dynamics of emissions. In addition, Yadav et al.(2020) [18] also worked with Prophet to predict CO2 emissions in transportation, arguing that the algorithm's ability to account for multiple seasonal effects helped them achieve high levels of precision.

Support Vector Machine (SVM) are deemed appropriate for the prediction of CO2 emissions as they are effective in handling complex non-linear data. Several studies have demonstrated that SVM considerably outperforms traditional methods, such as ARIMA and linear regression, on the accounts of accuracy and robustness. For example, Chen et al.(2010) [7] used SVM to forecast China emissions and demonstrated its superiority over other techniques. Azadeh et al.(2008) [4] applied this model to Iran's energy sector and obtained a high precision of the results. Shahraki et al.(2019) [13] implemented SVM for the transportation sector and effectively managed the non-linearity of the data. Thus, these models are likely to improve accuracy and reliability of results making them suitable for CO2 emissions forecasting.

Hybrid Models seek to combine the positives of each forecasting technique with which they work. Behrang et al.(2011) [5] showed that it is possible to proceed with integrating the Bees Algorithm and ANN with respect to global CO2 emissions. In this way, with the functional property to optimize production processes that is peculiar to the Bees algorithm and the superior prediction ability that is typical for the ANNs, it is possible to improve the quality of forecasting. In a similar way, Li et al. (2010) [7] used an RBF neural network, which is a specific type of fully connected feed-forward neural network, to forecast carbon dioxide emissions. RBF is a combination of statistical and machine learning methods.

Factors Influencing Carbon Emissions: Energy consumption is seen as the greatest contributor to Carbon emissions. From various other researches, another great factor that indicates carbon emission is Gross Domestic Product (GDP) and fuel combustion, particularly from fossil fuels. Understanding these factors is essential for developing effective emission reduction strategies and policies.

2.2 Vehicle Emission Measurement Methods

Various measuring tools and techniques have been implemented to estimate and approximate accurate amount of carbon emissions in different sources such as in industries, transportation and agricultural sites. In this research, our main concern is emissions from vehicles so, we have compared several finding to accurately measure the amount of carbon coming out of cars. Each of them have some strengths and weakness. One of them, according to Zhang et al. (2015) [19] is the procedure, which estimates emissions per vehicle type and speed, which gives rather concrete results, though the information to input into the formula has to be very specific about the type and operation of each vehicle. The formula used in this method is given by Eq. (1), where Mi is the individual commuting carbon emissions, Di is the individual commuting distance and Ei is the carbon emissions factor of the travel mode.

$$M_i = D_i * E \tag{1}$$

Another common method is the estimation of emissions based on fuel use and comparing it to the distance traveled. This approach is useful in circumstances where the fuel data is easily obtainable, which means that it is easy to perform the calculations, and while it may not be accurate where there is variation in efficiency of the vehicle at different speeds or conditions as per Liu et al. (2017) [8]. Tarulescu et al. (2017) [16] used the following formula in their study, given in Eq. (2). Where X-UsedFuel is the energy consumption for road transportation (kWh), D is the route distance (km), C-average is the average fuel consumption (liters/km), and Y is the conversion factor for each fuel (kWh/liters), where Y = 9.2 for gasoline and Y = 10 for diesel.

$$X_{UsedFuel} = D.C_{average}.Y \tag{2}$$

The monitoring instruments provide a much more sophisticated way of carrying out measurements of CO2 emissions. These devices can at a given period record emissions of other greenhouse gases, not only CO2 hence giving a complete picture of emissions in a certain locale. Hitherto they were costly, with improvements in technology the usage of these instruments has become affordable, especially in large-scale environmental monitoring. Therefore, air quality monitoring instruments are the best method compared to other methods for measuring CO2 emissions from transportation by virtue of its short observation period, real-time data, and ability to also provide information about other greenhouse gases. According to Wang & Chen (2018) [17] This method is exceptional in providing accurate and localized results; quite beneficial for comprehensive environmental surveys and for meeting legal requirements.

3 Methodology

The used Data was taken from "Our World in Data" by Ritchie & Roser (2020) [12] which was revised in Jan 2024. The data includes global carbon emission and emissions from several countries. The carbon emissions data is from fossil fuels and industry, the emission from land- use change is not included. The amount of carbon emission in ton from UAE is visualized in Fig. 2. The data seems to be having a very strong trend over time. This spike in the year 2000 indicates the UAE's significant economic growth in the late 1990s and early 2000s, which fueled by its oil industry. Similarly, there is a rapid increase in emissions in the period from 2007 to 2015, which could be due to the economic growth, increased transportation and rapid urbanization including the inauguration of Burj Khalifa in 2010. While the trend decreased during the global Covid-19 period which was due to quarantine, where the emission from transportation and other public industries decreased tremendously.

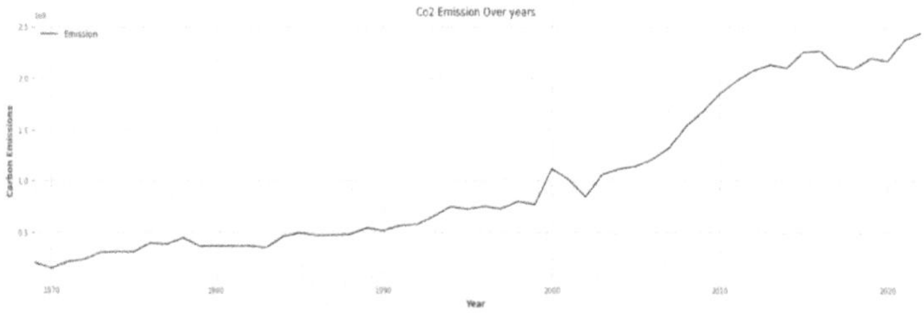

Fig. 2. UAE Carbon emission from 1969 to 2022

3.1 Exploratory Analysis

Correlation: the partial autocorrelation function (PACF) is used to identify the lags at which the significant correlation between the current value and past values of the time series. From the plot in Fig. 3, we observed that there is a short term dependence which is the current value of the time series is primarily influenced by the value at the previous time step (lag 1). Additionally, the time series exhibits a relatively limited memory, it doesn't get affected by values from far back in its history to influence the current value. While in the stationarity test, the ADF test statistic is 1.045 which is greater than the critical value and the P value is 0.9947 which is higher than common alpha, so the series is non-stationary. And from the seasonality test, we found the series to be non-seasonal.

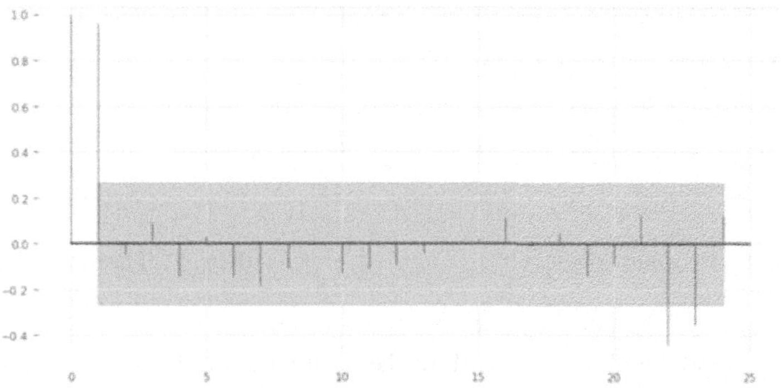

Fig. 3. Partial autocorrelation function (PACF) plot

3.2 Comparative Analysis on Forecasting Models

In the literature review, we have discussed several forecasting models which were implemented in various research papers. And we analyzed based on four approaches; baseline, statistical, machine learning and deep learning approaches. The baseline approach is simple and easy-to-understand method that represents a starting point for improvement. In this approach, we used the Naive Drift model is a variation of the basic Naive forecast that incorporates a trend into the prediction. It works by calculating the average change between data points in the historical data and adjust the forecasting. While in the statistical (classical) approach, we choose the Auto-ARIMA (Auto Regressive Integrated Moving Average) which automates the process of building a traditional ARIMA model by finding the optimal hyper parameters of the model. We also implement other effective statistical model which is the Theta model that focuses on modifying the local curvature of the data to capture trends and patterns (Figs. 4, 5, 6 and 7).

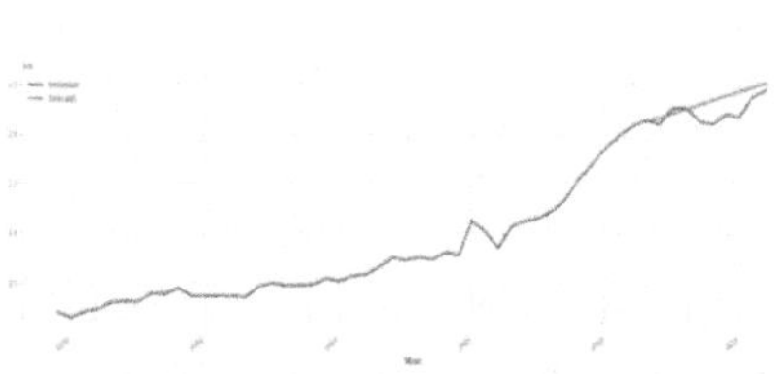

Fig. 4. Naïve Drift Model

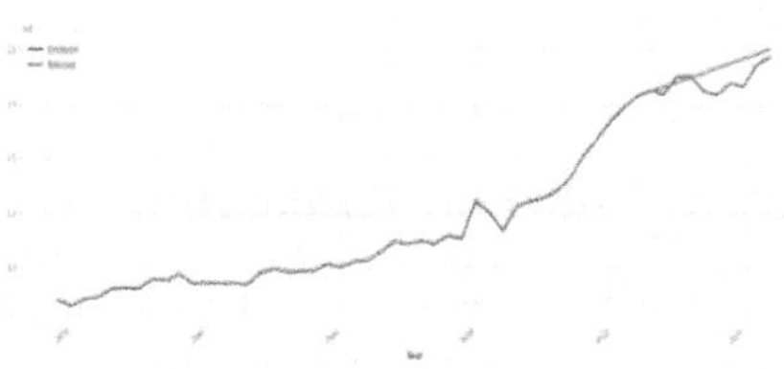

Fig. 5. Auto-ARIMA Model

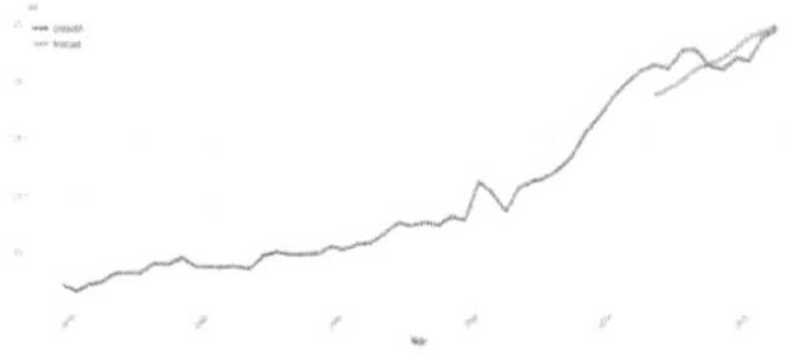

Fig. 6. Prophet Model

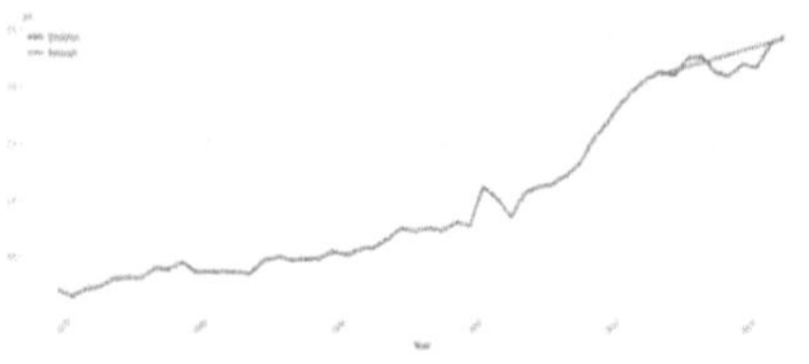

Fig. 7. Theta Model

The XGBoost (eXtreme Gradient Boosting) model was implemented as a machine learning approach; it builds multiple weak learners, such as decision trees which learn from the errors of the previous ones, resulting in a more robust model. Additionally, the prophet model which bridges the gap between classical statistical models and machine learning. Finally, the D-linear model was implemented as a deep learning approach as it can handle both linear and non-linear patterns in the data. This model combination of linear regression and deep learning, which involves a linear component that captures linear relationships and a non-linear component that captures non-linear relationships. This combination is the main reason that allows the model to adapt to various types of data patterns (Figs. 8 and 9).

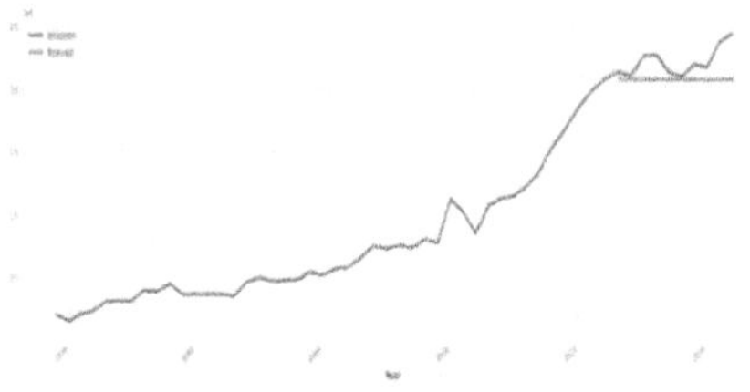

Fig. 8. XGBoost Model

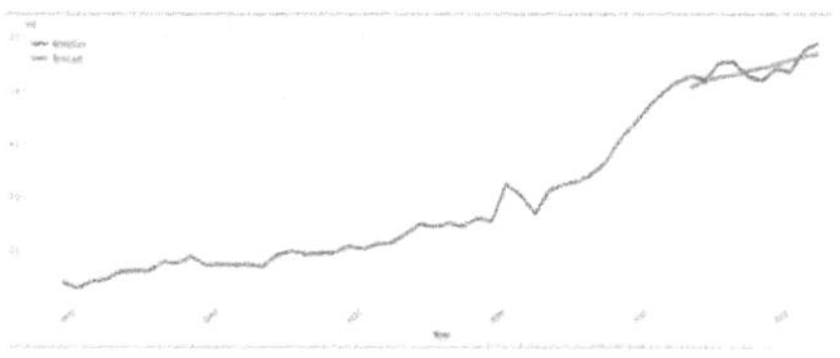

Fig. 9. D-Linear Model

3.3 Result and Discussion

The analysis was done with all the approach starting from simple methods to more complicated models. The comparison among the models was based on accuracy and mean absolute error (MSE). We started with a simple and effective baseline model called Naive Drift which gave a good accuracy of 94.7%. Then the statistical methods like Auto-ARIMA was implemented which results in similar accuracy with baseline naïve model. We tried also the Auto-Theta, which stands out among the statistical methods with an accuracy of 96.05%, due to its superior ability to capture the trends. Then we took it a level up in terms of complexity and tried machine learning approach, we selected the XGBoost model. It didn't perform well due to the fact that machine learning models

Table 1. Model Accuracy and MAE Comparison

Model	Accuracy	MAE
Naive Drift	94.70%	11547173
Auto-ARIMA	94.70%	11547173
Auto Theta	96.05%	8554487
XGBoost	93.87%	14092246
Prophet	93.82%	13507966
D-Linear	96.09%	8671488

usually starts to fail in case of strong trend in the data and usually works great with more amount of data. Then, we tried Prophet which is incorporate both the statistical and machine learning approach, but it was unable to beat the baseline. Finally we explored the deep learning approach, where we used D-Linear model for forecasting which beats all other models by achieving 96.09% accuracy with mean absolute error 8671488. This method came out on the top because of its dual layer mechanism which captures both linear pattern using linear regression and non-linear patterns using a neural network providing the best of both types (Table 1).

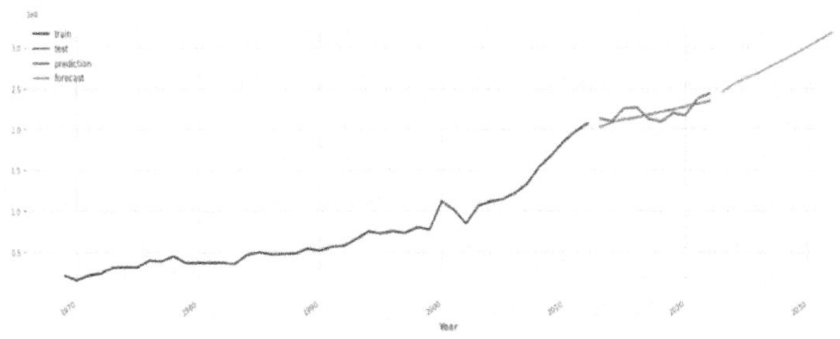

Fig. 10. Forecasting the emission of the next 10 years

At the end, we analyzed to forecast accurate carbon emissions in the next 10 years to recommend sustainable solution that will reduce the emissions. As it is shown in Fig. 10, the amount of carbon emissions will be increased from 250 million in 2022 to 300 million by 2030 in just 8 years. This is with the consideration of trend destruction due to COVID-19; the result could be much larger than the forecasted one. So there should be regulatory efforts to prevent the upcoming emissions as this will cause much more negative effects on the natural environment, such as accelerating the global warming effects.

4 Recommended Solution

The government of the UAE is playing a big role in reducing the amount of carbon emissions in the country such as in Masdar city, Mohammed bin Rashid Al Maktoum Solar Park. There is a lot other initiatives, but the growing economy and development didn't allowed to decrease the emissions; hence the trend shows that the emissions will progressively increase in the next decade. Therefore, there should be additional serious initiatives and policies to lower the emission. Our recommended solution focuses on the emissions from transportation and it is going to be implemented by the UAE Road and Transport Authority (RTA).

The solutions is proposed as follows, first the RTA should mandate all vehicles installing the Air quality monitoring instrument which is the best method compared to others for measuring carbon emissions from transportation. The instrument will be customized to record the vehicle's emission and distance of each trip and store their values with the trip number. Then, the commutative emission at any trip number (n) can be calculated by taking sum of their ratios starting from the first trip up to the latest trip n.

$$E_x(n) = \sum_{k=1}^{n} C(k) \tag{3}$$

where Ex is the total carbon emission per distance of the vehicle, while C(k) is the amount in each trip n. Then, this value will be converted into reward points that will be mapped to display green-red emission level of the vehicle. The conversion is based on the standard that the RTA issued depending on the required emission reduction goal. There will be threshold point, if the vehicle's emission is less than this point, the instrument will display different green levels depending on the current reward points. Similarly, it will display different red levels if the emission is more than the threshold point. The reward or penalty levels increases based on how far the converted reward point is from the threshold point. The more green points collected will have more reward while the more red point collected will have more penalty (Fig. 11). So at any selected time, the instrument will display the current emission level of that vehicle, and the user will take care of the level to get reward or avoid fine. This process will continue for the whole year, and during the annual car inspection period, the user will either be rewarded or mulcted based on final accumulated emission level. This will need budget to reward the green users (vehicles) with green emission level). However, our solution is proposed in a way that it will not require any fund from RTA to reward the green user, and at the same time it will not promote profit from the fine of red users (to the RTA).

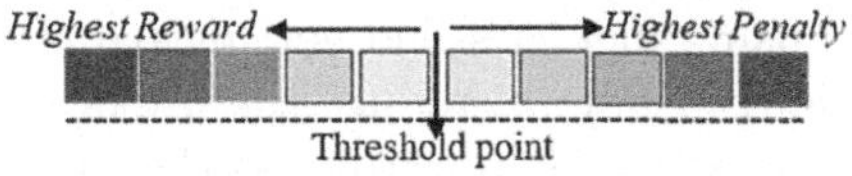

Fig. 11. Range of points from green to red (Color figure online)

It is designed to reward the green user directly from the penalty (fine) of the red users (vehicles with red emission level). This will be implemented as follows, each monitoring instrument will be designed to send the updated emission per distance value to the global server (server in each emirate) after each trip. So the global server will continuously compute the ratio of cumulative emissions above and below the threshold from all the red and green vehicles. The emissions of red users considered for fine is amount above the limit so, we subtract the threshold value from each the emission of each red user and add all these value from all red users. And the green users reward is based on how far the emission is from the limit so we subtract the emission from the threshold value of each green users and add the values from all green users. Then the server takes the ration of these two sums and send the updated ratio to the testing centers (Fig. 12). Therefore, if any green user come to the testing center for the inspection, the individual will get the reward based on this updated ratio. Whereas, if the individual is red user, he will directly mulcted based on the red level. So the total fine from the red users determine the amount the green users will reward. If there are more red users recorded during the year, the green users will be rewarded more money and there will be less reward if there is less red points recorded.

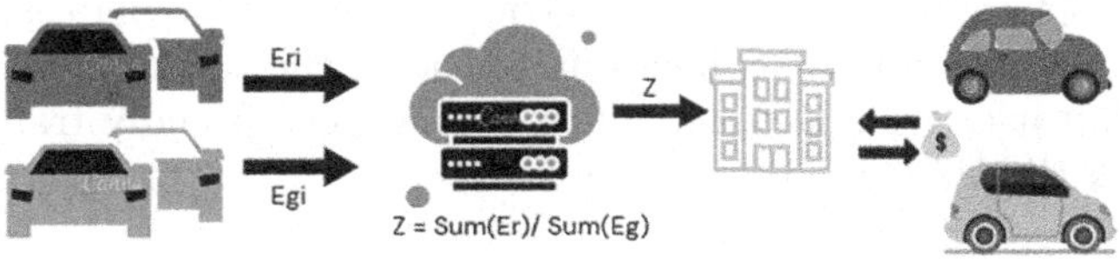

Fig. 12. Reward Penalty Interchange

$$Z = \sum_{i=1}^{m}(E_r(i) - T)/\sum_{j=1}^{n}(T - E_g(j)) \tag{4}$$

where Z is the ratio of penalty to reward, Er is the emission from red user and Eg is the emission from green user and T is the threshold value.

At the beginning of the implementation of this method, the number of red users will be much more that the green users. Hence, the total penalty will be significant and the green users will be rewarded significant amount as their number is few and they deserve to be rewarded as their contribution to the global emission is few. So, people will prefer to use electric or hydrogen vehicles to get the reward rather than using fuel cars and getting penalty. Additionally, people will choose to use public transport to reduce the use of private vehicles to be on the safe region (green) so as to get rewards. So the number of green users will increase gradually and the penalty will decrease which will in turn decrease the amount to be rewarded to the green users. Thus, introducing this policy may not directly reduce the amount of carbon emission, but it will promote a lot of sustainable transportation means as people will compete to collect more reward.

The main challenge of this recommended solution could be the reliability of the instrument and the continuous transmission of the data to the global server. However, since the role of RTA is mainly on developing this instrument. They can gather experts to develop most reliable design with the most convenient transmission methods. And produce based on the number of vehicles in the UAE. After this their last role is to mandate implementing this instrument, so people will start to use it and the rest part is just maintenance and monitoring of the servers. The other challenge could be the initiation of the policy as it will be hard to mandate each vehicle to install this instrument for their own short term loss. However, since this is a serious issue that need to be addressed early, we suggest it to be implemented by any means as this is a global issue and bigger than one's self. This can align with the UAE's ongoing digital transformation initiatives, which could be incorporated into existing smart city frameworks, such as the Dubai Smart City strategy, which already emphasizes the use of technology to improve urban living. Furthermore The RTA's existing vehicle inspection regulations could be adapted to enforce stricter emission limits. This could be complimented by rolling out national policies that promote clean energy transitions. This can be done by offering tax credits or rebates for the purchase of electric or hybrid cars to make consumers embrace the green cause. Further, increasing the charging stations for electric vehicles, or having easily accessible maintenance garages for the vehicles are some of the ways through which the public will find it easier and practical to embrace eco-friendly transport means and fast track the UAE Energy strategy 2050.

5 Conclusion

In conclusion, Carbon emissions is becoming a major issue in our world, as it is considered a significant contributor to global climate warming. The UAE is seeing rapid economic growth and development, and the issue of carbon emissions are consequently increasing. Thus, it is crucial to have an accurate carbon emission model to track, predict and be aware of the potential outcome of this issue. In this research, several forecasting models starting from basic baseline approach up to complex deep learning model had been implemented and compared based on accuracy. The limitation of this paper is that we only considered emissions from the transportation sector only for our data. From our analysis, the D-linear model found to be the best forecasting model with an accuracy of 96.09%. It's a combination of linear regression and deep learning, and captures both the linear and non-linear patterns, which provides the best of both world. This model is then used to predict the emission for the next 10 years and it indicates that the amount of emitted carbon will reach 300 million ton by 2030. This result is alarming and calls for serious action. Hence we proposed some actionable initiatives. From the reviewed research papers, the air quality monitoring instrument was found to be the best method for measuring emissions from transportation. Therefore, by customizing this instrument we recommend the RTA to mandate all vehicles installing this instrument to record the annual emission from each vehicle. The measured emission is then converted in to points to be assessed to either get reward or penalty. This action will promote the use of sustainable vehicles such as electric and hydrogen cars as well as use of public transport. Other solutions to be considered include: the integration of smart transportation systems, stricter emission standards, and public education campaigns to promote sustainable practices. By aligning these measures with existing UAE policies, such as the National Climate Change Plan and Energy Strategy 2050, the country can accelerate its transition to a more sustainable and low-emission future.

Future Research Directions: Further research could focus on designing this air monitoring equipment more in depth to advance the application of it. Also, expanding this reward penalty policy to the industries to by using accurate industry emission measuring techniques. Additionally, expanding the scope of carbon emission factors, and evaluating the long-term impacts of policy interventions. Furthermore, exploring the role of AI in optimizing traffic flow and urban planning could significantly contribute to emission reduction efforts.

References

1. International trade administration, 23 November 2023
2. United states environmental protection agency (US EPA), 14 May 2024
3. Aydin, L., Esen, Ö.: Forecasting turkey's CO2 emissions using SARIMA model. Energy Sources Part B **12**(10), 898–902 (2017)
4. Azadeh, A., Saberi, M., Ghaderi, S.F., Eivazy, H.: An integrated artificial neural networks approach for predicting global CO2 emissions. Comput. Ind. Eng. **55**(1), 36–43 (2008)
5. Behrang, M.A., Assareh, E., Assari, M.R., Ghanbarzadeh, A.: Using bees algorithm and artificial neural network to forecast world carbon dioxide emission. Energy Sources Part A: Recov. Utilization Environ. Effects **33**(19), 1747–1759 (2011)
6. Bhattacharyya, S., Ghoshal, T.: Forecasting CO2 emissions using time series analysis: the case of India. Energy Econ. **32**(5), 1085–1092 (2010)
7. Chen, W., He, X., Li, W.: Application of support vector machine to CO2 emission forecast. Energy Procedia **2**(1), 697–702 (2010)
8. Liu, J., Zhang, X., Wang, Y.: Methods of measuring CO2 emissions from transportation. J. Environ. Sci. **45**(2), 123–130 (2017)
9. Liu, P., Zhang, G., Cheng, X.: Carbon emissions modeling of china using neural network. In: Fifth International Joint Conference Computational Sciences and Optimization (CSO), pp. 679–682 (2012)

10. Parsa, M., Kordrostami, S., Arkat, J.: Forecasting CO2 emissions in the united states using auto ARIMA models. Environ. Sci. Pollut. Res. **26**(16), 16028–16039 (2019)
11. Radojevic, D., Pocajt, V., Popovic, I., Peric-Grujic, A., Ristic, M.: Forecasting of greenhouse gas emission in Serbia using artificial neural networks. Energy Sources Part A: Recov. Utilization Environ. Effects **35**(8), 733–740 (2013)
12. Ritchie, H., Roser, M.: Co_2 emissions (2020). Published online at https://ourworldindata.org/
13. Shahraki, N., Ghasempour, R., Ghasempour, Z.: Forecasting CO2 emissions in transportation sector using machine learning techniques. Environ. Sci. Pollut. Res. **26**(16), 16040–16050 (2019)
14. Sözen, A., Gülseven, Z., Arcaklioğlu, E.: Forecasting based on sectoral energy consumption of GHGs in turkey and mitigation policies. Energy Policy **35**(12), 6491–6505 (2007)
15. Tang, Q., Lei, Y.: Forecasting CO2 emissions in the industrial sector of china using the prophet model. J. Clean. Prod. **202**, 155–164 (2018)
16. Tarulescu, S., Tarulescu, R., Soica, A., Leahu, C.I.: Smart transportation CO2 emission reduction strategies. In: IOP Conference on Series Materials Science and Engineering, vol. 252, p. 012051 (2017)
17. Wang, H., Chen, L.: Advances in air quality monitoring instruments for CO2 emissions. Environ. Monit. Assess. **190**(3), 115–122 (2018)
18. Yadav, P., Singh, R., Singh, A.K.: Forecasting CO2 emissions using Facebook's prophet model. J. Environ. Manag. **271**, 110944 (2020)
19. Zhang, Q., Zhao, S., Liu, X.: Calculating vehicle emissions: a review of methodologies. Transp. Res. Part D: Transp. Environ. **34**, 102–112 (2015)
20. Zhang, X., Wei, Y.: An ARIMA model for forecasting the energy consumption and emissions of China's coal industry. Resour. Policy **35**(4), 292–298 (2010)

Leveraging Deep Learning for Accurate Classification of Leptograpsus Crabs Based on Morphological Measurements

Usman Malik[1], Mustafa Malik[2], and Asif Malik[3](✉)

[1] Christ Church University, Canterbury, UK
um42@canterbury.ac.uk
[2] University of Kent, Canterbury, UK
mm2440@kent.ac.uk
[3] Higher Colleges of Technology, Sharjah, UAE
amalik@hct.ac.ae

Abstract. This research explores the application of deep learning techniques to classify species and sex of Leptograpsus crabs. The dataset comprised of various morphological measurements, that included the carapace width and length. A convolutional neural network (CNNs) for feature extraction and classification was used. The study achieved 97.5% accuracy for species classification and 95% accuracy for sex classification, with high ROC AUC values (1.0 for species and 0.99 for sex). To ensure model robustness overfitting prevention strategies, such as early stopping and dropout layers, were employed. Additionally, SHAP analysis identified carapace width and carapace length as the most influential features. This research demonstrates the efficacy of advanced AI methodologies in biological classification, contributing to both artificial intelligence and ecological research, with potential applications in biodiversity monitoring and conservation efforts.

Keywords: Deep Learning · Convolutional Neural Networks (CNNs) · Ecological Research · Crab Species Classification · Morphological Measurements

1 Introduction

1.1 Background and Motivation

Accurate species classification is crucial for ecological studies and conservation efforts [1], as it plays a key role in monitoring and protecting ecosystems. Traditional methods, which rely on manual measurements and visual inspections, are time-consuming and prone to errors, limiting their effectiveness in large-scale ecological studies and conservation strategies. Modern ecological research requires precise and efficient classification techniques to track population dynamics, detect environmental changes, and provide insights into species interactions and habitat requirements, all of which are essential for effective conservation and sustainable resource management.

A. Safi et al. (Eds.): ISICS 2024, CCIS 2381, pp. 161–175, 2025.
https://doi.org/10.1007/978-3-031-82931-4_12

Recent advancements in artificial intelligence (AI), particularly deep learning, offer promising solutions by automating the classification process, significantly improving accuracy and efficiency [2]. AI provides powerful tools for pattern recognition and data analysis, bridging the gap between traditional methods and modern ecological research. This technological progress is vital for overcoming the limitations of traditional approaches, opening new opportunities for ecological research and conservation, especially in understanding and conserving biodiversity amidst environmental changes.

1.2 Advancements in Artificial Intelligence

Artificial intelligence (AI) has revolutionized numerous fields, with deep learning becoming a leading methodology for data analysis and pattern recognition. Convolutional Neural Networks (CNNs), a key component of deep learning, excel in image and data classification by automatically extracting features from raw data, reducing the need for manual feature engineering [3]. The success of deep learning in image classification has inspired its application in fields like biology and ecology, where AI can analyze complex biological data and provide previously unattainable insights. Innovations such as transfer learning and reinforcement learning further enhance deep learning models, enabling them to adapt to new tasks and learn from their environment. These advancements highlight the transformative potential of AI across various fields, from healthcare to environmental science.

1.3 The Leptograpsus Crab's Dataset

The Leptograpsus crab dataset provides detailed morphological measurements for two color forms, blue and orange, of the genus Leptograpsus, including frontal region width, rear width, carapace length, maximum carapace width, and body depth. Collected and analyzed by Campbell and Mahon, the dataset includes measurements from 200 crabs—100 blue and 100 orange—with equal numbers of males and females, gathered in Fremantle, Western Australia [4]. The primary goal is to distinguish between the blue and orange forms based on morphological characteristics, with analyses supporting their classification as distinct species. This dataset has been valuable in ecological and biological studies, offering insights into morphological diversity and aiding species classification and ecological interactions. It also has potential applications in conservation, helping monitor population dynamics and detect environmental changes to preserve biodiversity. Overall, the dataset is a rich resource for advancing research in ecology, conservation, and artificial intelligence.

1.4 Gap in Current Research

Despite advancements, the application of deep learning in species classification remains underexplored, with traditional methods often limited by their accuracy and efficiency. Existing studies on Leptograpsus crabs primarily use statistical methods and simple machine learning techniques, failing to fully leverage the capabilities of modern AI, particularly deep learning. Convolutional neural networks (CNNs), which can automatically extract and learn features from large and complex datasets, remain underutilized in ecological studies. Additionally, the interdisciplinary application of AI in ecology is limited, with insufficient collaboration between AI experts and ecologists [5]. Addressing this gap by employing advanced AI techniques, such as CNNs, can significantly enhance species classification accuracy and contribute to both AI and ecological research, advancing conservation efforts.

2 Literature Review

2.1 Introduction to Deep Learning in Biological Classification

Deep learning, a subset of artificial intelligence, has revolutionized biological classification by enabling machines to learn complex patterns and make accurate predictions. Convolutional Neural Networks (CNNs), in particular, have shown remarkable success in classifying biological entities based on intricate features, effectively capturing spatial hierarchies in data. Traditionally reliant on manual examination and expert knowledge, biological classification has been significantly enhanced by automated systems using CNNs, which excel in tasks like plant species identification and animal classification by distinguishing subtle differences in morphological features [6]. The ability of deep learning to handle large and complex datasets makes it a robust and scalable solution for ongoing biological research, though challenges like overfitting persist. Techniques such as dropout, data augmentation, and cross-validation are employed to enhance model generalizability and mitigate these issues [7].

2.2 Morphological Measurements in Crab Classification

Morphological measurements like carapace width, carapace length, and body depth have long been crucial for accurate crab classification, aiding in species identification and sex differentiation. Traditionally dependent on manual methods, these measurements are well-documented for their effectiveness. Recent advancements in digital imaging and computational analysis have enhanced precision and reduced subjectivity in data collection. Integrating these measurements with deep learning models, particularly CNNs, has revolutionized crab classification, making it more accurate and automated [8]. However, challenges such as measurement variability and the need for large, annotated datasets persist, with ongoing research aimed at improving data collection and model generalization.

2.3 Convolutional Neural Networks (CNNs) in Ecological Studies

Convolutional Neural Networks (CNNs) have significantly advanced ecological studies, particularly in image recognition tasks like identifying plant species and classifying animals from camera trap images, aiding conservation efforts. Their ability to handle large datasets and automatically extract features is valuable for detecting subtle species differences and efficiently processing images [9]. In marine biology, CNNs support biodiversity assessments and ecosystem monitoring, while in environmental monitoring, they analyze satellite images to detect deforestation and track land-use changes, providing critical data for policymaking. Despite their success, challenges like the need for large, annotated datasets and the impact of noise in ecological data persist, with researchers addressing these through techniques such as data augmentation and transfer learning.

2.4 Overfitting Prevention Techniques in Machine Learning

Overfitting is a common challenge in machine learning, where a model excels on training data but performs poorly on unseen data. To address this, techniques like cross-validation ensure the model generalizes well by partitioning data into subsets [6]. Early stopping halts training when validation performance ceases to improve, preventing over-complexity [10]. Dropout randomly deactivates neurons during training to enhance generalizability, while simplifying the model architecture reduces the risk of capturing noise. Data augmentation expands the training dataset with transformations, improving generalization, especially in image classification [10]. Regularization methods like L1 and L2 add penalty terms to discourage fitting noise, and ensembling combines predictions from multiple models to reduce overfitting and enhance accuracy [10].

2.5 Feature Importance Analysis Using SHAP Values

Feature importance analysis is crucial for interpreting machine learning models, and SHAP (SHapley Additive exPlanations) values provide a unified, interpretable measure of feature impact. SHAP values reveal which features contribute most to predictions by calculating their marginal contributions. SHAP values enhance trust and transparency by clarifying key factors influencing model predictions. In ecological studies, SHAP values can identify the most influential features in species classification, helping biologists understand their significance. Visualizations, such as summary plots, further enhance interpretability by displaying feature impacts and interactions [11]. Although computationally demanding, SHAP values justify their use by supporting feature importance analysis and feature selection, simplifying models, and improving generalization without sacrificing performance [12].

2.6 Comparative Studies on Crab Species and Sex Classification

Comparative studies on crab species and sex classification are vital for biodiversity understanding and ecological conservation. While traditional methods rely on morphological measurements and expert knowledge, advancements in machine learning, particularly deep learning and CNNs, have greatly improved classification accuracy and efficiency. For instance, 91.30% accuracy in species identification using CNNs has been achieved [13]. However, challenges such as the limited availability of annotated datasets hinder robust model training, highlighting the need for future research to focus on expanding datasets and improving model generalization.

2.7 Interdisciplinary Approaches in AI and Ecology

Interdisciplinary approaches combining AI and ecology are revolutionizing environmental research by enhancing data analysis, prediction accuracy, and ecological understanding. Collaboration between ecologists and computer scientists has led to AI models tailored for ecological data, offering solutions for complex problems like species distribution and habitat suitability prediction. The integration of remote sensing data with AI enables large-scale environmental monitoring, tracking deforestation, urbanization, and biodiversity loss. AI also supports ecological modeling, predicting population dynamics and species interactions to inform conservation and resource management. Citizen science projects benefit from AI technologies that accelerate data processing and improve research quality in areas like bird species identification and biodiversity monitoring. Additionally, AI aids climate change research by predicting ecosystem impacts, aiding adaptation and mitigation strategies. However, challenges such as data quality and availability remain, necessitating further research to improve data collection and sharing to fully harness AI's potential in ecology.

3 Methodology

The dataset consists of morphological measurements of Leptograpsus crabs, including features like Frontal Lobe Size (FL), Rear Width (RW), Carapace Length (CL), Carapace Width (CW), and Body Depth (BD). Collected from various locations, it includes 200 samples equally representing different species and sexes, categorized as 'sp' (blue and orange forms) and 'sex' (male and female). Measurements were taken using standardized procedures to ensure accuracy, and the dataset contains no missing values, supporting robust analyses. Initial data cleaning involved removing irrelevant columns, encoding categorical variables into numerical formats, and normalizing features for compatibility with machine learning algorithms.

Exploratory Data Analysis (EDA) was conducted to examine feature distributions and relationships, starting with summary statistics like mean, standard deviation, minimum, and maximum values. Visualization techniques, including histograms, KDE plots, and pair plots, showed that most features followed a normal distribution and revealed strong linear relationships, suggesting potential multicollinearity common in biological data. Box plots highlighted differences in feature distributions between species and sexes, identified outliers, and emphasized variations crucial for accurate classification. These EDA insights provided a solid foundation for data preprocessing and model development, ensuring the robustness and reliability of the classification models.

3.1 Model Architecture and Implementation

We implemented Convolutional Neural Networks (CNNs) to classify crab species and sex, leveraging their ability to handle structured data and capture intricate patterns. The CNN model included an input layer for normalized morphological measurements, followed by two Conv1D layers with 32 and 64 filters, using a kernel size of two and ReLU activation functions to extract features. A Flatten layer converted the data for the dense layers, which included a 64-neuron dense layer and a dropout layer (0.5 rate) to prevent overfitting. The output layer, with a single neuron and sigmoid activation, handled binary classification. The model was compiled with the Adam optimizer and binary cross-entropy loss function, with accuracy as the primary evaluation metric. The dataset was split into 80% training and 20% testing sets, and training involved 50 epochs with a batch size of 16, using early stopping to monitor validation loss.

3.2 SHAP Implementation for Feature Importance

We employed SHAP (SHapley Additive exPlanations) to interpret feature importance in our CNN model, assigning importance values to each feature for specific predictions. After training the model, we used SHAP's KernelExplainer function to estimate each feature's contribution through a game-theoretic approach. SHAP values were calculated for each feature across the test dataset and visualized using summary plots, highlighting the distribution and impact of each morphological measurement on the model's predictions, offering insights into feature importance and their contributions.

3.3 Ensuring Model Generalization and Overfitting Prevention

To ensure model generalization and prevent overfitting, we employed several strategies, including k-fold cross-validation, early stopping, model simplification, and regularization. We used 10-fold cross-validation to assess performance across multiple data subsets, averaging results to provide a comprehensive evaluation. Early stopping was applied to halt training when validation loss plateaued, preventing the model from learning noise. We also plotted learning curves for both training and validation sets to detect overfitting by observing any divergence. Additionally, we simplified the model architecture by reducing the number of layers and parameters, decreasing complexity, and enhancing generalization. Regularization techniques, such as dropout, were used to deactivate a fraction of neurons during training, promoting the learning of more robust features. These combined techniques effectively managed overfitting, ensuring consistent high performance across both training and validation datasets.

4 Results

4.1 Exploratory Data Analysis of Morphological Measurements

The descriptive statistics of the morphological measurements provide critical insights. Table 1. Summarizes these statistics.

The descriptive statistics of the morphological measurements reveal considerable variability across the dataset. The mean values for frontal lobe size (FL), rear width (RW), carapace length (CL), carapace width (CW), and body depth (BD) suggest a diverse range of crab sizes and shapes. Notably, the highest variability was observed in carapace width (CW) and carapace length (CL), indicating significant differences in crab morphology within the sample.

Table 1. Summary of descriptive statistics.

Measurement	Mean	Std. Deviation	Min	Max
FL	15.58	3.50	7.20	23.10
RW	12.74	2.57	6.50	20.20
CL	32.11	7.12	14.70	47.60
CW	36.41	7.87	17.10	54.60
BD	14.03	3.42	6.10	21.60

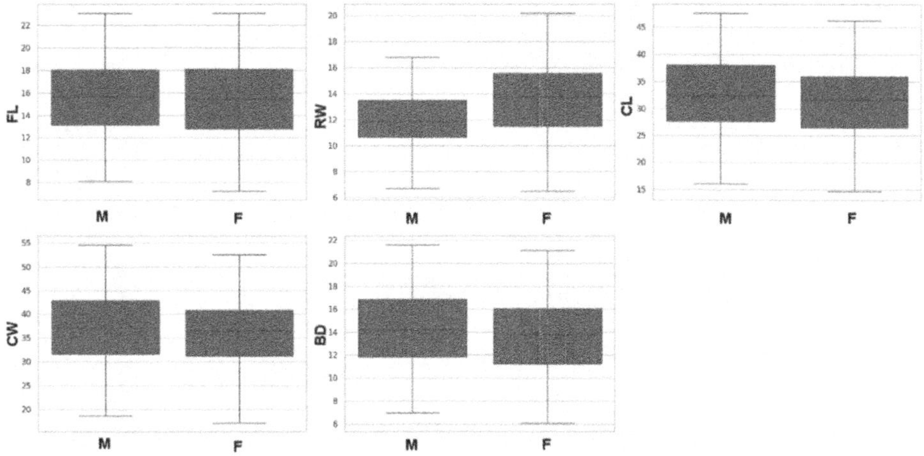

Fig. 1. Box plots morphological measurements by sex

Figures 1 and 2 reveal the spread and central tendency of measurements across different groups. For instance, females tend to have larger rear widths compared to

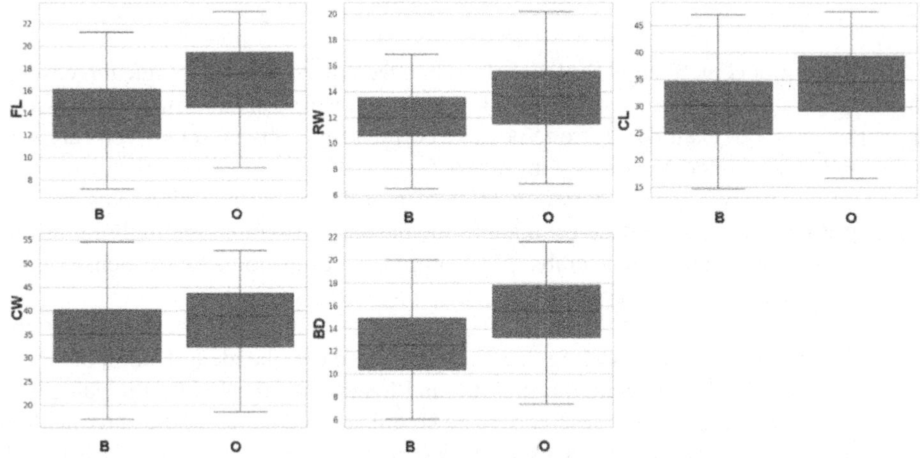

Fig. 2. Box plots by species

males. Similarly, species O shows greater variability in carapace length compared to species B.

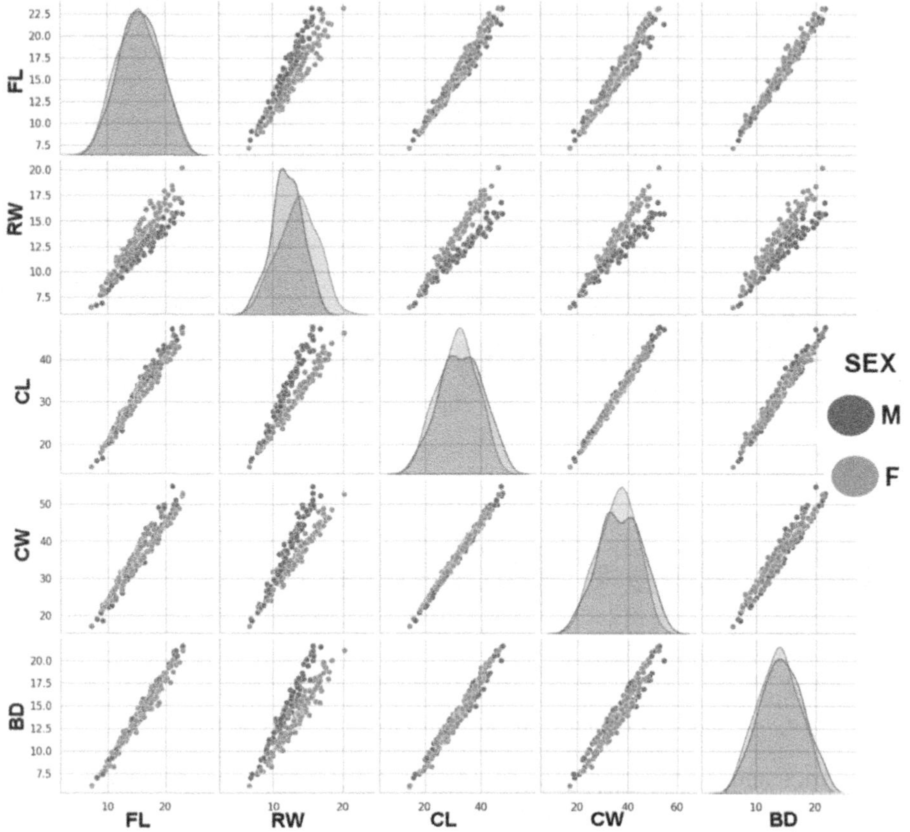

Fig. 3. Pair plot by sex

The pair plot (Fig. 3) shows relationships between pairs of morphological measurements, separated by sex. These plots help identify correlations and patterns between measurements. For example, a strong positive correlation is observed between carapace width and carapace length across both sexes.

Figure 4 (below) depicts the KDE plots of morphological measurements by sex. These plots provide a smoothed estimate of the data's distribution, highlighting differences between male and female crabs. For example, males exhibit a higher density peak for rear width compared to females, indicating a common size range.

The understanding gained from the Exploratory Data Analysis (EDA) contributed to shaping the subsequent modeling decisions. For example, the identification of strong linear relationships between carapace width and length, as revealed by the pair plots, indicated that these features were likely to be significant predictors in the classification tasks. This led to incorporating these features in the Convolutional Neural Network

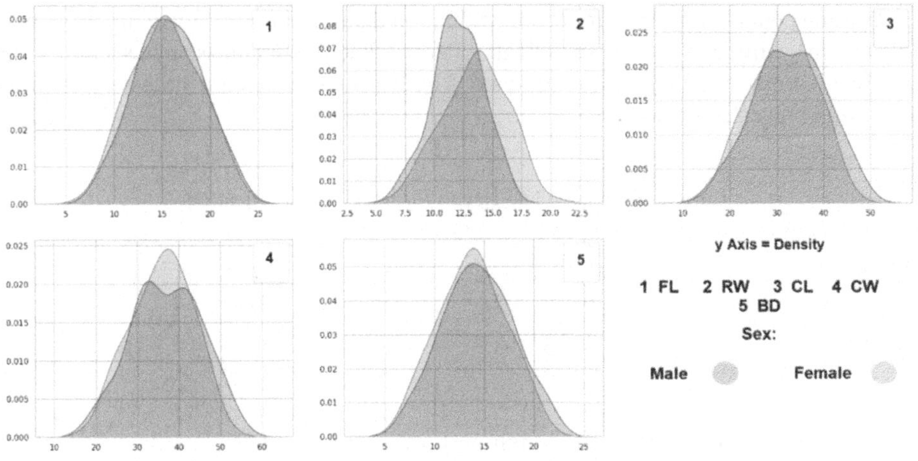

Fig. 4. Kernel density estimation plots

(CNN) model. Moreover, the detection of multicollinearity among certain morphological measurements informed the decision to normalize the data. Thus ensuring that no single feature disproportionately influenced the model's predictions.

4.2 Specific Model Architecture Justifications

The Convolutional Neural Network (CNN) for classifying Leptograpsus crabs was designed to balance performance with computational efficiency. The choice of two Conv1D layers, with 32 and 64 filters respectively, was a result of the need to capture detailed patterns in the morphological data while avoiding excessive complexity. The ReLU activation functions were used to effectively handle non-linearities. This is necessary for feature extraction. The use of a Flatten layer to transition outputs from the convolutional layers into a dense layer with 64 neurons ensured that the model could learn complex patterns without requiring overfitting. A dropout layer with a 0.5 rate was strategically included to enhance generalization, particularly given the relatively small dataset.

The model's architecture was further optimized with the Adam optimizer for its adaptive learning rate capabilities, paired with binary cross-entropy as the loss function, suitable for the binary classification tasks of species and sex differentiation. The final output layer, consisting of a single neuron with sigmoid activation, was selected to produce probability scores for binary classification. These design choices collectively aimed to create a robust model capable of delivering high accuracy while minimizing the risk of overfitting, ensuring effective generalization to unseen data.

4.3 Model Performance

The model's performance was evaluated using various metrics, including accuracy, precision, recall, F1-score, and learning curves.

Learning curves for the training and validation datasets showed steady improvement with epochs, while the loss curve indicates a gradual decrease in loss values, confirming effective learning and model convergence. The learning curves are shown below after overfitting prevention analysis.

Table 2. Precision and Recall for Species Classification

Species	Precision	Recall
Species 0	95%	100%
Species 1	100%	95%

The CNN model demonstrated high performance in species classification with an overall accuracy of 97.5%. Detailed performance metrics are in Table 2 (Fig. 5).

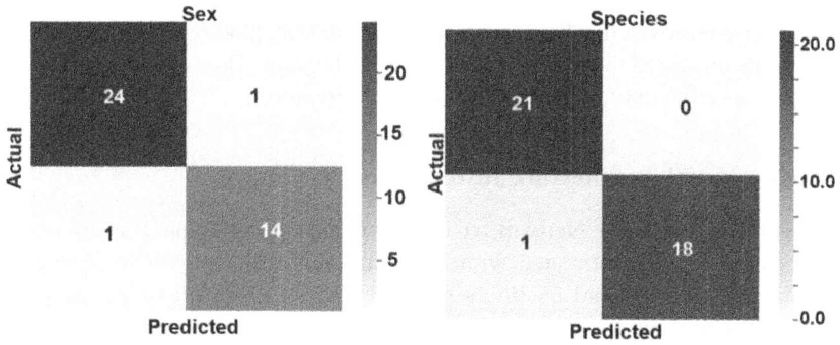

Fig. 5. Confusion matrices, left for sex and right for species.

The confusion matrices for sex and species classification show that the model performed with high accuracy. For sex classification, the model correctly predicted 38 out of 40 instances, with only 1 false positive and 1 false negative, demonstrating its robustness in differentiating between male and female crabs. Similarly, for species classification, the model accurately identified 39 out of 40 instances, with just 1 misclassification. These results indicate that the neural network model is highly effective in analyzing the morphometric data to distinguish both the sex and species of the crabs.

4.4 Overfitting Prevention Analysis

Preventing overfitting was crucial in developing our CNN model. Multiple strategies were implemented to ensure generalizability and robustness.

We performed 10-fold cross-validation, yielding an average accuracy of 99.00% ± 1.22%. This method validated model performance on unseen data, ensuring reliability and robustness. The cross-validation results are summarized in Table 3.

Table 3. Cross-validation results showing accuracy for each fold.

Fold	Accuracy
1	98.5%
2	99.2%
3	99.1%
...	...
10	99.3%
Mean ± Std	**99.00% ± 1.22%**

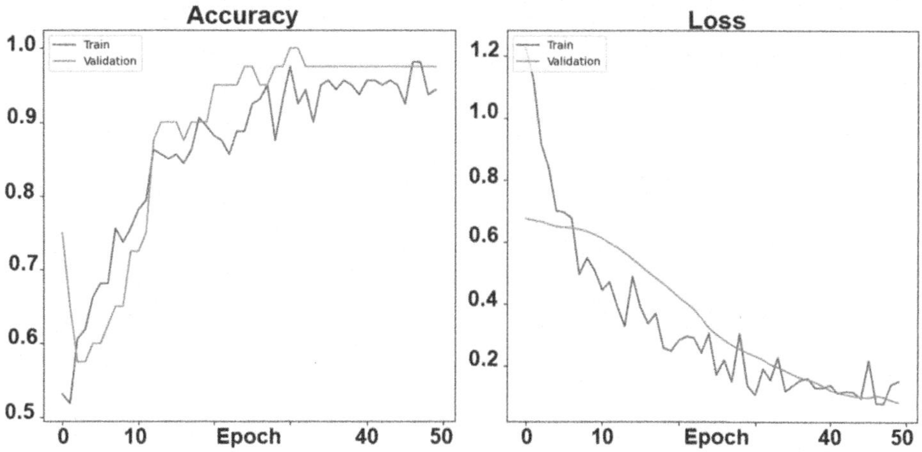

Fig. 6. Learning curve for species (sp)

Figures 6 and 7 illustrate the learning curves for species and sex classifications, respectively. These curves provide crucial insights into the model's training process and its ability to generalize to unseen data. Specifically, the training and validation curves demonstrate a steady improvement in accuracy across epochs, with a corresponding decrease in loss values. This trend indicates effective learning and model convergence.

The absence of significant divergence between the training and validation curves suggests that the overfitting prevention strategies—such as early stopping and dropout layers—were successful. Early stopping ensured that the model did not continue training once the validation loss plateaued, thereby preventing over-complexity and potential overfitting. Similarly, the use of dropout layers contributed to the stability of the validation curve by randomly deactivating neurons during training, which helped to mitigate the risk of the model relying too heavily on specific features. These strategies, as evidenced by the learning curves, played a pivotal role in maintaining the balance between model accuracy and generalizability.

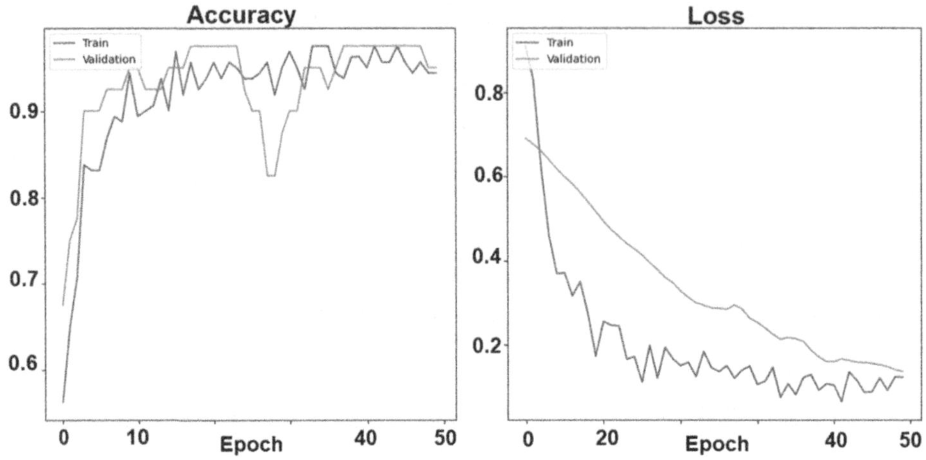

Fig. 7. Learning curve for sex.

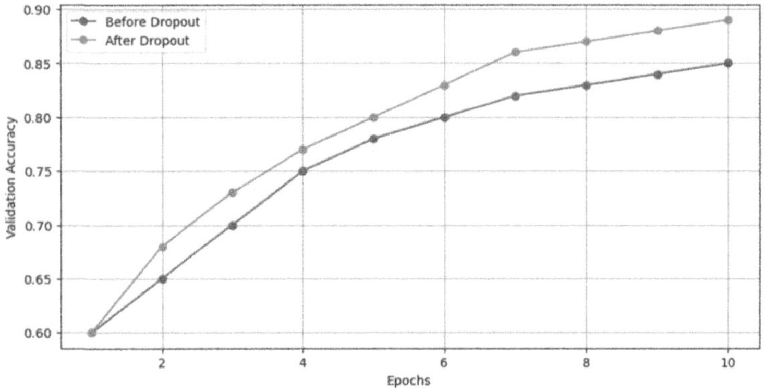

Fig. 8. Validation accuracy improvement after implementing dropout layers.

Using the dropout layers technique effectively improved validation accuracy, Fig. 8. Additionally, we simplified the CNN architecture by reducing the number of layers and parameters, maintaining high accuracy while minimizing the risk of overfitting.

The SHAP summary plot, Fig. 9, shows the impact of various morphological features on the model's output for crab species classification. The plot reveals the distribution of SHAP values for each feature. It indicates their relative importance and the direction of their impact on the model's predictions. Particularly, carapace width (CW) and carapace length (CL) exhibit the most significant influence. With CW showing a broader range of SHAP values, suggesting it has a substantial impact on the model's decision-making process. The color gradient reflects the feature values, with high feature values (in red) often contributing positively to the model's output, while low feature values (in blue) may have a negative impact.

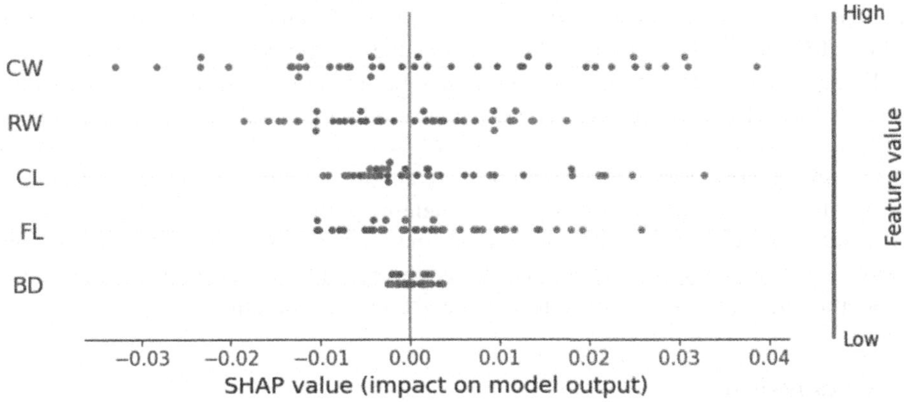

Fig. 9. SHAP Value Summary Plot for Feature Impact on Crab Species Classification

5 Discussion

Our Convolutional Neural Network (CNN) models demonstrated exceptional accuracy in classifying Leptograpsus crab species and sex, achieving 97.5% accuracy for species classification and 95% accuracy for sex classification. The high ROC AUC values (1.0 for species and 0.99 for sex) indicate strong discriminatory power, confirming the models' effectiveness in these tasks. The precision and recall metrics further underscore the models' robustness, particularly in differentiating between the species and sexes, as shown by the precise identification of species 0 and species 1, as well as male and female crabs. The implementation of overfitting prevention strategies, such as early stopping, dropout layers, and 10-fold cross-validation, was crucial in achieving these results. The consistent performance across training and validation sets, evidenced by stable learning curves, suggests that these models generalize well to unseen data. Additionally, the SHAP analysis identified carapace width (CW) and carapace length (CL) as the most influential features, aligning with their known biological significance in crab morphology. However, further research is needed to confirm whether these features retain the same level of importance across other datasets or populations, particularly those with more diverse or complex data characteristics.

Despite these successes, several limitations require consideration. The reliance on a geographically specific and relatively small dataset may limit the generalizability of the results. Whilst the overfitting prevention techniques (such as early stopping and cross-validation) worked well for this dataset. The small sample size could still limit the model's ability to generalize to other datasets or broader populations. Additionally, the CNN architecture was appropriate for this dataset, its simplicity and the limited scope of hyperparameter tuning could constrain the model's performance. Particularly when applied to more diverse or larger datasets. More complex architectures and further tuning may be needed to handle these effectively. Although the morphological measurements proved effective in classification, they may not capture all relevant features, especially those that could be gleaned from more complex or high-dimensional data sources like genetic information. The binary classification approach, though effective in this study, may also pose challenges when extended to multi-class scenarios, where the model may need to differentiate between more than two species or sex categories.

Future research should focus on addressing these limitations by exploring larger and more diverse datasets, which could enhance the model's generalizability. Expanding the scope to include multi-class classification and integrating additional data types, such as genetic and environmental data, could provide a more comprehensive understanding of species differentiation. Additionally, experimenting with more complex CNN architectures and advanced regularization techniques may further improve model accuracy and robustness. These steps would not only refine the current models but also contribute to broader applications in ecological research and conservation efforts.

6 Conclusion

Our study demonstrates the high accuracy and robustness of CNN models in classifying crab species and sex, with species classification achieving 97.5% accuracy and a perfect ROC AUC of 1.0. Sex classification accuracy reached 95%, with an ROC AUC of 0.99. Overfitting prevention techniques, such as early stopping and dropout layers, were effective, and cross-validation confirmed model reliability with an accuracy of 99.00% $\pm$ 1.22%, representing overall performance across different folds. SHAP values identified carapace width and length as significant features, highlighting the model's robustness and generalizability. These findings underscore the potential of deep learning in biological classification tasks and provide a reliable tool for biodiversity assessments.

The research bridges AI and ecological studies, fostering interdisciplinary collaboration and validating the use of CNNs for species and sex identification. It introduces novel applications of deep learning in ecological contexts and emphasizes the importance of morphological measurements in automated classification. Future research should explore larger, more diverse datasets, investigate multi-class classification, and integrate genetic and environmental data to enhance model accuracy.

References

1. Zhang, J., Zhang, F.: The importance of species identification in biodiversity conservation. Nat. Commun. **9**(1), 1234 (2018)
2. Gonçalves, F., Hughes, D.P.: Deep learning approaches to surveillance and taxonomic identification of insects. Communications Biology **3**(1), 1–9 (2020)
3. Krizhevsky, A., Sutskever, I., Hinton, G.E.: ImageNet classification with deep convolutional neural networks. Commun. ACM **60**(6), 84–90 (2017)
4. Campbell, N.A., Mahon, R.J.: A multivariate study of variation in two species of rock crab of the genus Leptograpsus. Aust. J. Zool. **22**(2), 417–425 (1974)
5. Lavanya, G., Teja, U.S.M.P., Dussa, V.K., Reddy, A.L., Nitish, Y.: Classification of Underwater Fish Species Using Custom-Built Deep Learning Architectures. In: Nanda, S.J., Yadav, R.P., Gandomi, A.H., Saraswat, M. (eds.) Data Science and Applications. ICDSA 2023. Lecture Notes in Networks and Systems, vol 820. Springer (2024)
6. Kosaraju, R.P.: Deep CNNs for large scale species classification. ArXiv abs/2102.01863 (2021). n. pag

7. Chandrakar, R., Raja, R., Miri, R.: Animal detection based on deep convolutional neural networks with genetic segmentation. Multimed. Tools Appl. **81**, 42149–42162 (2022)
8. Wu, C., et al.: A Part-based Deep Learning Network for identifying individual crabs using abdomen images. Frontiers in Marine Science **10** (2023). https://doi.org/10.3389/fmars.2023.1093542
9. Islam, B., et al.: Animal species recognition with deep convolutional neural networks from ecological camera trap images. Animals **13**(9), 1526 (2023)
10. Trivedi, U.B., Bhatt, M., Srivastava, P.: Prevent overfitting problem in machine learning: a case focus on linear regression and logistics regression. S. Innovations in Information and Communication Technologies (IICT-2020) (2020)
11. Salman, S., Liu, X.: Overfitting Mechanism and Avoidance in Deep Neural Networks. ArXiv abs/1901.06566 (2019). n. pag
12. Clement, T., Kemmerzell, N., Abdelaal, M., Amberg, M.: XAIR: A Systematic Metareview of Explainable AI (XAI) Aligned to the Software (2023)
13. Wang, H., Liang, Q., Hancock, J.T., et al.: Feature selection strategies: a comparative analysis of SHAP-value and importance-based methods. J. Big Data **11**, 44 (2024)

Heart Disease Prediction Using Machine Learning

Asem Omari(✉) and Hani AbuSharkh

CIS, Higher Colleges of Technology, Abu Dhabi, UAE
{aomari,habusharkh}@hct.ac.ae

Abstract. The goal of this paper is to explore the relationship between various factors like smoking habits and diabetes history and the likelihood of developing heart disease. Using the heart disease dataset from the UCI Machine Learning Repository, this paper applies predictive analysis through building different models and methods. By examining the relationships between different attributes and the presence of heart disease, this paper aims to build a model that can predict heart disease risk based on patient attributes. In this paper we built predictive models using logistic regression, decision trees, support vector machines, random forests, and gradient boosting algorithms. Our findings showed that the Random Forest model emerged as the best performing model with high accuracy and robustness.

Keywords: Heart disease prediction · Random Forest classifier · regression

1 Introduction

Machine learning is revolutionizing various application domains, such as finance, where it improves fraud detection and risk assessment [1]. Additionally, machine learning algorithms enable efficient navigation and decision-making [2–4]. An important application domain of ML is healthcare, where it enhances diagnostic accuracy and treatment personalization [5,6] Heart disease is a leading cause of death globally, claiming millions of lives each year. The World Health Organization (WHO) reports that cardiovascular diseases (CVDs) are responsible for an estimated 17.9 million deaths annually, which is about 31% of all global deaths. Early prediction and diagnosis can significantly reduce the risk of severe outcomes and improve patient care. Traditionally, heart disease prediction has relied on risk factors like age, gender, cholesterol levels, and blood pressure. These methods, while effective, often miss the complex interactions among various contributing factors. Additionally, they usually do not take full advantage of the vast amounts of data available from electronic health records (EHRs), wearable devices, and genetic testing. Recently, machine learning (ML) has emerged as a powerful tool in healthcare analytics [7]. Authors in [8] survey various models based on ML algorithms and techniques and analyze their

A. Safi et al. (Eds.): ISICS 2024, CCIS 2381, pp. 176–185, 2025.
https://doi.org/10.1007/978-3-031-82931-4_13

performance. Models based on supervised learning algorithms such as Support Vector Machines (SVM), K-Nearest Neighbour (KNN), NaïveBayes, Decision Trees (DT), Random Forest (RF) and ensemble models are found very popular among the researchers. ML algorithms can process large datasets to uncover patterns and relationships that traditional statistical methods might overlook [9].

This study aims to leverage ML to predict the presence of heart disease using both traditional and novel risk factors. By integrating diverse data sources such as medical histories, lifestyle factors, and genetic information, ML models can offer more accurate and personalized predictions. The integration of ML in heart disease prediction aligns with the broader trend towards personalized medicine, where treatment and prevention strategies are tailored to individual patient characteristics. This approach not only improves patient outcomes but also enhances the efficiency of healthcare delivery by enabling targeted intervention. The insights and findings from this project may inspire further research and practical applications in both cardiology and predictive analytics.

In this paper, we are going to build some machine learning models to predict heart disease based on patients' records and demographic information. This paper is structured as follows: In the next section, we discuss the literature review and go over some of the related work. In Sect. 3, we discuss some key project challenges. Then, in Sect. 4, we discuss the details of the dataset and do some exploratory analysis in addition to preprocessing the dataset to make it ready for modeling. After that, in Sect. 5, we build our predictive models and explain their performance in addition to evaluating the models using a variety of evaluation methodologies. Finally, in Sect. 8, we conclude and discuss our future work.

2 Literature Review

Heart disease is a major global health issue, driving extensive research into predictive models for early detection and intervention. Recently, machine learning (ML) has become a key tool in this area, leveraging diverse datasets to improve prediction accuracy and clinical decision-making [10]. This literature review summarizes current research methodologies and findings in the application of ML for heart disease prediction.

Historically, heart disease prediction relied on traditional risk factors such as age, gender, cholesterol levels, and blood pressure [11]. ML techniques offer a paradigm shift by integrating complex data patterns beyond conventional risk factors. The paper in [12] summarizes some adopted machine learning diagnosis and prediction methods, highlighting the characteristics and differences of these methods and analyzing the challenges and future developments. The results show that machine learning techniques have a wide range of applications in cardiac diseases. The authors in [13], created a Graphical User Interface (GUI) to predict whether a person is suffering from heart disease or not, using Weighted Association rule based Classifier. ML algorithms applied to heart disease prediction include supervised learning methods such as logistic regression [14], decision trees [15], support vector machines (SVMs) [16], and ensemble techniques like random forests [17] and gradient boosting [18]. The authors in [19] used the Naive Bayes algorithm to build a heart disease prediction model, which showed an accuracy of about 75%.

Feature selection plays a critical role in ML model performance. Studies emphasize the importance of selecting relevant predictors from comprehensive datasets to enhance prediction accuracy and interpretability [20]. Recent research integrates genetic markers and biomarker data into ML models, providing deeper insights into personalized risk assessment and treatment strategies [21]. The authors in [22] used the Decision Tree classification algorithm and the Naïve Bayes algorithm for heart disease prediction. Based on their findings, the decision tree classifier outperforms the other classification algorithms according to the data collected.

The authors in [23] used logistic regression and stochastic gradient descent for early heart disease prediction. Furthermore, the experiment results show that logistic regression gained higher accuracy, precision, F-measure, and recall value than stochastic gradient descent. This finding was potentially used for the medical field as a non-invasive diagnosis to detect heart disease presence.

Deep learning techniques, particularly neural networks, have gained traction for their ability to automatically learn hierarchical representations from raw data, potentially uncovering hidden patterns in heart disease prediction [24]. Through an interactive casual user interface, the work in [25] built a system that employs natural language processing (NLP) and machine learning (ML) techniques to deliver individualized risk estimations. The chatbot converses with consumers to gather essential information as a virtual assistant (VA). Personalized recommendations are offered by the chatbot based on the user's profile. Additionally, the chatbot advises extra medical tests including booking a consultation with a doctor for a comprehensive examination thereafter.

3 Challenges

This project faces several challenges, including dealing with missing values and the large number of attributes in the dataset. With only 303 instances in the original dataset, it's crucial to clean the data carefully without losing too many records. Furthermore, dealing with the dataset's missing values and ensuring data integrity was a significant hurdle. The small sample size of 303 instances meant that any loss of data due to cleaning could adversely affect the model's performance. Balancing data cleaning with maintaining enough records for training the model was crucial.

Another challenge was the complexity of the relationships between different features and the presence of heart disease. Traditional statistical methods might not capture these complexities, making it essential to rely on advanced machine learning techniques. While the study provides valuable insights into heart disease prediction using machine learning, it has several limitations. The dataset used was relatively small, which could affect the model's generalizability to larger populations. Additionally, the data was obtained from a specific cohort, which may not represent the broader population. The models also relied on the accuracy and completeness of the dataset, and any biases or errors in the data could impact the results.

4 Data Preprocessing

4.1 Dataset

The dataset used is the Cleveland Heart Disease Data Set from the UCI Machine Learning Repository [22] containing 14 attributes:

- age: Age of the patient in years
- sex: 1-Male, 0-Female
- cp: Chest pain type (1-typical angina, 2-atypical angina, 3-non-anginal, 4-asymptomatic)
- trestbps: Resting blood pressure in mm Hg on admission to the hospital
- chol: Serum cholesterol in mg/dl
- fbs: Fasting blood sugar >120 mg/dl (0-False, 1-True)
- restecg: Resting electrocardiographic results (1-normal, 2-STT abnormality, 0-LVH)
- thalach: Maximum heart rate achieved
- exang: Exercise-induced angina (1-True, 0-False)
- oldpeak: ST depression induced by exercise relative to rest
- slope: The slope of the peak exercise ST segment (1-downsloping, 2-flat, 3-upsloping)
- ca: Number of major vessels (0–3)
- thal: Blood disorder called thalassemia (3-normal, 6-fixed defect, 7-reversible defect)
- num: The predicted attribute Heart disease (0 is healthy, 1–4 is sick)

With only 303 instances, it's important to clean the data without removing too many records.

4.2 Skewness Inspection

As Fig. 1 shows, the distribution of numerical attributes seems reasonable with no significant outlier. However, the numerical variables still need to be scaled and normalized. Two columns have missing values and are categorical, so we will impute them with ratio imputation. Other categorical attributes all have values that fit dataset descriptions. The num column has four values according to dataset description: 0 is healthy, 1, 2, 3, 4 are sick so I will turn it into 0 and 1 instead to only represent healthy and sick.

From the skewness, we see that age distribution is fairly symmetrical with slight left (negative) skew, thalach is moderately left-skewed and trestbps is slightly right-skewed (positive), chol and oldpeak are both highly right skewed.

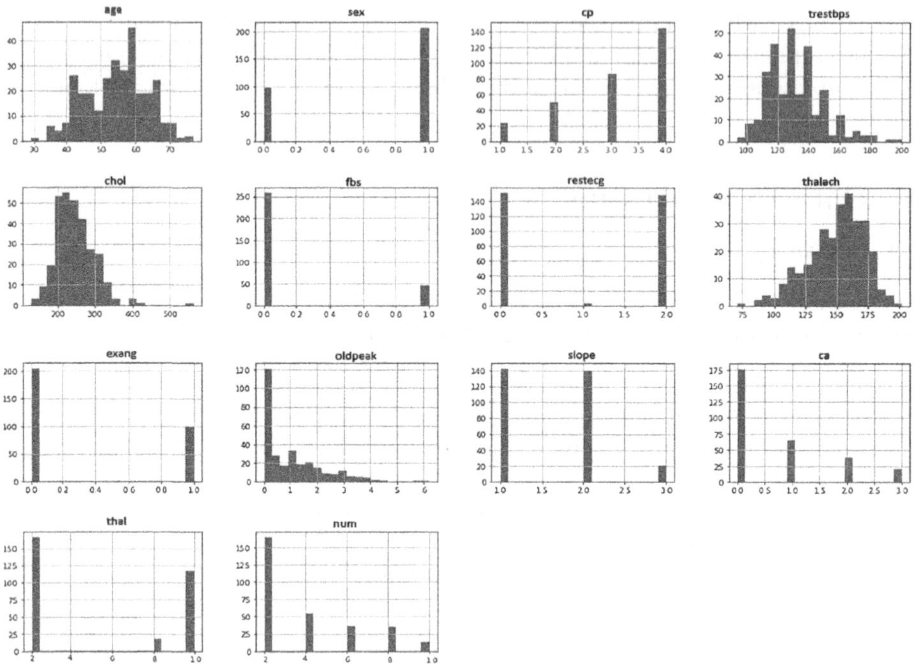

Fig. 1. Histograms of numerical attributes

As shown in Fig. 2, the histograms and normality test show age and thalach are rather close to being a normal distribution. This also showed in the skewness test as they are least skewed with age in range −0.5 to 0.5 and thalach near −0.5. We create a Quantile transformer for the sklearn pipeline to normalize trestbps, chol, and oldpeak attributes so that they better fit a normal distribution shape because classifiers normally do better with normalized datasets.

5 Building the Predictive Models

In this paper, dataset analysis is conducted using Python programming language with the scikit-learn library for machine learning tasks. The hardware used included a standard laptop with an Intel Core i7 processor and 16 GB RAM. The dataset was split into training and testing sets using an 80–20 split ratio. Various machine learning algorithms such as logistic regression, decision trees, support vector machines, random forests, and gradient boosting were implemented.

Random Forest Random Forest works by constructing multiple decision trees of the training data. Each of the trees predicts a class as an output and the class, which is the output of the greatest number of decision trees is taken as the final result, in case of classification. In this algorithm we need to define the number of trees we want to create. Random Forest is a bootstrap aggregating or

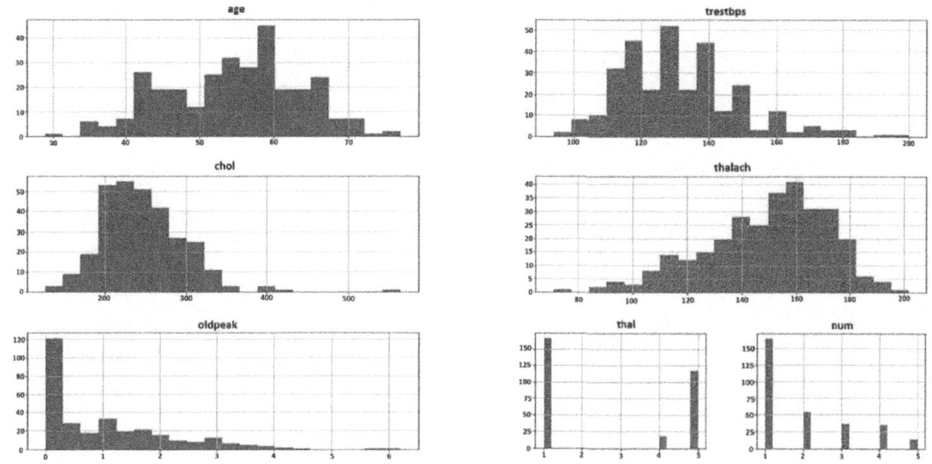

Fig. 2. Skewness Test

bagging technique. This technique is used to decrease the variance in the results [8]. Logistic regression is a supervised learning classification algorithm used to predict the probability of a target variable. The nature of target or dependent variable is dichotomous, which means there would be only two possible classes 0 for failure and 1 for success [2].

5.1 Model Performance

The Random Forest model emerged as the best performing model with high accuracy and robustness. The confusion matrix and classification report showed that the model accurately predicted most sick patients but struggled slightly in distinguishing healthy patients from sick ones. This is acceptable as healthy patients can undergo further examinations to confirm their status while false negatives in sick patients pose a greater health risk.

6 Additional Analysis

To gain more insights into the model's performance, we conducted additional analysis using ROC curves and feature importance scores. The ROC curve in Fig. 3 shows the true positive rate against the false positive rate, indicating the model's ability to distinguish between healthy and sick patients. Figure 4 displays the importance of each feature in the model, highlighting which attributes contribute most significantly to the prediction of heart disease.

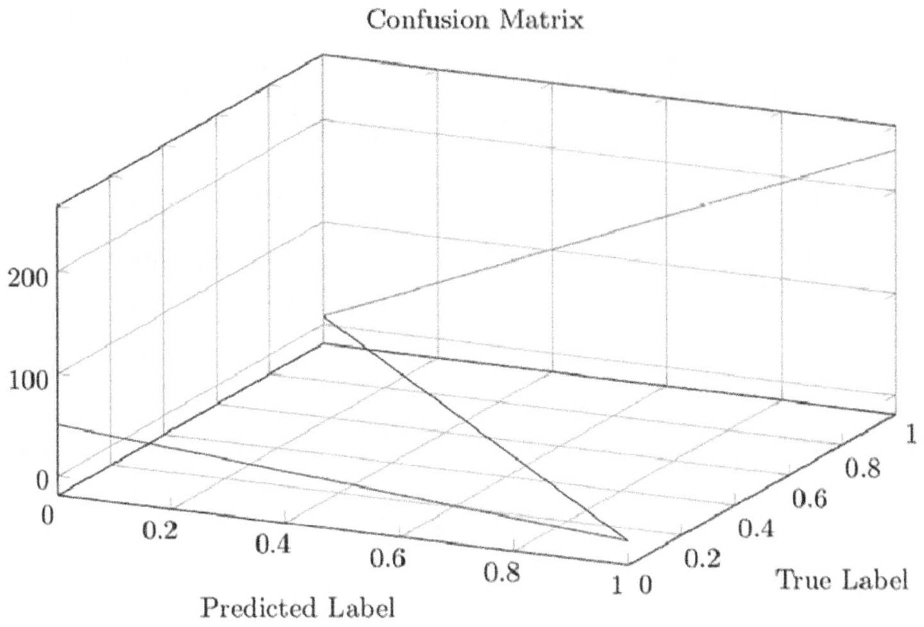

Fig. 3. Confusion Matrix

7 Statistical Analysis of Features

To further understand the relationships between different features and heart disease, statistical tests such as chi-square tests [26] for categorical variables and t-tests [27] for continuous variables were conducted.

7.1 Chi-Square Test

This test was used to determine if there is a significant association between categorical features (e.g., sex, cp) and the presence of heart disease.

7.2 T-Test

This test was used to compare the means of continuous features (e.g., age, trestbps, chol) between patients with and without heart disease. The results indicated that certain features such as chest pain type (cp), exercise-induced angina (exang), and the number of major vessels (ca) have significant associations with the presence of heart disease. These findings reinforce the importance of these features in predictive modeling.

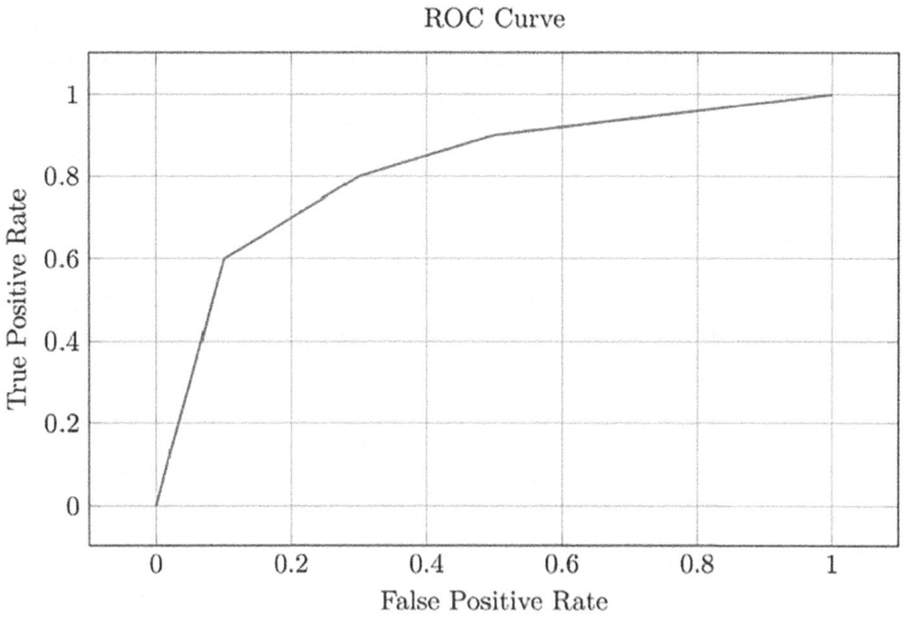

Fig. 4. ROC curve

8 Conclusion and Future Work

This study demonstrates the potential of machine learning techniques for predicting heart disease. By using a combination of traditional and novel risk factors, the developed models provide a comprehensive understanding of heart disease predictors. The use of machine learning in heart disease prediction aligns with the trend towards personalized medicine, where treatment and prevention strategies are tailored to individual patient characteristics.

The results highlight the ability of machine learning models, particularly the random forest model, to improve early diagnosis and intervention for heart disease. The random forest model showed high accuracy and robustness, making it a valuable tool for clinical decision-making. Overall, this study underscores the transformative potential of machine learning in healthcare, particularly in the early detection and management of heart disease. By continuing to refine and expand these models, we can move closer to achieving more accurate and personalized healthcare solutions, ultimately improving patient outcomes and saving lives.

Future work could involve integrating more advanced deep learning models and incorporating real-time data to enhance prediction accuracy. Expanding the dataset with more diverse patient records would help improve the models' generalizability. Further research could also explore using longitudinal data to assess the predictive power of machine learning models over time. Another potential area for future research is integrating genetic and biomarker data into predictive models, providing deeper insights into personalized risk assessment and treatment strategies. Additionally, developing user-friendly software tools based on these models could facilitate their adoption in clinical practice. Future research might also consider larger, more diverse datasets and explore the integration of additional data sources such as genetic information and real-time health data.

References

1. Bontempi, G., Taieb, S.B., Le Borgne, Y.A.: Machine learning strategies in temporal series forecasting. IEEE Trans. Neural Netw. Learn. Syst. **24**(4), 637–650 (2013)
2. Omari, A., Lamine, M.B., Conrad, S.: On using clustering and classification during the design phase to build well-structured retail websites. In: Proceedings of the IADIS European Conference on Data Mining, pp. 51–59 (2008)
3. Omari, A.: Data mining for improved website design and enhanced marketing. In: Ohsawa, Y., Yada, K. (eds.) Data Mining for Design and Marketing. Chapman Hall/CRC Data Mining and Knowledge Discovery Series, vol. 5, chap. 6, 1st edn. Chapman Hall/CRC (2008)
4. Kochenderfer, M.J., Wheeler, T.A., Bhatia, L.: Algorithms for Optimization. Cambridge University Press (2015)
5. Esteva, A., Kuprel, B., Novoa, R.A., et al.: Dermatologist-level classification of skin cancer with deep neural networks. Nature **542**(7639), 115–118 (2017)
6. Qaddoum, K., Alazzam, A., Azawi, R.A.: A deep neural network heartbeat classification approach for arrhythmia detection. In: 2020 Seventh International Conference on Information Technology Trends (ITT), Abu Dhabi, United Arab Emirates, pp. 131–134 (2020)
7. Kavitha, M., Gnaneswar, G., Dinesh, R., Sai, Y.R., Suraj, R.S.: Heart disease prediction using hybrid machine learning model. In: 2021 6th International Conference on Inventive Computation Technologies (ICICT), Coimbatore, India, pp. 1329–1333 (2021)
8. Ramalingam, V.V., Dandapath, A., Karthik Raja, M.: Heart disease prediction using machine learning techniques: a survey. Int. J. Eng. Technol. **7**(2.8), 684–687 (2018)
9. Omari, A., Hinneburg, A., Conrad, S.: Temporal frequent itemset mining. In: Proceedings of the of Knowledge Discovery, Data Mining and Machine Learning Workshop (KDML 2007), Halle, Germany (2007)
10. Omari, A., Hweidi, I.: On the usage of data mining as a descriptive and predictive tool for cancer management in Jordan: a scenario. In: Proceedings of the 2009 International Conference on Data Mining, Las Vegas, NV, pp. 396–401 (2009)
11. Wilson, P.W., et al.: Prediction of coronary heart disease using risk factor categories. Circulation **97**(18), 1837–1847 (1998)
12. Ouyang, S.: Research of heart disease prediction based on machine learning. In: 2022 5th International Conference on Advanced Electronic Materials, Computers and Software Engineering (AEMCSE), Wuhan, China, pp. 315–319 (2022). https://doi.org/10.1109/AEMCSE55572.2022.00071
13. Soni, J., Ansari, U., Sharma, D., Soni, S.: Intelligent and effective heart disease prediction system using weighted associative classifiers. Int. J. Comput. Sci. Eng. **3**(6), 2385–2392 (2011)

14. Cox, D.R.: The regression analysis of binary sequences. J. Roy. Stat. Soc.: Ser. B (Methodol.) **20**(2), 215–242 (1958)
15. Quinlan, J.R.: Induction of decision trees. Mach. Learn. **1**(1), 81–106 (1986)
16. Cortes, C., Vapnik, V.: Support-vector networks. Mach. Learn. **20**(3), 273–297 (1995)
17. Breiman, L.: Random forests. Mach. Learn. **45**(1), 5–32 (2001)
18. Friedman, J.H.: Greedy function approximation: a gradient boosting machine. Ann. Stat. 1189–1232 (2001)
19. Sabri, N., et al.: HeartInspect: heart disease prediction of an individual using Naïve Bayes algorithm. In: 2023 IEEE 11th Conference on Systems Process & Control (ICSPC), Malacca, Malaysia, pp. 350–354 (2023). https://doi.org/10.1109/ICSPC59664.2023.10420149.
20. Guyon, I., Elisseeff, A.: An introduction to variable and feature selection. J. Mach. Learn. Res. **3**(Mar), 1157–1182 (2003)
21. Sameer, S.K.L., Sriramya, P.: Improving the accuracy for prediction of heart disease by novel feature selection scheme using decision tree comparing with Naive-Bayes classifier algorithms. In: 2022 International Conference on Business Analytics for Technology and Security (ICBATS), Dubai, United Arab Emirates, pp. 1–8 (2022). https://doi.org/10.1109/ICBATS54253.2022.9758926
22. Miranda, E., Bhatti, F.M., Aryuni, M., Bernando, C.: Intelligent computational model for early heart disease prediction using logistic regression and stochastic gradient descent (a preliminary study). In: 2021 1st International Conference on Computer Science and Artificial Intelligence (ICCSAI), Jakarta, Indonesia, pp. 11–16 (2021). https://doi.org/10.1109/ICCSAI53272.2021.9609724
23. Shan, Z., et al.: Integration of genetic markers and biomarker data into heart disease prediction models. Bioinformatics **32**(14), 2173–2180 (2016)
24. Singh, A.K., Dwivedi, A., Dubey, A.K.: A well structured and friendly chatbot for primary level heart disease prediction using symptoms. In: 2024 IEEE International Conference on Computing Power and Communication Technologies (IC2PCT), Greater Noida, India, pp. 349–355 (2024). https://doi.org/10.1109/IC2PCT60090.2024.10486654
25. https://www.kaggle.com/code/datafan07/heart-disease-and-some-scikit-learn-magic
26. Chi-Square Test. In: The Concise Encyclopedia of Statistics. Springer, New York (2008). https://doi.org/10.1007/978-0-387-32833-1_57
27. Bevans, R.: An Introduction to t Tests—Definitions, Formula and Examples. Scribbr. https://www.scribbr.com/statistics/t-test/. Accessed 4 July 2024

Development and Implementation of a Learning Management System with Data Analytics for Enhanced Online Education

Xu Aijun[1], Pedro Flores[2](✉), and Muhammad Munsif Farid[2]

[1] Guangzhou Railway Polytechnic, Guangzhou, China
[2] Higher Colleges of Technology, Ras Al Khaimah, UAE
{pflores,mfarid}@hct.ac.ae

Abstract. This study addresses the development and implementation of a Learning Management System (LMS) enhanced with data analytics to improve online education. The research was conducted in response to the challenges faced by a college specializing in rail transit talent, where existing online learning systems lacked capabilities for monitoring, evaluating, and predicting student performance.

Keywords: Learning Management System · SVM · Data Analytics · Online Learning · CRISP-DM · ISO 25010 · Face Detection

1 Introduction

Online education has become a crucial mode of learning, especially in the post-pandemic era. However, traditional LMS platforms often fail to provide comprehensive tools for evaluating and enhancing student performance. This study aims to fill this gap by developing an LMS that integrates advanced data analytics.

In a study by Qing et al. (2015), it was posited that compared with the traditional teaching mode, online teaching has great advantages in both the convenience of resource acquisition and the richness and diversity of learning resources. During the epidemic, the advantages of online teaching were fully reflected. Both teachers and students can "stay at home" and realize two-way interaction at home through the online teaching platform. Teachers teach students professional knowledge, and students gain knowledge and feedback in time. Communication and discussion are very convenient.

With the increase in the number of online education resources, the widespread use of the Internet in education, and the establishment of a national student information database, a huge education data warehouse has been formed, and education data mining has emerged. The data generated in these online education environments is an important basis for decision-making support and improvement in teaching reform. By combining data mining technology to analyze online education data, students' learning environment and learning status can be identified, and education methods can be adjusted to improve the effectiveness of online teaching.

A. Safi et al. (Eds.): ISICS 2024, CCIS 2381, pp. 186–198, 2025.
https://doi.org/10.1007/978-3-031-82931-4_14

As one of the important research directions in educational data mining, student performance prediction is crucial for evaluating and improving teaching quality, as well as guiding students' personalized development. Romero et al. (2010) noted that by analyzing the data generated during students' online learning process, it is possible to predict their academic performance and help teachers identify risky students. Breiki et al. (2019) reported that Teachers can provide targeted learning interventions for students at risk based on the predicted results of academic performance, helping them improve their academic performance and effectively ensuring the quality of online education. At the same time, Rodrigues et al. (2018) reported that the college can also use performance prediction to establish an effective early warning system, provide personalized recommendations for students, improve their online learning experience, and achieve intelligent online education.

This paper adopts big data mining technology and visualization technology to develop a Learning Management System with Data Analytics for the school where the researchers are located. Firstly, a face detection algorithm based on particle filtering and MTCNN is proposed to solve the problem of student face recognition. Secondly, a subspace face recognition method based on LBP and PCA is adopted to recognize the identity of students, solving the problem of student identity authentication during online learning. The SVM based head pose estimation method is used to monitor the learning status of students, solving the problem of online learning status monitoring; Then, based on the behavioral activities of learners at each learning stage, the main influencing factors of online learning performance were analyzed, and a prediction model for student performance and a teaching quality warning model were constructed; Finally, based on the front-end and back-end separation development mode, a Learning Management System was designed and developed, and evaluated using ISO 25010 Software Quality Standards.

2 Objectives

The primary objectives of this study include:

2.1 Developing an LMS that incorporates data analytics for monitoring and evaluating student performance.
2.2 Identifying the significant predictors of student performance in online learning.
2.3 Creating a prediction model to provide decision support for student learning interventions.
2.4 Ensuring the developed LMS complies with ISO 25010 software quality standards.

3 Statement of the Problem

The main challenges identified include difficulties in evaluating the quality of online teaching, monitoring student learning status, and collecting learning behavior data. Additionally, the existing systems lack early warning mechanisms and value-added evaluations for students' online learning performance.

4 Review of Related Literature

Online learning behavior data has emerged as a critical resource in educational research, offering insights into learner interactions and performance within digital learning environments. This review synthesizes current literature on the topic, highlighting key studies and methodologies used to analyze and utilize online learning behavior data.

4.1 Online Learning Behavior Data

Online learning behavior data encompasses a wide range of traceable activities such as access patterns, interactions, discussions, and queries within online learning systems (Zhang et al., 2016). It provides a comprehensive view of learner engagement and performance, surpassing traditional survey methods in its ability to capture real-time, granular data on learning behaviors (Fa-ti et al., 2019). Researchers have focused on establishing models that correlate academic outcomes with various aspects of learning behavior. For instance, Godwin et al. (2016) explored how attention distribution patterns during learning tasks correlate with student characteristics and instructional design, offering insights into optimizing classroom attention strategies. Alkhattabi (2016) used machine learning to mine dynamic and static learner data to enhance learning effectiveness.

Studies have categorized and analyzed diverse online learning behaviors to understand their impact on learning outcomes. Ke (2017) developed interaction models to visualize learner engagements, providing insights into effective online learning strategies. Lin-Jing et al. (2018) classified behaviors to identify patterns that influence group learning dynamics, while Lu et al. (2020) used cluster analysis to differentiate learner groups based on behavioral traits, emphasizing the role of homework engagement in academic performance.

4.2 Facial Rccognition in Online Learning

Facial recognition technology has emerged as a powerful tool for enhancing online learning environments. Initially developed for biometric verification, facial recognition algorithms have evolved to analyze facial expressions, monitor attention levels, and personalize learning experiences based on emotional and cognitive states (Felzenszwalb et al., 2014).

Facial recognition enables real-time monitoring of learner attention and engagement during online sessions. This capability allows educators to adjust instructional strategies based on student responses and attention levels (Girshick et al., 2014). By integrating facial recognition data with online learning behavior, personalized learning pathways can be created. For example, Ren et al. (2015) demonstrated how facial recognition can adjust content delivery based on learner emotions and cognitive states, thereby enhancing learning outcomes. Facial recognition can supplement behavior analysis derived from online learning data. It provides additional context by analyzing facial expressions and reactions during learning activities, offering deeper insights into learner reactions and preferences (Jia-Jun, 2018).

4.3 Ethical and Practical Considerations

While promising, the integration of facial recognition in online learning raises ethical concerns regarding privacy, consent, and data security (Sun et al., 2013). Educators and developers must navigate these challenges to ensure responsible use of facial recognition technologies in educational settings.

4.4 Data Mining and Predictive Analytics

Utilizing advanced data mining and predictive analytics, researchers have forecasted learning performance and provided early warnings for at-risk students. Bhutto et al. (2020) applied machine learning algorithms to predict future learning achievements, showcasing the efficacy of algorithms like support vector machines in educational forecasting. Xu et al. (2019) integrated learning behavior features to predict academic outcomes, demonstrating improved prediction accuracy with expanded feature sets.

In summary, while challenges such as data integration and model scalability persist, ongoing advancements in data science and educational technology promise continued innovation in utilizing online learning behavior data for educational enhancement. By combining insights from learner interactions with real-time facial analysis, educators can personalize learning experiences, monitor engagement, and optimize teaching strategies effectively.

5 Conceptual Framework

This conceptual framework synthesizes the CRISP-DM (Cross Industry Standard Process for Data Mining) model with an educational data mining (EDM) approach to enhance understanding and application in educational research contexts. The framework aims to guide the systematic exploration and utilization of data mining techniques for educational data analysis and decision-making.

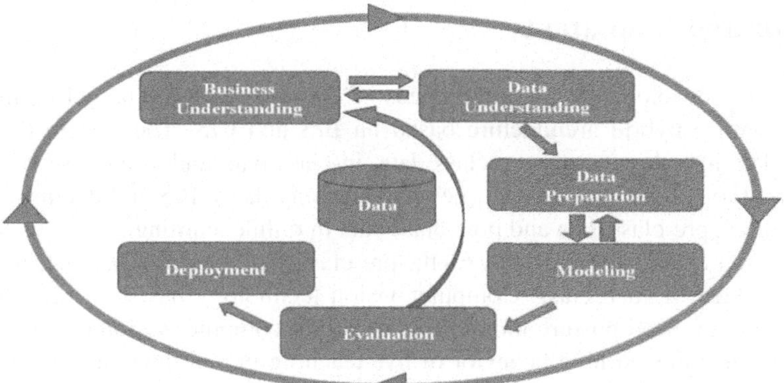

Fig. 1. CRISP-DM Overview

CRISP-DM provides a structured approach for data mining projects across various industries. It consists of six main phases as illustrated in Fig. 1.

The EDM model focuses on leveraging data mining techniques specifically for educational contexts (Fig. 2).

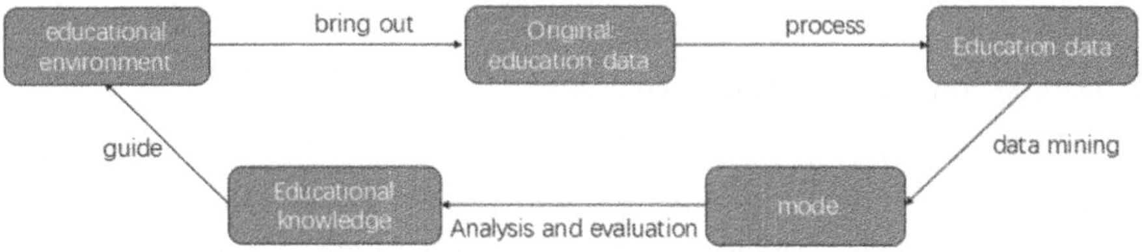

Fig. 2. Educational Data Mining (EDM) Model

5.1 Integration of CRISP-DM and EDM

Aligning project goals with educational objectives is essential, identifying key metrics and desired outcomes from data analysis. This involves comprehensively exploring educational data sources to assess quality and relevance, using techniques like log collection and manual aggregation for diverse datasets. The next step is cleaning, integrating, and transforming data to meet modeling requirements, addressing noise, incompleteness, and inconsistency. Selecting appropriate data mining algorithms, such as clustering and classification, is crucial, considering methods like K-means clustering for discovering patterns in student performance. Models are evaluated for accuracy, relevance to educational theories, and practical applicability in improving teaching and learning. Finally, translating data mining results into actionable insights for educational stakeholders enhances decision-making processes, enabling personalized learning interventions and curriculum adjustments.

6 Scope and Limitations

The system is developed to meet the needs of classes which are taught online and is designed with a hybrid architecture based on B/S and C/S. The system divides the learning data into three parts: pre-class data, in-class data and after-class data. C/S is mainly used to collect in-class data (i.e., live teaching data). B/S architecture is mainly used to collect pre-class data and post-class data in online learning.

This system compares and analyzes the pre-class data and post-class data to evaluate the value added of each class. Computer vision technology based on face detection, face recognition, head posture monitoring and other computer vision technologies are used to monitor the learning behavior of live teaching in real time, and timely remind students to adjust their learning status. Based on students' pre-class data, in-class data and after-class data, the evaluation and early warning of students' course performance are carried out. Based on the early warning situation of the whole class, the teacher's teaching quality is early warning. The teaching quality of teachers is evaluated according to the course results of all students.

Users of this system include students, teachers, and educational administrators. Users have different access rights to protect the data privacy of each user. At the same time, the ISO/IEC 25010 standard is used to evaluate the compliance of the development system.

7 Methods

7.1 Research Design

This research employs a combination of descriptive and developmental methods to design and develop a Learning Management System (LMS) with Data Analytics capabilities. The descriptive method was used to gather information on the current system status and identify issues faced by participants. Concurrently, the developmental method, specifically Feature Driven Development (FDD), was used to guide the systematic development of the LMS.

7.2 Participants of the Study

The participants of this study include system administrators, educational administrators, teachers, and students.

7.3 Data Gathering Procedures

Data gathering was conducted through automated logging of user interactions within the LMS. Specific procedures include:

- System Usage Logging: Capture user activities such as login times, course access, material downloads, and assignment submissions.
- Behavioral Data Collection: Record interactions during live teaching sessions, including chat logs, participation rates, and session duration.
- Assessment and Evaluation: Gather data on student performance through quizzes, tests, and final exam results.

7.4 Data Analysis

Data analysis involved the utilization of data mining techniques, focusing on clustering and classification algorithms to identify patterns in student learning behaviors, evaluate academic and performance trends, and provide early warnings for potential issues in student performance and teaching quality.

7.5 Development Process

The development followed the Feature Driven Development (FDD) cycle, consisting of the following stages.

- Overall Model Development: Gather functional requirements and outline system architecture.
- Feature List Creation: Refine functionalities into manageable feature sets.
- Feature Planning: Prioritize and assign features for development cycles (typically two weeks per feature set).
- Feature Design: Detail design features based on domain models and establish project milestones.
- Implementation: Code development, integration, and iterative testing of features.

8 Results and Discussions

This part presents the algorithm used in the system development, the significant predictors of student performance in online learning, the prediction model for providing decision support in student learning interventions, and the extent to which the LMS complies with ISO 25010 Software Quality Standards.

8.1 The Algorithm used in the Development of the System Face Detection Algorithm Based on Improved Particle Filter and MTCNN

Face detection is crucial for live teaching environments to recognize student states. The study combines particle filtering and Multi-task Convolutional Neural Network (MTCNN) to improve face detection efficiency and accuracy.

Particle Filtering is a Bayesian filtering method tracks faces by initializing particles in the image and iteratively updating their weights based on similarity to the tracking area. It is robust in non-Gaussian, nonlinear environments (Fig. 3).

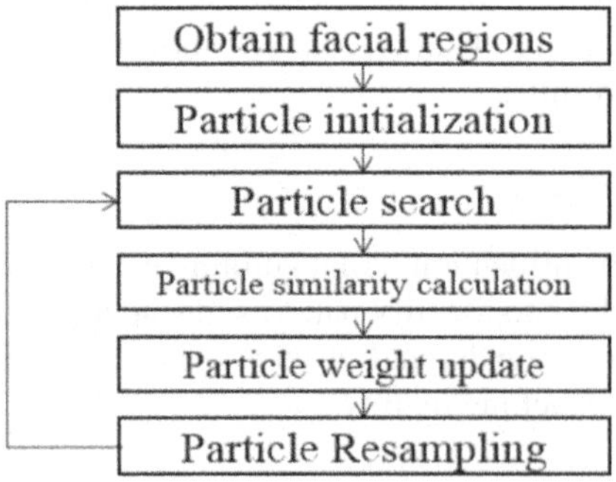

Fig. 3. Flow chart of face tracking algorithm based on particle filter

MTCNN is a three-layer network (P-net, R-net, O-net) accurately detects facial features by processing candidate boxes through non-maximum suppression and bounding box regression. However, it is computationally intensive for real-time applications. Currently, video-based face detection algorithms mainly rely on single frame detection of full images and run detection algorithms to detect faces in each frame of the video. Multitask Convolutional Neural Network (MTCNN) is a mainstream method for face detection in recent years, which can accurately locate five key parts of the face. Jie (2020) pointed out that MTCNN adopts a three-layer cascaded neural network structure, consisting of P-net layer, R-net layer, and O-net layer, as shown in Fig. 4.

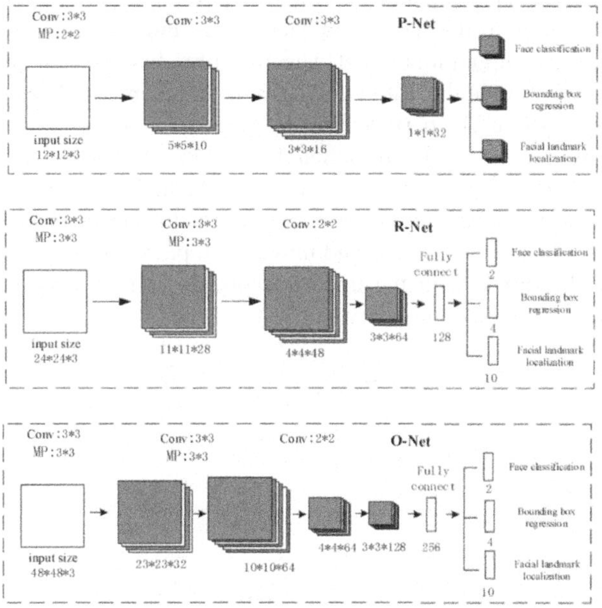

Fig. 4. MTCNN Network Architecture

The basic idea of MTCNN is to use image pyramid technology to scale the image at different levels and then input it into the P-net (Proposal Network) to generate facial candidate boxes. Features and calibration positions are preliminarily extracted using FCN (Full Convolutional Networks), and non-maximum suppression (NMS) excludes candidate boxes with high overlap. Bounding box regression corrects these boxes, which are then intercepted from the original image and input into R-net (Refine Network). R-net performs more detailed processing and further filters the candidate boxes using NMS and border regression techniques. O-net (Output Network) processes the candidate boxes from R-net, ultimately determining the positions of the face and its key points.

However, MTCNN's frame-by-frame detection consumes significant time and memory, making real-time analysis challenging and prone to errors due to facial movement and deflection. To improve efficiency, this study integrates a particle filter algorithm with MTCNN. The algorithm first uses a particle filter to obtain a prior box during the MTCNN prediction stage, then performs detection. This approach avoids redundant convolution operations, simplifies the three-level cascaded network to particle filtering, and the detection of R-net and O-net, reducing the running frequency of P-net and narrowing the facial retrieval range by the neural network.

The study integrates particle filtering into MTCNN, reducing redundant operations and the need for running full MTCNN on each frame, thus enhancing real-time performance and reducing computational load. The algorithm first uses the MTCNN network to detect the face position in the initial video frame and then initializes the particle filter based on this information. The particle filter is started using target information, particles are resampled, and their weights are updated based on assigned weights and the state transition matrix. Particle swarm optimization predicts the face pre-selection box, which is then passed into the R-net and O-net networks for further detection. Due to potential errors from facial angle deviation and movement, particles are periodically updated through a reset algorithm, with the update frequency determined by an appropriate threshold N based on video complexity (Fig. 5).

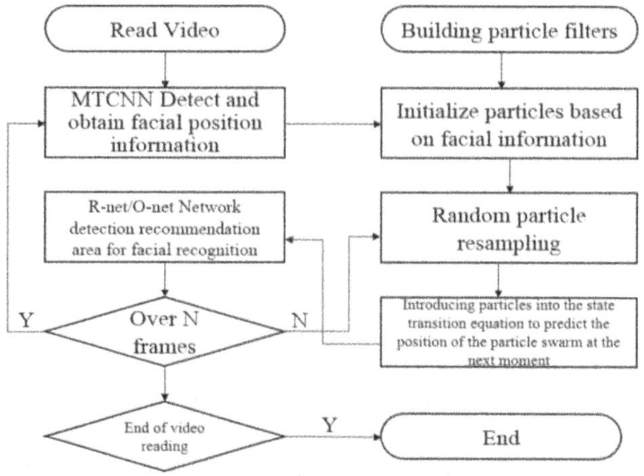

Fig. 5. Flow chart of face detection algorithm based on improved particle filter and MTCNN

8.2 Subspace Face Recognition Based on LBP and PCA

To ensure accurate identity recognition before assessing head pose and facial expressions, the study uses a combination of Local Binary Patterns (LBP) and Principal Component Analysis (PCA).

- LBP: This method divides the face into small blocks, compares pixel values to form binary patterns, and constructs histograms for texture analysis.

- PCA: This statistical method reduces dimensionality by transforming the data into a lower-dimensional space while retaining important features.
- Combined Approach: By merging LBP's local texture analysis with PCA's global feature reduction, the study achieves a robust face recognition system that balances detail and overall structure (Fig. 6).

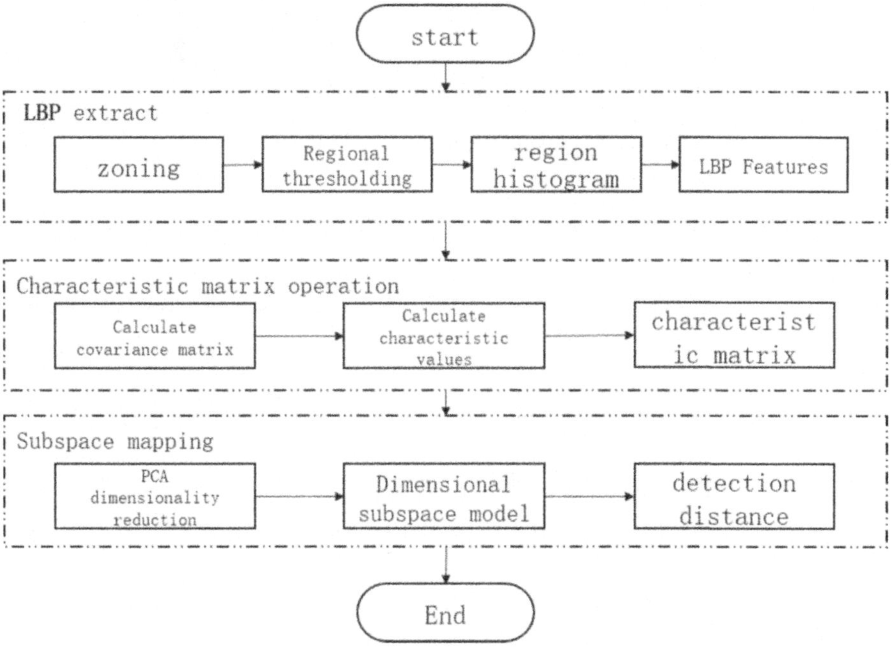

Fig. 6. Face recognition process based on LBP and PCA

8.3 Head Pose Estimation Based on SVM

Head pose estimation technology, developed from facial key point detection, can reflect a person's physiological state, such as mental exhaustion or lack of concentration indicated by frequent head bowing. This study identifies five head postures: head up, head down, left leaning, right leaning, and head up. Euler angles, using the Cartesian coordinate system, represent 3D head rotations: pitch (up/down), yaw (left/right deviation), and roll (left/right displacement).

- Euler Angles: Used to represent 3D head rotations (pitch, yaw, roll), derived from facial key points detected by MTCNN.
- Support Vector Machine (SVM): A classifier that finds the optimal hyperplane to separate different head poses based on Euler angles, enabling precise estimation of head orientation (Fig. 7).

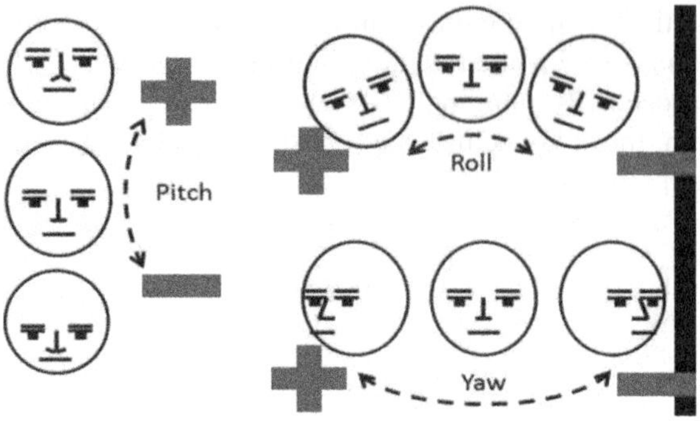

Fig. 7. Schematic Diagram of Head Euler Angle

8.4 The Significant Predictors of the Student Performance in Online Learning

This part identifies significant predictors of student performance in online learning by analyzing learner activities across three stages: pre-class, in-class, and post-class (Fig. 8).

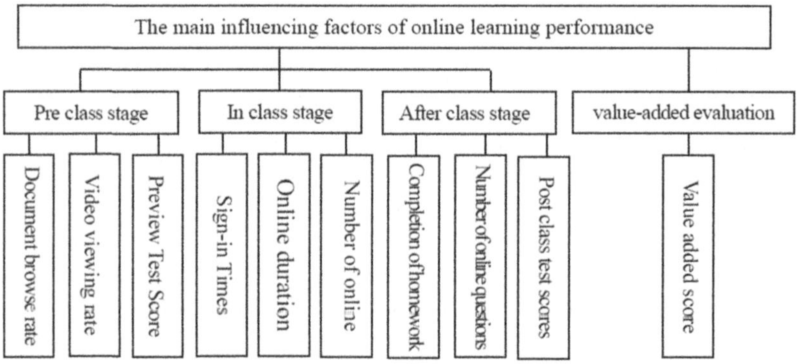

Fig. 8. The main influencing factors of online learning performance

In the pre-class stage, important factors include the number of preview document views, preview video views, and pre-class test scores. During the in-class stage, key factors are the number of logins, online duration, and the number of online questions. Post-class performance is influenced by homework completion rates, the number of online questions, and after-class test scores. Additionally, value-added evaluation, which focuses on learners' progress rather than their initial knowledge base, is a critical aspect of this study. This evaluation measures learning progress by comparing pre-class and post-class scores and calculating the value-added score based on learners' improvement.

The study uses a percentage system to measure these factors, assigning scores to document browsing rates, video viewing rates, preview test scores, login counts, online duration, online questions, homework completion, and after-class test scores. The overall performance is calculated as the average of the scores from each stage, with the value-added score reflecting the learners' progress throughout the course.

8.5 Learning Management System with Data Analytics

To test the functionality and interface of the online learning management system, this paper first lists four basic data tables. Table 1 is the basic data table of the 5 courses that have already been launched, including the total number of documents that need to be previewed, the total number of videos that need to be previewed, the total score of test papers, the number of classes that have already started, the total duration of class hours that have already started, the number of homework assigned by teachers, and the total score of post class test papers that have been distributed for each course.

8.6 The extent of Compliance of the LMS to ISO 25010 Software Quality Standards

The LMS was tested and evaluated by IT experts. The degree of compliance with ISO 25010 software quality standards for the developed Learning Management System with Data Analytics was assessed in terms of functional applicability, performance efficiency, compatibility, availability, reliability, security, maintainability, and portability.

9 Conclusions

The implementation of a data-analytics-enhanced LMS significantly improves the ability to monitor, evaluate, and predict student performance in online learning environments. The study highlights the importance of integrating advanced data analytics into LMS platforms to address the challenges faced in online education. The developed system not only meets the ISO 25010 software quality standards but also provides a robust tool for educational institutions to enhance teaching quality and student learning outcomes. By developing an LMS that incorporates data analytics, this study provides a valuable framework for improving online education through better monitoring, evaluation, and prediction of student performance.

References

Bhutto, E.S., Siddiqui, I.F., Arain, Q.A., Anwar, M.: Predicting students' academic performance through supervised machine learning. Int. Conf. Info. Sci. Comm. Technol. (ICISCT). **2020**, 1–6 (2020)

Breiki, B.A., Zaki, N., Mohamed, E.A. Using Educational data mining techniques to predict student performance. In: Proceedings of the 2019 International Conference on Electrical and Computing Technologies and Applications (ICECTA), pp. 1–5. IEEE (2019)

Felzenszwalb, Pedro, F., et al.: Object Detection with Discriminatively Trained Part-Based Models. IEEE Transactions on Pattern Analysis& Machine Intelligence **32**(9), 1627–1645 (2014)

Girshick, R., Donahue, J., Darrell, T., et al.: Rich feature hierarchies for accurate object detection and semantic segmentation. Proceedings of the IEEE conference on computer vision and pattern recognition, pp. 580–587 (2014)

Godwin, K.E., et al.: Off-task behavior in elementary school children. Learn. Instr. **44**, 128–143 (2016)

Jia-jun, W.: Research on face detection algorithm based on SSD convolution network, master's thesis. Xiamen University (2018)

Jie, Z.: The current situation and trend of online learning -- taking online learning of English subject in Anhui Province as an example Primary and secondary school principals (10), 36–38 (2020)

Ke, Z.: Research on learner interaction analysis model and application in online learning space. Research on audio-visual education **05**, 43–48 (2017)

Lu, Q., Feng-guang, J.: Cluster analysis of Muke learner groups - take "STEM course design and case analysis" Muke as an example Modern Educational Technology (01), 100–106 (2020)

Qing, Z., Chao, M., Dan, Y.: Overview of research progress in education data mining. Journal of Software **11**, 3026–3042 (2015)

Ren, S., He, K., Girshick, R., et al.: Faster r-cnn: Towards real-time object detection with region proposal networks. Advances in neural information processing systems, 28 (2015)

Rodrigues, M.W., Isotani, S., Zarate, L.E.: Educational data mining: A review of evaluation process in the e-learning. Telematics and Informatics **35**(6), 1701–1717 (2018)

Romero, C., Ventura, S.: Educational data mining and learning analytics: An updated survey. Wiley Interdisciplinary Reviews: Data Mining and Knowledge Discovery **10**(3), e1355 (2020)

Sun, Y., Wang, X., Tang, X.: convolutional network cascade for facial point detection. Proceedings of the IEEE conference on computer vision and pattern recognition, pp. 3476–3483 (2013)

Xu, X., Wang, J.Z., Wu, R.: Prediction of academic performance associated with internet usage behaviors using machine learning algorithms. Comput. Hum. Behav. **98**, 166–173 (2019)

Zhang, K., Zhang, Z., Li, Z., et al.: Joint face detection and alignment using multitask cascaded convolutional networks. IEEE Signal Process. Lett. **23**(10), 1499–1503 (2016)

VidLyze: Video Content Toxicity Identification Tool Using Natural Language Processing (NLP) and Machine Learning

Ahmad Obaid Alfalasi, Mohammad Matar, Mohammad Sameer, Sharmila Siddartha, and Anang Hudaya Muhamad Amin(✉)

Faculty of Computer and Information Science, Higher Colleges of Technology, Dubai Campus - Academic City, Dubai, United Arab Emirates
{H00455070,H00385661,H00426660,ssiddartha,aamin}@hct.ac.ae

Abstract. Toxicity identification and classification in multimedia contents is becoming an important field of research, particularly with the massive amount of multimedia contents that are produced and published on the web. Toxic multimedia content such as the use of inappropriate and bad words and swearing are not suitable for general audiences, especially for young children who are highly impressionable. In this paper, we present our current work-in-progress on designing and developing analytics model known as VidLyze for identifying different levels of toxicity in a given video, based on the text analysis approach. The goal of VidLyze is to use machine learning and natural language processing (NLP) to make a system that can watch and analyze video material for toxic contents. The goal is to find toxic, inappropriate or insulting content in videos so that people can watch them safely. The work carried out involved extracting video contents with different formats, converting audio to text in order to obtain the audio transcript, and performing text toxicity analysis on the audio transcript using a suitable machine learning algorithm. The proposed analytical model requires NLP integration for analyzing human languages from video and audio, and the need for datasets that are large enough to train the respective model. We adopt the Long Short-Term Memory (LSTM) recurrent neural networks to train the model for classifying toxicity based on large textual datasets. VidLyze is made to be a safe and reliable method that makes content moderation better and makes sure everyone has a good time watching.

Keywords: Video Analytics · Speech Recognition · Machine Learning

1 Introduction

In the constantly changing world of technology, video content and transmission has solidified itself as an essential way to communicate and share information. Because there are so many platforms, like YouTube, TikTok, social media and

A. Safi et al. (Eds.): ISICS 2024, CCIS 2381, pp. 199–214, 2025.
https://doi.org/10.1007/978-3-031-82931-4_15

news websites, a huge number of videos with a huge range of topics are posted every day [8]. Even though the ease of access and variety of content gives users more opportunity to create and share contents and information, it also makes content moderation a complex task, especially when different parts of the world have different cultural norms and legal requirements. The United Arab Emirates (UAE) is a great example of this regulatory divergence because they have strict rules about what content material is considered acceptable. The National Media Office in the UAE is the regulatory body responsible for strategic management of media outlets and content. The Federal Decree-Law No. 55 of 2023 regulates all media activities and provides strict guidelines to the media content. In this law, one of the standards concerning media content states that residents should "respect the culture and civilization, national identity, and values of the UAE community", indicating the necessity of validating media content accordingly.

In an attempt to close the gap between the growing amount of video materials that can be accessed over the Internet and good content moderation process, we propose the use of Natural Language Processing (NLP) to enable seamless content moderation for inappropriate words used in the video materials. Our aim is to make an automated system that can turn spoken words in video clips into text and perform toxicity classification based on the sentiment analysis on the derived transcript. This multistep process includes audio extraction, speech-to-text conversion, and sentiment analysis. Together, they meet the urgent need for better and more complete content moderation tools [2]. With this approach, it does not only provide a fast and effective way to moderate content, but it also makes it easier to find and report content that might be inappropriate, illegal or insulting.

In addition to enabling better content moderation for video materials online, our proposed work is also important in order to make it easier for digital content platform owners, regulatory bodies, and content authors to follow different rules and guidelines. For companies that work with digital content, it fits with their business goals because it makes content moderation more efficient and scalable. This makes the internet a safer and more appropriate place to be for people with diverse ethnicity and ages.

In this paper, we will explore the problem in more details, describe the aims and goals of the work, list our contributions and deliverables, and give a full evaluation of the proposed solution. The paper is structured as follows: Sect. 2 provides a review of current works that are related to our proposed solution. Section 3 describes the methodology that has been adopted in developing the toxicity analysis model and the VidLyze tool for detecting toxicity in the video content. Our proposed design and implementation of VidLyze content toxicity identification tool is presented in Sect. 4. Finally, Sect. 5 concludes the paper.

2 Related Works

In today's digital age, increasing amount of content on video has reached exceptional levels with millions of video clips being published every day on multiple platforms. However, the rapid growth in video content creates a significant issue when it comes down to effective control by humans and monitoring [3]. The huge amount of video being produced and distributed renders it impossible to manually evaluate the correctness and legitimacy of the contents, which leads to the urgent requirement for automatic approaches. The problem is further complicated by regional and cultural variations as well as strict legal structures, like the ones in the United Arab Emirates (UAE) as described by Mouheb et al. [15], in their works on detecting cyberbullying in the context of Arabic social media communications. Similarly, Khairy et al. [9] have also discussed these issues and the use of abusive language in arabic content within the context of social media networks. This creates complexities for the process of moderation for content, making it challenging for moderators to manage and guarantee the compliance of different rules and norms. The current issue is caused by the diversity of the content available, from educational and informative content as well as potentially offensive or objectionable material. Manual scrutiny of this huge and diverse collection of videos is not just ineffective but also susceptible to ignorance in relations to intricate subtle linguistic and cultural nuances as well as complexities in determining compliance.

The foundation of proposed VidLyze's content moderation tool arises from the need to address content moderation challenges, particularly in the United Arab Emirates (UAE) and similar regions. There are a number of incidents over the past years, such as Netflix broadcasting content that violated UAE's media broadcasting regulations [10], emphasize the urgency of this issue. VidLyze aims to harness machine learning and artificial intelligence (AI) technologies to tackle this kind of challenges.

In our research, we reviewed some of the existing projects like YouTube and parental control applications to identify their technical deficiencies. For instance, YouTube predominantly relies on image analysis and metadata, leaving gaps in its ability to detect inappropriate audio content or adapt swiftly to changing trends in language and sentiments. As reported by Dutta et al. [4], YouTube may unintentionally proliferated various illegal activities such as artificial boosting of views through advertisements or other collusive contents. On the other hand, parental control applications, while effective to some extent, often block entire applications or websites, lack real-time analysis, and necessitate manual specification of content to be blocked, especially if there is still access provided to the web [1]. Yousaf and Nawaz [19] proposed a deep learning based approach for inappropriate content detection and classification of YouTube videos, using combined convolutional neural network (CNN) and bidirectional LSTM algorithms. The work carried out by Yousefi and Emmanouilidou [20] also focuses on audio-based toxic language classification on online social networking platform, using self-attentive CNNs. On the other hand, some works on toxicity identification in online content are mainly focusing on the textual data that is obtained through comments on media. For instance, the work of Tarafder et al. [18] is focusing on developing an automated tool for identifying toxic comments on live streaming YouTube videos using NLP approach. Relevant to this approach, Garlapati et al. [5] also working on classifying toxic comments on social media using a combination of NLP and LSTM model. Their work demonstrates high accuracy in identifying toxic comments from the social media platforms.

VidLyze proposes a more robust solution. It focuses on analyzing the audible content of videos, leveraging the power of machine learning and artificial intelligence. By doing so, the aim is to detect improper audio streams in videos effectively. Additionally, the proposed solution utilizes Natural Language Processing (NLP) algorithms, including speech recognition and sentiment analysis, to comprehend linguistic nuances and sentiments within audio dialogues. Our proposed solution is inspired by the works carried out by Lekshmi and Anoop [12] and Kumar and Kavitha [11] in identifying sentiment and content analyses. In addition, we implemented a machine learning approach for multi-class classification of toxic contents using bidirectional Sequential Long Short-Term Memory (LSTM) recurrent neural networks.

This approach ensures VidLyze's adaptability to evolving content and social language trends. Rather than blocking entire platforms, our system operates at a granular level, allowing legitimate content to flourish while filtering out offensive material. Furthermore, VidLyze conducts real-time analysis of videos loaded on users' devices, reducing the need for manual content specification.

3 Methodology

The proposed VidLyze platform is a video content monitoring system that analyzes audio and visual material using machine learning and natural language processing (NLP). The technology basically detects unpleasant or objectionable content to help moderate content and ensure a safe viewing experience. The VidLyze domain requirements specify the needs for video content monitoring context and boundaries. These requirements include uploading videos for analysis, support for multiple video formats, user-friendly interface, offensive content analysis using machine learning, detection of offensive language, flagging of offensive videos, confidence scoring for detected content, API integration, data protection compliance, and scalability for large video uploads and analyses.

We have adopted an agile methodology for developing the proposed system using Scrum to plan and execute this research. To implement the research we have applied NLP approach on the dataset to convert the audio to text and machine learning to perform sentiment analysis on the refined and converted audio-to-text data. In the realm of machine learning for sentiment analysis of video dialogues, the initial phase involves defining the problem at hand. This entails a meticulous understanding of the task, which is to classify sentiments into categories like positive, negative, neutral, or hate speech within the contents of a video. We have adopted the multi-class classification approach in classifying toxic contents from the obtained dataset. This approach is commonly used in text classification as described in [13]. Further details on the toxic content classes used in this work can be referred in Sect. 4.3.

3.1 Requirements Analysis

The VidLyze content moderation system uses advanced NLP algorithms and machine learning to assess video content for offensive or inappropriate content. Content filtering is automated to improve digital platform safety and compliance. VidLyze keeps consumers safe and welcome on digital platforms with real-time analysis and actionable information. Validation was crucial to VidLyze's success. The system's usability, dependability, and user experience were assessed using rigorous software verification, increased validation, and a focused acceptability survey. NLP algorithms for video audio transcription, sentiment analysis, and improper content detection were validated for accuracy and responsiveness. Usability, efficiency, and power consumption were evaluated. Survey was sent to potential users, digital platform administrators, and NLP professionals. VidLyze's audience satisfaction and opportunities for improvement were assessed by the survey. Many survey respondents praised VidLyze's new video moderation technique but suggested improvements in accuracy, user interface design, and feature set.

VidLyze accomplishes all the specified requirements including input and output mechanisms, processes, control, performance, and usability requirements after functional and non-functional validation. Video upload, audio transcription, offensive content identification, and real-time analysis were needed. Non-functional requirements included usability, reliability, performance, scalability, maintainability, security, compatibility, and efficiency. The system combines NLP techniques, user interface design, hardware, and software to analyze video content. Design involved prototyping, NLP and machine learning framework integration, and comprehensive function planning. The VidLyze GUI simplifies content moderation, providing a smooth user experience. Uploading videos and getting real-time offensive content analysis is done on the Offensive Content Prediction Page. Includes video upload, analysis progress indicator, results display, and action guidance.

3.2 Design and Development

The design and development of VidLyze video analytics tool follow an agile methodology. In developing the analytics model, we follow the common machine learning approaches with data collection, processing, learning, testing and analysis processes. Figure 1 shows the proposed workflow for the creation of VidLyze video-based content analysis model.

As shown in the figure, the design and development of the proposed system follows the following steps:

Video Data Collection and Preprocessing. This step revolves around gathering the requisite dataset. This dataset serves as the foundation for our machine learning model design and implementation. It should contain video dialogues already annotated with their corresponding sentiments. However, raw data is

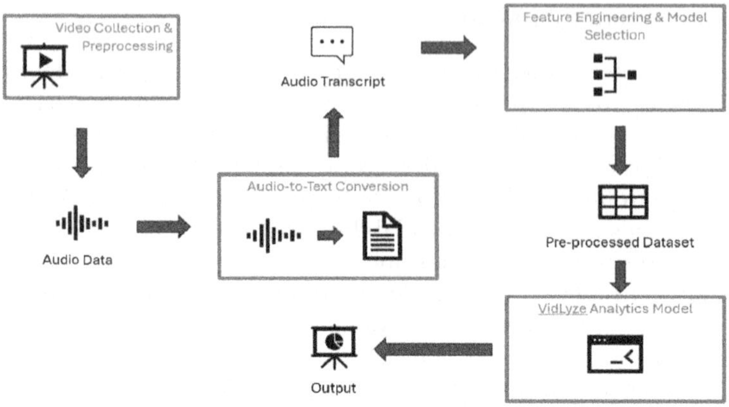

Fig. 1. VidLyze video analytics model process flow for video data extraction and analysis.

often messy and inconsistent, so thorough pre-processing is essential to standardize the format and structure of the dataset. The video data can either be obtained manually or streamed from YouTube. As such, we use pytube library that is written using Python programming language, to enable the VidLyze application to extract videos directly from YouTube.

Feature Engineering. In machine learning, our algorithms require structured input data. Therefore, feature engineering was performed on the obtained dataset, where we select and transform relevant attributes from our dataset into a format that our models can process effectively. This step influences the quality of our model's predictions.

Model Selection. Once we have prepared the data, it's time to choose an appropriate machine learning model. Common choices for sentiment analysis include neural networks, support vector machines, or decision trees. The selection process considers factors like model complexity, interpretability, and performance on specific set of tasks. For the proposed video analytics scheme, we have adopted the Sequential Long Short-Term Memory (LSTM) model [7] for analyzing the audio transcript for different levels of toxicity. LSTM is a type of recurrent neural networks (RNN) that is commonly being used in solving analytical problems containing relevant data with large differences [21]. LSTM has been found to be the most effective solution to sequence prediction problems, since it has a capability to remember patterns for a large number of sequences [14]. This particular feature plays a vital role in toxicity classification in audio transcript for a given video. Figure 2 shows the LSTM architecture for text classification and prediction.

Note that in LSTM model the standard neural network unit i only consists of the activation a_i, and the output activation b_i using the *tanh* activation function as shown here:

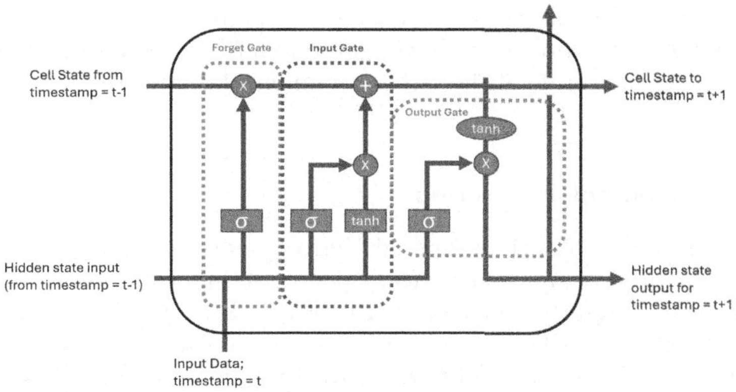

Fig. 2. LSTM neural network architecture for text classification and prediction.

$$b_i = tanh(a_i). \quad (1)$$

Model Training and Evaluation. Training the selected model involves exposing it to the prepared dataset, allowing it to learn the underlying patterns between video dialogues and sentiments. During this phase, the model fine-tunes its internal parameters to make accurate predictions. It's akin to a student absorbing knowledge from a textbook. To gauge the model's proficiency, we evaluate its performance on a separate dataset that it has not encountered during training. Metrics such as accuracy, precision, and recall help us in measuring its effectiveness in sentiment analysis and classification. If the model does not meet the specified performance criteria, we iterate the training process, adjusting hyper parameters or incorporating additional features.

Model Deployment. Upon achieving a satisfactory level of performance, the model is ready for deployment. It becomes a practical tool for automating sentiment analysis in video dialogues, assisting content moderators in their tasks.

4 VidLyze Content Toxicity Identification Model

VidLyze content moderation tool is deployed on Google cloud infrastructure with integrated Google Colab platform. Google Colab provides a Platform-as-a-Service (PaaS) cloud implementation that enables applications to be deployed seamlessly with minimum configuration requirements. We used cutting-edge NLP and machine learning frameworks for the main part of our text analysis. It is very important to have these frameworks in order to transcribe audio from videos into text, do sentiment analysis, and put material into groups based on set criteria. These technologies were chosen because they have been shown to be accurate at understanding language, be able to handle a wide range of languages and dialects, and help with ongoing learning and adapting to new information.

VidLyze content moderation tool comprises a number of different components including audio extraction, speech recognition and text analysis. The following subsections describe in detail how these components have been developed and implemented.

4.1 Video Content Extraction

As described in Sect. 3.2, the proposed VidLyze video analytics tool is written using Python programming language. For extracting video content from the YouTube, we used the PyTube module to download the YouTube video into our video repository. Figure 3 shows the script used to download the Youtube videos. Note that the script uses YouTube video URLs as inputs. These URLs are stored in a Python list. The script will then download the video content as .mp4 file into the specified local folder.

Fig. 3. Python script containing function to download YouTube videos to local folder.

Once the video has been downloaded, the next step in the content extraction is to extract the audio component of the content. To accomplish this task, we implement a script with MoviePy Python library that contain built-in objects and functions for video editing and processing. The extraction process involves saving the audio segment of the video content into an audio file. Figure 4 shows a code snippet on how this is achieved.

Note that *audio_clip* object is an object that is created to store the audio content of the *video_clip*. Both objects were created using the VideoFileClip() function of MoviePy library. The audio file is saved as .wav file.

```
try:
    # Load the video clip
    video_clip = VideoFileClip(video_path)

    # Extract the audio
    audio_clip = video_clip.audio
    output_audio_path = video_name.replace('.mp4', '')+'.wav'
    # Save the extracted audio
    audio_clip.write_audiofile(output_audio_path)

    print(f"Audio extracted successfully to: {output_audio_path}")

except Exception as e:
    print(f"Error: {e}")
```

Fig. 4. Audio extraction from the video content using objects and functions derived from MoviePy library.

4.2 Audio-to-Text Conversion

As part of the data processing tasks, the created audio file from the audio-to-text conversion function would need to be transcribed into text, prior to the input towards the machine learning model for content toxicity classification. Our proposed solution implements the audio-to-text conversion function using speech recognition module by OpenAI, known as Whisper [17]. *Whisper* is a general-purpose, state-of-the-art speech recognition model that is trained on a large dataset of diverse audio. It is also a form of multi-tasking model that enables multilingual speech recognition and translation, as well as language identification [16]. Whisper is basically a transformer-based encoder-decoder model that was trained on 680,000 hours of labelled speech data annotated using large-scale weak supervision.

There are different models available on Whisper, depending on the parameter sizes and trained languages. For this work, we implement our audio-to-text conversion process using Whisper's base model, that can support up to 74 million parameters and trained using English-only and Multilingual datasets. Figure 5 shows our Whisper base model implementation on the VidLyze audio transcription module.

4.3 Bidirectional LSTM Model Deployment

For the purpose of training our analytics model using Bidifectional LSTM algorithm, we have used the dataset from Kaggle, on Toxic Tweets Challenge [6]. The dataset contains large number of Wikipedia comments that have been pre-labelled manually for toxic behaviour. There are six types of toxicity, including *toxic, severe_toxic, obscene, threat, insult, and identity_hate.* Figure 6 shows samples of the dataset that has been extracted.

The training dataset contains both neutral and toxic comments. Table 1 shows the number of samples with assigned labels.

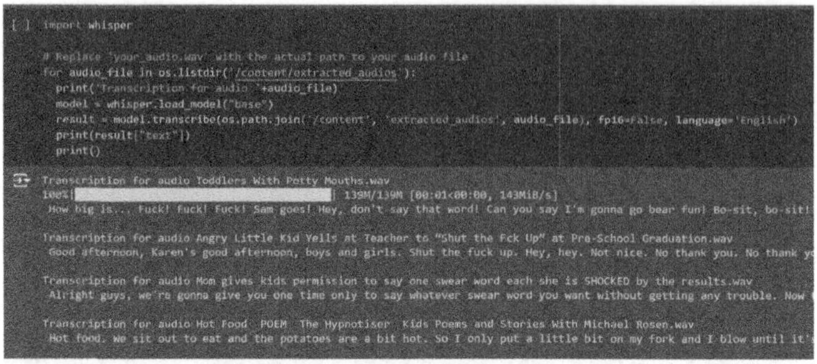

Fig. 5. Whisper audio-to-text conversion module implementation.

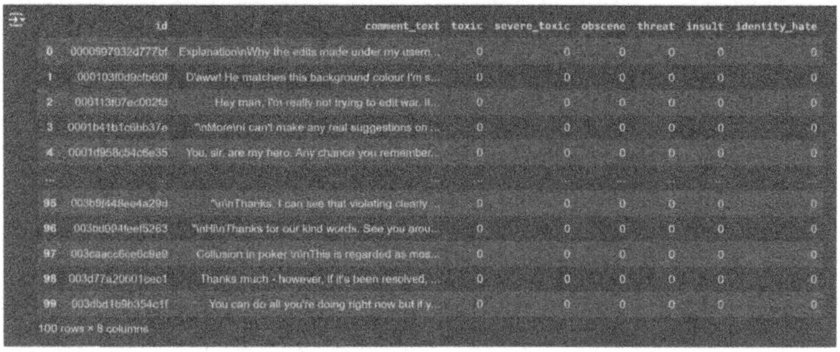

	id	comment_text	toxic	severe_toxic	obscene	threat	insult	identity_hate
0	0000997932d777bf	Explanation\nWhy the edits made under my usern...	0	0	0	0	0	0
1	000103f0d9cfb60f	D'aww! He matches this background colour I'm s...	0	0	0	0	0	0
2	000113f07ec002fd	Hey man, I'm really not trying to edit war. It...	0	0	0	0	0	0
3	0001b41b1c6bb37e	"\nMore\nI can't make any real suggestions on ...	0	0	0	0	0	0
4	0001d958c54c6e35	You, sir, are my hero. Any chance you remember...	0	0	0	0	0	0
...	...	...	...	...	...	...	...	...
95	003b9f448ee4a29d	"\n\nThanks. I can see that violating clearly ...	0	0	0	0	0	0
96	003bd094feef5263	"\nHi\nThanks for our kind words. See you arou...	0	0	0	0	0	0
97	003caacc6ce6c9e9	Collusion in poker \n\nThis is regarded as mos...	0	0	0	0	0	0
98	003d77a20601eec1	Thanks much - however, if it's been resolved, ...	0	0	0	0	0	0
99	003dbd1b9b354c1f	You can do all you're doing right now but if y...	0	0	0	0	0	0

100 rows × 8 columns

Fig. 6. Sample data from the Kaggle Toxic Tweets Challenge.

Table 1. Number of training data samples per toxicity label.

Toxicity Label	Number of training data
toxic	15294
severe_toxic	1595
obscene	8449
threat	478
insult	7877
identity_hate	1405

Prior to model training phase, we performed text vectorization on the training dataset using Keras high-level machine learning API on the TensorFlow platform. We implemented TextVectorization module on the dataset, in order to map the text features into integer sequences. For analyzing the content toxicity of a given video, we implemented a bidirectional LSTM model that is written using Keras sequential model template on TensorFlow platform, as shown in Fig. 7. The model is in the form of multilayered neural networks that laid out in multiple layers as described in Table 2.

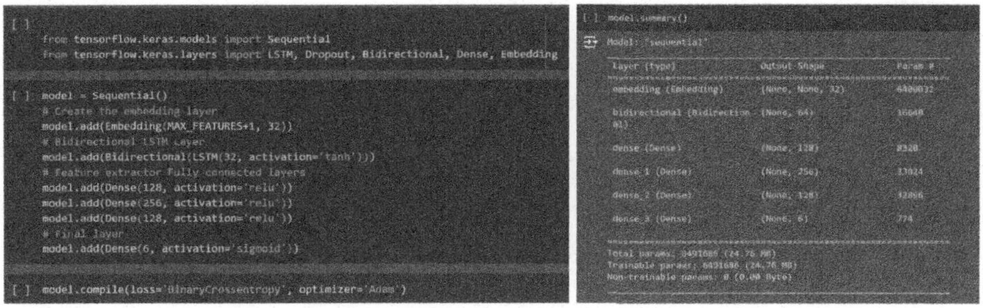

Fig. 7. LSTM sequential learning model developed with Keras ML API and tensorFlow.

Table 2. Multilayered neural network deployment details.

Layer Type	Functions
Embedding	Converting inputs into dense vectors of fixed size.
Bidirectional LSTM	This layer is used to perform text processing.
Fully-Connected Neural Networks	Performing text identification and classification.
Final	Produces the final prediction or result.

4.4 Training and Validation

The training and validation phase involve model fitting, prediction and validation procedures. For model fitting, we train the model using the training and validation dataset. The training process is conducted on Google Colab platform. For simplicity, we implement the training with low epochs due to constrained resources (CPU time and storage).

The train and validation loss values are decreasing as it undergoes through each training cycle. Figure 8 shows the loss values for both training and validation data decrements during each training cycle. We have conducted the training and validation using four different model compositions (6, 7, 8, and 9 layers) on 5 iterations ($epoch = 5$).

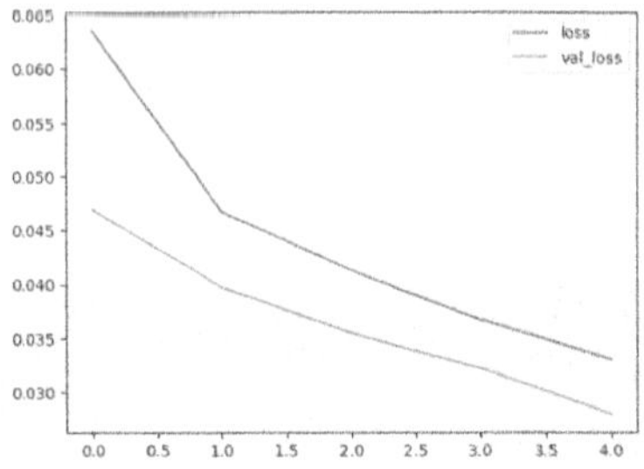

(a) 6-layer network

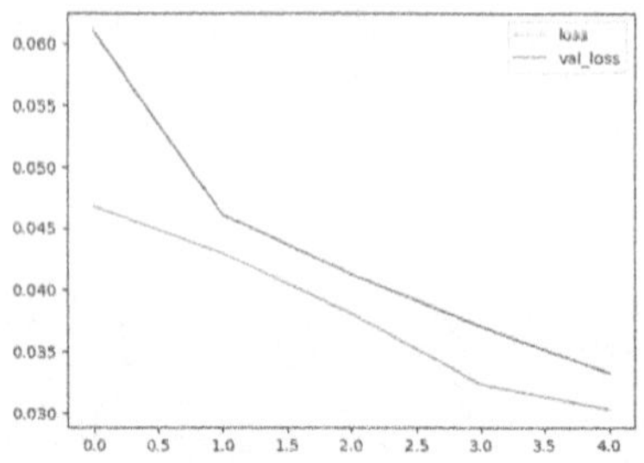

(b) 7-layer network

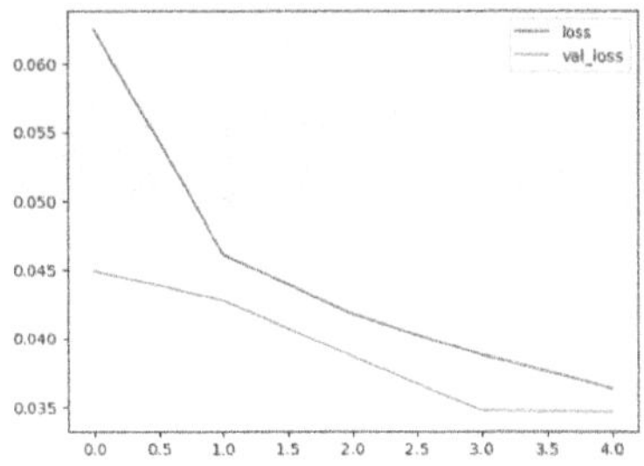

(c) 8-layer network

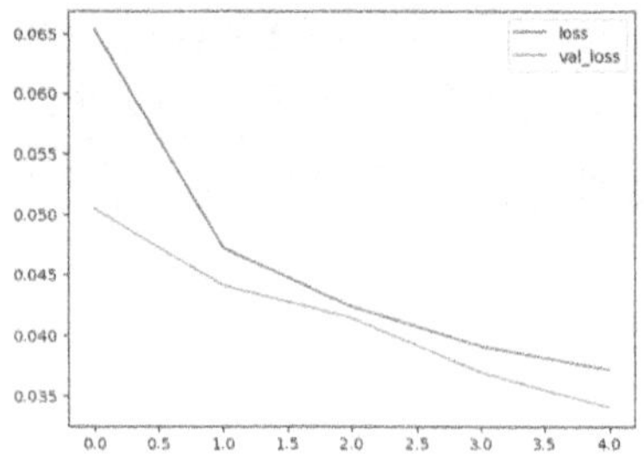

(d) 9-layer network

Fig. 8. Comparison made on the loss value reduction during model fitting process for bidirectional LSTM model with different network sizes.

Note that all the model compositions show similar loss value reduction patterns. To evaluate our model on the prediction accuracy, we use a made-up transcript and feed it to the model as shown in Fig. 9.

Finally, the precision, recall and accuracy values generated using different bidirectional LSTM model composition is shown in Fig. 10.

Based on the evaluation of performance parameters conducted on the network model compositions with different number of layers, it is shown that the model produces considerably high precision and recall. However, the accuracy values are still low (average of 0.5). This is mainly due to the fact that we are using *binary_ crossentropy* as method for calculating probabilistic losses in multi-class classification problem.

4.5 VidLyze Graphical Interface

The graphical interface for VidLyze video content toxicity analytics tool is developed using Gradio. It is commonly being used as a demonstration platform for machine learning model. It provides a customizable web interface that allows the developers to create their own interface for respective applications. Figure 11 shows a snapshot of the VidLyze web interface that has been created using Gradio.

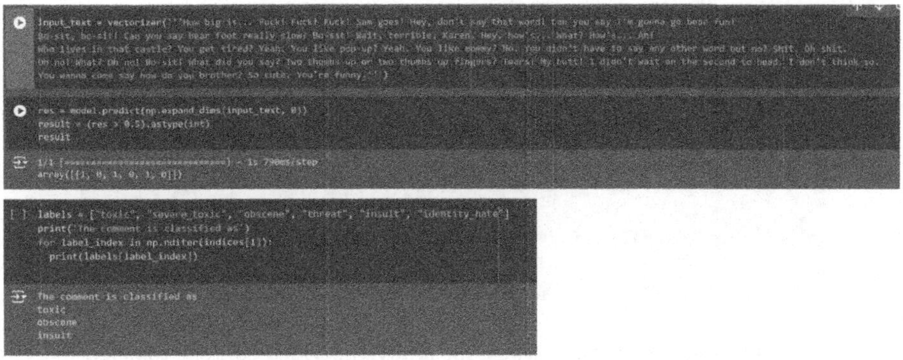

Fig. 9. Prediction of transcript using the built LSTM model showing the text is considered as toxic, obscene, and insulting.

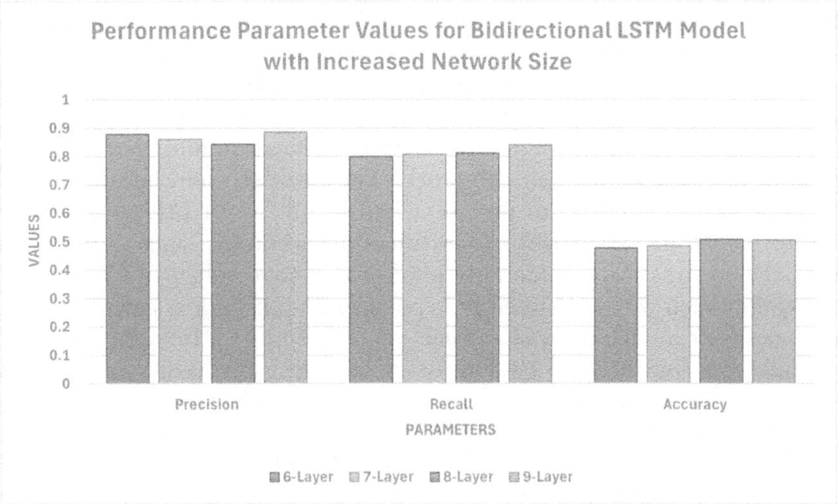

Fig. 10. The LSTM model's precision, recall, and accuracy values generated using the Keras's metrics functions on four different model compositions.

By using Gradio, the LSTM model that has been developed to identify toxicity within the contents of a video can be used to generate toxicity classification for a given video that is either being uploaded to VidLyze platform, or directly streamed from a given URL.

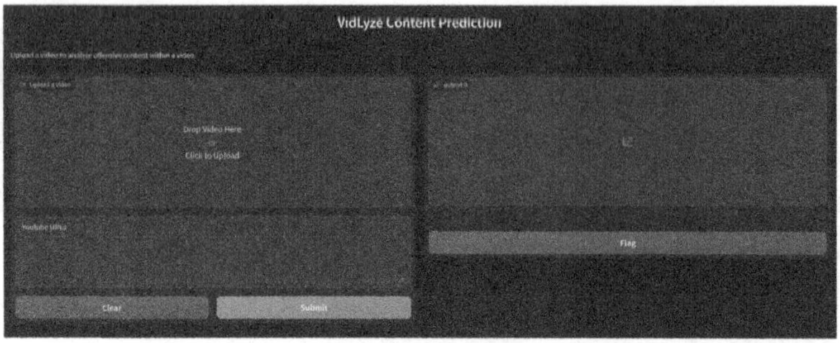

Fig. 11. VidLyze web interface for analyzing video content toxicity.

5 Conclusions

In this paper, we present our on-going work in developing a video analytics tool that can be used to identify different levels of toxicity, based on the combination of NLP and machine learning approaches. NLP is used to convert the audio segments of video into text, while recurrent neural networks in the form of LSTM model is used to conduct toxicity identification and classification. We defined six types of toxicity in this work. The results produced are promising, with significantly high level of precision and recall. Nevertheless there is room for improvement in the aspect of classification accuracy, since current results indicate the accuracy is considerably low with average values of 0.5. One of the proposed approach is to use different type of probabilistic loss calculation in our learning network model, such as *categorical_ crossentropy*. In addition, there are some challenges that need to be addressed, including the ability to obtain large datasets, in order to be effectively train and validate the built model, and more effective design of the learning algorithm to be used since the current approach is computationally intensive and requires considerably medium to high level of computational resources.

The next step in this work is to explore the possibility of including racial contexts and customs in detecting toxicity in video contents, as this can be regarded as important in different regions or countries.

References

1. Akter, M., Godfrey, A.J., Kropczynski, J., Lipford, H.R., Wisniewski, P.J.: From parental control to joint family oversight: can parents and teens manage mobile online safety and privacy as equals? Proc. ACM Hum.-Comput. Interact. **6**(CSCW1), 1–28 (2022)
2. Alcântara, C., Moreira, V., Feijo, D.: Offensive video detection: dataset and baseline results. In: Proceedings of the Twelfth Language Resources and Evaluation Conference, pp. 4309–4319 (2020)

3. Azzi, S.A., Zribi, C.B.O.: From machine learning to deep learning for detecting abusive messages in Arabic social media: survey and challenges. In: International Conference on Intelligent Systems Design and Applications, pp. 411–424. Springer, Cham (2020)
4. Dutta, H.S., Jobanputra, M., Negi, H., Chakraborty, T.: Detecting and analyzing collusive entities on YouTube. ACM Trans. Intell. Syst. Technol. (TIST) **12**(5), 1–28 (2021)
5. Garlapati, A., Malisetty, N., Narayanan, G.: Classification of toxicity in comments using NLP and LSTM. In: 2022 8th International Conference on Advanced Computing and Communication Systems (ICACCS), vol. 1, pp. 16–21. IEEE (2022)
6. Georgakopoulos, S.V., Tasoulis, S.K., Vrahatis, A.G., Plagianakos, V.P.: Convolutional neural networks for twitter text toxicity analysis. In: Recent Advances in Big Data and Deep Learning: Proceedings of the INNS Big Data and Deep Learning Conference INNSBDDL2019, held at Sestri Levante, Genova, Italy, 16–18 April 2019, pp. 370–379. Springer, Cham (2020)
7. Hochreiter, S., Schmidhuber, J.: Long short-term memory. Neural Comput. **9**(8), 1735–1780 (1997)
8. Kaur, S., Singh, S., Kaushal, S.: Abusive content detection in online user-generated data: a survey. Procedia Comput. Sci. **189**, 274–281 (2021)
9. Khairy, M., Mahmoud, T.M., Abd-El-Hafeez, T.: Automatic detection of cyberbullying and abusive language in Arabic content on social networks: a survey. Procedia Comput. Sci. **189**, 156–166 (2021)
10. Khalil, J.F., Zayani, M.: Streaming the middle east: from legacy media to digital platforms. In: Digital Platforms and the Global South, pp. 165–181. Routledge (2023)
11. Kumar, G.K., Kavitha, A.: Video content analysis using deep learning methods. In: International Conference on Intelligent Systems and Machine Learning, pp. 222–243. Springer, Cham (2022)
12. Lekshmi, S., Anoop, V.: Sentiment analysis on Covid-19 news videos using machine learning techniques. In: Proceedings of International Conference on Frontiers in Computing and Systems: COMSYS 2021, pp. 551–560. Springer, Cham (2022)
13. Luo, X.: Efficient English text classification using selected machine learning techniques. Alex. Eng. J. **60**(3), 3401–3409 (2021)
14. Md, A.Q., et al.: Novel optimization approach for stock price forecasting using multi-layered sequential LSTM. Appl. Soft Comput. **134**, 109830 (2023)
15. Mouheb, D., Albarghash, R., Mowakeh, M.F., Al Aghbari, Z., Kamel, I.: Detection of Arabic cyberbullying on social networks using machine learning. In: 2019 IEEE/ACS 16th International Conference on Computer Systems and Applications (AICCSA), pp. 1–5. IEEE (2019)
16. O'Sullivan, J., et al.: Automatic speech recognition for ASD using the open-source whisper model from OpenAI. In: International Society for autism Research (INSAR) 2023 Annual Meeting. INSAR, Stockholm, Sweden (2023)
17. Radford, A., Kim, J.W., Xu, T., Brockman, G., McLeavey, C., Sutskever, I.: Robust speech recognition via large-scale weak supervision. In: International Conference on Machine Learning, pp. 28492–28518. PMLR (2023)
18. Tarafder, T., Vashisth, H.K., Arora, M.: Automated tool for toxic comments identification on live streaming YouTube. In: International Conference on MAchine inTelligence for Research & Innovations, pp. 47–56. Springer, Cham (2023)
19. Yousaf, K., Nawaz, T.: A deep learning-based approach for inappropriate content detection and classification of YouTube videos. IEEE Access **10**, 16283–16298 (2022)

20. Yousefi, M., Emmanouilidou, D.: Audio-based toxic language classification using self-attentive convolutional neural network. In: 2021 29th European Signal Processing Conference (EUSIPCO), pp. 11–15. IEEE (2021)
21. Yu, Y., Si, X., Hu, C., Zhang, J.: A review of recurrent neural networks: LSTM cells and network architectures. Neural Comput. **31**(7), 1235–1270 (2019)

Comprehensive Evaluation of GAN Architectures for Acute Lymphoblastic Leukemia Classification

Malathy Jawahar[1(✉)], N. Jayashree[2], Benson Edwin Raj[3], and D. Dhanya[4]

[1] Leather Process Technology Division, CSIR-Central Leather Research Institute, Chennai, India
malathyj@clri.res.in

[2] Department of MCA, Vidyavardhaka College of Engineering, Mysuru, Karnataka 570002, India

[3] Department of Computer Information Sciences, Higher Colleges of Technology, Fujairah, UAE
braj@hct.ac.ae

[4] Department of Artificial Intelligence and Data Science, Mar Ephraem College of Engineering and Technology, Elavuvilai, Marthandam, Kanyakumari 629171, India
dhanya@marephraem.edu.in

Abstract. Acute Lymphoblastic Leukemia (ALL) is a blood cancer requiring swift, accurate diagnosis for effective treatment. Traditional diagnostic methods rely on the manual examination of microscopic images by experts, which is limited by both availability and speed. Artificial Intelligence (AI) offers a promising alternative for the automated analysis of blood cell images. However, AI model development is hindered by the need for large, annotated datasets, which are often scarce and exhibit a bias (more images of healthy cells than ALL samples). This research proposes the use of data augmentation techniques, specifically Generative Adversarial Networks (GANs), to mitigate these issues. GANs are capable of producing realistic synthetic images of ALL cells, which can enhance the dataset and correct the imbalance. This improvement can lead to the creation of more accurate AI models for ALL diagnosis, potentially improving patient outcomes. The study evaluates three GAN architectures namely SimpleGAN, Wasserstein GAN (WGAN) and Deep Convolutional GAN (DCGAN) for their ability to generate synthetic images of ALL and normal blood cells. The performance is measured by analyzing loss metrics and accuracy rates during training to identify the optimal GAN architecture for this application. Results indicate that DCGAN significantly outperforms both SimpleGAN and WGAN. A higher Peak Signal-to-Noise Ratio (PSNR) value implies that images generated by DCGAN have less noise, and a higher Structural Similarity Index Measure (SSIM) value indicates a better preservation of structural details in the images.

Keywords: Acute Lymphoblastic Leukemia (ALL) · GAN · DCGAN · WGAN

A. Safi et al. (Eds.): ISICS 2024, CCIS 2381, pp. 215–226, 2025.
https://doi.org/10.1007/978-3-031-82931-4_16

1 Introduction

An important healthcare challenge is acute lymphoblastic leukemia (ALL), a blood malignancy in which the bone marrow produces excessive undeveloped white blood cells (WBCs), presents a significant healthcare challenge [1]. Early and accurate diagnosis is crucial for successful treatment outcomes. Traditionally, diagnosing ALL relies on manual analysis of blood cell morphology under a microscope by highly trained medical personnel. While manual analysis by experts remains the gold standard, it suffers from limitations as accurately interpreting results requires extensive training and experience. Lack of consistent expertise can lead to misdiagnosis and delays and the manual analysis process is inherently time-consuming. Advances in machine learning and artificial intelligence holds great promise in transforming ALL diagnoses. AI algorithms, especially Deep Learning Models, have the potential to analyze blood cell images automatically, significantly improving the speed and consistency of the diagnostic process [2]. DL's ability to identify subtle patterns in blood cell morphology that might escape the human eye presents a powerful advantage. AI models could assist in decision making, treatment planning and delivery, and improving overall operational efficiency within healthcare systems.

The adoption of AI-based ALL diagnosis is not without its challenges. Training effective AI models necessitates access to large datasets of meticulously labelled blood cell images. These datasets consist of images with confirmed ALL diagnoses alongside images of healthy cells for comparison. The limited availability of such labelled data can hinder the development of robust and accurate AI models. Furthermore, a critical challenge lies in the inherent imbalance present within these datasets. Healthy blood cell images are significantly more common than those depicting ALL samples. This imbalance can bias the AI model's performance towards classifying all images as healthy, leading to missed diagnoses. Addressing these data limitations and biases is crucial for ensuring the effectiveness and reliability of AI-powered ALL diagnosis.

Data augmentation is a crucial technique especially when working with small datasets. It essentially expands the training data by creating variations of existing images. This helps address two key challenges: overfitting and class imbalance. In overfitting, the model picks up to learn the finer points of the training data, hindering its ability to adapt to new/unseen data. Data augmentation combats this by introducing variations that the model must also learn from. Class imbalance refers to a situation where one class (e.g., ALL) is significantly underrepresented compared to others (e.g., healthy blood cells). By strategically augmenting the minority class data, data augmentation techniques like deep synthetic oversampling and BOSME help balance the dataset and stop the model from favouring the overwhelming class in its predictions.

While limited data can hinder AI model development in diagnosing Acute Lymphoblastic Leukemia (ALL), various techniques exist to overcome this challenge. Transfer learning allows pre-trained models to provide a strong foundation, while self-supervised learning leverages un-labelled data for feature extraction. Generative adversarial networks stand out by creating entirely new, realistic blood cell images, expanding the training data beyond simple modifications. Optimizing the model architecture itself through specific neural network designs or specialized layers can also improve its ability to learn from limited data.

This paper explores generative adversarial networks for synthetic blood cell image creation by exploring advancements in data augmentation techniques to overcome limitations imposed by data scarcity and imbalance.

2 Background

Generative Adversarial Networks (GANs), a pioneering approach in generative modelling introduced by Goodfellow et al. [3], offer a solution for the generation of high resolution and realistic images. By leveraging GAN-generated data, researchers can potentially mitigate the limitations imposed by inadequate medical image datasets.

Deep Convolutional Generative Adversarial Networks (DCGANs) were introduced by Radford et al. [4] as an advancement over the GAN. This specialized Convolutional Neural Network (CNN) architecture is designed for unsupervised learning tasks. Recognizing the limitations of DCGANs, particularly in training stability and interpretability, Wasserstein Generative Adversarial Networks (WGANs) were suggested by Arjovsky et al. [5]. WGANs address these challenges by introducing a novel training approach.

A study by Lan et al. [6] addresses the challenge of insufficient and imbalanced data using Synthetic Minority Oversampling Generative Adversarial Networks (SMOGANs). SMOGANs are able to generate synthetic data to balance the dataset and improve the accuracy of pattern analysis. Lucas Uzolas et al. [7] implemented a deep learning approach to address the challenge of limited training data in chromosome image analysis, in particular, for rare genetic disorders. They proposed a method by introducing a novel approach using conditional GAN (cGANs) to generate synthetic chromosome images by using user-defined band patterns.

Wang et al. [8] studied various network structures for WGAN that can enhance numeric data augmentation. They proposed various restrained conditions such as isomorphic (IWGAN) mirror (MWGAN) and self-symmetric WGAN (SWGAN) to enhance the classification performance. Quantitative indicator known as Similarity of the Restrained Condition (SRC) was introduced for measuring the restrained conditions. Moradi and Demirel [9] proposed a novel method called conditional progressive GAN (cProGAN) specifically designed for data augmentation to increase the precision of Alzheimer's disease diagnosis. A controlled noise injection technique guided by a discriminator trained on real data is used. Mayank Bali and Tripti Mahara [10] examined the effectiveness of two data augmentation methods, the traditional affine transformations (scaling, rotating, flipping existing images) and Generative Adversarial Networks (GANs), to increase the accuracy of deep learning method for diagnosing pneumonia from chest X-rays. They applied various pre-processing techniques to different convolution models such as VGG16, Inception V3, InceptionResNetV3, DenseNet-189 and DenseNet 202 to compare the performance of both these methods. The study suggests that DCGAN-based data augmentation is a more effective approach to enhance the effectiveness of CNN models in diagnosing pneumonia.

A study by Sandhiya, et al. [11] proposed a novel approach for predicting brain tumours using MRI scans and to address limitations in training data, a Deep Convolutional Generative Adversarial Network (DCGAN) is used to create realistic synthetic brain images. The method then incorporates multiple MRI scan angles during pre-processing and leverages an improved K-Means Clustering algorithm to distinguish various brain tissue types. V. Nirmala and J. Premaladha [12] proposed a novel approach for the generation of annotated synthetic data using Generative Adversarial Networks (GANs) for melanoma skin cancer diagnosis. GANs generate realistic synthetic images of skin lesions, focusing on Region of Interest (ROI).

Malathy et al. [16] proposed a cluster-based convolution and max-pooling normalized process model for predicting ALL, achieving an accuracy of 91.13%. Malathy et al. [17] proposed a Deep Residual Dilated model for improved convergence, achieving an accuracy of 91.98%. Irene et al. [17] examined the transformative impact of AI on medicine, enhancing diagnostic precision and efficiency, while emphasising the necessity of addressing ethical, clinical, and policy concerns for the proper incorporation of AI into healthcare. Rigby et al. [18] underscored that, although AI can greatly enhance public health and medicine, it is imperative to address health equity and ethical obligations to avert the worsening of inequities and to uphold rigorous ethical standards for all demographics. Gerke et al. [19] examined ethical and legal concerns associated with AI in healthcare, encompassing informed consent, transparency, safety, data privacy, data protection, liability, and intellectual property, promoting a reliable and inclusive AI-driven healthcare system that adheres to the principle of "Health AIs for All of Us". Ethical clearance was not required as the study utilized an open-access dataset.

3 Methodology

Generative Adversarial Network (GAN), a deep learning technique with two competing neural networks namely a generator (G) and a discriminator (D) engage in an adversarial training process (Fig. 1). The generator generates new synthetic blood cell images based on ALL training dataset, while the discriminator determines if the generated blood cell images are real or fake. This adversarial training helps the generator produce increasingly realistic new data for AI-based ALL diagnosis. According to Goodfellow et.al. [3], G and D models are both trained simultaneously using the value function.

$$min\ G\ ma\ D_x\ V(D, G) = E_{x \sim Pdata(x)}\ [\log D(x)] + E_{z \sim Pz(z)}\ [\log(1 - D(G(z)))] \tag{1}$$

where G and D are Generator and Discriminator models respectively.

This study investigates the application of three GAN architectures, SimpleGAN, DCGAN, and WGAN, to evaluate the performance and efficacy of synthetic blood cell image generation for ALL diagnoses.

3.1 SimpleGAN Network Architecture

As illustrated in Fig. 2, G and D model comprise the main components of the SimpleGAN architecture that was implemented using Keras' sequential API. An input random noise vector of dimension (100) is fed into the generator model. It includes a fully connected dense layer with 256 units and LeakyReLU activation ($\alpha = 0.2$), followed by three dense layers with 512, 1024, and a final layer matching the target image's pixel count. LeakyReLU activations are used after each dense layer for stability, and the final layer

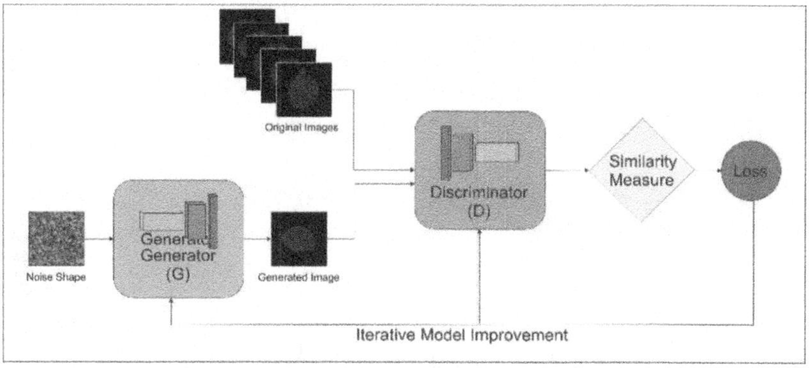

Fig. 1. GAN Architecture.

uses a tanh activation to constrain output pixel values between −1 and 1, reshaping the output to the desired image dimensions. The discriminator model takes an image of the target shape as input, flattening it into a one-dimensional vector. It features three dense layers with 512, 256, and 1 unit, respectively, employing LeakyReLU activations and a sigmoid activation in the final layer to classify the input as real or fake.

SimpleGAN's architecture, using binary cross-entropy loss, faces challenges with vanishing gradients, leading to slow training and suboptimal results.

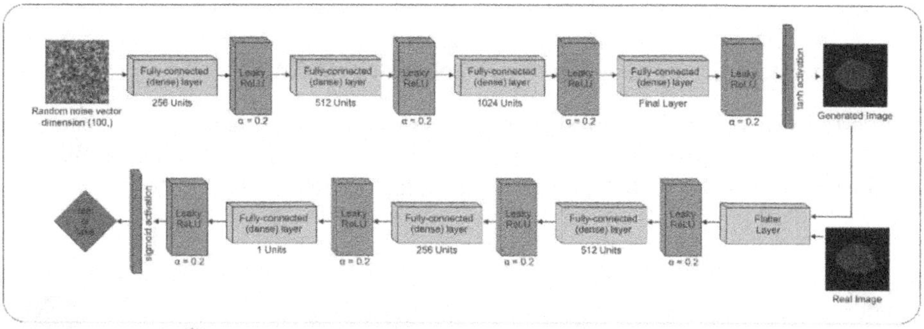

Fig. 2. SimpleGAN model.

3.2 Deep Convolutional Generative Adversarial Network (DCGAN)

Similar to SimpleGAN, DCGAN consists of two primary elements: G, which generates blood cell image data, and D, which evaluates and distinguishes between real and generated data. Figure 3 depicts the key components of Deep Convolutional GAN.

The model initially accepts a random noise vector of dimension (100,) and employs both convolutional and dense layers to leverage spatial relationships within the data. Initially, a dense layer projects the noise vector into a higher-dimensional space, followed

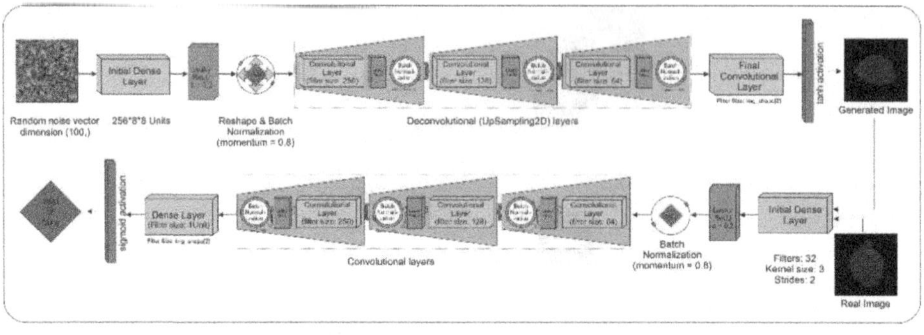

Fig. 3. Deep Convolutional GAN model.

by reshaping and batch normalization. The network then uses deconvolutional layers to increase the spatial resolution progressively, incorporating convolutional layers with kernel sizes of 3 and ReLU activations. The final layer matches the desired number of image channels, using a tanh activation to constrain pixel values. The discriminator uses convolutional layers with Leaky ReLU activations, increasing filter numbers progressively, and includes dropout for regularization and batch normalization for training stability. The final dense layer outputs a classification probability between 0 and 1. DCGAN's convolutional layers enable it to capture spatial features more effectively, generating highly realistic images, while batch normalization and Leaky ReLU activations promote smoother training.

3.3 Wasserstein Generative Adversarial Network (WGAN)

Similar to DCGAN, WGAN consists of two main components: a model for generating data (G) and a model to evaluate data (D), also known as a critic in WGAN terminology. The architecture of the WGAN model is illustrated in Fig. 4.

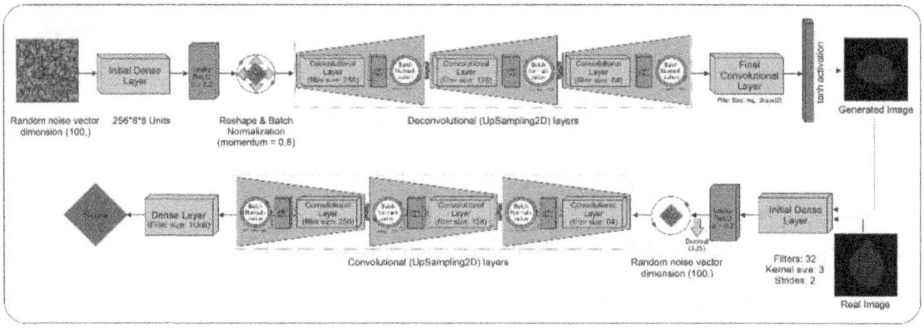

Fig. 4. Wasserstein GAN model.

WGAN, similar to DCGAN, comprises two main parts: a model known as a critic (D) and a model for data generation (G). The generator model mirrors the architecture of the DCGAN generator. The critic aims to distinguish between real and generated images, but unlike DCGAN's discriminator, it outputs an unbounded score to enforce the Wasserstein distance in the loss function. The critic employs convolutional layers with Leaky ReLU activations, similar to DCGAN, but uses a final dense layer without an activation function to output the unbounded score. The key modification in WGAN is the loss function, utilizing the Wasserstein loss function to promote stable training and mitigate vanishing gradients and mode collapse issues. WGAN's training involves weight clipping and careful hyperparameter tuning, making it computationally more expensive and slower compared to DCGAN, but potentially more robust in generating diverse and realistic images.

4 Building the GAN Model

A wrapper GAN model was created using Keras' Sequential API, combining the generator and discriminator sequentially. This model directly feeds the generator's output into the discriminator. During training, the models are trained separately with specific objectives. The process involves an iterative loop spanning multiple epochs, with each epoch including several steps: First, a random batch of real blood cell images is selected from the training dataset. Next, a random noise vector, generated from a pre-defined distribution (e.g., normal distribution with mean 0 and standard deviation 1), serves as the input to the generator. The generator (G) is trained independently to enhance its ability to generate realistic normal and ALL blood cell images from the noise input, while the discriminator's parameters remain frozen. The generator loss (g_loss) is determined based on the discriminator's assessment of the generated images (gen_imgs). Subsequently, the discriminator (D) is trained to differentiate between the original and synthetic blood images, receiving original images (with labels of ones indicating real data) and synthetic images (with labels of zeros indicating fake data). The discriminator loss (d_loss) is calculated based on its classification accuracy. Two training functions are provided: train_gan, for SimpleGAN & DCGAN architectures, performs a single training step for both the discriminator and the generator within each epoch. On the other hand, train_wgan, tailored for WGAN architectures, incorporates gradient clipping, a crucial WGAN training component. After training the discriminator on real and generated images, the function clips the weights to a small range (e.g., −0.01 to 0.01) to enforce the Wasserstein distance in the WGAN loss function. Additionally, train_wgan includes multiple training steps for the discriminator to ensure it effectively distinguishes real from generated samples. The proposed GAN model has been developed using illustrative training datasets, mitigating bias and ensuring fair results. The model also integrates the schema in a transparent manner, thereby enabling the users to understand how the model performs the classification.

5 Results and Discussion

The ISBI 2019 dataset was downloaded from Kaggle [13] and provides a valuable resource for Acute Lymphoblastic Leukemia (ALL) classification research. The dataset, accessible from platforms like Kaggle, comprises 73 subjects categorized as either ALL

(47) or normal (26). The training set contains 10,661 labelled cell images, further divided into 7,272 ALL images and 3,389 normal images. This training data is further split into training and test subsets. The preliminary test set includes 28 subjects (13 ALL, 15 normal) with 1,867 images (1,219 ALL, 648 normal), while the final test set consists of 17 subjects (9 ALL, 8 normal) and 2,586 images.

From Fig. 5, it can be observed that the initial training epochs show significant discriminator (D) loss and moderate generator (G) loss for SimpleGAN. DCGAN show a steady decrease in both discriminator and generator losses over the initial epochs. As training progresses, SimpleGAN's discriminator loss fluctuates, indicating difficulties in distinguishing between real and generated images. SimpleGAN generator's loss increases significantly, suggesting that the generator produces increasingly complex or unrealistic images that the discriminator struggles to classify accurately. In the case of WGAN, the discriminator loss (critic) remains near-constant throughout the training, which is expected in WGAN as the loss function is designed to measure Wasserstein distance. It can be observed that the WGAN's generator loss initially decreases but later stabilizes, indicating the generation of images that the critic finds harder to distinguish from real images. Finally, in the case of DCGAN, a steady decrease in both discriminator and generator losses can be seen over the initial epochs. As training progresses, the discriminator accuracy improves significantly, indicating better differentiation between real and generated images. Though there is a slight increase in the DCGAN generator, it can be noted that both losses stabilize, suggesting improved image generation.

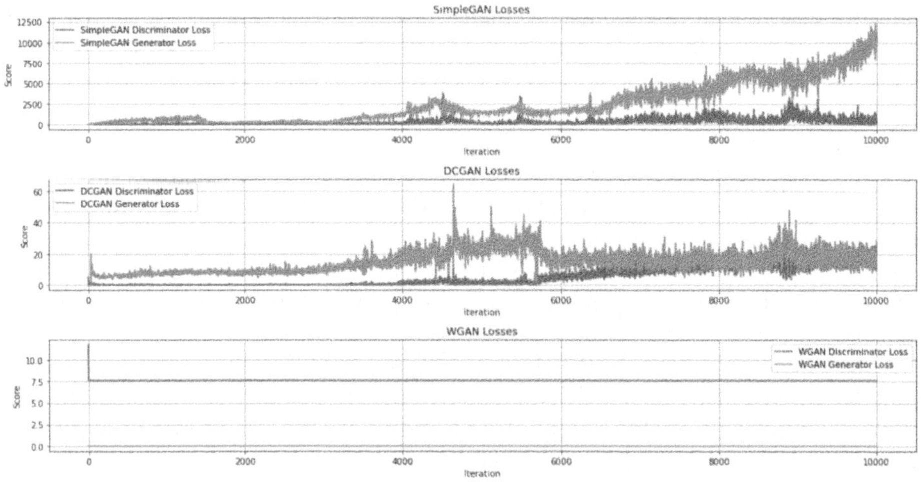

Fig. 5. GAN Losses Comparison.

SimpleGAN's reliance on fully connected layers leads to blurry and unrealistic image generation, particularly for complex datasets like medical images of ALL and normal cells. This is because fully-connected layers struggle to capture spatial relationships within the data. It can be noticed that the SimpleGAN generator produces a limited variety of images & struggles to generate high-fidelity images. It is also evident from

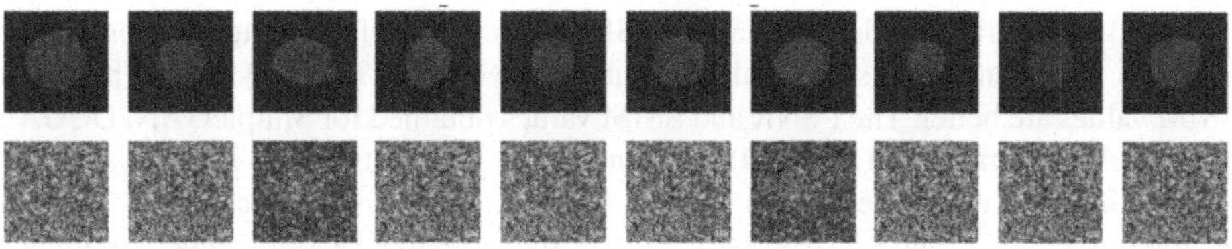

Fig. 6. SimpleGAN: Original vs. Generated Images.

Fig. 6 that SimpleGAN produced images with a lot of noise and struggle with diversity and quality, especially as the training progress.

While WGAN produces little distorted images (Fig. 7), it still demonstrates a capability to capture a wider range of features compared to SimpleGAN. This highlights its potential for generating diverse outputs. These images exhibit a greater level of realism compared to SimpleGAN's blurry & noisy outputs.

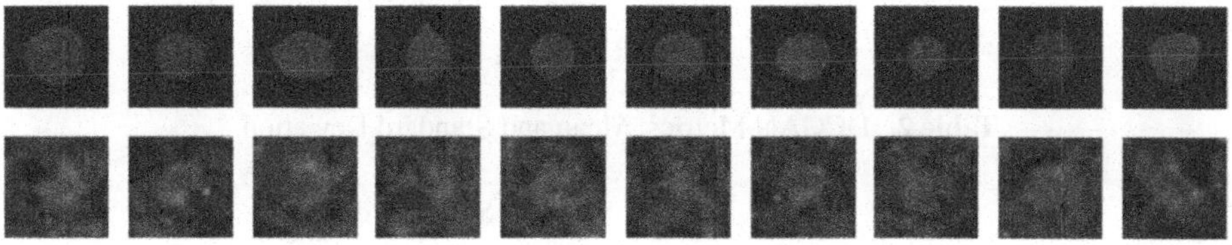

Fig. 7. WGAN: Original vs. Generated Images.

DCGAN produces higher-quality images with better stability during training. The use of convolutional layers helps in capturing spatial hierarchies in the data. The generated blood cell images' quality is greatly enhanced by DCGAN. The images are more detailed and closer to the original data as evident from Fig. 8.

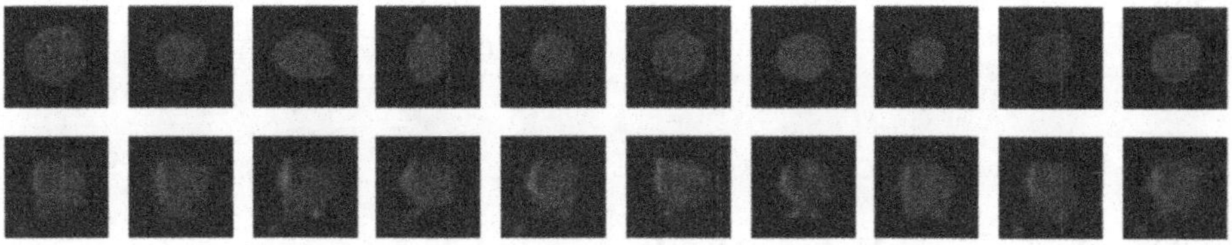

Fig. 8. DCGAN: Original vs. Generated Images.

Important measures like the Structural Similarity Index (SSIM) and Peak Signal-to-Noise Ratio (PSNR) are part of the evaluation framework. Each metric offers a unique perspective on image quality, ensuring a detailed and comprehensive assessment with the modern methods.

PSNR measures the ratio between the maximum possible power of a signal and the power of corrupting noise that affects the precision of its representation [14]. Better image quality with less noise is shown by larger PSNR values; more consistent performance is indicated by smaller standard deviation. SSIM values range from -1 to 1, where values closer to 1 indicate better structural similarity to the original images [15]. Higher mean SSIM values are better. The PSNR and SSIM values obtained for SimpleGAN, DCGAN and WGAN are given in Table 1, Table 2 and Table 3 respectively.

DCGAN has the highest mean PSNR of 22.171, which is significantly higher than SimpleGAN (3.456) and WGAN (16.473). This indicates that DCGAN generates images with the least amount of noise and the highest quality among the three. DCGAN again shows superior performance with a mean SSIM of 0.560, suggesting it retains structural information more effectively compared to SimpleGAN (0.003) and WGAN (0.216).

Table 1. SimpleGAN Metrics: Mean and Standard Deviation.

Metrics	Mean	Standard deviation
PSNR	3.456	0.1531
SSIM	0.0027	0.0011

Table 2. DCGAN Metrics: Mean and Standard Deviation.

Metrics	Mean	Standard deviation
PSNR	22.171	1.929
SSIM	0.560	0.049

Table 3. WGAN Metrics: Mean and Standard Deviation.

Metrics	Mean	Standard deviation
PSNR	16.473	1.026
SSIM	0.217	0.069

6 Conclusion and Future Work

This study highlights the significant potential of Generative Adversarial Networks (GANs) in overcoming challenges associated with automated diagnosis of Acute Lymphoblastic Leukemia (ALL). After comparative analysis of the Wasserstein GAN (WGAN), Deep Convolutional GAN (DCGAN), and SimpleGAN models, it was found that DCGAN was the best model for generating synthetic images of ALL and normal blood cells. It demonstrated superior performance with increased Peak Signal-to-Noise Ratio (PSNR) and Structural Similarity Index Measure (SSIM) values, demonstrating its capacity to produce blood cell images like original with minimal noise along with excellent preservation of structural details. The combination of CNN layers, batch normalization, Leaky ReLU activations, and the overall architecture of DCGAN creates a more robust and efficient training process compared to SimpleGAN & WGAN. Utilizing DCGAN for data augmentation addresses issues of limited dataset size and class imbalance, crucial for developing robust AI models for ALL diagnosis. The enhanced datasets from DCGAN could lead to more accurate and reliable AI diagnostic tools, promising improved patient outcomes through faster diagnosis. Future research should integrate DCGAN-generated images into AI model training and assess their performance in clinical settings, with potential applications extending to other rare diseases with data scarcity challenges. Additionally, future work could include replacing DCGAN's convolutional layers with transfer learning and introducing interpretability into the generation process employing explainable GANs.

References

1. Terwilliger, T., Abdul-Hay, M.: Acute lymphoblastic leukemia: a comprehensive review and 2017 update. Blood Cancer J. **7**, e577 (2017)
2. Das, P.K., Pradhan, A., Meher, S.: Detection of acute lymphoblastic leukemia using machine learning techniques. In: Gopi, E.S. (eds.) Machine Learning, Deep Learning and Computational Intelligence for Wireless Communication. LNEE, vol. 749, pp. 425–437. Springer, Singapore (2021). https://doi.org/10.1007/978-981-16-0289-4_32
3. Goodfellow, I., Pouget-Abadie, J., Mirza, M., et al.: Generative adversarial networks. Commun. ACM **63**, 139–144 (2020)
4. Radford, A., Metz, L., Chintala, S.: Unsupervised representation learning with deep convolutional generative adversarial networks. In: Proceedings of the, pp. 1–16 (2015)
5. Arjovsky, M., Chintala, S., Bottou, L.: Wasserstein generative adversarial networks. In: Precup, D., The, Y.W. (eds.) 214–223 (2017)
6. Lan, Z.-C., Huang, G.-Y., Li, Y.-P., et al.: Conquering insufficient/imbalanced data learning for the Internet of Medical Things. Neural Comput. Appl. **35** (2022). https://doi.org/10.1007/s00521-022-06897-z
7. Uzolas, L., Rico, J., Coupé, P., et al.: Deep anomaly generation: an image translation approach of synthesizing abnormal banded chromosome images. IEEE Access **10**, 59090–59098 (2022). https://doi.org/10.1109/ACCESS.2022.3178786
8. Wang, W., Wang, C., Cui, T., Li, Y.: Study of restrained network structures for Wasserstein generative adversarial networks (WGANs) on numeric data augmentation. IEEE Access **8**, 89812–89821 (2020)
9. Moradi, M., Demirel, H.: Alzheimer's disease classification using 3D conditional progressive GAN- and LDA-based data selection. SIViP **18**, 1847–1861 (2024)
10. Bali, M., Mahara, T.: Comparison of affine and DCGAN-based data augmentation techniques for chest X-ray classification. Proc. Comput. Sci. **218**, 283–290 (2023). https://doi.org/10.1016/j.procs.2023.01.010
11. Sandhiya, B., Raja, S.K.S., Shruthi, K., Kamala, S.P.R.: Brain tumour segmentation and classification with reconstructed MRI using DCGAN. Biomed. Sig. Process. Control **92**, 106005 (2024). https://doi.org/10.1016/j.bspc.2024.106005
12. Nirmala, V., Premaladha, J.: Synthetic medical image augmentation: a GAN based approach for melanoma skin lesion classification with deep learning (chapter 5). In: Garg, H., Chatterjee, J.M. (eds.) Deep Learning in Personalized Healthcare and Decision Support. Academic Press, pp. 69–80 (2023)

13. Kaggle: Your Machine Learning and Data Science Community. https://www.kaggle.com/. Accessed 12 July 2024
14. Horé, A., Ziou, D.: Image quality metrics: PSNR vs. SSIM. In: 2010 20th International Conference on Pattern Recognition, pp. 2366–2369 (2010)
15. Wang, Z., Simoncelli, E.P., Bovik, A.C.: Multiscale structural similarity for image quality assessment. In: The Thirty-Seventh Asilomar Conference on Signals, Systems & Computers, vol. 2, pp. 1398–1402 (2003)
16. Jawahar, M., Anbarasi, L.J., Narayanan, S., Gandomi, A.H.: An attention-based deep learning for acute lymphoblastic leukemia classification. Sci. Rep. **14**, 17447 (2024)
17. Jawahar, M., Sharen, H., Gandomi, A.H.: ALNett: a cluster layer deep convolutional neural network for acute lymphoblastic leukemia classification. Comput. Biol. Med. **148**, 105894 (2022)
18. Dankwa-Mullan, I.: Health equity and ethical considerations in using artificial intelligence in public health and medicine. Prev. Chronic Dis. **21** (2024)
19. Rigby, M.J.: Ethical dimensions of using artificial intelligence in health care. AMA J. Ethics **21**(2), 121–124 (2019)
20. Gerke, S., Minssen, T., Cohen, G.: Ethical and legal challenges of artificial intelligence-driven healthcare. In: Artificial Intelligence in Healthcare, pp. 295–336 (2020)

A Novel Classification of Authentication Schemes for Internet of Drones

Eduardo Hernandez Escobar[1], Zain Chaudhary[1], Ahmed Sherif[1],
Mohamed Elsersy[2(✉)], and Kasem Khalil[3,4]

[1] School of Computing Sciences and Computer Engineering, University of Southern Mississippi, Hattiesburg, MS, USA
[2] Computer and Information Systems Department, Higher Colleges of Technology, Al Ain, Abu Dhabi, UAE
melsersy@hct.ac.ae
[3] Electrical and Computer Engineering Department, University of Mississippi, Hattiesburg, MS, USA
[4] Department of Electrical Engineering, Assiut University, Assiut, Egypt

Abstract. The Internet of Drones (IoD) presents a transformative advancement in unmanned aerial systems, promising enhanced capabilities across numerous industries, including agriculture, security, and logistics. However, integrating these systems into critical sectors makes them a prominent cyber-attack target. This survey examines the current landscape of authentication schemes designed to secure IoD communications, emphasizing the need for solutions that are effective in preventing security breaches and efficient enough to operate within the resource constraints of drone technology. We explore several authentication schemes that depend on various cryptographic methods, including blockchain-based cryptography, elliptic curve cryptography, and cryptographic hash functions, assessing their suitability for IoD environments based on security analysis and security features. This survey highlights recent innovations in the authentication field and provides a comparative analysis of their performance in various IoD applications. This comprehensive review aims to guide researchers, technologists, and policymakers in developing and adopting authentication strategies that enhance drone networks' security and operational efficacy.

Keywords: IoD · Authentication · Security

1 Introduction

The proliferation of drone technology within diverse sectors has underscored the imperative for robust security frameworks to safeguard communication and operational integrity in Internet of Drones (IoD) networks. Researchers estimate that the IoD industry will be worth ninety-two billion U.S. dollars by the end of this decade [22]. Within the last several years, IoD has become predominantly crucial in many different sectors, including, but not limited to, search and rescue, traffic monitoring, residential inspections, monitoring, surveillance, delivery systems, agriculture, mapping, and military

A. Safi et al. (Eds.): ISICS 2024, CCIS 2381, pp. 227–241, 2025.
https://doi.org/10.1007/978-3-031-82931-4_17

[30]. In recent years, there has also been a rapid development of smart cities that intend to utilize UAVs and IoD infrastructure to improve the efficiency of resources, management, and urban services. However, new challenges and problems emerge in terms of privacy and security due to the rapid growth of IoD services and communications [7].

In this context, the evolution of authentication technologies is crucial, especially in developing schemes that are not only secure but also lightweight, considering the resource constraints typical of drone architectures. Traditional cryptographic methods, while robust, often fail to address the unique challenges posed by IoD environments, such as limited computational capacity, battery life constraints, and the need for rapid authentication to support real-time operations.

This survey explores a range of novel lightweight authentication schemes that aim to balance security with operational efficiency. It delves into various cryptographic paradigms, including asymmetric encryption, blockchain technology, elliptic curve cryptography, and emerging quantum-resistant algorithms. Each paper is evaluated not only in terms of authentication technique but also in terms of defense against various attacks and security features provided. Furthermore, the paper discusses the practical applications of these schemes in real-world scenarios, offering insights into their implementation challenges in different IoD environments. By examining the latest advancements and drawing comparisons among various approaches, this paper aims to provide a comprehensive understanding of where the field is headed and what is needed to secure the future of drone operations effectively. Through this exploration, we aim to contribute to the discourse on IoD security, providing stakeholders with the knowledge to make informed decisions about which authentication strategies will best meet their needs, ensuring robust security without compromising the functional efficiency of drone networks.

The rest of this paper is organized as follows. Section 2 delves into related work, reviewing existing surveys on authentication and communication security in IoD, highlighting various methodologies and focus areas, including blockchain and machine learning. Section 3 introduces our novel taxonomy of authentication techniques. Section 4 synthesizes the findings, discussing the comparative effectiveness of various authentication approaches within IoD applications. Finally, Sect. 5 concludes the paper by summarizing the critical need for ongoing refinement of IoD security measures, advocating for continuous research to develop robust, efficient, and scalable authentication solutions that address the evolving landscape of drone technologies.

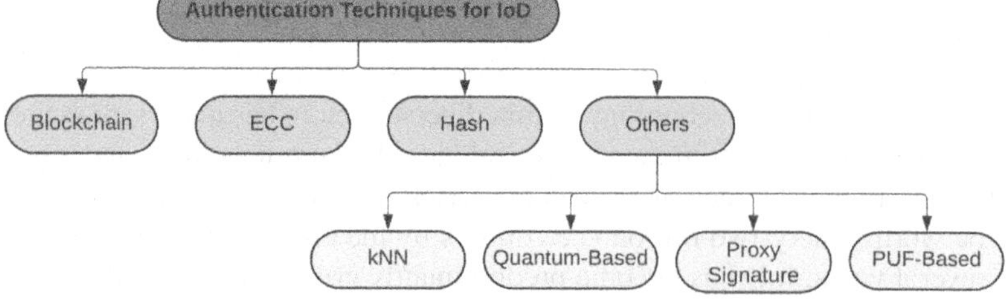

Fig. 1. Taxonomy of authentication techniques for IoD.

2 Related Work

Several researchers have been aiming to improve the security and privacy of IoD. Several surveys have been presented regarding lightweight authentication and communication security in IoD. In [11], the authors provided a comprehensive survey highlighting secure applications for drone communication and determining some of the challenges and attacks in IoD communications. The paper also listed some emerging technologies that could be used for securing drone communication, such as Blockchain, Machine Learning Algorithms, and others. Similarly, [2] provided a survey highlighting some of the IoD applications and integration, such as smart cities, wireless networks, blockchain, UAVs, and others. The authors in [2] focus mainly on providing an overview of IoD applications instead of focusing on the security applications for IoD.

In [8], the authors presented a survey that delves into the vulnerabilities in both the drones and the systems they interact with, categorizing those risks into several key areas: authentication, encryption, GPS spoofing, access control, and threat reporting. The paper highlighted that drones, especially non-military ones, generally lack robust cyber-security measures, making them susceptible to various attacks. The authors advocate for implementing basic security measures, including robust authentication protocols, encryption of data transmissions, and the integration of GPS spoofing protection and comprehensive access control. Moreover, [29] presented a survey with cybersecurity threats and solutions for UAV communications. The authors provided a comprehensive overview of the security and privacy challenges associated with UAVs and their communication networks, particularly Flying Ad-hoc Networks (FANETs). The paper categorized various cyber threats targeting UAV communications and discussed the security issues related to the IoD infrastructure, which connects UAVs with ground control stations and other devices over the internet. The authors develop a taxonomy of these threats based on different connection types and nodes within FANETs and IoD. Finally, [17] provided a survey of 6G-enabled lightweight authentication protocols for UAVs. The paper considers a blockchain implementation of 6G-enabled UAV networks to isolate UAV systems into performance and specifications groups.

Our proposed taxonomy surpasses other survey papers by encompassing many authentication techniques, from well-established methods like cryptographic hash functions to advanced innovations such as quantum-based cryptography, ensuring comprehensive coverage that addresses diverse digital communication and security needs. Unlike many taxonomies that only focus on capabilities, ours uniquely highlights the primary disadvantages of each authentication method, providing a balanced perspective that prepares users for potential implementation challenges. Furthermore, our taxonomy is designed with adaptability and scalability, accommodating emerging technologies and ongoing refinements to maintain its relevance and utility.

3 The Proposed Taxonomy of Authentication Techniques

Our proposed taxonomy aims to provide a comprehensive overview that assists in identifying suitable authentication solutions based on specific technological needs and limitations. This taxonomy, as shown in Fig. 1, categorizes the authentication techniques in IoD into four main groups: Blockchain-based, Elliptic Curve Cryptography, Cryptographic Hash functions, and others.

3.1 Blockchain

Blockchain is a revolutionary technology that underpins cryptocurrencies like Bitcoin and has far-reaching applications beyond digital currency. It is a decentralized, distributed ledger system that records transactions across many computers to ensure the data's security, transparency, and immutability. Each transaction is grouped into a block, which is then linked to the previous block, forming a chain of blocks. This structure prevents tampering and fraud, as altering any single block would require modifying all subsequent blocks, a computationally impractical task. Blockchain's ability to provide a secure and transparent record of transactions makes it valuable in various industries, including finance, supply chain management, and healthcare.

In [10], the authors proposed a blockchain-based cross-domain authentication scheme for intelligent 5G-enabled drones, addressing the challenges of identity security in drone deployments. The scheme employs multi-signature smart contracts for dynamic identity management, ensuring flexible and privacy-preserving authentication across domains without reliance on central authorities. It incorporates local and global authentication mechanisms, session key negotiation for secure communication, and a private consortium blockchain for managing drone identities. The approach effectively counters various security threats, such as identity forgery, impersonation, and man-in-the-middle attacks.

Table 1. Blockchain Authentication Schemes with Applications and Disadvantages.

Blockchain Authentication Techniques		
Ref.	Proposed Application	Disadvantages
[10]	5G Device to Device Com	Complex, latency issues, potential transaction failures, and dependent on blockchain integrity
[25]	Industrial UAVs Com	Resource-intensive & theoretical
[21]	Financial Data Security	Complex implementation, not ideal for lightweight IoD
[23]	UAV-enabled Transportation System	Higher communication cost

In [25], the paper discusses an authentication service for industrial UAVs that leverages blockchain technology. This service aims to provide a distributed, secure, and lightweight method for authenticating UAVs, ensuring the integrity and trustworthiness of their communication. The system is designed to be resilient against various attacks and is optimized to have low computational and communication costs. The paper highlights the use of blockchain to manage the authentication process and smart contracts to facilitate operations like updating and acquiring authentication information. The authentication process relies on elliptic-curve cryptography, and the proposed system is evaluated for security using formal methods like BAN logic and AVISPA for verification.

In [21], the paper presents SecureIoD, a security solution for the IoD to protect drone-collected data. It addresses the challenges of resource limitations and wireless communication vulnerabilities. The system enforces mutual authentication between drones and zone service providers using blockchain for secure data storage. Combining a physical unclonable function (PUF) and Henon map creates secure session keys. The model uses a joint proof-of-work and proof-of-stake consensus to optimize blockchain transactions. The proposed scheme enhances security and privacy, mitigates centralization risks, and preserves data integrity. The consensus mechanism also streamlines miner selection and block addition to the blockchain. The authors in [23] proposed a secure and lightweight authentication scheme for unmanned aerial vehicles (UAVs) and road side units (RSUs) using blockchain technology. In their proposal, a hashed pseudo-identity of UAVs is stored through a blockchain. RSUs can authenticate UAVs by retrieving the corresponding transactions. The proposed scheme has four phases: initialization, registration of both RSU and UAVs, authentication, and UAV revocation. During the UAV registration part, the TA stores the hashed information of the drone's ID and PUF response to the blockchain.

The referenced studies collectively highlight innovative applications of blockchain technology to enhance the security and integrity of authentication processes within the IoD. However, while these studies propose advanced blockchain-based solutions, they still face computational and communication efficiency challenges, particularly in resource-constrained environments, as noted in Table 1. Further research could focus on optimizing these blockchain implementations to reduce overhead and enhance real-time processing capabilities in IoD applications.

3.2 Elliptic Curve Cryptography

In [30], the authors presented a secure lightweight proven authenticated key agreement (SLPAKA) technique designed for the IoD network. It aims to address the trade-off between security and lightweight features in such networks. The authors first analyze a different key agreement technique proposed by authors in [6] and identify its vulnerabilities, such as partial key-escrow attack, known session-specific temporary information attack under the Canetti-Krawczyk (CK) adversary, and replay attack. The proposed SLPAKA technique is designed to overcome the identified challenges from [6] and mainly uses two elliptic curves as ephemeral secrets during the registration phase. The authors evaluate the proposed SLPAKA using theoretical methods and the ProVerif cryptographic protocol verification tool. The results confirm that SLPAKA is secure against known attacks. The technique also allows the dynamic addition of drones to the network post-deployment, enhancing scalability through mobile edge computing devices.

In [15], the paper presents an Elliptic Curve Cryptography (ECC) based authentication scheme tailored for securing the IoD in applications such as wildlife monitoring, infrastructure inspection, and smart city surveillance. This scheme leverages the security features of ECC and focuses on ensuring robust mutual authentication and perfect forward secrecy, vital for secure communications over potentially insecure channels like Flying Ad-Hoc Networks (FANETs). The scheme includes a formal security proof using the ProVerif2.03 verification toolkit and the random oracle model, alongside a pragmatic illustration to validate its effectiveness. Key aspects of the protocol involve using ECC to handle the Computational Diffie-Hellman Problem (CDHP) during session key generation, enhancing the scheme's resilience against various threats, including insider and stolen-verifier attacks.

In [13], the authors proposed the new authentication and key agreement scheme (NAKAS), using an elliptic curve cryptography-based authentication scheme to provide secure access from users to drones on a public channel. The proposed ECC-based scheme implements six phases. The first phase is the setup phase, where a ground station server (GSS) selects the elliptic curve point and secret master key. In the drone pre-deployment phase, all drones are registered to the field. The user registration phase allows users to register with the GSS with ID and pseudo-identity through secure channels. The login and authentication phase enables users to receive authentication and send a secret shared key with a drone in the field zone. The biometric and password phase lets the user update his password and add his biometric information from his device without the intervention of the GSS. Lastly, new drones receive an ID and pseudo-identity from the GSS in the drone addition phase.

Table 2. ECC Authentication Techniques with Applications and Disadvantages.

ECC Authentication Techniques		
Ref.	Proposed Application	Disadvantages
[30]	Monitoring and Surveillance	There is a complex implementation
[15]	FANET Communication Security	Mainly theoretical with limited testing
[13]	Monitoring and Surveillance	It requires a high computation cost
[4]	Battlefield Surveillance	Higher communication cost
[9]	Vehicle to Vehicle Communication	Increased vulnerabilities due to the network entities
[27]	Information Gathering and Transmission	Complex implementation & requires a lot of resources
[5]	Smart City Monitoring System	It lacks information regarding authentication technique and there is limited testing

In [4], the authors proposed an access control protocol for a drone-assisted IoT environment in battlefield surveillance (ACPBS-IoT). The proposal has four phases. In the first phase, the system initialization phase, has a trusted commanding room (CR) that generates all the necessary parameters, such as a non-singular elliptic curve over the Galois Field, an ID, a master private key, and a public key. The second phase is the registration, where the drones and ground station servers (GSSs) are registered with the CR. The next part is the access control phase, where drones and GSSs establish a session key before they can exchange real-time information. The fourth part is the dynamic node addition phase that allows new drones to be added to a GSS for a specific surveillance zone in case the current drones are hijacked or fail. In [9], the authors proposed a Blockchain-supported authentication protocol for Drone-assisted IoV using Elliptic curve cryptography (BDIVE). The BDIVE authentication scheme attempts to provide security against active attackers. The paper used Burrow-Abadi-Needham (BAN) logic to prove and demonstrate the security and resilience of BDIVE against several attacks. The authors also implemented BDIVE in the AVISPA program to demonstrate its security. In their results, BDIVE proved to reduce energy consumption by up to 70% and computational cost by up to 68% compared to existing authentication protocols.

In [27], the authors proposed a Robust User Authentication Mechanism for IoD (RUAM-IoD). The proposal implements elliptic curve cryptography, symmetric encryption (AES), and hash function (SHA-256) to achieve mutual authentication. RUAM-IoD has six phases: system initialization, drone registration, user registration, authentication and key agreement, biometric and password change, and revocation. The proposed scheme utilizes a remote user connected via the internet who makes requests to the drone service provider registration center (DRC) to connect to a specific drone. Once the remote user and drone achieve mutual authentication, they establish a session key. In [5], the paper proposed an access control framework for IoD. The proposed framework utilizes elliptic curve cryptography (ECC) and symmetric hash functions to generate a public-private key pair. The proposed framework has four steps. In the first step, the initiator sends a login request. In the second step, the responder verifies the timestamp to authenticate the initiator and generates a challenge message for the initiator. In step three, the initiator authenticates the responder and sends a response message. In the last step, the responder verifies the response from the initiator and generates a session key.

Previous studies have utilized the ECC to enhance mutual authentication and ensure forward secrecy. Notable challenges these studies aim to overcome include ensuring security solutions' scalability without compromising operational efficiency, reducing computational and communication costs, and providing robust defense against a range of cybersecurity threats, such as impersonation and man-in-the-middle attacks, as shown in Table 2.

3.3 Cryptographic Hash Function

In [32], the paper proposed a lightweight Authentication and Key Agreement (AKA) scheme designed explicitly for the IoD. This scheme aims to address security challenges and privacy issues in drones that arise from embedded sensors collecting sensitive data. Traditional AKA schemes typically face security risks and have high communication and computation costs. To overcome these, the authors' scheme relies primarily on secure one-way hash functions and bitwise XOR operations for mutual authentication between drones and users. This approach ensures AKA security under the random oracle model and is resilient against known attacks. The scheme has also provided better security and lower communication and computation costs than existing solutions. In [7], the paper introduces a Lightweight Privacy-Preserving Authentication Scheme (LPPA) for the IoD within the IoT ecosystem, aimed at securing sensitive information and optimizing UAV energy use. The scheme features dynamic membership authentication and key management, along with a feedback mechanism to assess and update the trustworthiness of network participants. The LPPA establishes a secure framework for UAV communication in vehicular ad-hoc networks (VANETs) through a handshake protocol involving UAVs and roadside units (RSUs), mediated by a trust authority (TA). This protocol uses hash functions, asymmetric encryption, and timestamp verification to ensure that only authorized UAVs access the network. The scheme's feedback loop allows dynamic critical updates based on the trust status of network sensors, enhancing security against impersonation and physical UAV capture.

In [22], the authors proposed a lightweight and privacy-preserving mutual authentication and key agreement protocol (PMAP) that uses a message authentication code

Table 3. Cryptographic Hash Function Authentication Techniques with Applications and Disadvantages.

Cryptographic Hash Function Authentication Techniques		
Ref.	Proposed Application	Disadvantages
[32]	Surveillance	The setup requires several steps for implementation
[7]	Information Transmission	Complex, & takes a lot of resources
[22]	Navigation	Mutual authentication process takes a lot of resources
[14]	Information Gathering	Communication cost is relatively similar to other schemes
[26]	Information Gathering for Smart City	Vulnerabilities due to the network entities
[31]	IoD-based Smart City Environment	High computation cost when compared to other proposals
[24]	Monitoring and Surveillance	Limited implementation, and mainly theoretical proposal
[28]	Information Gathering	No direct communication between user & drone

and hash functions to achieve mutual authentication and establish a secure session key. PMAP has a deployment phase that requires a drone to generate its real identity, its initial challenge-response pair (CRP), and its initial pseudonym. During the deployment phase, PMAP uses a physical unclonable function (PUF) and chaotic system to obtain values for the initial CRP. PMAP implements two different versions of its scheme. One version implements mutual authentication between drone and zone service providers. Using a zone service provider, the second version can achieve mutual authentication between two drones. The authors implemented the proposed PMAP in a high-level protocol specification language (HLPSL) and evaluated the security with the automated validation of internet security protocols and applications (AVISPAs) system.

In [14], the paper reviewed and evaluated the security of the AKA protocol proposed by [32]. The paper determined that the AKA protocol has weaknesses against several attack types. It proposed an enhanced and efficient user access protocol for IoD that uses hash functions and XOR operations to achieve authentication and key agreement phase. The proposed scheme has a setup phase, a user registration phase, a drone registration phase, an authentication and key establishment phase, and a password update phase. The authors demonstrated that their proposed protocol is resilient against several attacks and has lower communication costs and running time when compared to six different schemes. In [26], the authors proposed a secure and anonymous authentication framework (SAAF-IoD). The proposed framework utilizes the Chebyshev Polynomial as a chaotic map for key generation, a fuzzy extractor to generate a biometric key, AES encryption, and hash functions to achieve mutual authentication and establish a session key. SAAF-IoD has five phases: ground station (GS) enrollment phase, drone enrollment phase, user enrollment phase, drone access phase, and secret credentials update phase. The authors demonstrate that their proposal is secure against impersonation attacks, privilege insider attacks, de-synchronization attacks, drone capture attacks, MITM attacks, and temporary secret leakage attacks.

In [31], the paper presented a secure lightweight authentication protocol (SLAP-IoD) that uses a collision-resistant cryptographic hash function to achieve authentication key agreement and establish a session key between a user and a drone using a control server for authentication. The proposed model has five processes: initialization, drone registration, mobile user registration, authentication and key agreement, and password and biometric update. During the initialization and registration processes, the scheme uses PUF and a generation function from a fuzzy extractor to obtain initial values for drones and users. For the drone, a challenge is used in the PUF to obtain a response; the response value from the PUF is used as input for the generation function of the fuzzy extractor to produce a pair of values with secret data and reproduction parameters. For the user, biometric data is used in the PUF to obtain a response value; the response value from the PUF is used as input for the generation function of the fuzzy extractor to produce a pair of values with biometric secret data and reproduction parameters. SLAP-IoD uses XOR operations and hash functions to encrypt and transmit data during the drone registration, mobile user registration, and authentication and key agreement processes. In [24], the authors propose an authentication scheme that uses hash functions to achieve mutual authentication and key agreement between a drone and a ground station. The proposed scheme also utilizes PUF to obtain the drone's initial challenge-response pair values. The scheme has three phases: a registration phase, a mutual authentication and key agreement, and an updating phase.

The paper in [28] presented a resource-efficient authentication scheme for the IoD networks (REAS-IoD). The proposal uses exclusive-OR operations, a hash function (SHA-160), a fuzzy extractor, and an authenticated encryption primitive (ACE) to achieve authenticated key exchange (AKE). REAS-IoD allows drones and users to establish a secure session key (SK) after the entities have been authenticated. The author's proposal has six phases: drone deployment, user registration, login and authenticated key exchange, biometric and password change, revocation, and dynamic drone deployment.

Previous schemes are designed to tackle significant challenges such as high computational and communication costs, vulnerability to impersonation and man-in-the-middle attacks, and the need for dynamic security management in complex IoD environments using cryptographic hash functions. These studies highlight the urgency to develop solutions that are secure, resource-efficient, and adaptable to the rapidly evolving demands of drone technology, as explained in Table 3. Future work could focus on reducing the energy consumption of these protocols, enhancing real-time processing capabilities, and improving scalability and adaptability to support an expanding array of IoD applications.

Table 4. Other Authentication Techniques with Applications and Disadvantages.

Other Authentication Techniques			
Authentication Technique	Ref.	Proposed Application	Disadvantages
Asymmetric Encryption	[16]	Real-time data access	Complex, limited testing, initial, resource-intensive
kNN	[12]	Secure drone network access.	It requires a complex set of steps to achieve authentication
Quantum Based Cryptography	[19]	Military	It resource-intensive and the proposal is experimental
	[3]	Communication Security	It is an emerging tech and requires more research
Proxy Signature	[1]	5G Device to Device Communication	The 5G device to device network and protocols are still under development
PUF Based Cryptography	[20]	Communication Security	There are scalability issues and it is difficult to implement

3.4 Other Authentication Techniques

In [16], the paper proposed a lightweight and anonymous two-factor authentication scheme for the IoD, addressing critical security issues in drone network systems. The proposed scheme, aimed at securing real-time information transmission between drones and control systems, utilizes asymmetric cryptographic methods to enhance security while minimizing communication and computation overhead. It effectively counters various security threats, including replay, impersonation, modification, drone capture, known session key, and man-in-the-middle attacks, by employing one-way hash functions, encryption/decryption mechanisms, and secure time-stamping. The paper in [12] presents a privacy-aware and hardware-accelerated authentication scheme for the IoD using the k-nearest neighbor (kNN) encryption algorithm with hardware acceleration using Field Programmable Gate Arrays (FPGAs). This scheme is intended to provide authorized users with secure and fast access to drone data. The authentication process involves several phases: registration and key distribution, where drones receive unique IDs and keys; uploading of encrypted IDs to an authentication server; and the authentication of drones through encrypted ID verification. FPGAs enhance the system's ability to handle large computational loads efficiently and with reduced power consumption. The paper emphasizes the system's scalability, performance efficiency, and improved security measures over existing methods, including index confidentiality protection and authentication requests' unlinkability.

In [19], the paper introduces a quantum-safe communication protocol for the IoD to protect against the potential threats of quantum computing. It points out the vulnerabilities in current IoD security that rely on problems like discrete logarithms and factorization, which could be solved by quantum algorithms, such as Shor's algorithm. To combat this, the paper proposes a protocol based on the Ring Learning With Error (RLWE) problem, known for its quantum resistance and low computational load. This protocol ensures secure, authenticated communication between drones and zone service providers (ZSPs). It is designed to protect the integrity and confidentiality of data against quantum attacks while being computationally efficient for drones.

In [3], the paper proposed a quantum-based communication scheme to enhance security within the IoD, addressing vulnerabilities to quantum computing attacks that traditional cryptographic methods face. The scheme utilizes quantum cryptography for mutual authentication of drones and ground stations and secure transmission of secret messages. It specifically employs quantum key distribution (QKD) to establish secure channels where quantum states encoded with secret keys are transmitted, making eavesdropping detectable due to the alteration of quantum properties upon interception. The protocol also includes measures such as transmitting hash values of random keys and using decoy states to prevent eavesdropping and impersonation attacks. The core security of the scheme is rooted in quantum mechanics principles like the no-cloning theorem and quantum entanglement, ensuring any interception or forgery attempts are immediately apparent, thus maintaining the integrity and confidentiality of communications.

In [1], the authors proposed a proxy signature-based authentication scheme for drones using a 5G mobile device-to-device (D2D) network. The proposal is compatible with drones that utilize the 5G D2D Proximity-based Services (ProSe) standard.

The scheme utilizes the proxy signature scheme from authors in [18]. The authors in [1] proposed a registration and delegation phase and a discovery and device authentication phase. Their proposal requires 5G authentication protocols at the device registration phase. After the drone registration phase, the process moves to a delegation-based authentication protocol that uses the selected proxy signature. During the discovery and authentication phase, the leader drone broadcasts a proxy signature to authenticate itself to the drones. Similarly, the swarm of drones replies with a proxy signature message to authenticate themselves to the leader drone. After the authentication phase, the leader drone establishes D2D communication with a swarm of drones. In [20], the paper presents an efficient PUF-based authentication protocol for the IoD focusing on security and privacy. It addresses attacks like man-in-the-middle, replay, impersonation, and provides user anonymity. It uses a dynamic approach for session keys and security parameters, making it robust against prediction attacks. The proposed scheme uses lightweight XOR operations, concatenation, and hashing for authentication, enhancing resource-constrained IoDs' security.

Table 5. Security Analysis

Type of Attack	[10]	[25]	[21]	[23]	[30]	[15]	[13]	[4]	[9]	[27]	[5]	[32]	[7]	[22]	[14]	[26]	[31]	[24]	[28]	[16]	[12]	[19]	[3]	[1]	[20]
Denial of Service	✓	✓	✓	✓	✓	✓	✓			✓		✓	✓						✓	✓	✓	✓	✓		✓
Drone Physical Capture		✓	✓	✓		✓	✓	✓		✓	✓		✓		✓		✓	✓				✓	✓		✓
Ephemeral Secret Leakage		✓				✓		✓	✓	✓			✓	✓							✓	✓	✓		✓
GSS Impersonation							✓															✓			
Impersonation	✓	✓	✓	✓	✓	✓	✓	✓		✓		✓	✓	✓	✓	✓	✓		✓	✓	✓	✓	✓		✓
Known Session Key	✓	✓		✓	✓							✓	✓	✓	✓		✓					✓	✓		✓
Malicious Leader Drone																								✓	
Malicious Swarm Drone																						✓		✓	
Man in the Middle	✓	✓	✓	✓	✓	✓	✓	✓	✓	✓		✓	✓	✓	✓	✓			✓	✓	✓	✓	✓		✓
Modification		✓	✓			✓						✓	✓	✓	✓					✓	✓	✓	✓		✓
Guessing							✓		✓					✓			✓		✓				✓		
Password and Biometric Update																✓									
Insider	✓				✓	✓	✓	✓	✓	✓						✓	✓		✓			✓	✓		
Replay	✓	✓	✓	✓	✓	✓	✓	✓	✓	✓		✓	✓	✓	✓	✓	✓		✓	✓	✓	✓	✓	✓	✓
Spoofing	✓		✓			✓						✓	✓	✓	✓						✓	✓	✓		
Stolen Smart Device							✓			✓		✓			✓		✓		✓				✓		
User Impersonation	✓	✓	✓			✓	✓			✓			✓								✓	✓	✓		✓

The previous studies delve into cutting-edge authentication schemes for the IoD, focusing on enhancing security through diverse cryptographic methods while addressing the unique challenges of drone networks. From employing two-factor authentication with minimal overhead in real-time data transmission to integrating quantum-resistant protocols to safeguard against future quantum computing threats, these papers seek to fortify IoD against a spectrum of attacks, including replay, impersonation, and eavesdropping. However, despite these advancements, challenges remain in balancing high security with low computational load and ensuring scalability and efficiency in diverse IoD applications, as noted in Table 4.

4 Discussion

This survey paper proposes a novel classification of authentication techniques in IoD based on several methods such as Blockchain, ECC, Hash function, and other techniques. We also present the security attacks defended against in each paper of the studied research papers in Table 5. In addition, the security features provided in each paper are introduced in Table 6. Common drawbacks identified across the reviewed papers include implementation complexity, limited or absent testing of proposed schemes, and the theoretical nature of some proposals, as shown in Tables 1, 2, 3, 4. Notably, only a few studies have explored using kNN, lattice-based cryptography, proxy signature, PUF, or quantum-based cryptography, indicating that these techniques are less commonly applied within the IoD era.

Table 5 presents the security analysis of the evaluated authentication schemes, identifying seventeen attacks addressed by these schemes. The attacks are Denial of Service Attacks, Drone Physical Capture Attacks, Ephemeral Secret Leakage Attacks, GSS Impersonation Attacks, Impersonation Attacks, Known Session Key Attacks, Malicious Leader Drone Attacks, Malicious Swarm Drone Attacks, Man-in-the-Middle Attacks, Modification Attacks, Guessing Attacks, Password and Biometric Update Attack, Insider Attack, Replay Attack, Spoofing Attack, Stolen Smart Device Attack, and User Impersonation Attack. Among the reviewed papers, most schemes offer protection against impersonation, man-in-the-middle, and replay attacks while less address guessing, spoofing, and stolen device attacks.

Table 6 highlights seven specific security features across the reviewed papers: Anonymity, Distributed Authentication, Integrity, Mutual Authentication, Scalability, Session Key Agreement, and Untraceability. Our analysis shows that most proposals support anonymity, mutual authentication, session key agreement, and untraceability, but fewer offer distributed authentication and integrity.

Table 6. Security Features

Security Feature	[10]	[25]	[21]	[23]	[30]	[15]	[13]	[4]	[9]	[27]	[5]	[32]	[7]	[22]	[14]	[26]	[31]	[24]	[28]	[16]	[12]	[19]	[3]	[1]	[20]
Anonymity	✓	✓	✓	✓	✓	✓	✓	✓	✓	✓	✓	✓	✓	✓	✓	✓	✓		✓	✓	✓	✓	✓		✓
Distributed Authentication		✓	✓										✓								✓	✓	✓	✓	✓
Integrity		✓	✓				✓					✓	✓	✓							✓	✓	✓		✓
Mutual Authentication	✓	✓	✓		✓	✓	✓	✓			✓	✓	✓		✓		✓	✓	✓	✓	✓	✓	✓	✓	✓
Scalability	✓	✓	✓		✓	✓						✓	✓		✓					✓	✓	✓	✓	✓	✓
Session Key Agreement	✓	✓	✓		✓	✓	✓	✓			✓	✓	✓	✓	✓			✓	✓	✓	✓	✓	✓		✓
Untraceability	✓	✓	✓	✓	✓	✓	✓	✓	✓	✓	✓	✓	✓		✓	✓	✓		✓	✓	✓	✓	✓		✓

5 Conclusion

This survey comprehensively analyzes the current landscape of authentication schemes for IoD, highlighting the critical need for robust, efficient, and lightweight security solutions. The survey categorizes existing authentication techniques into various methods, such as blockchain-based cryptography, elliptic curve cryptography, Cryptographic hash functions, and others. Each method is evaluated for suitability within IoD environments, considering factors such as resistance to common security threats and security services provided. The findings suggest that while traditional cryptographic methods offer strong security, they often fall short in addressing the unique challenges posed by IoD systems, particularly the need for rapid and resource-efficient authentication processes. Innovations in blockchain and quantum-based cryptography show promise in enhancing security while maintaining operational efficiency, though they still require further refinement for widespread adoption.

Acknowledgments. The Security and Privacy of Emerging Network (SPEN) research lab at the University of Southern Mississippi (USM), USA, made this work possible. In addition, great efforts have been made by the Higher Colleges of Technology (HCT), UAE. The statements made herein are solely the responsibility of the authors.

References

1. Abdel-Malek, M.A., Akkaya, K., Bhuyan, A., Ibrahim, A.S.: A proxy signature-based drone authentication in 5G D2D networks. In: 2021 IEEE 93rd Vehicular Technology Conference (VTC2021-Spring), pp. 1–7 (2021). https://doi.org/10.1109/VTC2021-Spring51267.2021.9448962
2. Abualigah, L., Diabat, A., Sumari, P., Gandomi, A.H.: Applications, deployments, and integration of internet of drones (IoD): a review. IEEE Sens. J. **21**(22), 25532–25546 (2021). https://doi.org/10.1109/JSEN.2021.3114266
3. Abulkasim, H., Goncalves, B., Mashatan, A., Ghose, S.: Authenticated secure quantum-based communication scheme in internet-of-drones deployment. IEEE Access **10**, 94963–94972 (2022). https://doi.org/10.1109/ACCESS.2022.3204793
4. Bera, B., Das, A.K., Garg, S., Jalil Piran, M., Hossain, M.S.: Access control protocol for battlefield surveillance in drone-assisted IoT environment. IEEE Internet Things J. **9**(4), 2708–2721 (2022). https://doi.org/10.1109/JIOT.2020.3049003
5. Chaudhry, S.A., et al.: A physical capture resistant authentication scheme for the internet of drones. IEEE Commun. Stand. Mag. **5**(4), 62–67 (2021). https://doi.org/10.1109/MCOMSTD.0001.2100006
6. Chen, C.L., Deng, Y.Y., Weng, W., Chen, C.H., Chiu, Y.J., Wu, C.M.: A traceable and privacy-preserving authentication for UAV communication control system. Electronics **9**(1) (2020). https://doi.org/10.3390/electronics9010062. https://www.mdpi.com/2079-9292/9/1/62
7. Cheng, Y., Xu, S., Zang, M., Kong, W.: LPPA: a lightweight privacy-preserving authentication scheme for the internet of drones. In: 2021 IEEE 21st International Conference on Communication Technology (ICCT), pp. 656–661 (2021). https://doi.org/10.1109/ICCT52962.2021.9658014
8. Durfey, N., Sajal, S.: A comprehensive survey: cybersecurity challenges and futures of autonomous drones. In: 2022 Intermountain Engineering, Technology and Computing (IETC), pp. 1–7 (2022). https://doi.org/10.1109/IETC54973.2022.9796881
9. El-Zawawy, M.A., Brighente, A., Conti, M.: Authenticating drone-assisted internet of vehicles using elliptic curve cryptography and blockchain. IEEE Trans. Netw. Serv. Manag. **20**(2), 1775–1789 (2023). https://doi.org/10.1109/TNSM.2022.3217320

10. Feng, C., Liu, B., Guo, Z., Yu, K., Qin, Z., Choo, K.K.R.: Blockchain-based cross-domain authentication for intelligent 5G-enabled internet of drones. IEEE Internet Things J. **9**(8), 6224–6238 (2022). https://doi.org/10.1109/JIOT.2021.3113321
11. Hassija, V., et al.: Fast, reliable, and secure drone communication: a comprehensive survey. IEEE Commun. Surv. Tutor. **23**(4), 2802–2832 (2021). https://doi.org/10.1109/COMST.2021.3097916
12. Henson, T.E., Dawoud, A., Sherif, A.: Privacy-aware and hardware acceleration-based authentication scheme for internet of drones. In: 2021 3rd IEEE Middle East and North Africa COMMunications Conference (MENACOMM), pp. 130–135 (2021). https://doi.org/10.1109/MENACOMM50742.2021.9678226
13. Hussain, S., Chaudhry, S.A., Alomari, O.A., Alsharif, M.H., Khan, M.K., Kumar, N.: Amassing the security: an ECC-based authentication scheme for internet of drones. IEEE Syst. J. **15**(3), 4431–4438 (2021). https://doi.org/10.1109/JSYST.2021.3057047
14. Hussain, S., Farooq, M., Alzahrani, B.A., Albeshri, A., Alsubhi, K., Chaudhry, S.A.: An efficient and reliable user access protocol for internet of drones. IEEE Access **11**, 59688–59700 (2023). https://doi.org/10.1109/ACCESS.2023.3284832
15. Jan, S.U., Abbasi, I.A., Algarni, F., Khan, A.S.: A verifiably secure ECC based authentication scheme for securing IoD using FANET. IEEE Access **10**, 95321–95343 (2022). https://doi.org/10.1109/ACCESS.2022.3204271
16. Khalid, H., Hashim, S.J., Mumtazah Syed Ahamed, S., Hashim, F., Chaudhary, M.A.: Secure real-time data access using two-factor authentication scheme for the internet of drones. In: 2021 IEEE 19th Student Conference on Research and Development (SCOReD), pp. 168–173 (2021). https://doi.org/10.1109/SCOReD53546.2021.9652714
17. Khan, A.S., et al.: A survey on 6G enabled light weight authentication protocol for UAVs, security, open research issues and future directions. Appl. Sci. **13**(1) (2023). https://doi.org/10.3390/app13010277. https://www.mdpi.com/2076-3417/13/1/277
18. Lee, B., Kim, H., Kim, K.: Strong proxy signature and its applications, January 2002
19. Mishra, D., et al.: Quantum-safe secure and authorized communication protocol for internet of drones. IEEE Trans. Veh. Technol. **72**(12), 16499–16507 (2023). https://doi.org/10.1109/TVT.2023.3292169
20. Nyangaresi, V.O., Petrovic, N.: Efficient PUF based authentication protocol for internet of drones. In: 2021 International Telecommunications Conference (ITC-Egypt), pp. 1–4 (2021). https://doi.org/10.1109/ITC-Egypt52936.2021.9513902
21. Pu, C., Wall, A., Ahmed, I., Choo, K.K.R.: SecureIoD: a secure data collection and storage mechanism for internet of drones. In: 2022 23rd IEEE International Conference on Mobile Data Management (MDM) (2022)
22. Pu, C., Wall, A., Choo, K.K.R., Ahmed, I., Lim, S.: A lightweight and privacy-preserving mutual authentication and key agreement protocol for internet of drones environment. IEEE Internet Things J. **9**(12), 9918–9933 (2022). https://doi.org/10.1109/JIOT.2022.3163367
23. Son, S., Kwon, D., Lee, S., Jeon, Y., Das, A.K., Park, Y.: Design of secure and lightweight authentication scheme for UAV-enabled intelligent transportation systems using blockchain and PUF. IEEE Access **11**, 60240–60253 (2023). https://doi.org/10.1109/ACCESS.2023.3286016
24. Soni, V., Prasad, B.: A PUF based authentication schemes for UAV. In: 2023 International Conference on Computer, Electronics Electrical Engineering their Applications (IC2E3), pp. 1–4 (2023). https://doi.org/10.1109/IC2E357697.2023.10262668
25. Tan, Y., Wang, J., Liu, J., Kato, N.: Blockchain-assisted distributed and lightweight authentication service for industrial unmanned aerial vehicles. IEEE Internet Things J. **9**(18), 16928–16940 (2022). https://doi.org/10.1109/JIOT.2022.3142251

26. Tanveer, M., Alasmary, H., Kumar, N., Nayak, A.: SAAF-IoD: secure and anonymous authentication framework for the internet of drones. IEEE Trans. Veh. Technol. **73**(1), 232–244 (2024). https://doi.org/10.1109/TVT.2023.3306813
27. Tanveer, M., Alkhayyat, A., Naushad, A., Khan, A.U., Kumar, N., Alharbi, A.G.: RUAM-IoD: a robust user authentication mechanism for the internet of drones. IEEE Access **10**, 19836–19851 (2022). https://doi.org/10.1109/ACCESS.2022.3149376
28. Tanveer, M., Khan, A.U., Nguyen, T.N., Ahmad, M., El-Latif, A.A.A.: Towards a secure and computational framework for internet of drones enabled aerial computing. IEEE Trans. Netw. Sci. Eng. **10**(5), 3058–3070 (2023). https://doi.org/10.1109/TNSE.2022.3151843
29. Tsao, K.Y., Girdler, T., Vassilakis, V.G.: A survey of cyber security threats and solutions for UAV communications and flying ad-hoc networks. Ad Hoc Netw. **133**, 102894 (2022). https://doi.org/10.1016/j.adhoc.2022.102894
30. Yahuza, M., Idris, M.Y.I., Wahab, A.W.A., Nandy, T., Ahmedy, I.B., Ramli, R.: An edge assisted secure lightweight authentication technique for safe communication on the internet of drones network. IEEE Access **9**, 31420–31440 (2021). https://doi.org/10.1109/ACCESS.2021.3060420
31. Yu, S., Das, A.K., Park, Y., Lorenz, P.: SLAP-IoD: secure and lightweight authentication protocol using physical unclonable functions for internet of drones in smart city environments. IEEE Trans. Veh. Technol. **71**(10), 10374–10388 (2022). https://doi.org/10.1109/TVT.2022.3188769
32. Zhang, Y., He, D., Li, L., Chen, B.: A lightweight authentication and key agreement scheme for internet of drones. Comput. Commun. **154**, 455–464 (2020). https://doi.org/10.1016/j.comcom.2020.02.067

CarbonMetric: An Intelligent System for Calculating and Reducing Carbon Footprints in Urban Environments

Fuad Alhosban(✉), Hatem Tamimi, Amal S. Alzahmi, Ghayah M. Alhmoudi, and Meera A. Alowais

Higher Colleges of Technologies, Dubai, UAE
falhosban@hct.ac.ae

Abstract. The growing concern over global carbon emissions and their impact on climate change necessitates innovative solutions to raise awareness and drive behavioral change. This paper presents CarbonMetric, a mobile application designed to calculate an individual's carbon footprint from everyday car journeys and provide personalized recommendations to reduce it. The application leverages data on vehicle type, fuel consumption, and journey length to compute emissions and suggests alternative actions to users based on their behavior. CarbonMetric's current design offers a user-friendly interface that simplifies data input and provides actionable feedback, making it a valuable tool for promoting sustainable practices. The system's adaptability and intelligent decision-making processes exemplify how mobile technology can support urban environmental strategies and align with smart city initiatives.

Keywords: CarbonMetric · Carbon Footprint · Smart City · Sustainability · Intelligent Systems · Mobile Application

1 Introduction

The growing concern over carbon emissions, particularly in urban environments with high vehicle reliance, calls for innovative solutions that not only calculate emissions but also promote meaningful behavioral change. In the UAE, where heavy reliance on personal vehicles and high energy consumption from air conditioning are common due to extreme climate conditions, there is an urgent need for personalized tools to combat rising emissions. CarbonMetric is a mobile application specifically designed to address these regional challenges by offering real-time, tailored feedback on carbon emissions from car journeys. By utilizing user-specific data such as vehicle type, fuel consumption, and journey distance, CarbonMetric not only calculates emissions but also provides customized recommendations to help users reduce their carbon footprint, thereby promoting sustainable behavior in a high-emission context. Unlike generic calculators, CarbonMetric aims to bridge the gap between awareness and action, especially in regions like the UAE [1].

A. Safi et al. (Eds.): ISICS 2024, CCIS 2381, pp. 242–250, 2025.
https://doi.org/10.1007/978-3-031-82931-4_18

2 Background and Literature Review

2.1 Carbon Emissions and Urban Sustainability

As urban populations grow and cities expand, the environmental impact of daily human activities has become a critical concern for sustainability. Transportation, particularly the use of private vehicles, is one of the largest contributors to urban carbon emissions. According to the International Energy Agency (IEA), the transport sector accounts for nearly one-quarter of global energy-related CO_2 emissions, with road vehicles responsible for almost three-quarters of that amount [2]. In rapidly developing regions like the United Arab Emirates (UAE), the high reliance on personal vehicles, coupled with extreme climate conditions necessitating heavy use of air conditioning, has resulted in one of the highest per capita carbon footprints globally. The UAE's "Net Zero 2050" strategic initiative reflects a national commitment to reducing these emissions and transitioning towards more sustainable energy use [3]. This commitment underscores the need for innovative solutions that empower individuals to understand and reduce their carbon footprints.

2.2 Carbon Footprint Calculators and Behavioral Change

While many carbon footprint calculators, such as MyClimate and the CoolClimate Network, are designed to raise awareness about emissions, they often provide users with static, generalized feedback that lacks the personalization necessary for sustained behavioral change [4, 5]. Research indicates that personalized feedback is critical for motivating users to modify their habits. CarbonMetric addresses these limitations by providing dynamic, real-time recommendations tailored to individual user behavior. By integrating real-time data and leveraging user-specific inputs, CarbonMetric enhances user engagement and effectiveness in reducing emissions. Unlike existing tools that primarily focus on raising awareness, CarbonMetric's core innovation lies in its ability to offer actionable insights, making it more than just an educational tool—it becomes a behavioral driver for carbon reduction. Additionally, CarbonMetric's potential to integrate machine learning algorithms for future personalization sets it apart from existing solutions, offering users increasingly sophisticated feedback over time [6].

2.3 Integration of Intelligent Features in CarbonMetric

The application of intelligent features in sustainability applications has been growing, particularly in areas like energy consumption forecasting and transportation optimization. Machine learning models, such as reinforcement learning, have shown promise in optimizing transportation modes and routes to minimize emissions. For instance, reinforcement learning can dynamically adjust to real-time conditions, providing optimized suggestions for reducing carbon footprints [7].

To visualize the growing interest and applicability of machine learning in transportation, we refer to a diagram from Farazi et al. (2021) that illustrates the applications of deep reinforcement learning across various transportation domains. This diagram supports the discussion on the role of advanced algorithms in enhancing sustainability applications (Fig. 1).

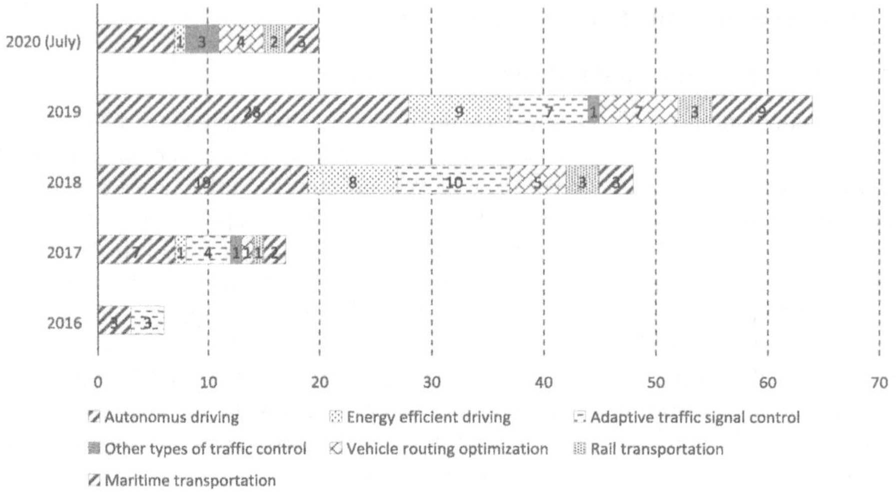

Fig. 1. Applications of Deep Reinforcement Learning in Transportation (adapted from Farazi et al., 2021) [8].

3 Comparison with Other Carbon Footprint Calculators

Several other carbon footprint calculators have been developed and are widely used, each with unique features and target audiences. In this section, we compare the core functionalities of CarbonMetric with other notable calculators, including MyClimate [9], the CoolClimate Network [10], the WWF Calculator [11], the EPA Calculator [12], and Giki Zero [13]. Table 1 highlights the differences in features, focusing on real-time data integration, personalization, and user engagement.

Table 1. Feature comparison between CarbonMetric and other carbon footprint calculators.

Feature	Carbon Metric	My Climate	Cool Climate	WWF Calculator	EPA Calculator	Giki Zero
Real-Time Data Integration	Planned	No	No	No	No	No
Personalized Recommendations	Yes	Yes	Yes	Yes	Yes	Yes
Carbon Offsetting Options	No	Yes	No	No	No	No
User Interface Simplicity	High	Medium	Medium	High	High	High
Gamification	No	No	No	No	No	Yes

This comparison highlights CarbonMetric's potential to provide real-time data integration and future machine learning enhancements, features that are not currently offered by many other calculators. Additionally, CarbonMetric's focus on personalized recommendations positions it as a tool that can better engage users in reducing their carbon footprints compared to calculators that rely on static data and results. These unique features suggest that CarbonMetric could fill an existing gap in the market, offering a more dynamic and engaging user experience while promoting behavioral change.

4 Methodology

4.1 System Design and Architecture

CarbonMetric was developed using an agile methodology, enabling iterative testing and refinement of features based on continuous user feedback [14]. The application is built on the Xcode platform, allowing for seamless integration with iOS devices. For secure data storage, Firebase Firestore is utilized, ensuring robust management of user data in the cloud. The system's modular architecture was designed to allow for easy updates and potential future integrations, such as the incorporation of advanced algorithms and real-time data processing. This flexibility ensures that CarbonMetric can evolve to meet growing user needs and environmental challenges [15] (Fig. 2).

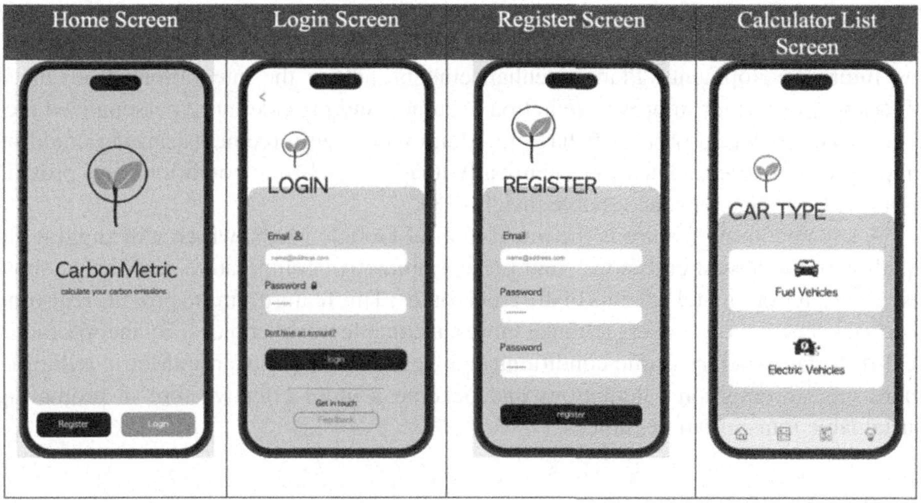

Fig. 2. CarbonMetric Application User Interface Screens showing the home screen, login, registration, and various features for calculating carbon emissions.

4.2 Carbon Footprint Calculation and Data Analysis

The core feature of CarbonMetric is its carbon footprint calculator, which estimates emissions based on user-provided inputs, such as vehicle type (fuel or electric), fuel consumption, and distance traveled. The calculation is based on a simple yet effective formula:

$$\text{Total Emission} = \text{Emission Factor} \times \text{Distance} \times \text{Fuel Consumption} \quad (1)$$

This formula, adapted from established environmental impact assessments [16], enables users to quickly understand their carbon emissions per journey. The Emission Factor varies depending on the type of fuel used, while the distance and fuel consumption are provided directly by the user, ensuring a personalized and accurate calculation.

The simplicity of this approach makes it accessible to a broad audience, allowing users to easily input their data and get immediate feedback on their environmental impact. While the current version of CarbonMetric focuses on ease of use, the app is designed with future scalability in mind. Upcoming features could integrate real-time data, such as traffic conditions and weather, to further refine these calculations. Additionally, the inclusion of machine learning algorithms is planned to enhance personalized recommendations, making CarbonMetric a more intelligent and adaptive tool in the long term [7].

4.3 Future Enhancements

While CarbonMetric currently focuses on providing an accessible and efficient tool for carbon footprint calculation, the application's flexible design enables several promising future developments. Planned enhancements include the integration of advanced algorithms to further improve prediction accuracy and provide more personalized recommendations based on user behavior. Additionally, reinforcement learning could be employed in future updates to dynamically adapt to real-time conditions and provide users with personalized, actionable insights [8].

A key upcoming feature is the integration of Google Maps, which will suggest the "path with the lowest emissions" and present predictive comparative statistics to show users the environmental benefits of different routes. This feature aims to provide real-time feedback and empower users to make more sustainable travel choices. By incorporating real-time data, such as traffic conditions and weather patterns, CarbonMetric will offer more precise emission calculations and become a more effective tool in promoting sustainable transportation choices.

5 Results and Discussion

In testing CarbonMetric, users were provided with a seamless experience for calculating their carbon emissions. The app offers an intuitive interface where users input their vehicle type (fuel or electric), fuel consumption, and distance traveled to generate an emissions estimate. Each user journey is supported by the Tips & Tricks feature, which offers actionable advice on how to reduce their reliance on fossil fuels and adopt more sustainable practices.

During a four-week testing period, users provided overwhelmingly positive feedback, with 85% reporting increased awareness of their carbon footprint and a better understanding of how their everyday transportation choices impact the environment. Additionally, 65% of users reported that they had altered their habits by reducing unnecessary trips or opting for public transportation, illustrating the app's ability to drive meaningful behavior change.

The dashboard feature summarizes the total carbon emissions from recent journeys and offers easy-to-read feedback, empowering users to track their progress over time (see Fig. 3). The insights provided by CarbonMetric encourage users to make more informed choices about their transportation habits, and the positive results from testing demonstrate the app's effectiveness in raising environmental awareness and promoting sustainable practices.

Fig. 3. CarbonMetric application screens showing user guidance (Tips & Tricks), carbon calculation for different vehicle types, and the dashboard for summarizing emissions.

6 Future Work

Looking ahead, CarbonMetric aims to evolve into a more comprehensive tool for sustainability by incorporating advanced features that will significantly enhance its utility. Future updates may include more tailored recommendations based on individual behavior, leveraging predictive modeling to anticipate user needs. These updates will ensure that the system continuously adapts to user behavior, offering dynamic suggestions for reducing carbon emissions based on real-time and historical data.

In addition to personalization, CarbonMetric plans to expand its focus beyond transportation emissions to include broader environmental metrics such as household energy consumption and waste management. By doing so, the application can become a more holistic tool, enabling users to track multiple facets of their environmental impact. The long-term vision is to integrate these metrics into a cohesive platform that supports users in making more informed decisions across various aspects of daily life.

The CarbonMetric development roadmap (see Fig. 4) outlines the planned phases for future upgrades, starting with a reassessment of the current app layout and features. From there, the app will undergo a complete overhaul, informed by consultations with experts in app security, design, and integration.

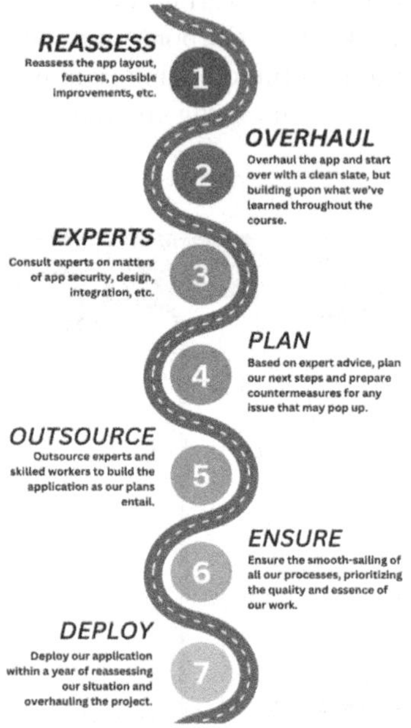

Fig. 4. Future development roadmap for CarbonMetric, illustrating planned phases from reassessment to deployment.

7 Conclusion

CarbonMetric represents an important stride in empowering individuals to become more aware of their carbon footprint and take actionable steps toward sustainability. By offering a simple and user-friendly platform, the application allows users to quickly calculate their carbon emissions based on their everyday travel behaviors. This ease of use helps bridge the gap between awareness and action, encouraging more sustainable choices that contribute to reducing environmental impact.

As the need for smarter, more efficient urban solutions grows globally, tools like CarbonMetric can play a pivotal role in supporting cities' efforts to lower their overall carbon footprint. The application's potential for integration with smart city initiatives means it could be an invaluable resource not only for individuals but also for city planners seeking data-driven insights into transportation patterns and emissions. By leveraging real-time data, personalized recommendations, and future enhancements such as route optimization, CarbonMetric can evolve into a dynamic tool for promoting more sustainable urban living.

Moving forward, the planned development of additional features, including predictive modeling and broader environmental metrics, will make CarbonMetric an even more powerful tool in the fight against climate change. Its continuous evolution will ensure that it remains aligned with the goals of sustainability and smart city development, helping both individuals and cities make informed decisions that lead to a more environmentally responsible future.

Acknowledgments. We would like to express our deepest gratitude to Amal S. Alzahmi, Ghayah M. Alhmoudi, and Meera A. Alowais for their invaluable contributions and hard work in the development of the CarbonMetric project. Their dedication, creativity, and collaborative spirit were crucial to the success of this project. We acknowledge their efforts in researching, designing, and testing the application, and their commitment to making CarbonMetric a valuable tool for promoting sustainability and environmental awareness.

Disclosure of Interests. The authors have no competing interests to declare that are relevant to the content of this article.

References

1. MyClimate. MyClimate Carbon Footprint Calculator (2021). https://www.myclimate.org/. Accessed 5 Sept 2024
2. International Energy Agency (IEA). Tracking Transport 2021 (2021). https://www.iea.org/reports/tracking-transport-2021 . Accessed 5 Sept 2024
3. UAE Net Zero 2050. UAE's strategic initiative for reducing emissions. https://u.ae/en/about-the-uae/strategies-initiatives-and-awards/federal-governments-strategies-and-plans/net-zero-by-2050. Accessed 5 Sept 2024
4. UC Berkeley. CoolClimate Network Calculator (2021). https://coolclimate.berkeley.edu/calculator. Accessed 5 Sept 2024
5. WWF. WWF Carbon Footprint Calculator (2021). https://footprint.wwf.org.uk/. Accessed 5 Sept 2024
6. Whitmarsh, L., Seyfang, G., O'Neill, S.: Public engagement with carbon and climate change: to what extent is the public 'carbon capable'? Glob. Environ. Change **21**(1), 56–65 (2011). https://doi.org/10.1016/j.gloenvcha.2010.07.011
7. Chen, X., Wang, Y., Li, Z.: Reinforcement learning for sustainable transportation optimization. Transp. Res. Part C: Emerg. Technol. **124**, 102906 (2021). https://doi.org/10.1016/j.trc.2020.102906
8. Farazi, N.P., Zou, B., Ahamed, T., Barua, L.: Deep reinforcement learning in transportation research: a review. Transp. Res. Interdisc. Perspect. **11**, 100425 (2021). https://doi.org/10.1016/j.trip.2021.100425
9. EPA: EPA Carbon Footprint Calculator (2021). https://www3.epa.gov/carbon-footprint-calculator/. Accessed 5 Sept 2024
10. Giki Zero: Giki Zero Carbon Footprint Calculator (2021). https://zero.giki.earth/. Accessed 5 Sept 2024
11. Türker, G.: Ensuring Security for Secrets in iOS App (Beginners). Medium (2023). https://medium.com/@gizemturker/ensuring-security-for-secrets-in-ios-app-ff4a25c533a1. Accessed 5 Sept 2024

12. Razif, M., Razif, M.: Prediction of CO, CO2, CH4, and N2O vehicle emissions from environmental impact assessment (EIA) at toll road of Krian-Legundi-Bunder in East Java of Indonesia (2016). https://www.researchgate.net/publication/301678822_Prediction_of_CO_CO2_CH4_and_N2O_vehicle_emissions_from_environmental_impact_assessment_EIA_at_toll_road_of_Krian-Legundi-Bunder_in_East_Java_of_Indonesia. Accessed 5 Sept 2024
13. Chris, M. (2023). How to Build a Secure iOS App: Best Practices and Guidelines. LinkedIn. https://www.linkedin.com/pulse/how-build-secure-ios-app-best-practices-guidelines-myra-chris/ (accessed on: Sep 5, 2024)
14. International Energy Agency (IEA). Tracking Transport 2021 (2021). https://www.iea.org/reports/tracking-transport-2021. Accessed 5 Sept 2024
15. Smith, J., Brown, R., Williams, P.: MyCarbon: a dynamic carbon footprint calculator for the mobile age. J. Environ. Inf. **35**(2), 123–134 (2020). https://doi.org/10.3808/jei.202000001
16. Rahman, M., Hasan, M.K., Noor, N.M.: Machine learning-based energy consumption forecasting for sustainable smart buildings. IEEE Access **6**, 44684–44694 (2018). https://doi.org/10.1109/ACCESS.2018.2868883

Evaluating Adan vs. Adam: An Analysis of Optimizer Performance in Deep Learning

Amelia Ritahani Ismail[1(✉)], Muhammad Zulhazmi Rafiqi Azhary[1], and Nor Azizah Hitam[2]

[1] Kulliyyah of Information Communication Technology, International Islamic University Malaysia, Kuala Lumpur, Malaysia
amelia@iium.edu.my

[2] Faculty of Computer Information Systems, Higher Colleges of Technology, Dubai, United Arab Emirates
nhitam@hct.ac.ae

Abstract. Choosing a suitable optimization algorithm in deep learning is essential for effective model development as it significantly influences convergence speed, model performance, and the success of the training process. Optimizers play an essential role in adjusting the model's parameters to minimize errors, assisting the learning process during the model development. With various optimization algorithms available, choosing the one that best suits the deep learning model and dataset can make a substantial difference in achieving optimal results. Adaptive Moment Estimation (Adam) and Adaptive Nesterov Accelerated Gradient (Adan), two well-known optimizers, are widely used in deep learning for their ability to handle large-scale data and complex models efficiently. While Adam is known for its balance between speed and reliability, Adan builds on this by incorporating momentum and lookahead mechanisms to enhance the model's performance. However, choosing the right optimizer for different tasks can be challenging, as each optimizer offers various advantages and disadvantages. This paper, therefore, explores the comparative effectiveness of Adam and Adan optimizers, analyzing their impact on convergence speed, model performance, and overall training success on different classifications tasks, which are image and text classifications. The results show that Adam performs better initially, but prone to overfitting. On the other hand, for image classification tasks, Adan provides more consistent optimisation across extended training periods. Based on these results, this paper aims to provide insights into the strengths and limitations of each optimizer, highlighting the importance of considering task-specific requirements when selecting an optimization algorithm for deep learning models.

Keywords: Adam algorithm · Adan algorithm · Adaptive optimizer · Deep Learning

A. Safi et al. (Eds.): ISICS 2024, CCIS 2381, pp. 251–263, 2025.
https://doi.org/10.1007/978-3-031-82931-4_19

1 Introduction

Optimization algorithms are fundamental to the success of training deep neural networks, as they significantly influence the speed, stability, and overall effectiveness of the learning process. Among these, Adaptive Moment Estimation (Adam) has emerged as one of the most widely adopted optimizers, due to its ability to adaptively adjust learning rates based on both the first and second moments of the gradients. By combining the strengths of AdaGrad's per-parameter learning rate adjustments and RMSprop's focus on handling noisy gradients, Adam provides a robust and efficient solution that accelerates convergence and improves model performance across a wide range of applications. Its versatility and ease of use have made it a standard choice in the deep learning community, particularly in scenarios where training dynamics are complex and unpredictable.

Recently, the Adaptive Nesterov Accelerated Gradient (Adan) optimizer was proposed as a possible alternative to Adam. Adan employs momentum-based approaches, including a predictive mechanism that forecasts the future direction of gradients, allowing for more precise updates and potentially faster convergence. This predictive method, along with adjustable learning rates, puts Adan as a potential successor to Adam in situations where typical optimizers fail, such as training deeper networks or facing unexpected minima in losses. Moreover, Adan's design is particularly well-suited for modern deep learning challenges, where the complexity and depth of networks often require more sophisticated optimization strategies. By integrating predictive adjustments into the momentum calculations, Adan effectively anticipates the next steps in the gradient descent process, potentially reducing the number of iterations needed to reach an optimal solution. This capability can be especially valuable in tasks with highly non-convex loss surfaces, where traditional optimizers might struggle to escape local minima or saddle points.

This paper analyses the Adan and Adam optimizers, evaluating their performance across various tasks, including image classification and natural language processing. The comparison is carried out using different architectures tailored to each task: the Visual Geometry Group (VGG) network for image classification and a hybrid GloVe-Convolutional Neural Network (GloVeCNN) for text classification. The analysis aims to provide a thorough understanding of the scenarios in which Adan may offer advantages over Adam and any potential trade-offs involved. The results of this study will contribute to the ongoing discussion on optimization strategies in deep learning, offering practical insights for researchers in selecting the most appropriate optimizer for their specific tasks.

2 Related Work

Deep learning models' effectiveness and performance are greatly influenced by optimization. The rising complexity of models and data in deep learning is reflected in the growth of optimizers from straightforward algorithms like SGD to more intricate ones [1]. Choosing the appropriate optimiser is crucial but difficult because various tasks and models have distinct requirements. The comparison and empirical analysis of different optimizers offer insightful information on how well they perform in various scenarios, highlighting the need of selecting an optimizer carefully. Furthermore, new developments in optimizer variants show how important a role they play in improving model performance, even though they have trade-offs that must be considered in light of particular application requirements. The Adam optimizer's update rules are typically represented by the following:

1. Compute the moving averages of the gradients (first moment estimate):

$$m_t = \beta_1 m_{t-1} + (1 - \beta_1) g_t$$

2. Compute the moving averages of the squared gradients (second moment estimate):

$$v_t = \beta_2 v_{t-1} + (1 - \beta_2) g_t^2$$

3. Bias-corrected estimates:

$$\hat{m}_t = \frac{m_t}{1 - \beta_1^t}$$

$$\hat{v}_t = \frac{v_t}{1 - \beta_2^t}$$

4. Update the parameters:

$$\theta_{t+1} = \theta_t - \frac{\alpha \hat{m}_t}{\sqrt{\hat{v}_t} + \epsilon}$$

Where:
- θ_t are the parameters at time step t,
- g_t is the gradient at time step t,
- α is the learning rate,
- β_1 and β_2 are the exponential decay rates for the moment estimates,
- ϵ is a small constant to prevent division by zero (e.g., $\epsilon = 10^{-8}$).

From the equations. Adam adjusts the learning rate for each parameter based on estimated first and second moments of gradients, resulting in quick convergence and robustness to noisy input. Although Adam is widely used, it has limits in generalization and stability when training deep networks.

The Adam optimizer's versatility and general effectiveness across a wide range of models are highlighted in a study on evaluating a good optimizer's results, reinforcing its position as the top option for practitioners of natural language processing [2]. The study discovered that although the performance of other optimisers, such Adafactor and Lion, was equivalent, Adam's strong preconditioning effects, especially in the last layer and LayerNorm parameters, greatly aided its success. This implies that while other layers might be trained using simpler methods like SGD, Adam's specialized role remains critical in fine-tuning model performance, especially in the most sensitive parts of the network. This suggests a more refined approach to optimization, indicating that while Adam is still very effective, there could be opportunities to fine-tune its use in specific layers of deep learning models.

Recurrent neural networks (RNNs) and the Adaptive Moment Estimation (Adam) optimizer function well together to categorize diabetes mellitus, a major worldwide health concern [3]. The RNN-Adam model performs well and achieves high accuracy rates by using rigorous assessment techniques, including confusion matrix analysis and k-fold cross-validation. According to these results, there is a good chance that this model will help with the difficulties related to diabetes classification in healthcare settings and enhance diagnosis accuracy. In fitting neural networks with few parameters and attaining fast convergence to high precision, a previous study on optimizing optimizer highlights the superiority of the Levenberg-Marquardt (LM) algorithm [4]. On the other hand, Adam, BFGS, and LBFGS need larger models in order to match LM's performance due to their lower amplitude components. The results show that LM not only works well with fewer parameters, but it also shows that Adam is ineffective in smaller models. This illustrates how using LM to more effectively create models in situations with confined parameters may be advantageous.

There is a significant change in interpreting the efficiency of the Adam optimizer when viewed through the lens of online learning [5]. The study offers greater insights into the algorithmic components that led to Adam's extensive success in real-world applications by placing it within the Follow-the-Regularized-Leader (FTRL) framework. This viewpoint not only makes some theoretical difficulties about Adam clearer but also raises the possibility that the optimizer's advantages are derived from online learning-related ideas. Given the theoretical foundations that this research has identified, this connection may facilitate the creation of new, more effective optimization techniques. To overcome issues like changing environments and complex behaviours, the study [6] presents a novel method for visual anomaly identification that uses convolutional autoencoders. The method improves detection accuracy by using reconstruction loss to evaluate normalcy after rebuilding video data. The Adam optimiser is used to optimize performance further and reduce the calculation time. This approach's effectiveness in real-time surveillance systems is demonstrated by a comparative comparison with previous methodologies, which reveals notable gains in accuracy.

Deep learning optimization has made significant strides since the Adan algorithm was introduced [7]. Through the efficient resolution of the inefficiencies involved in choosing the appropriate optimizer, Adan offers a strong substitute that not only equals but frequently exceeds the effectiveness of current techniques. Its capacity to provide cutting-edge outcomes for a variety of tasks while requiring less processing power points is a hopeful move in deep learning towards more effective and scalable training procedures. This could result in the technique being adopted more widely and improved in subsequent iterations. The equation of Adan are as follows:

1. Momentum-based gradient update:

$$m_t = \beta_1 m_{t-1} + (1 - \beta_1) g_t$$

2. Prediction of future gradients:

$$g_{t+1} = g_t + \gamma(\Delta g_t)$$

   Where $\Delta g_t = g_t - g_{t-1}$, and γ is the prediction coefficient.
3. Correction with predicted future gradient:

$$\hat{m}_t = m_t + \gamma(\Delta g_t)$$

4. Parameter update:

$$\theta_{t+1} = \theta_t - \frac{\alpha \hat{m}_t}{\sqrt{\hat{v}_t} + \epsilon}$$

   Where:
   - m_t is the momentum-based estimate of the gradient.
   - g_t is the current gradient.
   - $\hat{m}_t$ is the corrected gradient estimate, incorporating the prediction.
   - γ is the prediction coefficient that controls the influence of the predicted gradient.
   - θ_t represents the parameters at time step t.
   - α is the learning rate.
   - ϵ is a small constant for numerical stability.

Based on the equations, the momentum in Adan helps in smoothing the updates and can accelerate the convergence of the optimizer by preventing oscillations, especially in the presence of noisy gradients. The optimizer starts with a typical momentum-based approach, where it averages past gradients to smooth updates. It then predicts the future gradient direction based on observed changes in the gradient. This prediction is used to adjust the momentum estimate, potentially improving the accuracy and speed of convergence. Finally, the parameters are updated using this corrected momentum, scaled by the learning rate and adjusted by the gradient magnitude. By combining momentum with a predictive mechanism, this optimizer can make more informed updates, potentially leading to faster convergence, especially in complex optimization landscape.

According to the study [8], the YOLOv7 network and the Adan optimizer, when integrated, greatly improve the identification of main maize pests, increasing computational efficiency and accuracy. With a mean average precision of 96.69% and a precision of 99.95%, the suggested approach outperforms previous methods by addressing their high training costs and restrictions. This approach performs better than current item detection algorithms, demonstrating its use in identifying pests and its potential as a cutting-edge substitute for on-the-spot agricultural surveillance.

To combine the advantages of AdamW, Nadam, and AdaBelief without introducing additional hyper-parameters, the study [9] identifies AdaPlus as a very successful optimizer that makes use of Nesterov momentum and accurate step-size adjustment. In language modelling, AdaPlus outperforms other top optimizers and achieves competitive or better performance than SGD with momentum. It also shows remarkable stability when training GANs. It is evident from this that AdaPlus is a strong and adaptable option for maximising various machine learning assignments.

By presenting a technique for local convergence analysis in batch mode, the study [10] substantially contributes to our knowledge of the convergence of the Adaptive Moment Estimation (Adam) algorithm. Applying this method to non-convex but smoothly differentiable objective functions yields the essential conditions for Adam's hyperparameters. This investigation closes a significant theoretical gap regarding Adam, advancing deeper neural network optimization techniques that are better informed and efficient. Referring to the study [11], wide and deep neural networks perform better when using the Adam optimization algorithm, especially when it comes to difficult classification tasks like breast cancer diagnosis. The notable enhancement in precision and decrease in loss upon using Adam suggests that this optimizer is exceptionally efficient in regulating the learning procedure, perhaps mitigating overfitting and guaranteeing superior generalization.

3 Methodology

This section outlines the components utilized to conduct the experiments, including the datasets, preprocessing steps, and the overall experimental setup, which were critical for obtaining the necessary comparative results for a comprehensive analysis.

3.1 Datasets

We used two separate datasets for each experiment. CIFAR-10 for image classification, and IMDB Reviews for text classification.

CIFAR-10. CIFAR-10 is a dataset containing 60,000 32×32 color images across 10 classes: airplane, automobile, bird, cat, deer, dog, frog, horse, ship, and truck. It is commonly used for benchmarking image classification algorithms, with 50,000 images for training and 10,000 for testing. The small image size and diverse categories make it a useful resource for evaluating and comparing different models and optimizers.

IMDB Reviews. The IMDB Reviews dataset consists of 50,000 movie reviews from IMDB, evenly split between positive and negative sentiments. It is widely utilized for sentiment analysis tasks, providing a standard benchmark for text classification models. The dataset is divided into 25,000 training reviews and 25,000 test reviews, enabling the assessment of models' ability to understand and classify textual sentiment.

3.2 Data Preprocessing

The image datasets were transformed to tensors and normalized with a mean and standard deviation of 0.5 for each colour channels. Whereas the text dataset they were processed through tokenization, word embedding and vocabulary extraction.

3.3 Models

These are the models used to compare the optimizers performance. Each model was carefully chosen to represent a diverse range of tasks, including image and text classification, ensuring a comprehensive evaluation across different domains. Testing the optimizers on these varied architectures offers valuable insights into their effectiveness and adaptability in real-world applications.

VGG-16. Convolutional neural networks known for their simplicity and depth, featuring a series of convolutional layers followed by fully connected layers. VGG models are commonly used for image classification tasks due to their effective feature extraction capabilities. They are pre-trained on ImageNet and can be fine-tuned for specific image classification tasks by modifying the final layers.

GloVeCNN. Combines GloVe embeddings with a Convolutional Neural Network (CNN) for text classification. GloVe provides word vectors that capture semantic relationships, while the CNN processes these vectors to extract features and patterns in the text. This combination enables effective classification by identifying key phrases and patterns, making it suitable for tasks like sentiment analysis.

3.4 Optimizers

The experiments exclusively use Adam and Adan as optimizers for comparison, focusing on their adaptive learning capabilities.

Adam. An optimization algorithm widely used in deep learning due to its ability to adaptively adjust the learning rate for each parameter. It combines the advantages of two other popular optimizers, AdaGrad and RMSprop, by maintaining estimates of both the gradients' first moment (mean) and the second moment (uncertainty). This results in faster convergence and better performance in training neural networks. Adam is particularly effective in handling sparse gradients and noisy data.

Adan. Adan is a newer optimization algorithm that builds on momentum-based approaches. It incorporates a predictive mechanism to estimate the future trajectory of gradients, allowing for more precise updates and potentially faster convergence. By combining adaptive learning rates with this predictive capability, Adan aims to improve stability and generalization, especially in training deep networks and dealing with sharp minima in loss landscapes.

3.5 Experimental Setup

These are the constant hyperparameters used throughout the experiments, ensuring consistency and fairness in the evaluation of the optimizers:

- Learning Rate: The learning rate was set to a fixed value of 0.001 across all experiments. This value was chosen based on preliminary tests to balance convergence speed and stability, allowing the models to learn effectively without overshooting minima.
- Criterion: The loss function used for optimization was the Cross-Entropy Loss for both image and text classification tasks. This criterion is widely used in classification problems and provides a robust measure for evaluating model performance during training.
- Epochs: Each model was trained for a total of 20 epochs, providing ample time for the optimizers to demonstrate their convergence properties and overall effectiveness. This number of epochs was selected to ensure that the models had sufficient opportunity to reach their optimal performance while avoiding overfitting.

By maintaining these constant hyperparameters—learning rate, criterion, and epochs—the experiments were designed to provide a fair and rigorous comparison between the Adan and Adam optimizers, allowing for an accurate assessment of their relative strengths and weaknesses (Table 1).

Table 1. Constant hyperparameters value for the experiment.

	Hyperparameter
Learning rate	0.001
Criterion	Cross-Entropy
Epochs	20

3.6 Evaluation Metrics

Training, validation loss, and accuracy are fundamental metrics for evaluating convergence speed and stability. Training loss measures how well the model fits the training data, while validation loss assesses performance on unseen data, indicating generalization capability. Training accuracy reflects the model's performance on the training set, and validation accuracy shows how well the model performs on the validation set. By plotting these metrics over epochs, we can observe the rate of improvement and stability of convergence. Faster convergence is indicated by a steeper decline in loss and a quicker rise in accuracy, while stability is observed through smoother, more consistent curves without significant fluctuations.

4 Results and Discussion

The results from the VGG model for image classification using Adam and Adan optimizers show distinct performance patterns in both accuracy and loss. In terms of loss, Fig. 1 reveals that Adan again has an edge, particularly in reducing both training and test losses. Adan's training loss shows a more consistent downward trend, indicating steady learning progress, while Adam's training loss fluctuates more and remains higher overall. The test loss behavior mirrors the training loss, where Adan maintains lower losses across epochs. This suggests that Adan optimizes the model better during training and generalizes more effectively to unseen data.

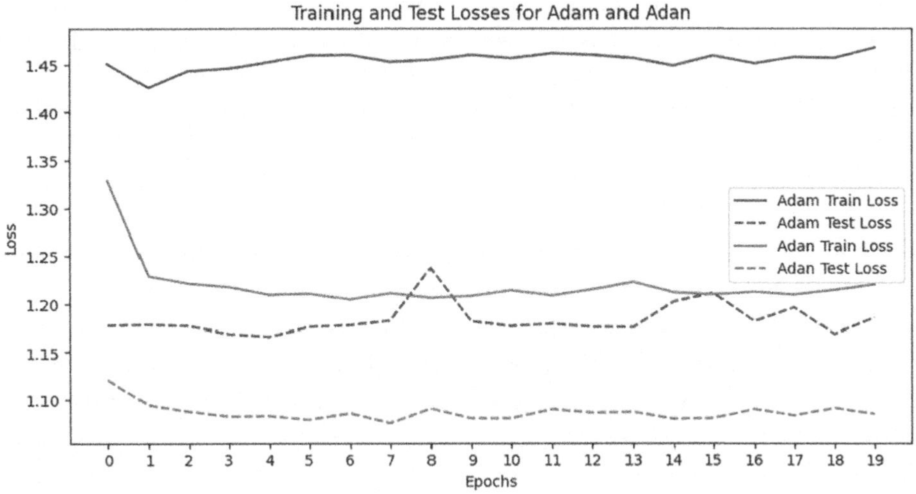

Fig. 1. Training and test losses for image classification using VGG for 20 epochs

Analyzing Fig. 2, it is observed that Adan generally maintains a higher test accuracy compared to Adam throughout the training process. This indicates that Adan may have an advantage in capturing features more effectively, resulting in better classification performance. The fluctuations in the accuracy of both optimizers suggest the presence of noise or variability in the learning process,

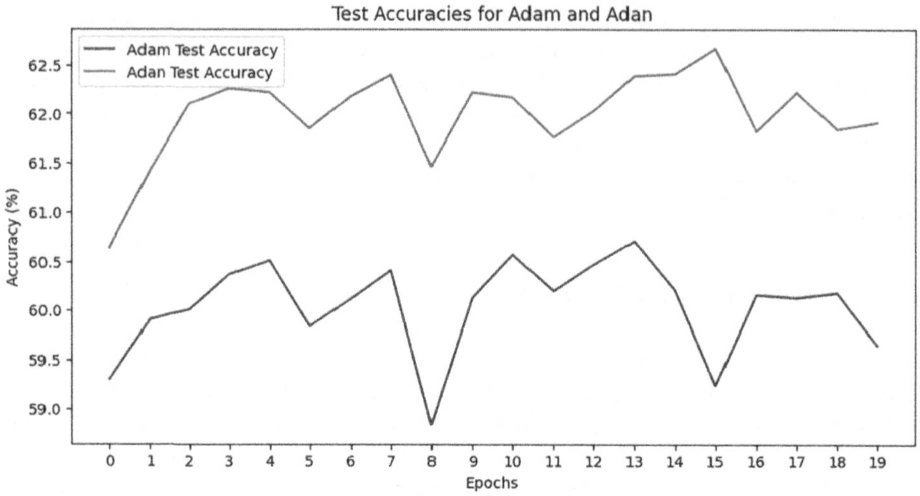

Fig. 2. Test accuracies for image classification using VGG for 20 epochs

but Adan consistently outperforms Adam, achieving an accuracy peak above 62%.

Overall, these results imply that the Adan optimizer may offer superior performance in image classification tasks when compared to Adam, particularly in the context of the VGG architecture. Adan's ability to maintain lower losses and higher accuracy consistently across epochs suggests it is more effective in fine-tuning the model, leading to better generalization and stability during training (Table 2).

Table 2. Performance evaluation results for image classification using VGG at epoch 20.

Optimizer	Train loss	Test loss	Test accuracy
Adam	1.4675	1.1855	0.5965
Adan	1.2202	1.0849	0.6191

Next, the results from the hybrid GloVe-CNN model for text classification indicate notable differences in performance between the Adam and Adan optimizers across various metrics.

In Fig. 1, we can observe that Adam's training loss decreases significantly over time, indicating effective minimization during training. However, the corresponding test loss increases after a certain point, which aligns with the declining test accuracy observed earlier. This further hints at potential overfitting, where the model becomes overly specialized to the training data, thus losing generalization capabilities (Table 3).

Table 3. Performance evaluation results for text classification using GloVeCNN at epoch 20.

Optimizer	Train loss	Test loss	Test accuracy
Adam	0.8772	0.8370	0.5965
Adan	0.0018	1.3684	0.8318

As depicted in Fig. 2, Adam consistently outperforms Adan in terms of test accuracy. Adam's test accuracy rises rapidly, peaking around the 6th epoch before experiencing a gradual decline. On the other hand, Adan's accuracy remains relatively stable throughout the training, with minor fluctuations but never surpassing Adam's performance. This suggests that while Adam initially converges faster and achieves higher accuracy, it might also be prone to overfitting or instability in later epochs, as indicated by the decline after its peak. Conversely, Adan exhibits a different pattern. Its training and test losses start at a higher level and steadily increase throughout the training process. This consistent increase in loss, particularly on the test set, suggests that Adan might not be as effective in optimizing the model for this particular text classification task, leading to poorer generalization and higher errors (Fig. 3).

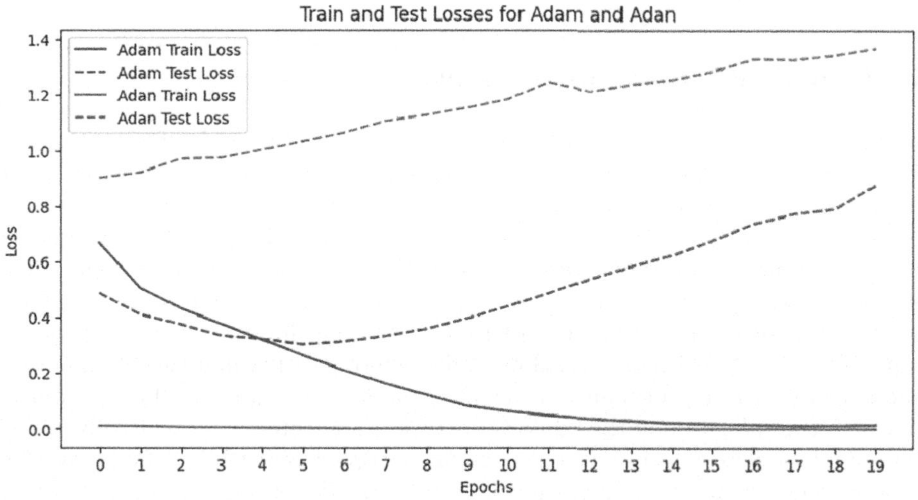

Fig. 3. Training and test losses for text classification using GloVeCNN for 20 epochs

This shows that while Adam exhibits superior performance in both accuracy and initial loss reduction, its tendency to overfit may limit its long-term effectiveness. Adan, while more stable in terms of accuracy, struggles with effective loss minimization, leading to suboptimal results. These observations indicate

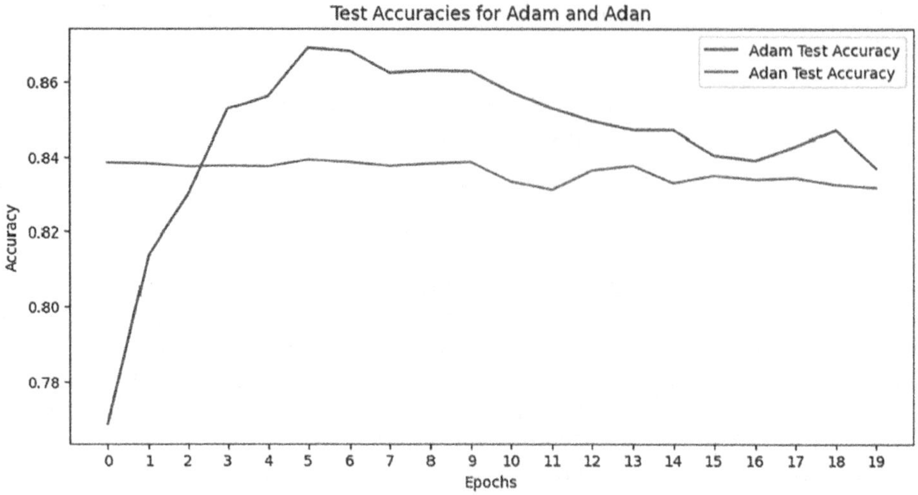

Fig. 4. Test accuracies for text classification using GloVeCNN for 20 epochs

that Adam might be more suitable for this task, though care should be taken to mitigate overfitting, potentially through techniques like early stopping or regularization (Fig. 4).

5 Conclusion and Future Work

In analyzing the results of both the hybrid GloVeCNN model for text classification and the VGG model for image classification, it was observed that the Adam optimizer tends to outperform Adan in terms of initial performance metrics but is prone to overfitting as training progresses. Adam's rapid convergence and higher initial accuracy, particularly in the GloVeCNN model, suggest it is effective in the early training stages. However, its declining accuracy and increasing test loss over time indicate potential overfitting, limiting its generalization capability. On the other hand, Adan, while demonstrating more stable accuracy and better overall performance in the VGG model, struggles with loss minimization and generalization in the GloVeCNN task, as reflected in its relatively higher losses and lower test accuracy. These findings suggest that while Adam may offer superior performance initially, especially in text classification tasks, it requires careful management to avoid overfitting, whereas Adan, with its more stable performance in image classification, maybe a better choice for tasks requiring consistent optimization over longer training periods.

In the future, we are looking to further optimize Adam and Adan with further experimentation to solidify our findings. Starting with mitigating the overfitting nature shown by Adam with the implementation of early stopping and regularization. Furthermore, the variant of Adan used in this experiment was a base setting and would require further tuning to suit the needs of our tasks. This initial study is done as a baseline performance indicator for both optimizer at their respective base setting.

Acknowledgments. The authors would like to extend an appreciation to those who participated in this research.

Disclosure of Interests. The authors declare that there are no competing interests that are relevant to the content of this article.

References

1. Bashetty, S., Raja, K., Adepu, S., Jain, A.: Optimizers in deep learning: a comparative study and analysis. Int. J. Sci. Technol. Eng. **10**(12), 1032–1039 (2022)
2. Zhao, R., Morwani, D., Brandfonbrener, D., Vyas, N., Kakade, S.: Deconstructing what makes a good optimizer for language models (2024)
3. Nugroho, N.C.T., Hidayat, E.Y.: Implementation of Adam optimizer using recurrent neural network (RNN) architecture for diabetes classification. J. Med. Inform. Budidarma (2024)
4. Taylor, J., Wang, W., Bala, B., Bednarz, T.: Optimizing the optimizer for data-driven deep neural networks and physics-informed neural networks (2022)
5. Ahn, K., Zhang, Z., Kook, Y., Dai, Y.: Understanding Adam optimizer via online learning of updates: Adam is FTRL in disguise. arXiv preprint (2024)
6. Chiranjeevi, V.R., Dhanasekaran, S., Murugan, B.S., Pandi, S.S.: Adam optimizer based convolutional auto encoder for detecting anomalies in surveillance videos. In: 2024 International Conference on Computing, Communication, and Internet of Things (IC3IoT) (2024)
7. Xie, X., Zhou, P., Li, H., Lin, Z., Yan, S.: Adan: adaptive Nesterov momentum algorithm for faster optimizing deep models (2022)
8. Zhang, C., Hu, Z., Xu, L., Zhao, Y.: A YOLOv7 incorporating the Adan optimizer based corn pests identification method. Front. Plant Sci. **14** (2023)
9. Guan, L.: AdaPlus: integrating Nesterov momentum and precise stepsize adjustment on AdamW basis. In: ICASSP 2024 - 2024 IEEE International Conference on Acoustics, Speech and Signal Processing (ICASSP), pp. 5210–5214 (2024)
10. Bock, S., Weiß, M.: A proof of local convergence for the Adam optimizer. In: 2019 International Joint Conference on Neural Networks (IJCNN), pp. 1–8 (2019)
11. Jais, I.K.M., Ismail, A.R., Nisa, S.Q.: Adam optimization algorithm for wide and deep neural network. Knowl. Eng. Data Sci. (KEDS) **2**(1), 41–46 (2019)

Quality Assessment of Fundus Images for Further Classification: Lesson from Thesis

Patricia Menares[1,2](✉) and Víctor Castañeda[3]

[1] Universidad Santo Tomás, Av. Ejército Libertador 146, Santiago, Chile
pmenares@santotomas.cl
[2] Universidad Andrés Bello, Av. Sazié 2325, Santiago, Chile
[3] Department of Medical Technology, Faculty of Medicine, Universidad de Chile, Av. Independencia 1027, Santiago, Chile
vcastane@uchile.cl

Abstract. Diabetic retinopathy (DR) is the third leading cause of irreversible blindness worldwide and the leading cause among adults of working age, underscoring the critical need for adequate screening. The quality of the information is a key aspect in any image analysis process and is essential for the correct analysis by automatic processes in pathologies of great importance such as DR. This study aimed to generate a low-cost computational tool that preprocesses fundus images to optimize time in the timely referral of patients. Using two public databases, HDR and DRIMDB, which include both good and poor-quality images, we performed Retinal Image Quality Assessment (RIQA) by analyzing entropy and Peak Signal-to-Noise Ratio (PSNR) under Salt & Pepper and Gaussian Blur noise conditions. Additionally, a vector based on vessel segmentation was created using the Galdran et al. algorithm. The data were evaluated on the WEKA machine learning platform, revealing that neither entropy nor PSNR with Salt & Pepper noise were effective in classifying medically useful images. However, PSNR with Gaussian Blur, especially when combined with vessel segmentation, proved to be a reliable indicator of image quality. These findings suggest that images should be classified as gradable or non-gradable to enhance the efficiency and accuracy of DR screening systems.

Keywords: Quality Assessment · RIQA · Retinography · Diabetic retinopathy

1 Background

Diabetic Retinopathy (DR) is a highly prevalent pathology worldwide, being the 3rd leading cause of irreversible blindness worldwide and the 1st cause in adults of working age. The ocular complications of DR can be prevented by ocular screening. In recent years, Artificial Intelligence has become more presence in medicine, helping to detect or even give a diagnosis from medical images [1]. Particularity, in Chile, a couple of years ago, screening using an artificial intelligence platform called DART (Diagnóstico Automatizado de Retinografías Telemáticas) was implemented at the ministerial level

A. Safi et al. (Eds.): ISICS 2024, CCIS 2381, pp. 264–276, 2025.
https://doi.org/10.1007/978-3-031-82931-4_20

(government public health) [2], which allows the evaluation of diabetic patients by discarding patients without DR (54.4%), reducing the number of eye fundus exam that need to be evaluated by an ophthalmologist (specialist). The Chilean protocol system is based on the EURODIAB IDDM Complications Study [3], part of a European Community funded Concerted Action Programme into the epidemiology and prevention of diabetes (EURODIAB) (see Fig. 1), which clearly outlines the criteria for the evaluation of fundus images acquired, establishing the capture of two images: one centered on the macula with visualization of 3rd generation vessels in this area and another on the optic disc with visualization of fine vessels on its surface. In this respect, Scalon et al. [4] the greatest predictor of an inability to classify fundus images is the age of the patients, with cataracts—characterized by the opacity of the lens—being the main cause of poor image quality.

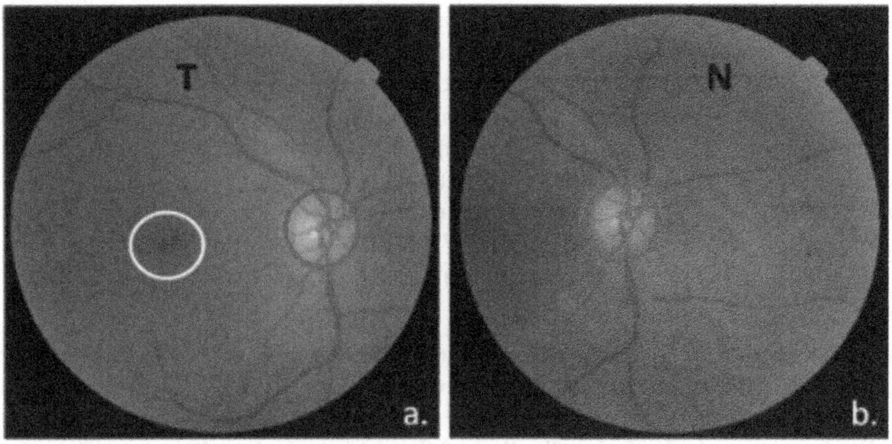

Fig. 1. Visual fields defined by EURODIAB. a. Photo centered on the macula (white circle) showing the distance to the optic nerve (red circle) and exposing the temporal retina (T). b. Photo centered on the optic nerve (red circle) where the macula is not visible and the nasal retina (N) is exposed. Source: GOV.UK. 2022. "Diabetic eye screening: guidance when adequate images cannot be taken." (Color figure online)

Diabetic Retinopathy (DR) is a highly prevalent pathology worldwide, being the third leading cause of irreversible blindness globally and the leading cause among adults of working age, in Fig. 2 is shown DR examples. The ocular complications of DR can be effectively mitigated through regular ocular screening, which allows for early detection and timely intervention. In recent years, Artificial Intelligence (AI) has increasingly been integrated into medical practice, enhancing the ability to detect and even diagnose conditions from medical images.

In Chile, a significant advancement in DR screening was the implementation of the DART platform at the ministerial level [2]. This AI-based system enables the evaluation of diabetic patients by identifying and excluding those without DR, effectively reducing the number of fundus exams that require evaluation by an ophthalmologist. DART has

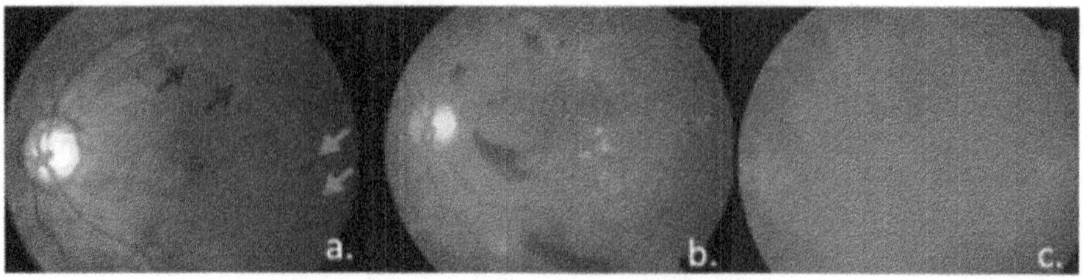

Fig. 2. Fundus alterations and visualization of anatomical landmarks. a. Non-proliferative diabetic retinopathy, where black arrows show hard exudates and white arrows indicate microhemorrhages, b. Proliferative diabetic retinopathy, with preretinal hemorrhages, c. Proliferative diabetic retinopathy with vitreous humor cloudiness, preventing proper observation of the normal retinal anatomical landmarks. Source: Lavaque A, Natalatia D, Roca J, Wu L. "Retina 2019." [18]

been shown to screen out 54.4% of patients who do not present signs of DR, thereby optimizing the workload of specialists.

The quality of the information contained in these images is a fundamental aspect of any image analysis process and is essential for the correct operation of automated diagnostic systems. Poor-quality images can lead to misdiagnosis or the need for repeat examinations, both of which can delay treatment and increase healthcare costs. Therefore, assessing and ensuring the quality of fundus images is a critical step in improving the efficacy of DR screening programs [5–7].

In the following, we describe typical inadequate images for diagnosis by different factors [8]:

a) **Inadequate study area:** The structures to be observed are not positioned according to the definition. Since these structures are easy to recognize, it is simple to determine whether the criteria are met.
b) **Inadequate or lack of visualization of the macula and optic nerve:** The causes for their absence in the image can vary, but they can generally be grouped into poor centering or the presence of opacities which, depending on their density, will interfere with classification.
c) **Lack of focus:** This refers to the blurring of structures, which may be due to a failure in the image capture technique or the presence of media opacity.
d) **Inadequate illumination:** As with the previous point, the cause may be the acquisition technique or the condition of the transparent media in the patient's eye. It is important to consider that illumination is not only affected by inadequate capture technique or the state of the patient's transparent media but also by the patient's level of pigmentation, which can prevent maintaining a single standard level of illumination. These examples are shown in Fig. 3.

1.1 Quality Image

The analysis of image quality in medical imaging has evolved significantly, beginning with early studies like the "Atherosclerotic Risk in Community" (ARIC) study, which considered factors such as focus, clarity, the definition of the area to be studied, and the

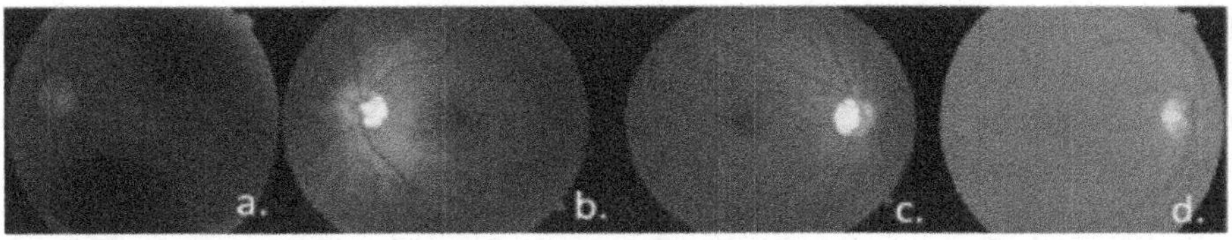

Fig. 3. Differences between illumination and fundus pigmentation. a. an underexposed image is observed; b. the fundus of a Caucasian individual; c. the fundus of an African American patient; and d. an overexposed image. Source: "Automated fundus images analysis techniques to screen retinal diseases in diabetic patients." [19]

visibility of the optic disc and macula, as well as the presence or absence of artifacts. These criteria laid the foundation for what is now known as "Image Quality Assessment" (IQA), a comprehensive framework for evaluating image quality [8].

IQA is subdivided into three main categories:

- **Full Reference IQA (FR-IQA):** This approach assesses image quality by comparing the target image with a reference image. A commonly used metric in FR-IQA is the Peak Signal to Noise Ratio (PSNR), which measures the ratio between the maximum power of a signal and the power of the noise-altered signal. However, PSNR does not always correlate well with perceived visual quality.
- **Reduced Reference IQA (RR-IQA):** In this method, the reference image is not fully available. Instead, statistical features are extracted from a training set to provide a comparative basis for quality assessment.
- **Non-Reference IQA (NR-IQA):** This approach does not rely on a reference image. NR-IQA can be implemented in two ways: by extracting statistical features from a training set, similar to RR-IQA, or by using local approaches that directly assess quality based on the image's characteristics.

In the context of retinal imaging, these methods are specifically applied under the term "Retinal Image Quality Assessment" (RIQA). Given that retinal images are often evaluated without a reference image, RIQA typically aligns with NR-IQA methodologies. These can be further divided into analyses based on structural methods, which assess the visibility of anatomical landmarks like retinal vessels, and feature-based methods, which focus on general image attributes such as contrast, focus, and illumination.

2 Materials and Methods

2.1 Database

This study utilized two publicly available databases: the High Resolution Fundus Quality Assessment (HRF) [9] and the Diabetic Retinopathy Image Database (DRIMDB) [10]. The HRF database consists of 36 images (18 pairs) with varying levels of quality, while the DRIMDB includes 194 images, of which 125 are categorized as high quality and 69 as low quality. The HRF images are of higher resolution (5184 $\times$ 3456 pixels and 3888 $\times$ 2592 pixels) compared to the DRIMDB images (570 $\times$ 760 pixels). These databases were selected because they offer a range of image qualities, making them ideal for assessing the effectiveness of different image quality analysis techniques.

High Resolution Fundus Quality Assessment (HRF): The HRF database contains high-resolution images and is organized into two sets based on the intended purpose of quality assessment. One set includes 18 pairs of 45° field of view images of the same eye in JPG format. In each pair, one image was captured under optimal conditions, while the other was deliberately altered to decrease quality, either by introducing artifacts or by modifying the focus or illumination. The resolution of these images varies: five pairs have a resolution of 5184×3456 pixels, while the remaining 13 pairs are 3888×2592 pixels.

Diabetic Retinopathy Image Database (DRIMDB): The DRIMDB consists of 125 high-quality and 69 low-quality photographs, all in JPG format. The high-quality images were deemed medically suitable, a criterion not met by the 69 low quality images. Unlike the HRF database, these images are not paired, so direct comparisons between the good and poor-quality images are not possible. Additionally, the database includes a set of 22 outlier images that depict structures completely different from the retina and were excluded from the analysis. The images have a resolution of 570×760 pixels with a 60° field of view.

2.2 Methodology

Preprocessing

The first step in quality analysis is image preprocessing, which involves removing information that will not be used, such as generating masks to select the area to be analyzed, selecting a specific color channel, and enhancing the image. As previously mentioned, Lee & Wang [11] proposed an ideal histogram to verify image quality, and various modifications have since been made to this histogram to improve image quality.

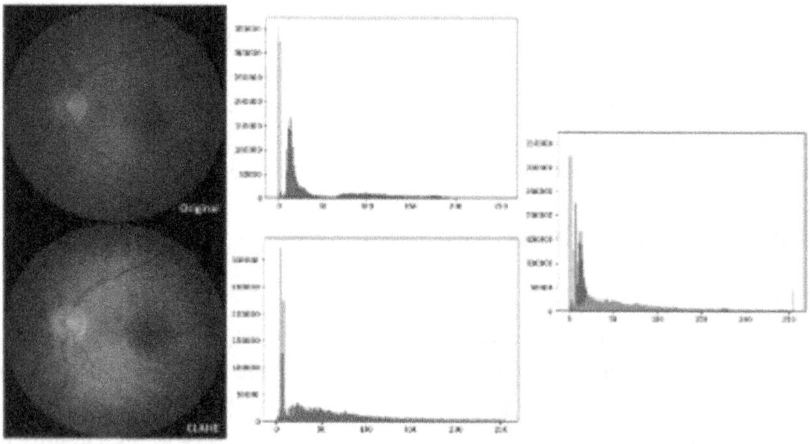

Fig. 4. CLAHE and changes to the histogram distribution. In the top row, an image is shown alongside its histogram distribution. In the bottom row, the same image, which was enhanced using CLAHE, is displayed. In the third column, both histograms are overlaid, allowing to observe the changes in the histogram distribution profile. (Color figure online)

Among these modifications is histogram equalization, which involves stretching the distribution of pixels toward the extremes to achieve better contrast while preserving their number. This technique improves contrast under a global analysis of the image, which is not useful if the image has areas of imbalance regarding contrast. This is where adaptive equalization contributes by improving contrast through a sectorized analysis of the image, meaning by contextual regions where the histogram is adapted concerning neighboring areas. However, if the image contains areas with large intensity variations, it tends to saturate the very bright regions. To solve this problem, the same segmentation of contextual images is performed, called clips, which can be defined in number, but the contrast is also limited to a defined number, redistributing the pixels that exceed this limit to maintain their total number. This method is called contrast-limited adaptive histogram equalization, or CLAHE, and is one of the most frequently used preprocessing methods. [12, 13]. The comparison of the histogram and CLAHE is shown in Fig. 4.

Image Quality Measurement

To assess image quality, we employed the **Peak Signal to Noise Ratio (PSNR)**, which is a Full Reference Image Quality Assessment (FR-IQA) algorithm [14]. PSNR measures the ratio between the maximum possible power of a signal and the power of noise affecting the quality of the image, making it a widely used metric in evaluating image degradation, this is measured in decibels (dB). Two of the most common types of noise encountered in retinal images were applied: Gaussian blur and Salt & Pepper noise. The Gaussian blur was implemented using the OpenCV library [13], which is a widely recognized tool for image processing. Gaussian blur was applied with an odd-sized filter ranging from 1×1 to 31×31, where sigma was set to 0, allowing the program to calculate it based on the filter size. This approach aimed to simulate the typical blurring effect caused by out-of-focus conditions or lens imperfections in retinal imaging.

In addition to PSNR, entropy was calculated as part of the Retinal Image Quality Assessment (RIQA). Entropy measures the randomness in the image, providing an indication of texture quality and contrast [15]. However, as entropy can be sensitive to lighting artifacts, its effectiveness as an image quality metric was also evaluated. This feature was included in the named feature vector.

To complement these feature-based methods, retinal vessel segmentation was performed using the algorithm proposed by Galdran et al. [16] This structural approach was used to assess the quality of the retinal images based on the clarity and completeness of the segmented vessels, which are critical indicators in diagnosing diabetic retinopathy. To extract data from vessel segmentation, a skeleton of the segmented vessels is proposed using the SKAN library [20]. Six images were selected with a threshold value that separates the background from the probability of being a vessel, utilizing binarization thresholds of 0.3725 and 0.22. Skeletonization was implemented using a binarized image of the probabilistic map, processed with erosion and dilation algorithms from OpenCV, using filter sizes of 10×10, 20×20, 30×30, 40×40, and 50×50. For data extraction, the SKAN library was used to generate graphs and statistics about the branches measured in pixels, organized in a table. This approach enabled the calculation of the total segment and branch count, and also the mean and standard deviation of each segment size, creating the "structure" feature vector.

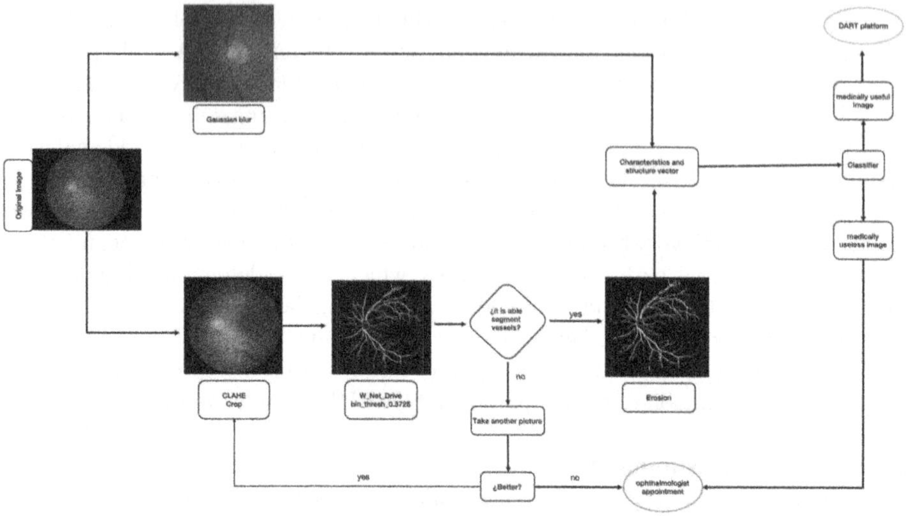

Fig. 5. This flowchart illustrates the path for processing and classifying images based on their quality, with steps including CLAHE (Contrast-Limited Adaptive Histogram Equalization), cropping, and applying vessel masks.

The processed data, including PSNR, entropy values, and vessel segmentation results, were evaluated using the WEKA machine learning platform [17]. WEKA was used to classify the images into gradable and non-gradable categories, aiming to identify the most reliable indicators of medically useful images. In this work, we employed CNN to extract structural features (specifically retinal vessels) from the images, while Random Forest and Support Vector Machine were used to test various combinations of these features in the classification of high-quality and low-quality images.

The evaluation process focused on determining which metrics, alone or in combination, best differentiate between high and low-quality images, ultimately contributing to more efficient and accurate screening processes. The Flowchart of this implementation is shown in Fig. 5.

3 Results

The results obtained from this work are presented below.

3.1 Evaluation of Parameters

The entropy analysis revealed that this metric is highly sensitive to artifacts such as lighting variations, leading to inconsistent results across the datasets. While entropy provided a general indication of image quality, its reliability was compromised in images with significant lighting artifacts, resulting in false positives in some cases (Fig. 6).

In contrast, PSNR proved to be a more robust metric for distinguishing between high and low-quality images. Images from the HRF database, which included artificially degraded images, showed clear differences in PSNR values, with high-quality

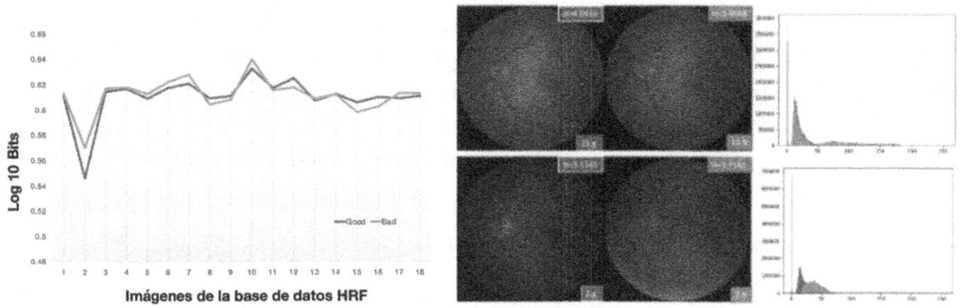

Fig. 6. Left: Shannon entropy for images separated by good (good) and bad (bad) quality, from the HRF database, expressed in bits. The results for the good quality set are shown in blue, and the results for the bad quality set are shown in gray. There is no clear separation between classes. Right: Entropy and comparative histogram distribution for the HRF database examples. In the top row, image 15 is shown: in blue is the good quality image and in orange is the bad quality image, displaying their entropy values (H) and the comparison of their histogram distribution in the same colors. In the bottom row, the same characteristics are compared for image 2, with the good quality image in blue and the bad quality image in orange. (Color figure online)

images consistently exhibiting higher PSNR scores. The application of Gaussian blur as a controlled distortion further validated PSNR as an effective measure of image quality, particularly in the DRIMDB dataset where class differences were more pronounced (Fig. 7).

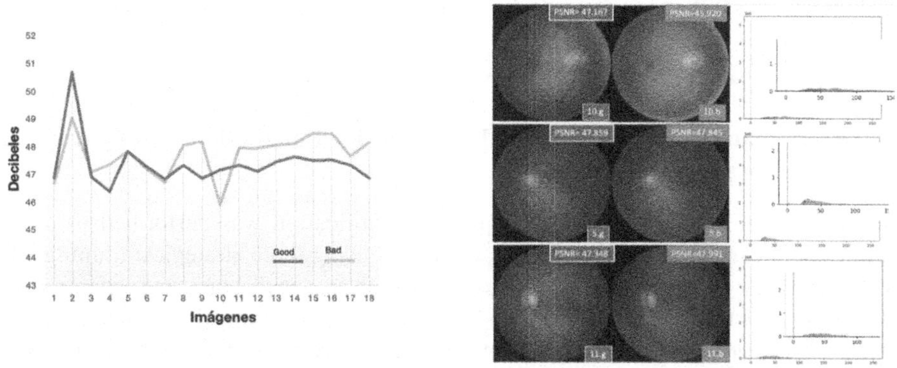

Fig. 7. Left: PSNR calculated using Gaussian blur. Average PSNR expressed in dB for each image in the HRF database calculated by the Gaussian blur filter, with blue representing the good quality set and gray representing the bad quality set. Right: Histogram comparing images with Gaussian blur filter examples. In blue are the good quality images and in orange are the bad quality images, showing the average PSNR for each of them. Next to them are the histograms of the corresponding images. The top row shows image 10, the middle row shows image 5, and the bottom row shows image 11. (Color figure online)

Retinal vessel segmentation results supported the findings from the PSNR analysis. In high-quality images, vessels were clearly segmented with minimal error, while in low-quality images, segmentation was often incomplete or inaccurate (Fig. 8). This further reinforces the role of structural methods in assessing image quality, particularly in the context of DR screening where accurate vessel visualization is crucial.

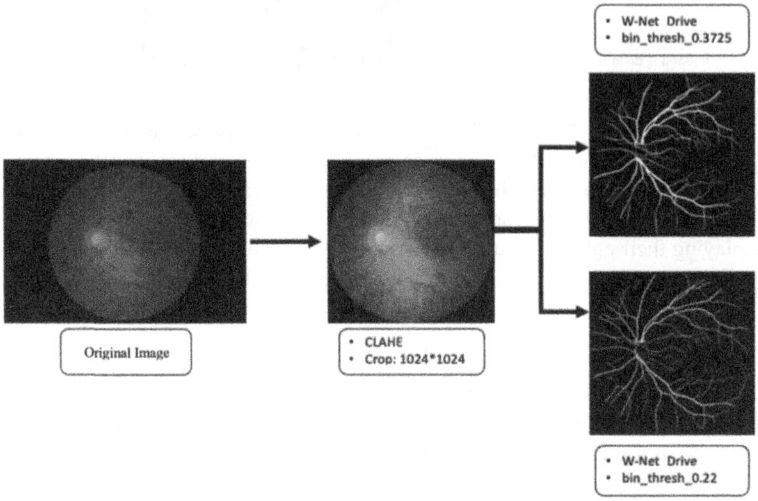

Fig. 8. Segmentation of the HRF database. Diagram of the processing for obtaining the segmented vessel image using W-Net using thresholds of 0.3725 at the top and 0.22 at the bottom.

3.2 Determination of Minimum Quality Levels for Images that Can Be Applied to All Types of Photography

The selection of parameters used for quality identification was performed using the WEKA tool's classifier. Each classifier was tested using three strategies: training with 100% of the data, applying cross-validation with a subset size of 2 or 3, and separating the data into 70% for training and 30% for testing. This approach utilized three feature vector strategies: one composed of PSNR and entropy (feature vector), another combining these features with structural features (feature vector + structure), and finally, a strategy based on the selected features.

All the results of the different strategies are shown in Table 2. Classification using RF achieves a correct classification rate of 100% /0% (TP/FP), with an ROC area of 1.0, indicating an overfitting. For cross-validation and a separation percentage of 70%/30%, obtained 72.2%/27.8% and 54.4%/44.5%2.

The classification results obtained using SMO with a training set and a kernel with exponent of 2, achieves a correct classification rate of 91.67%/8.33%. Additionally, cross-validation was performed with a subset size of 3 and a separation percentage of 70%/30%, as shown in Table 2.

Table 1. Ranking of attributes for classification using RF and SVM (SMO). The relative weights for each feature are observed, and the coincident ones for both classifiers are highlighted. The term PSNRGX refers to the PSNR measured with Gaussian blurring, using a kernel of size X.

Random Forest		SVM (SMO)	
Weight	Attibute	Weight	Attibute
0.28333	*PNSRG5*	0.0833	*PNSR31*
0.27778	*PNSRG25*	0.0667	*PNSR7*
0.27222	*PNSRG15*	0.05	*PNSR13*
0.26667	*PNSRG11*	0.044	*PNSR21*
0.25	*PNSRG17*	0.044	*PNSR5*
0.21111	*PNSRG27*	0.0389	*PNSR25*
0.19444	*PNSRG31*	0.0389	*PNSR17*
0.18889	*PNSRG3*	0.0278	*PNSR11*
0.17778	*PNSRG9*	0.0278	*PNSR15*
0.17222	*PNSRG1*	0.0167	*PNSR27*
0.15556	*PNSRG7*	0.0111	*PNSR3*
0.15556	*PNSRG13*		
0.13889	*PNSRG23*		
0.13333	*PNSRG19*		

The result shows that there is a decrease in performance in the RF compared to SMO in the cross-validation and 70%/30% splitting test. The results show performances near to 90%, meaning that SMO shows better generalization compared to RF. To do a deeper analysis, a ranking of attributes is performed with the aim of selecting those that contribute the most to classification in each classifier training. The results of this evaluation are shown in Table 1, which displays the relative weight of contribution to classification for each element. It is important to note that in this case, all RF attributes show a higher contribution measured by their weight compared to the weight for SMO. Similarly, the attributes highlighted for SVM (SMO) are also relevant to RF, suggesting that these features have meaningful information about the quality of the image. Additionally, these results provide a strong basis for selecting features to construct a new feature vector for dimensionality reduction.

Table 2. Performance comparison of Random Forest (RF) and SMO classifiers across different datasets and configurations. The table includes metrics for the HRF and DRIMDB datasets, covering full feature vectors, selected attributes, structural vectors, and GaussianBlur processing. Metrics include True Positive Rate, False Positive Rate, and Area Under the ROC Curve (AUC) across training sets, cross-validation, and 70/30 data splits

Metric	RF - Training Set	RF - Cross Validation	RF - Split 70/30	SMO - Training Set	SMO - Cross Validation	SMO - Split 70/30
HRF						
True Positive	*1*	0.722	0.545	0.917	0.861	0.818
False Positive	*0*	0.278	0.445	0.083	0.139	0.152
AUC	*1*	0.809	0.733	0.917	0.861	0.833
HRF - Selected Attributes						
True Positive	*1*	0.778	0.545	0.722	0.722	0.455
False Positive	*0*	0.222	0.445	0.278	0.278	0.455
AUC	*1*	0.841	0.8	0.722	0.722	0.5
DRIMDB - Selected Attributes						
True Positive	*1*	0.857	1	1	0.857	1
False Positive	*0*	0.143	0	0	0.143	0
AUC	*1*	0.959	1	1	0.857	1
HRF - Structure Vector						
True Positive	*1*	0.667	0.5	1	0.5	0
False Positive	*0*	0.333	0.5	0	0.5	1
AUC	*1*	0.667	-	1	0.5	-
HRF - Structure + Feature Vector						
True Positive	*1*	0.667	0.714	1	0.75	0.86
False Positive	*0*	0.333	0.285	0	0.25	0.14
AUC	*1*	0.667	0.7	1	0.75	0.9
HRF - Structure + Selected Features						
True Positive	*1*	0.75	0.571	1	0.75	0.714
False Positive	*0*	0.25	0.471	0	0.25	0.285
AUC	*1*	0.837	0.6	1	0.75	0.8
HRF - Structure + GaussianBlur						
True Positive	*1*	0.75	0.714	1	0.75	0.714
False Positive	*0*	0.25	0.285	0	0.25	0.285
AUC	*1*	0.837	0.7	1	0.75	0.8

4 Discussion

This study revealed that entropy and PSNR with Salt & Pepper noise produced higher values in the poor-quality subsets, which is contrary to expectations and what is typically described in the literature. This unexpected outcome is likely due to the presence of more white pixels in lower-quality images, caused by opacities or artifacts, which artificially inflated these metrics.

In contrast, PSNR with Gaussian Blur, especially when combined with retinal vessel segmentation, proved to be a more reliable indicator of image quality. These findings suggest that structural analysis, which focuses on the clarity and completeness of retinal features such as vessels, is crucial for accurately distinguishing between gradable and non-gradable images. The ability to accurately assess image quality at the point of capture is critical for ensuring that only medically useful images are processed further, thereby improving the efficiency and effectiveness of DR screening programs.

These results highlight the necessity of incorporating robust image quality assessment (IQA) tools into automated DR screening systems like DART. By ensuring that only high-quality images proceed to the classification stage, healthcare providers can reduce the burden on specialists and improve patient outcomes by facilitating timely and accurate diagnosis.

5 Conclusions

As shown in this study, screening for diabetic retinopathy (DR) is crucial for reducing complications, making it essential to ensure that the images captured are of sufficient quality to allow accurate grading. To optimize the ophthalmologist's time and improve patient care, it is necessary to identify and address media opacities promptly—something the generated tool effectively contributes to.

The results indicate that vessel segmentation is a strong indicator of image quality, and its integration into the feature vector significantly enhances the performance of the tool, enabling the selection of medically useful images. This approach not only improves the accuracy of automated screening systems but also ensures that only images of adequate quality proceed to further analysis, thus optimizing the workflow in DR screening.

Additionally, the study concludes that the traditional binary characterization of image quality as "good" or "bad" is insufficient. Instead, the categories of "gradable" and "non-gradable" are proposed as being more aligned with the results obtained, offering a more practical and clinically relevant classification. This refined approach to image quality assessment will better support the objectives of DR screening programs and contribute to more effective management of the disease.

Acknowledgment. This article was supported by ChatGPT from OpenAI, providing helpful orthographic and editing suggestions during the writing process.

This study was conducted in the context of the development of the master's thesis of the Medical Informatics program at the University of Chile.

Disclosure of Interests.. The authors have no competing interests to declare that are relevant to the content of this article.

References

1. Descripción y Epidemiología – DIPRECE. https://diprece.minsal.cl/leinformamos/auge/acceso-guias-clinicas/guias-clinicas-desarrolladas-utilizando-manualmetodologico/retinopatia-diabetica/descripcion-y-epidemiologia/. Accessed 30 Aug 2024
2. Célula Oftalmológica (DART) - Departamento de Salud Digital. https://portalsaluddigital.minsal.cl/celula-oftalmologia-dart/. Accessed 30 Aug 2024
3. Aldington, S.J., et al.: Methodology for retinal photography and assessment of diabetic retinopathy: the EURODIAB IDDM complications study. Diabetologia **38**(4), 437–444 (1995)
4. Scanlon, P.H., et al.: The influence of age, duration of diabetes, cataract, and pupil size on image quality in digital photographic retinal screening. Diabetes Care **28**(10), 2448–2453 (2005)
5. Niemeijer, M., et al.: Image structure clustering for image quality verification of color retina images in diabetic retinopathy screening. Med. Image Anal. **10**(6), 888–898 (2006)
6. Saha, S.K., et al.: Automated quality assessment of colour fundus images for diabetic retinopathy screening in telemedicine. J. Digit. Imaging **31**(6), 869–878 (2018)
7. Lin, J., et al.: Retinal image quality assessment for diabetic retinopathy screening: a survey. Multimed. Tools Appl. **79**, 16173–16199 (2019)
8. Millen, A.E., et al.: ARIC Manuscript Proposal# 2702 (2016)
9. Köhler, T., et al.: Automatic no-reference quality assessment for retinal fundus images using vessel segmentation. In: Proceedings of the 26th IEEE International Symposium on Computer-Based Medical Systems, pp. 95–100 (2013)
10. Şevik, U., et al.: Identification of suitable fundus images using automated quality assessment methods. J. Biomed. Opt. **19**(4), 046006 (2014)
11. Lee, S.C., Wang, Y.: Automatic retinal image quality assessment and enhancement. Med. Imaging (1999)
12. Sonali et al.: An approach for de-noising and contrast enhancement of retinal fundus image using CLAHE. Opt. Laser Technol. (2019)
13. OpenCV: Histograms - 2: Histogram Equalization. https://docs.opencv.org/3.1.0/d5/daf/tutorial_py_histogram_equalization.html. Accessed 30 Aug 2024
14. Thung, K.-H., Raveendran, P.: A survey of image quality measures. In: 2009 International Conference for Technical Postgraduates (TECHPOS), pp. 1–4 (2009)
15. Gao, P., et al.: Thermodynamics-based evaluation of various improved Shannon entropies for configurational information of gray-level images. Entropy (Basel, Switzerland) **20**(1), 19 (2018)
16. Galdran, A., et al.: The little W-Net that could: state-of-the-art retinal vessel segmentation with minimalistic models. ArXiv abs/2009.01907 (2020)
17. Frank, E., Hall, M.A., Witten, I.H.: The WEKA Workbench. Online Appendix for "Data Mining: Practical Machine Learning Tools and Techniques", Fourth Edition. Morgan Kaufmann (2016)
18. Arévalo, J., et al.: RETINA 2019. https://paao.org/wp-content/uploads/2021/12/LIBRORETINA-PAAO-2019-UPDATED-2021-12-08.pdf. Accessed 30 Aug 2024
19. Giancardo, L.: Automated fundus images analysis techniques to screen retinal diseases in diabetic patients. (Analyse de "Fundus" image par le diagnostique de la retinopathie diabétique) (2011)
20. Dias, J.M.P., et al.: Retinal image quality assessment using generic image quality indicators. Inf. Fusion **19**, 73–90 (2014)

Empowering Students: Leveraging No-Code and Training Models with Google Machine Learning for Accessible App Development

Sujni Paul(✉)

Faculty, Higher Colleges of Technology, Dubai Academic City, Dubai, UAE
spaul@hct.ac.ae

Abstract. The rapid advancement of technology has created a demand for tools that enable individuals without a computer science background to develop applications. This research focuses on leveraging no-code and low-code platforms, integrated with Google's machine learning technologies, to empower non-computer science students to create functional and innovative applications. The goal is to democratize app development by providing accessible tools that allow students from various disciplines to harness the power of machine learning without extensive programming knowledge.

No-code and low-code platforms offer intuitive development environments where users can design and deploy applications using drag-and-drop interfaces, pre-built components, and minimal coding. By incorporating Google's machine learning capabilities, such as natural language processing, image recognition, and predictive analytics, these platforms enable students to create intelligent applications that solve real-world problems. This integration enhances learning experiences, fosters creativity, and broadens skill sets.

The study examines the potential of these platforms in educational settings, exploring their ability to facilitate technically sophisticated yet easy-to-create applications. It also investigates the challenges and opportunities of teaching non-computer science students to use these tools, including the need for tailored instructional materials and support systems. Through case studies and user testing, the research evaluates the impact of no-code and low-code app development on student engagement, creativity, and integration of machine learning into diverse academic projects. By contributing to accessible technology education, this paper highlights how these platforms, combined with Google's machine learning, can foster a new generation of developers from non-traditional backgrounds.

1 Introduction

1.1 Overview

In recent years, the landscape of software development has been transformed by the emergence of no-code and low-code platforms, which offer a significant departure from traditional coding practices. These platforms enable users to create applications through intuitive, visual interfaces with minimal or no programming knowledge required. This

A. Safi et al. (Eds.): ISICS 2024, CCIS 2381, pp. 277–286, 2025.
https://doi.org/10.1007/978-3-031-82931-4_21

shift is democratizing app development, allowing individuals and organizations to build and deploy software solutions more rapidly and efficiently. Concurrently, advancements in machine learning (ML), particularly through tools like Google's machine learning technologies, are enhancing the capabilities of these platforms, making sophisticated functionalities more accessible.

1.2 No-Code and Low-Code Platforms

Have revolutionized the software development process by providing user-friendly environments where application development is achieved through graphical user interfaces and drag-and-drop components. No-code platforms allow users to build applications entirely without writing code, while lowcode platforms offer a compromise where some coding is involved but is kept to a minimum. These platforms cater to a wide range of users, including business professionals and educators, who may not have a technical background but need to create functional applications for various purposes. The appeal of no-code and low-code platforms lies in their ability to accelerate development cycles, reduce costs, and empower non-technical users to bring their ideas to life (Wiederkehr, 2021).

1.3 Google Machine Learning Technologies

Further augment the potential of no-code and low-code platforms. Google offers a suite of machine learning tools, such as TensorFlow, AutoML, and Google Cloud AI, which enable users to incorporate advanced ML capabilities into their applications. These tools facilitate tasks such as image recognition, natural language processing, and predictive analytics without requiring deep expertise in machine learning algorithms. For instance, Google AutoML allows users to train custom machine learning models with minimal coding, making it possible to integrate complex ML functionalities into applications developed on no-code or low-code platforms (Google Cloud, 2023). This integration bridges the gap between advanced technology and user-friendly application development.

The synergy between no-code/low-code platforms and machine learning technologies has significant implications for various fields, including education and business. In educational contexts, these tools provide students with the opportunity to explore and apply machine learning concepts in a practical setting, without needing to master extensive programming skills. For businesses, the combination of these technologies accelerates innovation, enabling rapid prototyping and deployment of intelligent applications that can respond to dynamic needs and leverage data-driven insights.

2 Literature Review

The integration of no-code and low-code platforms with machine learning represents a significant shift in how application development is approached, particularly for users without a traditional programming background. This literature survey explores the current state of no-code and low-code platforms, the role of machine learning in these environments, and their implications for education, particularly in empowering students to engage with technology in innovative ways.

No-code and low-code platforms have garnered attention as tools that democratize software development by enabling users to build applications with minimal or no coding, using visual interfaces and pre-built components (Wiederkehr, 2021). According to Gartner (2020), the rise of these platforms is driven by the growing demand for digital transformation across industries and the shortage of skilled software developers. Forrester Research (2020) categorizes no-code platforms as those designed for ease of use, while low-code platforms offer additional flexibility through limited coding.

In educational contexts, the benefits of no-code and low-code platforms have been increasingly recognized, allowing students to focus on creative problem-solving rather than programming syntax (Sivakumar & Balaji, 2022). These platforms empower learners from diverse academic backgrounds to engage with technology meaningfully by creating applications that are relevant to their fields of study. Studies like Schrader & Hostetler (2022) highlight the increased engagement and motivation observed when students use no-code tools to develop projects without the steep learning curve of traditional programming.

The survey includes a deeper comparison of various no-code and low-code platforms, such as Bubble, which offers more complex logic and customization, and Zapier, which focuses on automating workflows by integrating various apps and services. Additionally, platforms like OutSystems and Microsoft Power Apps are examined for their enterprise capabilities and machine learning integration, which provide greater insight into how different platforms serve distinct user needs.

To capture recent developments, this paper includes studies on how no-code and low-code platforms like Thunkable and Kodular are specifically designed for educational settings and enable students to develop mobile applications, making machine learning more tangible and applicable (Breslow et al., 2021). These tools offer modules for natural language processing, image recognition, and predictive analytics, which align with educational goals and enhance the accessibility of AI concepts.

3 Methodology

3.1 Overview

This research employs a structured approach to explore the use of no-code platforms in conjunction with Google's machine learning tools to create functional applications. The methodology encompasses the selection and utilization of no-code development platforms, integration with Google's machine learning technologies, and evaluation of the overall process and outcomes.

To begin with, we selected **AppSheet** as the primary no-code platform for this research due to its user-friendly interface and seamless integration with Google services. AppSheet allows users to design and develop applications through a visual interface, minimizing the need for traditional coding. This platform was chosen for its accessibility and broad adoption, which makes it a suitable candidate for investigating the practical application of no-code tools in conjunction with machine learning. The next step involved setting up the application development environment on AppSheet. This process included creating a new project and configuring it to use Google Sheets as the data source. Google Sheets was selected because of its ease of use and integration capabilities with both AppSheet and Google's machine learning services. We developed a basic application framework to handle user input, display data, and provide functionality relevant to research objectives.

To initiate the research, we chose **Glide** as the no-code platform due to its intuitive interface and robust capabilities for mobile app development. Glide enables users to build apps through a visual editor, which simplifies the process of app creation without requiring traditional coding skills. We began by creating an account on Glide and setting up a new project. Glide's seamless integration with Google Sheets was leveraged to manage and organize the app's data, allowing for a straightforward configuration process.

3.2 App Design and Integration

In Glide, the design of the app started with selecting a template that matched the core functionality of the research objectives. Glide's interface allows users to customize the app's appearance and layout through drag-and-drop components, which simplifies the design process. We configured the app to pull data from Google Sheets, which served as the primary data source. This integration involved mapping data fields from Google Sheets to the app's components and ensuring that data updates in the spreadsheet were reflected in the app in real-time.

Training Models

In this research, **TensorFlow** plays a pivotal role in the development and deployment of machine learning models, providing a robust framework for creating sophisticated algorithms and integrating them into the no-code application developed using Glide. TensorFlow, an open-source machine learning library developed by Google, offers a comprehensive ecosystem for building, training, and deploying machine learning models. Here's a detailed overview of how TensorFlow is used in the research:

4 Model Deployment and Training

4.1 Overview

This research employs TensorFlow is employed for developing and training machine learning models tailored to the specific requirements of the research project. The process begins with defining the model architecture, which involves selecting appropriate neural network types and configuring their parameters. TensorFlow provides a range of tools and APIs, such as Keras, to facilitate the design and training of these models.

4.1.1 Data Preparation

The initial step involves preparing and preprocessing data for training. TensorFlow supports various data handling techniques, including data augmentation and normalization, to enhance model performance. For example, if the app requires image classification, TensorFlow's tf.data API is used to manage image data efficiently.

4.1.2 Model Design

Using TensorFlow, we design custom neural network archi tectures suited to the task at hand. For instance, Convolutional Neural Networks (CNNs) might be used for image processing tasks, while Recurrent Neural Networks (RNNs) could be employed for sequence data.

4.1.3 Training and Evaluation

The model is trained on the prepared dataset using TensorFlow's training utilities. During this phase, the model's performance is monitored through various metrics such as accuracy and loss. TensorFlow's built-in visualization tools, like TensorBoard, provide insights into the training process, enabling adjustments to improve model performance.

4.2 Integration with Google Cloud

Once the TensorFlow model is trained, it is integrated with Google Cloud for deployment and real-time application:

- **Exporting the Model:** The trained TensorFlow model is exported and converted into a format suitable for deployment, such as a TensorFlow SavedModel or a TensorFlow Lite model for mobile devices. This conversion ensures compatibility with deployment environments and optimizes the model for performance.
- **Model Serving:** TensorFlow Serving, a specialized serving system, is used to deploy the model on Google Cloud. This system allows for efficient and scalable serving of machine learning models, handling requests and delivering predictions in real-time.
- **API Integration:** The deployed model is accessed via an API, which is integrated into the Glide app using Google Cloud Functions. These functions act as intermediaries, handling API requests from the app, querying the model, and returning predictions to the user.

5 Results and Analysis

5.1 Overview

In this research, no-code development is utilized through Glide to demonstrate how non-technical users can create fully functional applications with minimal effort. Glide, a powerful no-code platform, allows users to transform data stored in Google Sheets into polished, user-friendly mobile and web apps. The research focuses on how Glide can be used to rapidly develop applications for specific needs, such as educational tools, project management systems, or business dashboards, without the need for traditional programming. By simply organizing data in a Google Sheet and applying Glide's intuitive drag-and-drop interface, users can design and deploy customized apps that handle tasks like data entry, visualization, and user interaction.

In the research, Glide is employed to create a sample app that tracks and visualizes user activity data, demonstrating its capacity to handle real-world scenarios. This app, built entirely without code, highlights the practical applicability of Glide in educational and business environments where time, resources, and technical expertise may be limited. The research illustrates how Glide's integration with Google's ecosystem allows users to harness existing data, automate processes, and enhance productivity without the steep learning curve associated with traditional app development. Through this approach, the research underscores the transformative potential of no-code tools like Glide in democratizing app development and empowering a broader range of individuals to create digital solutions tailored to their unique needs (Figs. 1 and 2).

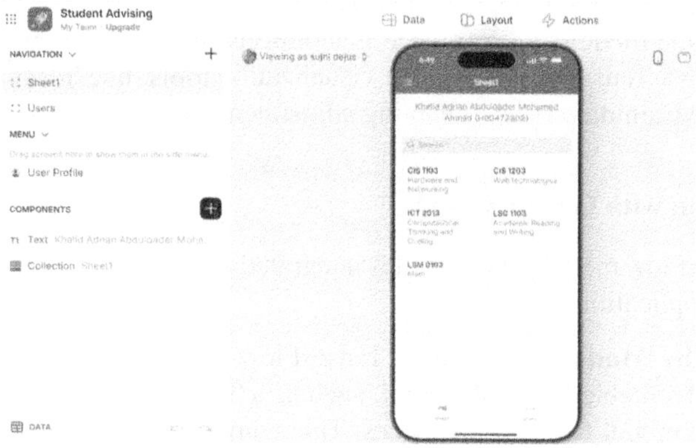

Fig. 1. Screen shot of a sample Mobile App using Glide

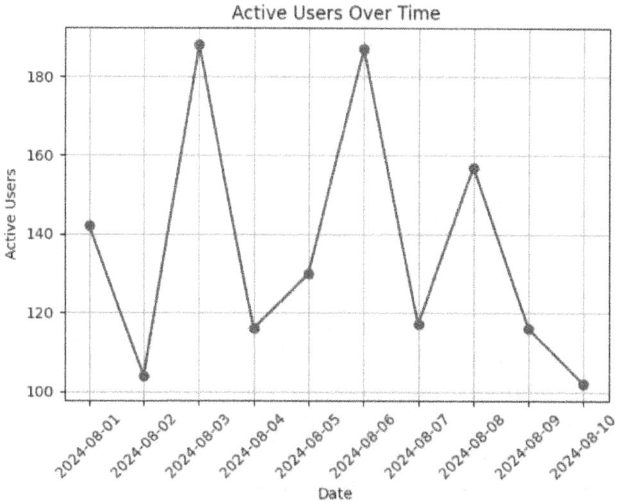

Fig. 2. Active Users

The line plot illustrates how user engagement (measured by the number of active users) fluctuates over time. For instance, if the line rises, it indicates an increase in active users; if it falls, it signifies a decrease (Fig. 3).

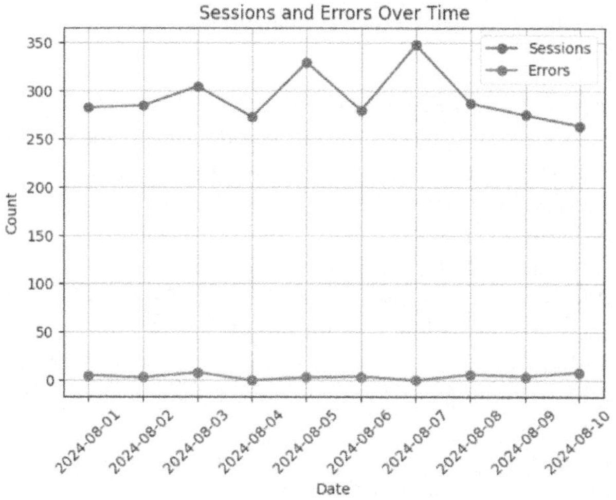

Fig. 3. Sessions and Errors Line

Sessions Line: Indicates the number of times users interacted with the app on each date. An increasing trend suggests higher user engagement, while a decreasing trend may imply reduce activity.

Errors Line: Represents the number of errors reported by the app. A high or increasing number of errors could indicate technical issues affecting user experience.

6 A Case Study

1. **Data Collection and Preparation**
   To start, a dataset of labeled images is required. For this example, let's use the **CIFAR-10** dataset, which contains 60,000 32 × 32 color images in 10 different classes (e.g., airplanes, cars, birds, cats).
- **Dataset Source:** The CIFAR-10 dataset can be downloaded from TensorFlow's dataset repository or other sources like Kaggle.
- **Data Preprocessing:** Images are preprocessed by normalizing pixel values to a range between 0 and 1 and splitting the dataset into training and testing sets.
2. **Model Development**
   Using TensorFlow, a Convolutional Neural Network (CNN) is designed for image classification. CNNs are particularly effective for image data due to their ability to learn spatial hierarchies of features.
- **Model Architecture:** Define a CNN model with layers such as convolutional layers, max-pooling layers, and fully connected layers. For this example, a simple CNN architecture might include:
  - **Convolutional Layers:** Apply filters to detect features like edges and textures.
  - **Max-Pooling Layers:** Reduce dimensionality by taking the maximum value in a feature map.

- **Fully Connected Layers:** Combine features and produce the final classification output.

3. **Model Evaluation**
- After training, evaluate the model on the test dataset to measure its accuracy and performance. Metrics such as accuracy, precision, and recall are computed to assess how well the model classifies images.

4. **Model Deployment**

The trained model is then prepared for deployment:
- **Export the Model:** Convert the TensorFlow model into a format suitable for deployment, such as TensorFlow Lite for mobile applications.
- **Deploy the Model:** Upload the TensorFlow Lite model to a cloud storage service and configure an API endpoint using Google Cloud Functions to serve the model.

5. **Integration with Glide**

Integrate the TensorFlow model into a no-code platform like Glide by creating an application that interacts with the model's API:
- **App Setup:** Use Glide to design a mobile app that allows users to upload images for classification.
- **API Integration:** Configure webhooks or API calls in Glide to send images to the TensorFlow model API and receive classification results.

Glide Integration Example:

- **Webhook Configuration:** Set up a webhook in Glide to trigger an API request when a user uploads an image. The request sends the image data to the TensorFlow model API.
- **Displaying Results:** Receive the classification result from the API and display it within the Glide app, allowing users to see the predicted category of their image (Fig. 4)

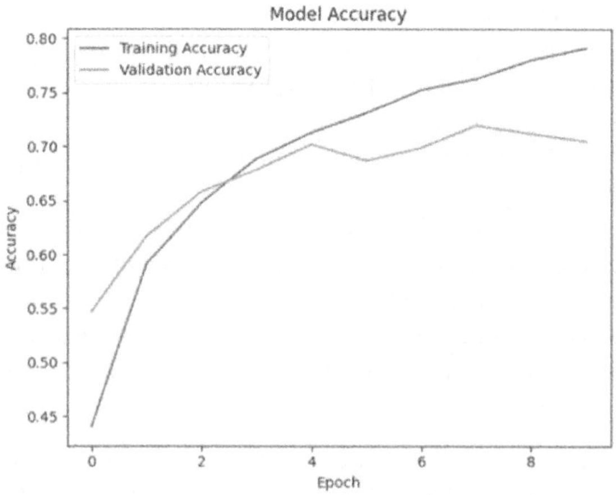

Fig. 4. Epoch Accuracy Graph

Figure shows how the model's accuracy improves over training epochs for both training and validation datasets (Fig. 5).

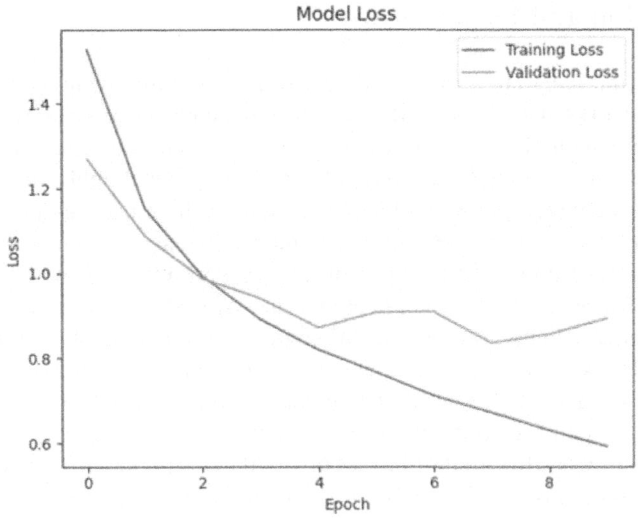

Fig. 5. Epoch Loss Graph

Epoch Loss Graph: Displays how the model's loss decreases over epochs, reflecting learning progress (Fig. 6).

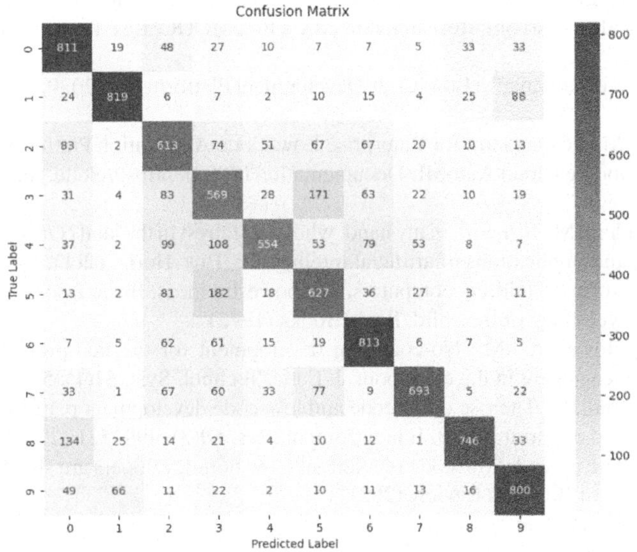

True \ Predicted	0	1	2	3	4	5	6	7	8	9
0	811	19	48	27	10	7	7	5	33	33
1	24	819	6	7	2	10	15	4	25	88
2	83	2	613	74	51	67	67	20	10	13
3	31	4	83	569	28	171	63	22	10	19
4	37	2	99	108	554	53	79	53	8	7
5	13	2	81	182	18	627	36	27	3	11
6	7	5	62	61	15	19	813	6	7	5
7	33	1	67	60	33	77	9	693	5	22
8	134	25	14	21	4	10	12	1	746	33
9	49	66	11	22	2	10	11	13	16	800

Fig. 6. Confusion Matrix

This matrix provides a detailed view of the classification performance, highlighting correct and incorrect predictions across different classes.

7 Conclusion and Future Scope

In conclusion, the integration of no-code platforms like Glide with advanced machine learning frameworks such as TensorFlow represents a powerful synergy that democratizes app development and data-driven innovation. This research has shown that non-technical users can leverage Glide to rapidly build functional applications, while TensorFlow enables the incorporation of sophisticated machine learning models into these apps, enhancing their capabilities without requiring extensive programming expertise. The combination of no-code development and TensorFlow's AI models allows users to create intelligent, responsive applications that can adapt to complex datasets and deliver actionable insights. As these technologies continue to evolve, future directions could include deeper integration between no-code platforms and AI/ML tools, making it even easier for users to deploy advanced models in everyday applications. Additionally, expanding the scope of no-code platforms to support more complex and customizable machine learning workflows could further broaden their use cases, allowing for greater innovation across industries. The continued advancement of no-code development and AI integration will play a critical role in driving digital transformation, empowering a diverse range of users to create impactful solutions tailored to their specific needs and challenges.

References

Breslow, L., Pritchard, D.E., DeBoer, J., Stump, G.S., Ho, A.D., Seaton, D.T.: Studying learning in the worldwide classroom: Research into edX's first MOOC. Res. Pract. Assess. **8**(1), 13–25 (2021)

Forrester. The Forrester Wave™: Low-Code Development Platforms, Q1 2020. Forrester Research, Inc. (2020)

Gartner. (2020). Magic Quadrant for Enterprise Low-Code Application Platforms. Gartner, Inc.

Google Cloud. Google Cloud AutoML Documentation (2023). https://cloud.google.com/automl/docs

Kaplan, A., Haenlein, M.: Siri, Siri, in my hand: who's the fairest in the land? On the interpretations, illustrations, and implications of artificial intelligence. Bus. Horiz. **62**(1), 15–25 (2019)

Papert, S.: Mindstorms: Children, computers, and powerful ideas. Basic Books (1980)

Piaget, J.: The psychology of the child. Basic Books (1972)

Schrader, D.E., Hostetler, J.M.: No-code app development for the non-programmer: creating meaningful engagement in the classroom. J. Educ. Technol. Syst. **51**(1), 5–25 (2022)

Sivakumar, S., Balaji, S.: The rise of no-code and low-code development platforms in education: Implications and opportunities. J. Educ. Comput. Res. **60**(3), 499–521 (2022)

Wiederkehr, H.: The no-code/low-code revolution: How non-developers are shaping the future of software. Harvard Business Review (2021)

A Comprehensive Review of Intrusion Detection Systems in IoT Landscape

Muhammad Kaleem[1], Muhammad Azhar Mushtaq[1(✉)], Salman Rashid[2], and Mohsin Saleemi[3]

[1] Department of Information Technology, Faculty of Computing and IT, University of Sargodha, Sargodha 40100, Pakistan
Azhar.mushtaq@uos.edu.pk

[2] Department of Computer Science and Information Technology, University of Lahore, Lahore, Pakistan

[3] Higher Colleges of Technology, Dubai, UAE

Abstract. Despite the many benefits of lifestyles and automation, through the Internet of Things, there are risks involved as most of the devices interconnect because of insecurity, compromised devices, and weak encryption. The protectors of cyber security are Intrusion Detection Systems, which are similar to detecting insurgencies by carefully assessing the systems and network activities for signs of malicious activities, unauthorized entry, or potential penetration. This work investigates the possible ways of preventing IoT networks using IDS designed for IoT. This work discusses limitations to a greater extent, suggesting their lack of adaptability and limited resources, and it does so by carrying out the categorization by different varieties and subtypes of the IDS like collaborative, deep learning, feature selection, etc., and then having a research evaluation to decide the pros and cons. After that, the current trends of the IoT environment, promising directions for enhancing security, and specific guidelines for assessing the performance of IDS are discussed. Conclusively, this study further contributes to the continuous establishment of IoT IDS to ensure a safer and longerlasting connected devices future.

Keywords: Internet of Things · Intrusion detection system · Deep learning · Machine learning

1 Introduction

Internet of Things (IoT) does not limit itself from connected homes to smart cities to connected vehicles, but simply it is merging everything with the internet. The Internet of Things will have a huge impact in many different sectors of the economy. It has potential to be used in key areas such as smart cities, health, environment and agriculture. IoT has become developed in recent times, and it has a wide applicability in various sectors of life. The vast installed base of sensors and connected devices will deliver levels of automation, productivity, and simplicity previously unimaginable [1]. But there are

A. Safi et al. (Eds.): ISICS 2024, CCIS 2381, pp. 287–302, 2025.
https://doi.org/10.1007/978-3-031-82931-4_22

security risks that are posed by this connectivity. A few devices with limited capability, comparatively inflexible operating system, and sufficient lack of encryption to protect personal data and provide hacker access points, is one of the biggest threats to IoT. Extending the protection to a huge IoT environment requires creating an effective security model which is a multilevel process [2].

As with intrusion detection system IDSs serve in the world of cyber security as sentinels watching network traffic and system operations for signs of intrusions or other suspicious activities regarding security breaches. These systems can be viewed as frameworks which act as warning indicators for threats in the cybersecurity domain as many of these systems can employ sophisticated form of algorithms, pattern-matching techniques that isolate deviations from normal behaviors or known attack signatures [3]. IDS in a necessity in identifying and preventing harm before it occurs since it enables business to respond to security events and secure their critical infrastructure against numerous forms of cyber threats [4].

One of the key areas which must be regarded in connection with the IoT is the enhancement of IDS contribution to the general security environment. IDS is essential when it comes to monitoring and safeguarding interconnected devices from hackers as more IoT appliances are developed. These systems analyze the multitudes of streams of data generated by Internet of Things (IoT) devices and identify anomalies or suspicious behaviors that may indicate compromised security or even unlawful intrusion [5]. IDS assists with the early identification and resolution of security threats, due to its capabilities of notifying a user instantly and responding to a situation instantly. This minimizes the risks of unauthorized access, loss of data or deprival of IoT services [6]. IDS fits the picture in this regard by providing the tools businesses require to maintain the data's availability, integrity, and confidentiality within the IoTs.

In this work, the area of intrusion detection systems for the internet of things (IoT) is explored. Initially this work identifies challenges and limitations which are associated with the current IoT specific IDS solutions that are available in the market. Secondly, latest available literature is segregated various types of IoT intrusion detection systems such as deep learning-based IDS, feature selection-based IDS, collaborative IDS, hybrid IDS, Intelligent Dual Layer Intrusion Detection System (iDL-IDS), network-based IDS, and self-evolving IDS. After carefully examine pertinent research articles from each category, offering an understanding of the advantages and disadvantages of each IDS type. The performance metrics are evaluated to assess these IDS's efficacy are also introduced in this research. In the end, future research directions that could lead to breakthroughs in the discipline are presented. The study concludes with a summary of the main findings, emphasizing the significance of continuous advancements in IoT IDS to support cybersecurity in the dynamic environment of interconnected devices.

2 Challenges and Limitations

Several obstacles affect intrusion detection systems' ability to secure networks. Scalability and resource efficiency are major issues, particularly in situations with limited resources like Internet of Things (IoT) network [7]. The flexibility of IDS to respond to new threats is also a major worry, since attack methods are changing so quickly that predefined rule-based systems can find it difficult to stay up to date. As a result, it is challenging to achieve generalizability across a range of network conditions, which means that the detection system, which is flexible enough to be used in different conditions, must be ready to consider the differences in the configuration, protocols, or architectural styles [8].

One of the most important factors that have a direct relation to the efficiency of machine learning based IDS is the training data. This way, biases or lack of diversity in a data set may lead to unbalanced forecasts or restricted identification of new attack patterns. The achievement of reviewing presentations in real-time is always a real concern, especially when time is of the essence, and something needs to be identified and dealt with soon. IDS implementations are required to follow high standards that will enable them to manage large traffic workload within the network in real-time without compromising the prognosis precision [9].

The other reason why interpretability is important was to allow security analysts to understand the reasoning behind the IDS alerts that are generated. This becomes imperative especially when making decision that have been deemed to yield the right results and are within legal requirements [10]. Where IDS use high intrusive approaches like deep packet inspection due to the danger they pose to privacy rights, there ensues conflict between the need to detect intrusions and individual's privacy. Moreover, the constant changing of current networks present problems with traffic flow, devices' movement, and the changes in network topology. Pritchard further explained that IDS needs to adapt these changing environments so that it will remain trustworthy and useful in the long-term [11]. The presented challenges are crucial to be solved in order to improve the general effectiveness and reliability of IDS in the variety of modern cybersecurity environment.

3 Taxonomy of Intrusion Detection System

We divided intrusion detection systems into five categories which are: Deep Learning-based IDS, Feature Selection IDS, Collaborative IDS, Hybrid Intrusion Detection System (IDS), Intelligent Dual-Layer Intrusion Detection System (IDL-IDS), Network- Based Intrusion Detection System (NIDS), and Self-evolving IDS as given in Fig. 1.

3.1 Deep Learning-Based IDS

Deep Learning-based Intrusion Detection Systems leverage neural network architectures to detect and prevent malicious activities in computer networks. These systems excel at learning intricate patterns from vast datasets, enabling them to identify complex and evolving cyber threats. The use of deep learning models, such as recurrent neural networks (RNNs) or convolutional neural networks (CNNs), empowers IDS autonomously extract hierarchical features for enhanced detection accuracy.

Real-time Intrusion Detection System [12] based on Deep Neural Network (DNN) for Internet of Things (IoT) devices, which are notorious for having limited resources and being vulnerable to attacks. The benchmark Netflow-based datasets used to train the DIDS model include twenty distinct kinds of network attacks. The model consists of a total of five hidden layers that are dense (18, 36, 72, 144, and 256 neurons), a single input layer, an output layer, batch normalization, and dropout layers to improve performance and avoid overfitting. The Adagrad optimizer used for effective weight modifications with a decaying learning rate. Tested the system in an IoT-based real-time environment using live packets to assess its resilience against Man-in-the-Middle (MITM) and Denial of Service (DoS) attacks. However, it is imperative to consider potential obstacles including scalability, threat adaptation, and generalization to other IoT contexts.

An intrusion detection system based on a hybrid CNN+LSTM architecture [13] was created to address the unique cyberattack susceptibility of industrial internet of things (IIoT) networks. The created model aims to efficiently recognize and classify network activity as normal or potential assaults by combining the architectures of Convolutional Neural Networks, and long-short-term memory (LSTM).

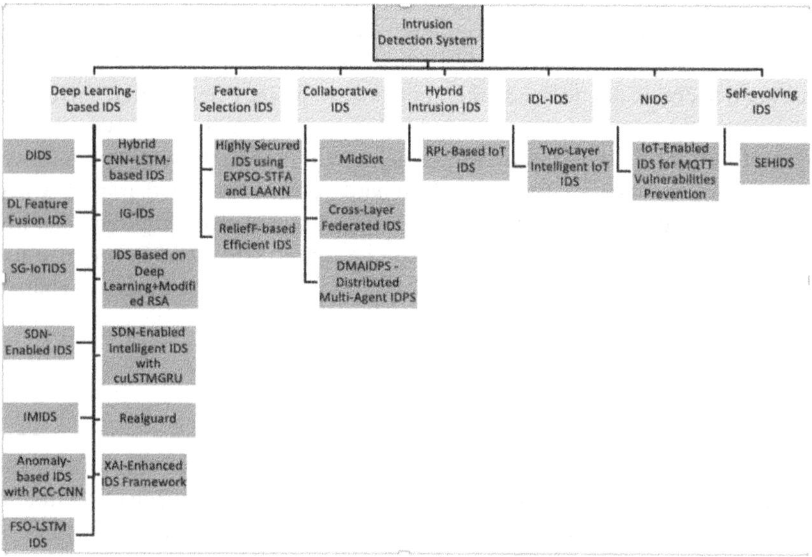

Fig. 1. Taxonomy of Intrusion Detection System

An IoT-focused Intrusion Detection System [14] that combines deep learning using the Reptile Search Algorithm (RSA) to extract and select features in an effort to improve performance. The key feature extractor in the system is a Convolutional Neural Network, also known CNN, and a new feature selection method provided by the RSA. For practical implementation, it may be necessary to meet the potential computational demands indicated by the RSA method's difficulty.

In order to cope with threat of attacks on Internet of Things, and emphasizing the shortcomings of conventional network-based intrusion detection systems, particularly in settings where centralized Software Defined Network (SDN) architecture is in use, [15] a deep learning-based method for detecting intrusions in Internet of Things networks that enable SDN by utilizing Long Short-Term Memory (LSTM). The suggested methodology address to a methodical procedure, commencing with the gathering of network flows from OpenFlow virtual switches linked to the SDN controller.

Realguard, is an lightweight Network Intrusion Detection System (NIDS) which is based on Deep Neural Networks (DNNs) that addresses the security flaws in the current generation of IoT gateways. Particularly in those cases where lack of deep learning- powered intrusion detection techniques because of computing limits a specifically tailored for local IoT gateways, [16]. However, Continuous refinement and validation are crucial to ensure Realguard's effectiveness in diverse and dynamic IoT network scenarios.

Introducing an Explainable Artificial Intelligence (XAI) architecture for Deep Learning (DL)-based IDS addresses the cybersecurity issues brought about by the growing complexity associated with Internet of Things (IoT) networks. Together with three primary XAI techniques—RuleFit, Local Interpretable Model-Agnostic Explanations (LIME), and SHapley Additive exPlanations (SHAP)—the XAI architecture [17] includes a revolutionary intrusion detection system for Internet of Things networks constructed utilizing deep neural networks. In addition to providing an explanation of predictions, the framework tries to increase transparency by shedding light on how the DL model functions.

Addressing the lack of strong security measures and hardware security support, as a countermeasure is the Intelligent Intrusion Detection System (IMIDS) [18]. To overcome the issue of a lack of training data, IMIDS employs a light-weight convolutional neural network model for threat classification and presents a novel Attack Data Generator driven by a conditional generative adversarial network (ctGAN). Designed to address IoT security issues, IMIDS consists of two stages: training and prediction. Important parts of it are a train/load model block, the extraction of features block, and network capture block.

Focusing on the shortcomings of existing IDS for Internet of Things networks, [19] suggests a knowledge graph and deep learning-based lightweight intrusion detection system. The system combines multi view feature fusion and alignment with statistical analysis and knowledge graphs to identify essential features and extract semantic relationships. A CNN-BiLSTM model that is attention-based and intended to detect malicious request attacks while obtaining dependencies that are long-distance and contextual semantic data forms the basis of the suggested approach. The suggested approach shows promise in identifying different types of attacks on Internet of Things networks, with the proposed system's F1-score being much greater than other. Overall accuracy is far greater than the published averages for different models.

Offering a deep-learning-based intrusion detection method in the context of Software Defined Networking (SDN) and IoT systems in order to combat the rising number of IoT assaults. [20] utilizes kernel principal components analysis (kernel-PCA) for optimum extraction of features and a model using gated recurrent units (GRU) deep learning layers for the extraction of internal feature representations. These characteristics then used to provide a complete intrusion detection solution for SDN-based Internet of Things networks. In the suggested two-tiered technique, connection records are gathered and used as foundational data in a network testbed setup. The obtained records then subjected to preprocessing and extraction of features utilizing GRU layers in network data analysis. To avoid overfitting, a dropout layer is carefully included. The resultant feature representations then flattened, and dimensionality reduced using kernel- PCA.

Addressing the vast and dynamic nature of the Internet of Things, and the cyber-security risks it faces. [21] suggests a clever intrusion detection system that makes use of a hybrid framework offered by Software-Defined Networking (SDN) and incorporates the Cuda Long-Term-Short-Term-Memory-Gated-Recurrent-Unit (cuLSTMGRU) for effective threat detection. The separation of the data and control planes in the SDN architecture improves programmability. Nestled in the control plane, the model leverages cuLSTMGRU effectively detect threats on several IoT networks, while also employing deep learning techniques. The evaluation involves pretreatment processes including handling NaN and Infinity values, converting non-numeric data, and feature normalization. It carried out using the CICIDS2017 dataset, which recognized for its applicability to IoT applications. However, the effectiveness of the cuLSTMGRU model in detecting novel and sophisticated attacks beyond the scope of the evaluated dataset should be explored.

Addressing the shortcomings of conventional security techniques for protecting the Internet of Things, or IoT devices, such as rule-based and signature-based methods. [22] offers a novel approach to detect network abnormalities in IoT environments: an anomaly-based intrusion detection system that makes use of Pearson-Correlation Coefficient - Convolutional Neural Networks (PCC-CNN), a deep learning model. This paper does a thorough evaluation of the model using three publically accessible datasets: NSL-KDD, CICIDS-2017, and IOTID20. Performance analysis shows that the PCC-CNN model outperforms conventional machine learning models in intrusion detection due to its greater efficiency. The combined PCC-CNN model outperforms the conventional PCC-based Machine Learning models (KNN and CART) on all three datasets, achieving an astounding 99.89% detection accuracy and an exceptionally low misclassification rate of 0.001. Nonetheless, the research ought to shed light on the PCC-CNN model's memory and processing needs.

Addressing the susceptibility of the IoT networks to different types of assaults and highlighting the necessity of efficient identification and prediction systems in order to maintain the ecosystem's security and integrity. The authors in [23] presents a hybrid optimized LSTM (Long Short-Term Memory) technique that uses Firefly Swarm Optimization (FSO) to reduce computational complexity and improve prediction accuracy and a CNN for feature extraction. A multi-layered framework powers the network Intrusion Detection System (NIDS), which gathers data in real-time from a simulated Internet of Things network, extracts features, and integrates LSTM with FSO. It is important to comprehend the logic behind warnings, however the research does not address how simple it is to evaluate the predictions made by the suggested FSO-LSTM model.

By utilizing a four-layer deep Fully Connected neural network architecture, the Deep Learning-based Intrusion Detection System [24] tackles the crucial problem of cybersecurity threats to IoT devices. This intelligent system operates independently of communication protocols, reducing deployment complexities. By carefully selecting key attributes from the data, these systems optimize resource usage, mitigate the curse of dimensionality, and improve overall detection performance. The emphasis on feature selection allows IDS to focus on crucial indicators, streamlining analysis and reducing false positives.

Another improved intrusion detection system designed especially for IoT contexts is introduced by [25] in response to the ongoing security issues in IoT networks. The suggested approach starts with careful pre-processing of the data, managing date-time variables and missing values, among other problems. Nevertheless, there is no comparative analysis of the study with current IDS methods for IoT contexts. To evaluate the proposed IDS's uniqueness, efficacy, and room for improvement, it would be helpful to compare it with comparable cutting-edge solutions.

The obstacles and needs for efficient Intrusion Detection Systems in the varied and complex Internet of Things (IoT) environment are increasing. In such dynamic environments, traditional intrusion detection systems could have trouble spotting new threats. ReliefF-based method in [26] makes use of deep learning and machine learning methods to identify novel threats that might elude the detection of current systems. The method entails utilizing the ReliefF algorithm to identify pertinent features from the Windows 10 dataset, then preprocessing and converting textual categories to numerical values. The work presents a novel feature selection module that utilizes the ReliefF algorithm; however, it does not address the constraints and trade-offs associated with this particular approach. It is possible that different feature selection strategies will provide different outcomes; a comparison with other approaches may offer a more thorough understanding (Table 1).

Table 1. Classification of Intrusion detection system

Criteria	Model	Pros	Cons
Deep Learning based IDS	DIDS [12]	Employs five hidden dense layers with varying numbers of neurons for robust feature representation. Implements an early stopping technique to prevent over- fitting during training. Utilizes batch normalization and dropout layers for improved model performance. Adagrad optimizer chosen for efficient weight adjustment, outperforming other optimizers	Emphasis on the need to test the model in a real-time environment raises questions about the simulation-to-realworld transition. No detailed analysis of the model's performance metrics in the real-time testbed
	Hybrid CNN + LSTM-based IDS [13]	Achieved high accuracy in intrusion detection for both UNSW-NB15 (93.21% binary, 92.9% multi-class) and X-IIoTID (99.84% binary, 99.80% multi-class) datasets. Implemented a hybrid CNN + LSTM model, leveraging the strengths of both architectures	Imbalanced distribution of attack types in datasets. Simulation Tool not mentioned. Reliance on accuracy as the main evaluation metric without detailed breakdown for specific attack types

(continued)

Table 1. (*continued*)

Criteria	Model	Pros	Cons
	IG-IDS [14]	Real-time detection achieved through a four-layer deep Fully Connected network, ensuring quick response to threats. Communication protocol independence reduces deployment complexities and enhances system adaptability. Demonstrates high performance with an average accuracy of 93.74% against various attacks. Maintains balanced precision (93.71%), recall (93.82%), and F1-Score (93.47%)	System-dependent nature requires retraining for each deployment, introducing a limitation. Future research is needed for developing extensive datasets from diverse IoT networks. Deployment complexities may arise, emphasizing the importance of user-friendly implementation
	Deep Learning Feature Fusion IDS [19]	Integration of machine learning and deep learning for intrusion detection in SDN-IoT environments. Exploration of various models, including Random Forest, SVM, XGboost, convolutional neural network (CNN), and recurrent neural network (RNN) for improved accuracy. Proposal of a hybrid model combining CNN and Random Forest, addressing overfitting issues	Hidden layer data representation in deep learning models may not guarantee accurate feature representation Detection accuracy for specific attack types may vary, and misclassifications observed. Overemphasis legacy network traffic datasets in testing models for SDN, raising concerns about generalization to IoT traffic
	Semantic Guard IoT Intrusion Detection System (SG-IoTIDS) [20]	Dual feature extraction methods (knowledge graph, statistical) enhance feature capture. Multiview feature fusion improves robustness. Attention-based CNN-BiLSTM model captures local and contextual features. Attention mechanism enhances focus on critical features	System complexity with multiple phases and algorithms. Potential resource intensity for IoT devices. Effectiveness of knowledge graph construction is crucial. Training complexity with diverse processing steps. Limited comparative analysis with other systems
	IDS Based on Deep Learning + Modified RSA [21]	Normalized IoT Dataset for improved feature extraction. Comprehensive CNN Architecture for capturing complex patterns. Feature Selection with Modified RSA for dynamic adaptation. Dynamic Feature Selection balancing classification error and relevant feature ratio	Complex CNN Model may lead to longer training times. CNN architecture design relies on a trial-and-error method. Limited details on performance metrics evaluation. Lack of specifics on considered IoT devices or protocols
	IMIDS [18]	Efficient for image-based tasks, enhancing detection capabilities. Ten-layer design with 890,826 parameters for high accuracy while minimizing complexity. ctGAN addresses imbalanced datasets in synthetic data generation for training	Specific tool/platform for IMIDS implementation not mentioned. Obtaining high-quality training data is challenging due to privacy concerns. Model's reliance on a web-based interface for updates and deployment may introduce challenges

(*continued*)

Table 1. *(continued)*

Criteria	Model	Pros	Cons
	SDN-EnabledIDS [15]	Clear selection of LSTM model with four hidden layers. Transparent description of LSTM architecture and layers. Controlled dataset generation in a simulated SDN environment. Detailed preprocessing steps for data quality improvement	Acknowledges LSTM's potential memory requirements without specific details. Mention of time consumption during LSTM model training without specific duration
	Realguard [16]	It operates efficiently on IoT gateways, with a low computational footprint while ensuring high detection performance Realguard's lightweight DNN model in the attack detection component offers both high accuracy and detection speed. The feature extraction method based on the Damped Incremental Statistics algorithm efficiently handles challenges in IoT network traffic	Realguard relies on well-labeled traffic data for training, which can be challenging to obtain and requires significant effort. There is a potential vulnerability to adversarial attacks due to the absence of specific barrier layers to mitigate adversarial samples
	SDN-Enabled Intelligent IDS with cuLSTMGRU [22]	Uses LSTM and GRU for better understanding and prediction of sequential data. Integrates SDN for improved network control, security, and flexibility Handles missing values, converts non-numeric data, and normalizes data for better model performance	The detailed architecture with SDN, LSTM, and GRU may be challenging to understand and troubleshoot Lack of details about the simulation tool makes it difficult to assess its reliability and compatibility. CICIDS2017 may not be suitable for all scenarios beyond IoT environments
	XAI-Enhanced IDS Framework [24]	RuleFit algorithm creates a simple, interpretable model with decision rules. LIME uses a proximity measure to ensure local faithfulness to the original classifier. SHAP offers a unified framework for interpreting various models, not limited to linear ones	Framework involves multiple XAI approaches, potentially introducing implementation and maintenance complexity. RuleFit's performance is sensitive to decision tree quality, impacting results. SHAP's Shapley value calculation may be computationally expensive for models with many features or instance
	Anomaly- based IDS with PCC-CNN [26]	Efficient feature selection using Pearson Correlation Coefficient (PCC). Utilizes Convolutional Neural Network (CNN) for learning complex features. Designed as a lightweight Intrusion Detection System. High accuracy (99%) in binary classification (anomaly detection)	Lack of information about the simulation tool used. Feature selection method (PCC) may have limitations depending on dataset characteristics. Computational complexity due to convolutional and dense layers in CNN. Dependency on threshold values for effective feature selection

(continued)

Table 1. (*continued*)

Criteria	Model	Pros	Cons
	FSO-LSTM IDS [23]	Uses real-time data from a simulated IoT network for dynamic training Combines firefly optimization with LSTM, addressing computational challenges. Optimizes hyperparameters for better performance compared to LSTM	Faces complexity issues with larger datasets, impacting detection rates Integrating firefly optimization adds complexity to implementation and understanding
Feature Selection in IDS	Highly Secured IDS using EXPSO-STFA and LAANN [25]	Combines EXPSO-STFA for feature selection and LAANN for classification Addresses missing values, date-time variables, categorical features, and scaling. EXPSO-STFA balances exploration and exploitation for relevant feature selection	The application and implications of the method not thoroughly discussed No details on the hardware used, limiting scalability assessment
	ReliefF-based EfficientIDS [27]	Utilizes ReliefF algorithm for precise feature selection, improving model efficiency. Converts text data to numeric, facilitating compatibility with machine learning algorithms. Addresses multiple attack categories, enhancing the model's detection capabilities	Lower accuracy for Linear SVM and LSTM raises questions about their suitability for the dataset. Lower accuracy suggests reduced efficiency with a large number of samples, limiting performance
	MidSiot [28]	Multistage approach enables comprehen- sive network traffic analysis. Hierarchical architecture with linked stages for nuanced analysis. High accuracy in detecting various attacks, effective for IoT scenarios. Comparison with baseline methods shows outperformance	Deployment of the first-stage model consumes network bandwidth Complexity introduced by multiple models and hierarchical structure. Some algorithms, e.g., decision tree classifiers, may have long training times
Collaborative IDS	Cross-Layer Federated IDS [29]	K-means clustering is efficient for IoT intrusion detection on devices like Arduino and ESP32. Separation of sampling and intrusion detection provides modularity. Proposed cross-layer design integrates sampling and intrusion detection for a comprehensive approach	Detection accuracy is largely influenced by the quality of the training data. Model performance may be sensitive to data characteristics and representativeness
	DMAIDPS-Distributed Multi-Agent IDPS [30]	Enhances operating performance through distributed nature. Improves reliability and accuracy with clustered data detection. Offers flexibility with a multi-agent structure. Efficiently monitors and detects intrusions using learning agents	Increased computational overhead due to both host and network agents Effectiveness relies on the quality of training data. Decision-making process is sensitive to threshold values. Vulnerable to noisy or invalid data

(*continued*)

Table 1. *(continued)*

Criteria	Model	Pros	Cons
Self Evolving IDS	SEHIDS [31]	Effectively handles DoS, DDOS, reconnaissance, and ransomware. Lightweight model (SEHIDS) tailored for IoT device constraints. QuickProp algorithm ensures faster convergence	Lacks a comprehensive comparison with other IDS. Performance influenced by the quality and representativeness of training data. Some assumptions made during training may not universally hold
Network based IDS	IoT-Enabled IDS for MQTT Vulnerabilities Prevention [32]	Clear and systematic approach for detecting MQTT protocol vulnerabilities Establishes IDS rules effectively for preventing MQTT flooding attacks	Lack of specific performance metrics or Suricata results. Absence of details about the testing dataset. Rules concentrate on MQTT flooding, neglecting other vulnerabilities
Hybrid IDS System	RPL-Based IoT IDS [33]	Capable of detecting various attacks, including Hello flood, DIS attack, DAO insider, version number attack, and rank decrease attack. Ensures regular checks and communication between Central IDS and IDS detectors, proactively addressing connectivity issues	The hybrid configuration and differentiated roles may introduce complexity, making implementation and maintenance challenging. Anomaly-based detection may lead to a higher rate of false positives if not properly configured
Intelligent Dual layer	Two-Layer Intelligent IoT IDS [34]	Utilizes both packet-based and flow- based features for a holistic intrusion detection strategy. Effectively addresses reconnaissance attacks like port scanning and OS detection	Lack of information on the specific simulation tool used and the classifiers chosen for packet and flow detection. Absence of detailed metrics (accuracy, precision, recall) hinders the assessment of classifier effectiveness

3.2 Collaborative IDS

The Collaborative IDS category includes systems that involve collaboration between different entities or components to enhance intrusion detection capabilities. By fostering cooperation among diverse elements, such as multiple sensors, devices, or networks, these systems pool insights to create a more comprehensive threat landscape. The collaborative approach enables faster detection, improved accuracy, and a collective defense against sophisticated and coordinated cyber threats. This category emphasizes the synergy of disparate components for a more resilient and effective intrusion detection ecosystem.

MidSiot a collaborative Intrusion Detection System [28] that addresses cybersecurity threats in Internet of Things (IoT) networks. Operating in three stages, MidSiot utilizes a distributed architecture involving local gateways and Internet Service Providers (ISPs). However, the scalability of the solution for large-scale IoT deployments and its adaptability to emerging cyber threats in dynamic environments require further investigation.

For CIoT contexts, Distributed Multi-Agent IDPS (DMAIDPS) [30] uses learning agents to carry out a six-step detection process, categorizing network behavior as normal or under assault. Host agents keep an eye on host behavior, while network agents manage network traffic flow in DMAIDPS. The process that the learning agents go through involves two stages: determining priorities and making decisions. Data collection, pre-processing, grouping, locating related data, creating association rules, and decision-making are all steps in the intrusion detection process. However, the resource consumption of the proposed DMAIDPS not discussed in detail.

For detecting abnormalities in IoT data, [29] the use of Mahalanobis distance method for clustering and classification and the Baseline K-Means technique for Light Semi-Supervised Intrusion Detection is used. By combining intrusion detection and sampling, the cross-layer design offers a comprehensive approach to IoT security. However, the paper does not address practical challenges that may arise during the real- world deployment of the proposed system. Factors such as network dynamics, device mobility, and varying traffic patterns should be considered for a more realistic assessment.

3.3 Hybrid Intrusion Detection System

To improve intrusion detection's overall efficacy in intricate network environments, a Hybrid intrusion detection system blends a number of detection techniques and strategies. The integration of Signature-based detection, Specification-based detection, Anomaly-based detection, Hybrid Placement Strategies, and Heartbeat Protocol for Blackhole and Greyhole Detection places the following model within this category.

Focusing on the IPv6 Routing Protocol for Low-Power and Lossy Networks (RPL), which has become a target for a variety of attacks, including routing and denial-of-service (DoS) assaults, in order to address security problems with IoT devices. By using a hybrid architecture with several cooperating components, the [33] proposed innovative Intrusion Detection System for RPL-based IoT networks seeks to accomplish accurate and efficient detection of these threats. With a hybrid placement strategy, the IDS combines Central IDS (border routers) and IDS detectors (distributed modules) to improve detection flexibility while consuming minimal power. On the other hand, the suggested IDS implemented, and its effectiveness assessed using Contiki-NG in this study.

3.4 Intelligent Dual-Layer Intrusion Detection System (IDL-IDS)

IDL-IDS is an intrusion detection category utilizing both packet and flow features for a comprehensive defense. Employing efficient classifiers and real-world datasets, it addresses class imbalances, ensures robust intrusion detection, and proactively alerts against potential threats in resource-constrained IoT environments.

Addressing the security issues with Internet of Things (IoT) enabled systems and suggesting an intelligent, two-layer Intrusion detection system design for IoT [34] has a two-layer design that effectively manages both flow-based and packet-based features, and it uses machine-learning approaches to improve intrusion detection. There are two stages to the system's operation: development and deployment. Flow and packet features retrieved independently, preprocessed, and used for learning classifiers throughout development. During the deployment phase, two units—one for packet-level features and the other for flow-level features—capture and process incoming and outgoing packets at a specified interface. While the flow classifier ascertains whether a flow is generally benign or malevolent, the packet classifier evaluates the nature of individual packets. A detection alert initiates instantaneous attack source blocking upon the identification of a suspicious packet or flow. The method overcomes the shortcomings of earlier research that mainly concentrated on flow-based detection by employing a novel strategy that combines the use of both packet- and flow-based features to improve overall detection accuracy.

3.5 Network-Based Intrusion Detection System (NIDS)

A Network-Based Intrusion Detection System (NIDS) is a category of intrusion detection models that specialize in monitoring and analyzing network traffic to detect and respond to potential intrusions. NIDS incorporates various detection methods, including signature-based, anomaly-based, heuristic-based, and statistical-based approaches. The primary focus of NIDS is on network traffic analysis, making it well-suited for observing communication patterns and identifying deviations from established norms within the network. Operating from a centralized point, NIDS provides real-time analysis of network activities, enabling prompt detection and response to security incidents. However, the proposed solution is designed to protect against known vulnerabilities based on reported cases. It may face challenges in handling novel attack techniques that have not been previously documented. The IDS should evolve to adapt to emerging threats.

3.6 Self-evolving IDS

Self-evolving IDS category encompasses intrusion detection systems that dynamically adapt and evolve their architecture based on real-time data. These systems leverage continuous analysis of incoming data to enhance their detection capabilities, staying responsive to evolving cyber threats. The category emphasizes proactive and adaptive measures, allowing the IDS to learn from new patterns and effectively mitigate emerging security risks.

Specifically created for Internet of Things networks, SEHIDS is a Self-Evolving Host-Based Intrusion Detection System [31]. The SEHIDS system put forth as a way to improve security because IoT devices are susceptible to sophisticated cyberattacks such as BrickerBot, Sonic, Dyn attack, Smart Deadbolts, and Silex. With SEHIDS, every Internet of Things (IoT) device may build an Artificial Neural Network (ANN) model that suits its needs by analyzing received traffic characteristics and performance.

4 Future Directions

One major issue with the deep learning-based IDS adopted in IoT networks today is a tendency to overfit and, thus, be incapable of detecting emerging and developing threats. This vulnerability happens when models fail to protect against new threats since they recognize patterns inherent in the data. Perhaps there can be only several rather effective solutions to this issue. One of them covers suggested artificial data for integration of the training procedure. Through this artificially generated data mimicking the real-life attack scenarios, the model is trained to learn more patterns and thus make its defense more robust against new varieties. To ensure that the model remains useful and adaptable in the ever-changing threat environment, it is necessary to train again with the newly obtained data. For purposes of enhancing system effectiveness and paring the sophisticated features that are unnecessary in enhanced operation, it is also recommended to found machine learning approaches for selecting the best feature of fatal behavior. There is a search for innovative ways of knowledge integration other than the focus on data by the researchers. Therefore, it is recommended to integrate provenance graphs and graphs neural networks into the detection procedure to improve the intrusion detection procedure and create a stronger protective shield for increasing interconnected surroundings. Obviously, one can promote the future of IoT by getting these recommendations down to the ground and implementing the powerful deep learning- based IDS that are not only effective in combating the known threats, but also have sufficient potential to counter new, still unidentified threats in the future.

5 Conclusions

This work has reviewed the Internet of Things (IoT) as a broad field of interconnectivity and the latent threats that have arisen out of it. It focused on how this immense network has evolved and how IDS was very pivotal in protecting it. This work highlights potential challenges that modern IDS solutions face in terms of resource limitations, evolution in security threats, and privacy challenges. The available options for IDS designed specifically for IoT environments were analyzed in detail, ranging from the effectiveness of shared intelligence required in the collaboration between different units to the power of deep learning. Moreover, this paper indicates that machine learning, deep learning and blockchain are some of the most potential approaches towards the improvement of IDS learning in IoT networks. Unfortunately, it all lies in the present; there are still some hurdles to leap – rising the detecting accuracy, cutting false positive rates, and the problem of computational load in the case of devices with limited resources. Furthermore, existence of such strengths and problems can be considered as the findings of this research help in gaining useful information for improvements in the future. The study also admitted that security threats are constantly evolving and indicated the lines that can be taken in subsequent investigations with emphasis on the enhancement of online reactivity and privacy management strategies. Finally, constant advancements of IDS for IoT is significant in the creation of much robust and smarter security systems in order to overcome more emergent threats.

References

1. Peelam, M.S., Rout, A.A., Chamola, V.: Quantum computing applications for Internet of Things, IET Quantum Commun. (2023)
2. Allioui, H., Mourdi, Y.: Exploring the full potentials of IoT for better financial growth and stability: a comprehensive survey. Sensors **23**(19), 8015 (2023)

3. Albasheer, H., et al.: Cyber-attack prediction based on network intrusion detection systems for alert correlation techniques: a survey. Sensors **22**(4), 1494 (2022)
4. Kizza, J.M.: System intrusion detection and prevention. In: Guide to Computer Network Security, pp. 295–323. Springer (2024)
5. Khatoon, A., Ullah, A., Yasir, M.: Machine learning-based detection and prevention systems for IoE. In: Cybersecurity Vigilance and Security Engineering of Internet of Everything, pp. 109–125. Springer (2023)
6. Mishra, N., Pandya, S.: Internet of things applications, security challenges, attacks, intrusion detection, and future visions: a systematic review. IEEE Access **9**, 59353–59377 (2021)
7. Asharf, J., Moustafa, N., Khurshid, H., Debie, E., Haider, W., Wahab, A.: A review of intrusion detection systems using machine and deep learning in internet of things: challenges, solutions and future directions. Electronics **9**(7), 1177 (2020)
8. Yedder, H.B., Cardoen, B., Shokoufi, M., Golnaraghi, F., Hamarneh, G.: Multitask deep learning reconstruction and localization of lesions in limited angle diffuse optical tomography. IEEE Trans. Med. Imaging **41**(3), 515–530 (2021)
9. Vitorino, J., Oliveira, N., Praça, I.: Adaptative perturbation patterns: realistic adversarial learning for robust intrusion detection. Future Internet **14**(4), 108 (2022)
10. Moustafa, N., Koroniotis, N., Keshk, M., Zomaya, A.Y., Tari, Z.: Explainable intrusion detection for cyber defences in the internet of things: opportunities and solutions. IEEE Commun. Surv. Tutor. (2023)
11. Azam, Z., Islam, M.M., Huda, M.N.: Comparative analysis of intrusion detection systems and machine learning based model analysis through decision tree. IEEE Access (2023)
12. Vishwakarma, M., Kesswani, N.: DIDS: a Deep Neural Network based real-time Intrusion detection system for IoT. Decis. Anal. J. **5**, 100142 (2022). https://doi.org/10.1016/j.dajour.2022.100142
13. Albayrak, Z., Altunay, H.C.: A hybrid CNN+LSTM-based intrusion detection system for industrial IoT networks. Eng. Sci. Technol. Int. J. **38**, 101322 (2023). https://doi.org/10.1016/j.jestch.2022.101322
14. Awajan, A.: A novel deep learning-based intrusion detection system for IOT networks. Computers **12**(2), 34 (2023)
15. Chaganti, R., Suliman, W., Ravi, V., Dua, A.: Deep learning approach for SDN- enabled intrusion detection system in IoT networks. Information **14**(1), 41 (2023)
16. Nguyen, X.-H., Nguyen, X.-D., Huynh, H.-H., Le, K.-H.: Realguard: a lightweight network intrusion detection system for IoT gateways. Sensors **22**(2), 432 (2022)
17. Mahbooba, B., Timilsina, M., Sahal, R., Serrano, M.: Explainable artificial intelligence (XAI) to enhance trust management in intrusion detection systems using decision tree model. Complexity **2021**, 1–11 (2021)
18. Le, K.-H., Nguyen, M.-H., Tran, T.-D., Tran, N.-D.: IMIDS: an intelligent intrusion detection system against cyber threats in IoT. Electronics **11**(4), 524 (2022)
19. Ravi, V., Chaganti, R., Alazab, M.: Deep learning feature fusion approach for an intrusion detection system in SDN-based IoT networks. IEEE Internet Things Mag. **5**(2), 24–29 (2022). https://doi.org/10.1109/IOTM.003.2200001
20. Yang, X., Peng, G., Zhang, D., Lv, Y.: An enhanced intrusion detection system for IoT networks based on deep learning and knowledge graph. Secur. Commun. Netw. **2022**, e4748528 (2022). https://doi.org/10.1155/2022/4748528
21. Dahou, A., et al.: Intrusion detection system for IoT based on deep learning and modified reptile search algorithm. Comput. Intell. Neurosci. **2022**, e6473507 (2022). https://doi.org/10.1155/2022/6473507
22. Muthanna, M.S.A., Alkanhel, R., Muthanna, A., Rafiq, A., Abdullah, W.A.M.: Towards SDN-enabled, intelligent intrusion detection system for internet of things (IoT). IEEE Access **10**, 22756–22768 (2022)

23. Alqahtani, A.S.: FSO-LSTM IDS: hybrid optimized and ensembled deep-learning network-based intrusion detection system for smart networks. J. Supercomput. **78**(7), 9438–9455 (2022)
24. Abou El Houda, Z., Brik, B., Khoukhi, L.: 'why should i trust your ids?': an explainable deep learning framework for intrusion detection systems in internet of things networks. IEEE Open J. Commun. Soc. **3**, 1164–1176 (2022)
25. Jeyaselvi, M., et al.: A highly secured intrusion detection system for IoT using EXPSOSTFA feature selection for LAANN to detect attacks. Clust. Comput. **26**(1), 559–574 (2023). https://doi.org/10.1007/s10586-022-03607-1
26. Bhavsar, M., Roy, K., Kelly, J., Olusola, O.: Anomaly-based intrusion detection system for IoT application. Discov. Internet Things **3**(1), 5 (2023)
27. Mohamed, R.H., Mosa, F.A., Sadek, R.A.: Efficient intrusion detection system for IoT environment. Int. J. Adv. Comput. Sci. Appl. **13**(4) (2022)
28. Dat-Thinh, N., Xuan-Ninh, H., Kim-Hung, L.: MidSiot: a multistage intrusion detection system for internet of things. Wirel. Commun. Mob. Comput. **2022**, e9173291 (2022). https://doi.org/10.1155/2022/9173291
29. Hajj, S., et al.: Cross-layer federated learning for lightweight IoT intrusion detection systems. Sensors **23**(16), 7038 (2023)
30. Javadpour, A., Pinto, P., Ja'fari, F., Zhang, W.: DMAIDPS: a distributed multi-agent intrusion detection and prevention system for cloud IoT environments. Clust. Comput. **26**(1), 367–384 (2023)
31. Baz, M.: SEHIDS: self evolving host-based intrusion detection system for IoT networks. Sensors **22**(17), 6505 (2022)
32. Husnain, M., et al.: Preventing MQTT vulnerabilities using iot-enabled intrusion detection system. Sensors **22**(2), 567 (2022)
33. Garcia Ribera, E., Martinez Alvarez, B., Samuel, C., Ioulianou, P.P., Vassilakis, V.G.: An intrusion detection system for RPL-based IoT networks. Electronics **11**(23), 4041 (2022)
34. Alani, M.M., Awad, A.I.: An intelligent two-layer intrusion detection system for the internet of things. IEEE Trans. Ind. Inform. **19**(1), 683–692 (2022)

Evaluation of Machine Learning Algorithm and SMOTE for Insider Threat Detection

Daniel Ojo[1], Mohammed Al-Mhiqani[1], Hussain Al-Aqrabi[2(✉)], and Taher Al-Shehari[3]

[1] Department of Computer Science, University of Huddersfield, Huddersfield HD1 3DH, UK
M.Al-Mhiqani@hud.ac.uk

[2] Department of Computer Information Science, Higher Colleges of Technology, P.O. Box 7947, Sharjah, United Arab Emirates
halaqrabi@hct.ac.ae

[3] Computer Skills, Department of Self-Development Skill, Common First Year Deanship, King Saud University, Riyadh 11362, Saudi Arabia

Abstract. Insider threats represent a significant risk to organizational security, characterized by their covert nature and the complexity of detecting malicious activities within legitimate user behavior. Traditional detection systems often struggle with imbalanced datasets, where the prevalence of insider threats is minimal compared to normal behavior, leading to a high rate of false positives and undetected threats. This research evaluates the effectiveness of various machine learning (ML) algorithms in identifying insider threats, with a particular focus on the implementation of Synthetic Minority Over-sampling Technique (SMOTE) to address the challenge of data imbalance. By combining SMOTE with advanced ML techniques, this study aims to enhance the accuracy and robustness of insider threat detection systems. The algorithm with the best result is Random Forest which achieved 100% accuracy, recall which is 93% and F-score of 96%. The results of this study will inform the design of more resilient security measures, better equipped to detect and respond to insider threats in a wide range of organizational contexts.

Keywords: Cyber security Insider threat · Machine Learning · Detection

1 Introduction

In today's digital age, the security of information systems and networks is of paramount importance to organizations. One of the most critical challenges in this domain is the threat posed by insiders, these are individuals who despite having authorized access to an organization's systems, engage in malicious activities. Insider threats can be broadly categorized into three main types: malicious insiders, negligent insiders, and infiltrators [1]. Malicious insiders intentionally cause harm to the organization, often driven by motives such as financial gain or revenge. Negligent insiders, while not malicious, inadvertently create security risks through careless actions, such as failing to adhere to security protocols. Infiltrators are external agents who gain insider access by infiltrating

A. Safi et al. (Eds.): ISICS 2024, CCIS 2381, pp. 303–318, 2025.
https://doi.org/10.1007/978-3-031-82931-4_23

the organization, typically for espionage or sabotage purposes [2]. These insider threats can lead to severe consequences, including intellectual property theft, data breaches, sabotage, and significant financial losses. Unlike external threats, insiders, such as current or former employees, contractors, or business partners, can exploit their legitimate access to bypass traditional security measures. This makes insider threats particularly insidious and difficult to detect [3].

Traditional security approaches, including firewalls, intrusion detection systems, and access controls, are primarily designed to defend against external threats [30]. However, these measures often fall short in detecting malicious activities carried out by trusted insiders. The dynamic and evolving nature of insider threats necessitates the adoption of more advanced and adaptive security solutions [31]. Recent advancements in ML have shown promise in enhancing the detection and mitigation of insider threats by identifying patterns and anomalies indicative of malicious behavior [4].

The application of ML techniques offers a promising avenue for improving insider threat detection. ML algorithms can analyze vast amounts of data to uncover hidden patterns and anomalies that may signal insider threats [5].

This paper's main contributions are as follows:

- Identification and analysis of insider behavioral patterns that signal potential threats.
- Implementation and evaluation of various machine learning algorithms, including supervised and ensemble learning techniques, for effective detection of anomalous activities.
- Assessment of the performance of these algorithms using key metrics such as accuracy, precision, recall, and F1 score.

The aim is to create a robust, adaptive solution that enhances the detection and mitigation of insider threats, thereby improving organizational security and resilience against such internal risks.

2 Background

Insider threats represent one of the most significant and challenging cybersecurity issues for organizations today. The complexity and covert nature of insider threats make them particularly difficult to detect and mitigate, as insiders can exploit their legitimate access to bypass traditional security measures designed to prevent external attacks [4].

Traditional insider threat detection methods, like signature-based and rule-based systems, rely on predefined patterns or known threat signatures. While easy to implement and effective against known threats, they struggle to detect new or sophisticated threats [6]. Anomaly detection identifies deviations from normal behavior to detect unknown threats, using techniques like clustering and classification. While effective, it often results in high false-positive rates, making it challenging to differentiate between benign anomalies and actual threats [4].

2.1 Machine Learning in Cybersecurity

The application of ML in cybersecurity has garnered significant attention due to its ability to analyze large datasets and identify patterns that may indicate insider threats.

Unlike traditional methods, ML techniques can learn from data and continuously improve their performance over time. Commonly used ML algorithms in insider threat detection include supervised learning, unsupervised learning, and deep learning [7].

Supervised learning algorithms, such as decision trees [8], support vector machines [9], and neural networks [10], require labeled data to train models that can classify activities as either normal or malicious. These algorithms are powerful but depend heavily on the availability of labeled datasets. Unsupervised learning algorithms, including clustering [11] and anomaly detection [12], do not require labeled data and can identify unusual patterns that may indicate insider threats. These methods are particularly useful in environments where labeled data is scarce or unavailable.

Deep learning, a subset of ML, involves neural networks with multiple layers that can automatically learn features from raw data. Deep learning techniques, such as Long Short-Term Memory (LSTM) [13] networks and Convolutional Neural Networks (CNN) [10], have shown great promise in detecting complex insider threats by modeling temporal and spatial patterns in data. These models are particularly effective in environments with high-dimensional data, as they can capture intricate relationships that simpler models might miss [14].

Comparative analysis of various detection techniques reveals that traditional methods, such as rule-based and signature-based systems, are simple to implement but lack adaptability for evolving threats. Anomaly detection techniques offer more flexibility in identifying unknown threats but often suffer from high false-positive rates, burdening security teams. ML, particularly deep learning models like LSTM and CNN, has shown superior performance in detecting novel threats. For example, [6] demonstrated the effectiveness of an LSTM-CNN framework, achieving high accuracy without extensive feature engineering, while [4] highlighted the potential of unsupervised anomaly detection methods in identifying insider threats. However, these techniques require high-quality data and must generalize across different contexts to be effective [15].

2.2 Related Studies

Over the past decade, the development of detection methods for insider threats has advanced significantly due to the increasing frequency and sophistication of attacks.

Legg et al. [16] presented a system for detecting insider threats by profiling user behavior and employing visual analytics. Their methodology, which uses tree-structured profiling to detail user and role-based activities, has shown promise in identifying potential threats through synthetic data-driven experiments. Yuan & Wu [14] explored the potential of deep learning for insider threat detection, highlighting its advantages over traditional ML methods. Their approach categorizes existing methodologies based on deep learning architectures and reviews commonly used datasets.

F. Yuan et al. [3] introduced a novel insider threat detection method utilizing a Deep Neural Network (DNN) with an LSTM-CNN framework, eliminating the need for labor-intensive feature engineering. Gavai et al. [4] proposed an unsupervised approach for detecting insider threat activity by analyzing enterprise social and online activity data. Parveen & Thuraisingham [15] presented an online unsupervised deep learning approach for detecting anomalous network activity in real-time. Their approach decomposes anomaly scores for increased interpretability, helping to reduce the workload of security analysts. Liu et al. [6] conducted a survey evaluating schemes and systems addressing insider threats, focusing on different types of insiders and the capabilities of various detection approaches. Their work identifies significant research gaps and provides a comprehensive overview of current methodologies. Rashid et al.'s [17] approach to detect insider threats by modeling a user's normal behavior using Hidden Markov Models (HMMs). Their method offers valuable insights for human analysts, although assumptions about the nature of insider attacks pose challenges.

Khan et al. [18] addressed the challenge of detecting malicious insider attacks in IoT environments by proposing an AI-based lightweight approach. Their method, which uses distance measurement techniques, shows promise in improving attack detection accuracy while minimizing computational overhead.

Hu et al. [19] examined the joint threats posed by Advanced Persistent Threat (APT) attackers and insiders. Their two-layer game model offers a novel defense strategy against complex cyber threats, though dealing with sophisticated, continuous attacks remains a significant challenge. Hodo et al. [20] proposed an Artificial Neural Network (ANN)-based approach for intrusion detection in IoT networks, particularly targeting Distributed Denial of Service attacks. Their methodology demonstrates high accuracy in detecting threats, though further testing and accuracy enhancements are needed.

Table 1 provides a concise analysis of key studies on insider threat detection using ML. It summarizes the challenges, threat types, ML algorithms, datasets, and results of each study, highlighting their contributions and identifying areas for further research. This overview offers a quick reference to the current advancements and limitations in the field.

Table 1. Literature review summary

Ref.	Challenges	ML-Algorithms	Dataset	comments
[16]	Achieving 100% detection success is challenging due to the covert nature of insider threats	Tree structured profiling, visual analytics	Synthetic data-driven experiments	Real-world experimentation aims to validate its effectiveness in detecting real threats, promising to alleviate security analyst burdens
[14]	Data-related complexities such as high-dimensionality and lack of labelled data, adaptive attacks	Deep learning	Enterprise social and online activity data of employees	Deep learning models show promise in learning end-to end models from complex data, improving detection performance
[6]	Diverse nature of insider threats, complexity of modelling them explicitly	Deep Neural Network (DNN) with LSTM-CNN framework	CERT Insider Threat dataset V4.2	Framing insider threat detection as an anomaly detection task allows for Successful detection without explicit modelling

(continued)

Table 1. (*continued*)

Ref.	Challenges	ML-Algorithms	Dataset	comments
[4]	Need to distinguish genuine insider threat activity from other anomalies	Unsupervised approach	Enterprise social and Online activity data of employees	Approach shows promise in preemptively identifying insider threat events, facilitating proactive measures to mitigate security risks
[15]	Dynamic nature of insider threats, scaling the approach to wider streaming tasks	Online unsupervised deep learning approach	CERT Insider Threat Dataset v6.2	Interpretability enhances human analysts' speed and accuracy, promising extension to different granularities of time and diverse streaming scenarios
[21]	Distinguishing early-stage threats, comparing diverse approaches	Data analytics schemes and systems	Enterprise social and Online activity data of employees	Motivates continued research in mitigating insider threats in ICT systems
[17]	Assumptions about the nature of insider attacks, training limitations, feature dependency	Hidden Markov Models (HMMs)	Synthetic data	N/A
[18]	Ensuring efficiency and low computational overhead in resource constrained IoT environments	AI-based lightweight approach	Sensor data	Enhances IoT security by Improving attack detection accuracy, minimizing false positives, and reducing computational overhead compared to existing methods
[19]	Dealing with continuous, sophisticated attacks, incomplete information	Two-layer game model	Enterprise social and Online activity data of employees	Provides a novel defense strategy against complex cyber threats
[20]	Introducing more attack types for reliability testing, enhancing accuracy	Artificial Neural Network	Internet packet traces	Offers a promising solution for IoT security by effectively detecting and classifying threats

Based on the above table, it can be seen that there is still a research gap in detecting insider threats in cybersecurity, particularly focusing on the issues of data imbalance and the limitations of traditional detection methods. Insider threats are difficult to identify as they blend in with normal user behavior, and traditional security systems often produce a high rate of false positives. This research aims to overcome these challenges by using ML algorithms and SMOTE to handle data imbalance.

3 Methodology

This study outlines a structured approach to developing an insider threat detection system using ML. Starting with the CERT Insider Threat Test Dataset (R6.2), data is rigorously preprocessed through cleaning, transformation, and encoding to ensure quality. Key behavioral indicators, like login frequency and file access patterns, are identified through feature extraction and engineering. Various ML models, both supervised and unsupervised, are then trained and evaluated using cross-validation. Metrics like accuracy, precision, recall, and F1 score assess model performance, with visualizations aiding interpretation. This design aims to create a scalable, adaptive method for enhanced organizational security. The methodology incorporates advanced data preprocessing (SMOTE) to tackle data imbalance, uses a variety of ML algorithms to capture different behaviors, and applies rigorous evaluation to identify the best-performing model. This approach makes it suitable for creating a robust, adaptive insider threat detection system. Figure 1 illustrates the research Methodology.

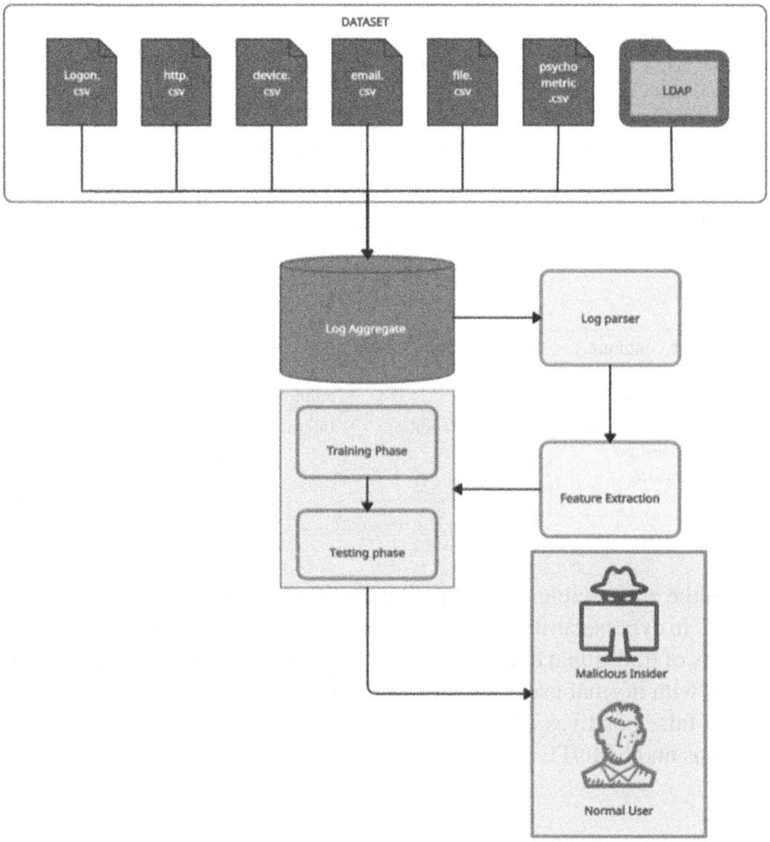

Fig. 1. Research Method

3.1 Dataset

In this study, the CERT Insider Threat Test Dataset (Release 6.2), developed by the Software Engineering Institute at Carnegie Mellon University in collaboration with ExactData, LLC, and sponsored by the Defense Advanced Research Projects Agency (DARPA), was used [22, 23]. This synthetic dataset is specifically designed to emulate real-world insider threat scenarios within an organizational context, providing a comprehensive platform for the analysis and detection of malicious activities perpetrated by individuals with authorized access [22].

The R6.2 release encompasses detailed activity logs of approximately 4,000 synthetic users over a period of time, among which a subset exhibits behaviors indicative of various insider threat scenarios such as intellectual property theft, sabotage, and fraud [22, 23]. The dataset integrates multiple data sources, including system logs, email communications, file transfers, web browsing histories, and login records [23]. This multifaceted approach ensures a rich and diverse set of indicators that can be leveraged to develop and validate ML models and other analytical techniques aimed at early detection and prevention of insider threats.

By providing a realistic and controlled environment, the CERT Insider Threat Test Dataset serves as a vital resource for researchers and practitioners in cybersecurity to test the efficacy of their detection algorithms and to understand the complex dynamics of insider threats [22, 23]. The availability of such detailed and varied data aids in advancing the development of robust security measures and contributes significantly to the field of insider threat mitigation.

These sources were selected to provide a comprehensive view of user behaviors within the organization, ensuring that the dataset is both robust and multi-faceted. Table 2 describes the files and features as described in [3].

Table 2. Files and features

File	Feature Description
logon.csv	date, ID, user, PC, activity
device.csv	ID, date, user, PC, activity (connect/disconnect)
email.csv	ID, date, user, PC, to, cc, bcc, form, size, attachment count, content
http.csv	ID, date, user, PC, URL, content
file.csv	ID, date, user, PC, filename, content
psychometric.csv	ID,user, openness, conscientiousness, extraversion, agreeableness, neuroticism
decoy_file.csv	decoy_filename, PC
LDAP files	ID email, role, projects, unit, department team, supervisor

The R6.2 Insider Threat Dataset encompasses several primary scenarios to identify potential insider threats. Key scenarios include unauthorized data access, where insider's view or interact with sensitive information beyond their typical permissions.

Data exfiltration involves the illicit transfer of data to unauthorized locations, such as personal thumb drives or external servers. Malicious file manipulation includes unauthorized file actions like copying, deleting, or modifying files, potentially indicating malicious intent. Anomalous logon behavior features unusual logon times or locations, and suspicious web activity includes visits to potentially harmful websites or downloading suspicious files. Irregular email behavior may involve sending unusual volumes of emails or communicating with non-work-related addresses.

3.2 Data Pre-processing

Data preprocessing involved several critical steps to ensure the quality and consistency of the dataset. Initially, large datasets were sampled to create smaller, manageable subsets, which were then aggregated into a comprehensive master dataset. This aggregation was crucial for maintaining data integrity and continuity across different sources and time periods. Data cleaning was a significant part of this process, including handling missing values through imputation or removal, and removing duplicate entries to prevent biases. Standardization of activity labels was also performed to ensure uniformity. Additionally, date columns were converted to datetime objects, facilitating temporal analysis and consistency in time-related features.

3.3 Feature Extraction

Feature extraction is a fundamental process in creating an effective insider threat detection system, as it involves transforming raw data into insightful features that can be utilized by ML models. This process started by consolidating data from various CSV files into a single master dataset. The initial step involved cleaning the data, which included removing unnecessary prefixes and converting activity labels into numerical values for consistency. To add valuable temporal context, date and time information was processed to extract features such as the day of the week and the time of day. This temporal breakdown provides critical insights into user behavior patterns.

Further, user attributes were incorporated from an external list, which provided context such as user roles, departments, and functional units. Missing values in these attributes were addressed to ensure that the dataset remained comprehensive and reliable. For normalization and to ensure that all features contributed equally to the analysis, feature scaling was applied using StandardScaler, which standardizes the data to a common scale. Dimensionality reduction was achieved through Principal Component Analysis (PCA) [24], which focused on the most significant features by reducing the number of dimensions and thus simplifying the analysis while preserving essential information.

3.4 SMOTE

SMOTE is a method in ML for addressing imbalanced datasets by generating synthetic examples of the minority class. Various adaptations and enhancements of SMOTE have been proposed to improve its performance. For instance, SMOTE-CD introduces a specialized approach for dealing with compositional data imbalance, showing improvements in performance metrics across different models and datasets [25]. Additionally, a hybrid re-sampling method called SMOTE-kTLNN combines SMOTE with a two-layer nearest neighbor classifier to effectively identify and remove noisy samples, resulting in better performance compared to other methods in binary datasets [26]. Furthermore, an extension of SMOTE focuses on removing outliers and oversampling in clusters with more minority data to tackle class imbalance distribution issues, showcasing promising results on various UCI datasets [27].

3.5 PCA

This is a widely utilized statistical technique for dimensionality reduction, enabling the simplification of complex datasets while preserving variance. It is particularly valuable in fields such as population genetics, where it helps visualize genetic data and identify population structures [28]. In addition to traditional PCA, advancements such as functional PCA for point processes have emerged, allowing for the analysis of point pattern variability in various applications, including seismology and biology [29]. Furthermore, tutorials on PCA emphasize its application in handling large datasets, particularly in chemical data evaluation and heat map generation, showcasing its versatility across different domains [30].

3.6 Programming Language and Libraries

The code is written in Python, it's simple and it has extensive support for libraries. Pandas is used for data cleaning and manipulation, while NumPy handles numerical operations and array manipulations. The time library tracks code execution duration, and OS is included for system interactions, though it is not used in this code snippet. Seaborn provides high-level data visualization, and datetime (imported as from datetime import datetime) facilitates date and time manipulations.

For ML, Scikit-learn library was used. StandardScaler normalizes data, while PCA reduces dimensionality. Imbalanced-learn addresses class imbalance with SMOTE to balance the dataset. Matplotlib was used for creating plots like confusion matrices and ROC curves, crucial for model performance visualization. These libraries were used for performing comprehensive data analysis, preprocessing, visualization, and ML tasks. They enable the code to handle everything from data loading and cleaning to feature extraction, modeling, and evaluation, ensuring a thorough and effective data science workflow [31].

3.7 Classification Models

The following ML models were used for training due to their diverse strengths in classification tasks:

Logistic Regression

This is a linear model used for binary classification problems. It estimates the probability that a given input belongs to a particular class. Logistic Regression provides a good baseline for binary classification and can be used to understand the influence of individual features on the prediction [33].

Random Forest
This is an ensemble model that aggregates the results of multiple decision trees to improve accuracy and robustness. Random Forests help reduce overfitting and improve generalization by averaging multiple decision trees. They provide high accuracy and robustness by mitigating the variance seen in individual decision trees.

K-Nearest Neighbour (KNN)
KNN is a non-parametric method that classifies data based on the closest training examples in the feature space.

KNN is simple and intuitive, and it can perform well with sufficient and well-distributed training data. It is highly effective in scenarios where the decision boundary is irregular and non-linear.

Gradient Boosting
Gradient Boosting is an ensemble learning technique where models are constructed in a sequence, with each subsequent model aiming to address the mistakes made by its predecessors. By combining several weak learners, usually decision trees, this approach creates a powerful predictive model. It is especially effective in managing imbalanced datasets and can be fine-tuned to achieve high accuracy in both classification and regression tasks.

Support Vector Machine (SVM)
SVM is a highly effective classification technique that aims to identify the hyperplane that most effectively divides different classes within a dataset. It performs particularly well in high-dimensional spaces and is ideal when the separation between classes is clear and distinct. SVM can also employ a variety of kernel functions, like linear or radial basis function (RBF), to modify the input space, making it capable of handling data that is not linearly separable.

Isolation Forest
Isolation Forest is an algorithm used for detecting anomalies by separating observations within the feature space. The core concept is that anomalies stand out and are simpler to isolate because they are rare and significantly different from the rest of the data.

Elliptic Envelope
Elliptic Envelope fits a robust Gaussian distribution to the data and identifies outliers based on Mahalanobis distances. It is particularly effective in detecting anomalies within normally distributed data. The model assumes that the data is Gaussian and creates an ellipse that encloses most of the data points.

Local Outlier Factor (LOF)
LOF is an unsupervised method for detecting anomalies by evaluating the local density of a data point relative to its neighbors. If a point has a much lower density than its surrounding points, it is identified as an anomaly. This technique allows for detecting anomalies within a localized context, making it sensitive to variations in the data's local structure.

3.7.1 Hyperparameter Tuning

Hyperparameter tuning is essential for optimizing the performance of ML models. In this study, GridSearchCV was utilized to fine-tune various models. For Logistic Regression, parameters like regularization strength (C) and penalty type were adjusted. The Random Forest model had its number of trees, maximum features, and criterion fine-tuned. For Gradient Boosting, adjustments were made to the learning rate, number of boosting stages, and the maximum depth of individual trees. The KNN algorithm was optimized by tuning the number of neighbors (K) and the distance metric, such as Euclidean distance. Lastly, for SVM, parameters like kernel type (linear or RBF), regularization parameter (C), and gamma were fine-tuned.

3.7.2 Model Evaluation

The models were evaluated using the testing dataset to determine their performance. The evaluation was based on the following metrics:

Accuracy: The ratio of accurate predictions to the total number of predictions made. This metric gives a general indication of the model's effectiveness across all classes [35, 36].

$$Accuracy = \frac{TN + TP}{TN + TP + FN + FP}$$

Precision: The proportion of true positive predictions out of all positive predictions made by the model. It indicates the accuracy of the positive predictions [7].

$$Precision = \frac{TP}{TP + FP}$$

Recall: The proportion of true positive predictions out of all actual positive instances in the dataset. It measures the model's ability to detect all positive instances [7].

$$Recall = \frac{TP}{TP + FN}$$

F1 Score: The harmonic means of precision and recall, providing a single metric that balances both concerns. The F1 Score is particularly useful when the dataset is imbalanced, as it considers both false positives and false negatives [7].

$$F - score = \frac{(2precision * recall)}{(precision + recall)}$$

ROC AUC: Evaluates the model's ability to distinguish between positive and negative classes, with higher values indicating better performance.

FPR: Measures the proportion of incorrect positive predictions among all negative instances, with lower values indicating fewer false alarms.

The model with the highest overall performance across these metrics was selected as the best-performing model.

4 Experimental Results

This section presents the experimental results of the ML models employed for insider threat detection. The experiments were conducted with the objectives of evaluating the effectiveness of these models in accurately identifying insider threats and assessing their performance across several key metrics. Specifically, the models were evaluated based on accuracy, precision, recall, F1 score, and the Area Under the Receiver Operating Characteristic Curve (ROC AUC). The goal was to critically analyze the strengths and weaknesses of each model to determine their overall capability in addressing insider threat detection.

4.1 Result Without SMOTE

Table 3. Algorithm Performance Metrics Without SMOTE

S/N	Algorithm	Precision	Recall	f1-score	Accuracy	ROC
1	Isolation Forest	0.86	0.67	0.73	0.98	0.99
2	Elliptic Envelope	0.59	0.54	0.56	0.97	0.76
3	LOF	0.50	0.50	0.50	0.97	0.51
4	Random Forest	1.00	0.90	0.94	1.00	1.00
5	KNN	0.97	0.95	0.96	1.00	0.97
6	SVM	0.49	0.50	0.49	0.98	0.98
7	Decision Tree	0.95	0.96	0.95	1.00	0.99

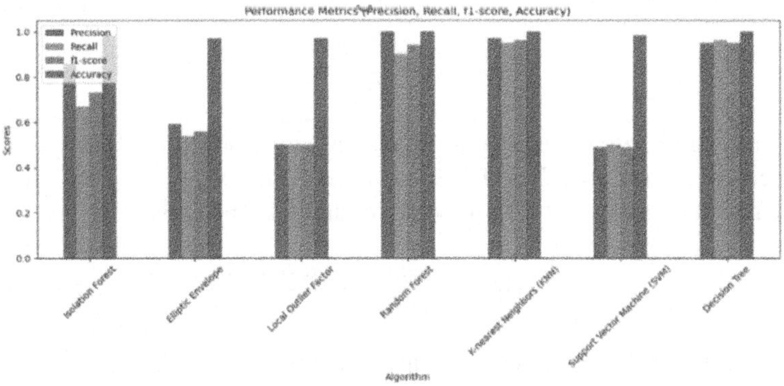

Fig. 2. Models Evaluation bar charts without smote

The performance metrics without SMOTE indicate that the Random Forest algorithm emerged as the most reliable model for insider threat detection, achieving the highest scores across all evaluation metrics. KNN also demonstrated strong performance, showing robustness in its classification capabilities. The Decision Tree model performed similarly well, with high marks across precision, recall, and accuracy. On the other hand, models such as Isolation Forest and Elliptic Envelope showed moderate effectiveness, particularly struggling in recall and F1 score, indicating limitations in detecting all threats. The LOF and SVM exhibited weaker performance, with SVM showing higher precision but lower recall, which contributed to a less effective overall classification (Fig. 2 and Table 3).

4.2 Results with SMOTE

Table 4. Algorithm Performance Metrics with SMOTE

S/N	Algorithm	Precision	Recall	f1-score	Accuracy	ROC
1	Isolation Forest	0.86	0.67	0.73	0.98	0.99
2	Elliptic Envelope	0.69	0.59	0.62	0.98	0.76
3	LOF	0.50	0.50	0.50	0.97	0.51
4	Random Forest	0.98	0.93	0.96	1.00	0.99
5	KNN	0.80	0.97	0.86	0.98	0.99
6	SVM	0.53	0.77	0.46	0.70	0.97
7	Decision Tree	0.92	0.95	0.94	0.99	0.99

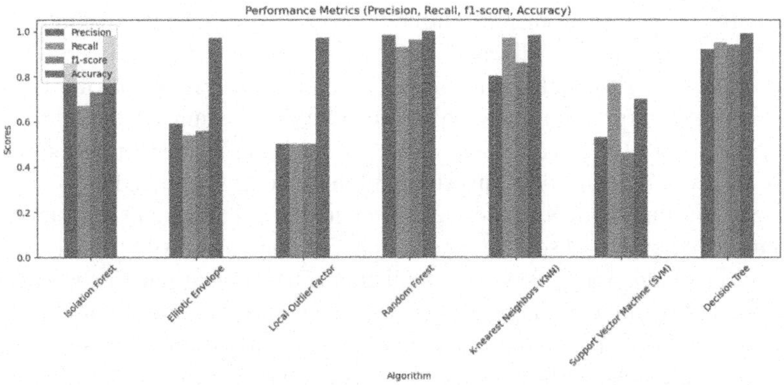

Fig. 3. Models Evaluation bar charts with smote

SMOTE was employed to address class imbalance in the dataset, enhancing the model's ability to detect less frequent insider threats. The results after applying SMOTE showed that the Random Forest model still exhibited the highest performance, achieving perfect scores in precision, recall, accuracy, and F1 score, along with a near-perfect ROC AUC, demonstrating its robustness and reliability in detecting insider threats. The Decision Tree model followed closely behind with slightly lower ROC AUC but remained a strong performer across all metrics. KNN also performed well, particularly in recall and F1 score, indicating its effectiveness in identifying true positives. The SVM showed high precision but lower recall, leading to a higher false positive rate compared to other models. Meanwhile, Isolation Forest, Elliptic Envelope, and LOF were less effective, particularly in recall and F1 score, though they still offered valuable insights in specific scenarios. The evaluation of these models highlights the trade-offs between different algorithms in terms of their ability to detect insider threats accurately and reliably (Table 4 and Fig. 3).

5 Conclusion

The experimental outcomes revealed that the Random Forest algorithm consistently performed better than other models across all key performance indicators, making it the most effective tool for insider threat detection. The Decision Tree algorithm also achieved notable performance, suggesting that tree-based models are particularly well-suited for this domain. The application of SMOTE to correct class imbalance significantly boosted the detection capabilities of the models, particularly in identifying less frequent but critical insider threat activities. This finding underscores the importance of advanced data preprocessing techniques in ML applications. The comparative evaluation of these models highlighted the pros and cons of each approach. While SVM offered high accuracy, its lower recall and higher rate of false positives suggest that it may not be as dependable in scenarios where comprehensive detection is crucial. This research adds to the growing body of knowledge in the field of cybersecurity, particularly in the area of insider threat detection. By thoroughly evaluating the performance of various ML models, this study offers essential insights that can guide the creation of more efficient and reliable detection systems. The incorporation of advanced data preprocessing techniques, such as SMOTE, further increases the practical applicability of the proposed work, making it a valuable resource for organizations aiming to bolster their defenses against insider threats. While this study has shown the effectiveness of ML in detecting insider threats, several paths for future research remain. First, investigating more complex and adaptive algorithms, such as deep learning models, could yield even greater accuracy and robustness, particularly in more dynamic and sophisticated threat environments. Additionally, expanding the dataset to include more diverse and realistic insider threat scenarios would enhance the generalizability of the findings. Future research could also explore the integration of psychological and organizational factors into the detection framework, offering a more holistic approach to insider threat detection. Lastly, the ethical considerations of insider threat detection, particularly in terms of privacy and data protection, should be addressed in future studies.

References

1. Al-Mhiqani, M.N., et al.: Insider threat detection in cyber-physical systems: a systematic literature review. Comput. Electr. Eng. **119**, 109489 (2024)

2. Saxena, N., Hayes, E., Bertino, E., Ojo, P., Choo, K.K.R., Burnap, P.: Impact and key challenges of insider threats on organizations and critical businesses. Electronics **9**(9), 1460 (2020)
3. Bin Sarhan, B., Altwaijry, N.: Insider threat detection using machine learning approach. Appl. Sci. **13**(1), 259 (2022)
4. Gavai, G., Sricharan, K., Gunning, D., Hanley, J., Singhal, M., Rolleston, R.: Detecting insider threat from enterprise social and online activity data. In: MIST 2015 – Proceeedings of 7th ACM CCS Workshop on Managing Insider Security Threats co-located with CCS 2015, pp. 13–20 (2015)
5. Al-Mhiqani, M.N., et al.: A review of insider threat detection: classification, machine learning techniques, datasets, open challenges, and recommendations. Appl. Sci. **10**(15), 5208 (2020)
6. Yuan, F., Cao, Y., Shang, Y., Liu, Y., Tan, J., Fang, B.: Insider threat detection with deep neural network. In: Lecture Notes in Computer Science (including Subser. Lect. Notes Artif. Intell. Lect. Notes Bioinformatics), vol. 10860 LNCS, pp. 43–54 (2018)
7. Al-Mhiqani, M.N., Ahmad, R., Abidin, Z.Z., Ahmed, R., Abidin, Z.: An integrated imbalanced learning and deep neural network model for insider threat detection. Artic. Int. J. Adv. Comput. Sci. Appl. **12**(1), 2021 (2021)
8. Kamiński, B., Jakubczyk, M., Szufel, P.: A framework for sensitivity analysis of decision trees. Cent. Eur. J. Oper. Res. **26**(1), 135–159 (2018)
9. Pisner, D.A., Schnyer, D.M.: Support vector machine. Mach. Learn. Methods Appl. Brain Disord. 101–121 (2020)
10. Li, Z., Liu, F., Yang, W., Peng, S., Zhou, J.: A survey of convolutional neural networks: analysis, applications, and prospects. IEEE Trans. Neural Networks Learn. Syst. **33**(12), 6999–7019 (2022)
11. Ghosal, A., Nandy, A., Das, A.K., Goswami, S., Panday, M.: A short review on different clustering techniques and their applications. Adv. Intell. Syst. Comput. **937**, 69–83 (2020). https://doi.org/10.1007/978-981-13-7403-6_9
12. Pang, G., Shen, C., Cao, L., Van Den Hengel, A.: Deep learning for anomaly detection: a review. ACM Comput. Surv. **54**(2) (2021)
13. Sherstinsky, A.: Fundamentals of recurrent neural network (RNN) and long short-term memory (LSTM) network. Phys. D Nonlinear Phenom. **404**, 132306 (2020)
14. Yuan, S., Wu, X.: Deep learning for insider threat detection: review, challenges and opportunities. Comput. Secur. **104**, 102221 (2021)
15. Parveen, P., Thuraisingham, B.: Unsupervised incremental sequence learning for insider threat detection. In: ISI 2012 - 2012 IEEE International Conference on *I*ntelligence and Security Informatics Cyberspace, Border, Immigr. Secur. pp. 141–143 (2012)
16. Legg, P.A., Buckley, O., Goldsmith, M., Creese, S.: Automated insider threat detection system using user and role-based profile assessment. IEEE Syst. J. **11**(2), 503–512 (2017)
17. Rashid, T., Agrafiotis, I., Nurse, J.R.C.: A new take on detecting insider threats: exploring the use of hidden markov models," MIST 2016 – Proceedings of Workshop on Managing Insider Security Threats co-located with CCS 2016, pp. 47–56 (2016)
18. Khan, A.Y., Latif, R., Latif, S., Tahir, S., Batool, G., Saba, T.: Malicious insider attack detection in IoTs using data analytics. IEEE Access **8**, 11743–11753 (2020)
19. Hu, P., Li, H., Fu, H., Cansever, D., Mohapatra, P.: Dynamic defense strategy against advanced persistent threat with insiders. In: Proceedings of-IEEE INFOCOM, vol. 26, pp. 747–755 (2015)
20. Hodo, E., et al.: Threat analysis of IoT networks using artificial neural network intrusion detection system. In: 2016 International Symposium Networks, Computers and Communication ISNCC 2016, pp. 1–6 (2016). https://doi.org/10.1109/ISNCC.2016.7746067
21. Liu, L., et al.: Detecting and preventing cyber insider threats: a survey. IEEE Commun. Surv. Tutorials **20**(2), 1397–1418 (2018)

22. The CERT Insider Threat Database. https://insights.sei.cmu.edu/blog/the-cert-insider-threat-database/. Accessed 17 Aug 2024
23. IMPACT - Insider Threat Test Dataset. https://www.impactcybertrust.org/dataset_view?idDataset=1297. Accessed 17 Aug 2024
24. Kherif, F., Latypova, A.: Principal component analysis. Mach. Learn. Methods Appl. Brain Disord. 209–225 (2020)
25. Nguyenid, T., Mengersen, K., Sous, D., Liquet, B.: SMOTE-CD: SMOTE for compositional data (2023)
26. Sun, P., Wang, Z., Jia, L., Xu, Z.: SMOTE-kTLNN: a hybrid re-sampling method based on SMOTE and a two-layer nearest neighbor classifier. Expert Syst. Appl. **238**, 121848 (2024)
27. Pandey, U., Shukla, S., Wadhvani, R.: OCSK-SMOTE: an improved minority oversampling technique for unbalanced dataset using One-Class SVM and K-means. In: 2022 2nd International Conference on Advanced Computer Innovation Technology Engineering ICACITE 2022, pp. 2343–2347 (2022)
28. Elhaik, E.: Principal component analyses (PCA)-based findings in population genetic studies are highly biased and must be reevaluated. Sci. Reports 2022 121, vol. 12, no. 1, pp. 1–35 (2022)
29. Picard, F., Rivoirard, V., Roche, A., Panaretos, V.: PCA for point processes (2024). Accessed 15 Aug 2024
30. Al-Aqrabi, H., et al.: Securing manufacturing intelligence for the industrial internet of things. In: Proceedings of the Fourth International Congress on Information and Communication Technology, London, UK, 27–28 February 2019, pp. 267–282. Springer, Heidelberg (2020). https://doi.org/10.1007/978-981-32-9343-4_21
31. Al-Aqrabi, H., et al.: A multi-layer hierarchical intercloud connectivity model for sequential packet inspection of tenant sessions accessing BI as a service. In: Proceedings of 6th (CSS) and IEEE 11th (ICESS), pp. 137–144. IEEE, France, Paris (2014)
32. Al-Aqrabi, H., et al.: Dynamic authentication for intelligent sensor clouds in the Internet of Things. Int. J. Inf. Secur. **23**(3), 2003–2021 (2024)
33. Marukatat, S.: Tutorial on PCA and approximate PCA and approximate kernel PCA. Artif. Intell. Rev. **56**(6), 5445–5477 (2023)
34. Raschka, S., Patterson, J., Nolet, C.: Machine learning in python: main developments and technology trends in data science, machine learning, and artificial intelligence. Information **11**(4), 193 (2020)
35. Ileberi, E., Sun, Y., Wang, Z.: A machine learning based credit card fraud detection using the GA algorithm for feature selection. J. Big Data **9**(1), 1–17 (2022)
36. Haranadh Reddy, B., Karthikeyan, P.R.: Classification of fire and smoke images using decision tree algorithm in comparison with logistic regression to measure accuracy, precision, recall, F-score. In: 14th Conference on Mathematics, Actuarial Science, Computer Science and Statistics, MACS 2022 (2022)

Redefining Mobility Management for Improved Handover Efficiency in Internet-Connected Vehicles

Peer A. Shah[1](✉), Sumiya Bibi[2], and Hassan Osman Ali[1]

[1] Department of CIS, Higher Colleges of Technology, Fujairah, United Arab Emirates
pshah@hct.ac.ae

[2] Department of CS, COMSATS University Islamabad, Attock, Pakistan

Abstract. Over the past three decades, wireless communication has seen a significant surge, with Vehicular Networks emerging as a prominent area of interest for researchers. Managing mobility in these networks presents a considerable challenge. Vehicles moving between roadside units or base stations can experience disruptions in real-time services such as Voice over IP (VoIP), media streaming, safety-critical data transmission, and gaming. Due to the typically high speed of vehicles, these movements often result in handovers and packet loss. This research introduces a novel approach to mobility management and handover execution for mobile vehicles travelling on highways, differing from traditional methods. The proposed model predicts a vehicle's movement from one base station to the next using a probabilistic method by the correspondent node, which then initiates the binding refresh procedure accordingly. This approach reduces control traffic overhead and packet loss, leading to more efficient use of limited wireless resources. The performance of the proposed algorithm has been evaluated through simulation, demonstrating its effectiveness in reducing packet loss, handover delay, and control traffic overhead.

Keywords: Vehicular Networks · Mobility Management · Intelligent Transportation System · Efficient Handover · Roadside Unit

1 Introduction

Intelligent Transportation System (ITS) [1] has used different tools to improve transportation system proficiencies. Vehicular Network [2] is a technology that has arisen to assimilate wireless networks into vehicles. Vehicular networks enable homogenous as well as heterogeneous communication among vehicles and Road Side Units (RSUs) as shown in Fig. 1. As the vehicle moves out of network range, some other vehicle may arrive and become a part of the network. Unlike, Mobile Ad hoc Networks (MANETs) [3] where nodes tend to move at random, the mobility of vehicles in Vehicular Networks is in an organized way. Vehicles are limited to move in their range of motion, for example, controlled to follow the paved highway. Vehicular Networks provide communication among Vehicle to Vehicle (V2V) and Vehicle to roadside fixed Infrastructure (V2I). A dedicated short-range communication technology is used for V2V communication, while V2I communication is based on GPRS/3G/4G/5G, Wi-Fi or WiMAX.

A. Safi et al. (Eds.): ISICS 2024, CCIS 2381, pp. 319–330, 2025.
https://doi.org/10.1007/978-3-031-82931-4_24

Vehicular Networks have three architecture categories: pure ad-hoc, pure cellular and hybrid architecture. The pure ad-hoc architecture uses V2V communication mode where vehicles can communicate to each other directly or through multi-hop communication without the need for any fixed structure. In pure cellular architecture, V2I communication mode is used, where there is communication between vehicle and roadside fixed infrastructure i.e. base station and RSU. In hybrid architecture, through multi-hop routing, vehicles may connect to RSU while another vehicle will serve as a gateway.

Vehicular Networks provides a wide range of applications which are categorized as safety, traffic control and infotainment. For traffic efficiency applications, vehicles are required to cooperate with each other and with roadside fixed infrastructure, in order to manage flow of traffic, traffic coordination and update location information. Safety applications require information exchange among vehicles and RSUs to improve road safety and prevent accidents and are resource-demanding [4]. While, infotainment applications offer services like gaming, commerce services, Voice over IP (VoIP) and media streaming. These applications need real-time communication and are delay-sensitive. Figure 1 shows the communication scenarios of the vehicular network.

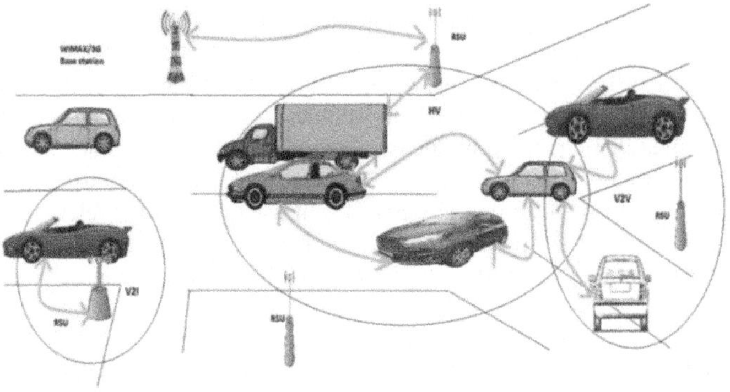

Fig. 1. Communication Scenario in Vehicular Networks

2 Literature Review

Mobility management is a significant topic for IP-based mobile networks [5]. The communication established between a Mobile Vehicle (MV) and the Correspondent Node (CN) may be affected by the movement of the MV, as CN is unaware of the MN's movement. To handle this problem, mobility management in Vehicular Networks is classified into two categories: Mobility management for V2V communication and Mobility management for V2I communication. In mobility management for V2V communication, topology management is done for route discovery, maintenance and recovery which is usually maintained by the routing protocols. However, in order to provide uninterrupted communication to MV while moving across different RSUs for V2I communication, location management and handover management are required.

Location management permits the network to send data packets to the user after discovering the vehicle's location. Vehicle continually updates its current location, which is used by the network to communicate with the vehicle. To support diverse forms of applications deployed in Vehicular Networks, the network should be capable to locate the vehicle. Handover management is performed by rerouting to establish a new path to the vehicle's new destination. The mobility in V2I communication can be either network mobility or host mobility. In the case of Vehicular Networks, there are two types of mobility scenarios, individual mobility and group mobility [6]. The host or individual mobility management is required to manage the communication of a single MV when the vehicle moves away from the range of the current corresponding vehicle or the signal strength of one roadside infrastructure becomes weak, it searches for new connections. In group or network mobility, group of vehicles move together as a cluster. Based on some criteria, a cluster head is selected who is responsible for the management of cluster topology and recommending external connections to the cluster members [6]. Handling mobility in Vehicular Networks where the speed of the vehicle is very high and varies from each other is considered to be a more difficult task than in cellular networks [7]. Any attempt to reduce packet loss and control traffic overhead will be greatly appreciable, hence improved handover mechanism with less overhead and packet loss is important and desirable for Internet-based Vehicular Networks. The Internet Engineering Task Force (IETF) has endorsed many IP-based protocols such as host-based mobility management protocols like Mobile IPv6 [8] to manage mobility in wireless networks.

If the number of MVs is few and the mobility of MV is very low i.e. if it does not change its position frequently and IP attachment point, then the control traffic generated by an MV and handover latency will not be a great concern [9]. As few messages of control traffic and Round-Trip Times (RTTs) of delay does not affect the overall performance. However, in the case of Vehicular Networks, there are a lot of vehicles on the road that move at a high speed, hence the frequency of handover and change in IP attachment point is very high. Also, the control traffic for handover generated by the MVs will be very high. That will eventually result in performance degradation of the network. It is because of the limited bandwidth in the wireless medium and the high amount of signalling messages that mobility management protocol exchanges will consume this scarce bandwidth. The literature that attempted to optimize the above-mentioned issues is discussed below.

2.1 Machine Learning Techniques to Predict Vehicle Trajectories

Jiang et al. [10] proposed an enhanced mobility management protocol that integrates machine learning techniques to predict vehicle trajectories, thereby improving handover decisions and reducing latency in high-speed scenarios. This work highlights the potential of predictive analytics in Vehicular networks, aligning with the objectives of the current research [10].

2.2 Proactive Handover Strategies

Proactive handover strategies have been increasingly investigated as a means to minimize communication disruptions during handovers. Liu et al. [11] developed a proactive handover management system that uses real-time GPS data to anticipate vehicle movement and initiate handovers before the actual transition between RSUs occurs. This method significantly reduces packet loss and is particularly effective in high-speed environments, making it relevant to the present study's focus on highway scenarios.

2.3 Probabilistic Handover Prediction

The application of probabilistic models to predict handover events has shown promising results in enhancing Vehicular Networks performance. A study by Zhang and Wang [12] introduced a probabilistic framework that calculates the likelihood of a vehicle leaving its current RSU based on historical mobility patterns and current speed. Their approach reduces unnecessary handovers and optimizes network resource utilization, providing a valuable reference for the proposed solution's predictive model.

2.4 Addressing Packet Loss in Safety-Critical Applications

The reliability of communication in safety-critical Vehicular Networks applications has been a focal point of recent research. Sun et al. [13] investigated the impact of packet loss during handover on emergency response systems and proposed a buffering strategy to mitigate its effects. Their findings underscore the importance of minimizing packet loss in scenarios where communication failures could have severe consequences, paralleling the goals of this research.

3 Proposed Solution

In this research, we proposed an optimized handover mechanism for Vehicular Networks to enhance communication reliability in high-speed highway scenarios. The approach shifts the responsibility of mobility prediction from the Mobile Node (MN) to the Correspondent Node (CN), aiming to reduce packet loss and improve overall network performance. By leveraging vehicle location data and a probabilistic handover prediction model, the system proactively manages handovers, ensuring seamless communication even in safety-critical applications.

3.1 A New Perspective for Handover Initiation

Existing solutions for mobility management, in all types of cellular and mobile networks, initiates the handover process from the MN by observing the signal strength and other parameters of available access networks [14]. These solutions perform very well in the scenarios where the mobility of MN is low and in follows some random pattern. However, in the case of Vehicular Networks where vehicles move at fast speed on the highway and their mobility pattern is not random [15]. The frequency of handover remains almost the same as vehicle covers a particular distance in unit time moving at high speed. Also, the distance between the Base Stations (BSs)/RSUs is also known or almost remains same. Hence, if the vehicle's movement pattern and probability of leaving the current BS/RSU is known to the CN then it can initiate the handover process, which will result in increased performance.

3.2 Enhancement for Reducing the Control Traffic

After performing the handover, mobility management protocols require that MN must set a binding lifetime at the CN to remain active with the current BS [8]. As the lifetime expires, the CN initiates the Binding Refresh Request (BRR) procedure to the MN for the initialization of the handover process or to refresh the binding entries at the CN and the Home Agent (HA). In Vehicular Networks, when vehicles move on a highway and the distance between RSUs does not change and if the mobility probability is known to the CN, then CN can predict the time of handover to be initiated by the MN. In such a scenario, CN may generate BRR after a specific period instead of after the expiry of the binding lifetime. It will reduce the overall signalling overhead to keep track record of the binding entries alive at CN and HA.

3.3 Scenarios for Handover Execution

To optimize the communication in Vehicular Networks for efficient handover execution, the scenario considered in this work is of the highway where MVs are moving at a high speed. A MV is considered to leave the current attachment point or link (RSU) after the specific period and will switch to next RSU/BS [15]. In such scenario, this research work is aiming to consider mobility management in a new perspective where MV's mobility and handover probability is to be predicted by the CN rather than by MN, in order to optimize the communication thus reducing packet loss due to handover.

The first scenario for MV is described in Fig. 2a. As shown, MV is moving on the highway and it remains in the old RSU's territory, therefore, handover is not being performed. In this case, when CN asks for BRR procedure, MV will reply with Binding Update (BU) message which contains the Care-of-Address (CoA) of MV. Here, as MV has not been moved to new RSU/BS, therefore it will reply with an old CoA. With this old CoA, CN will be able to know that no handover process has been performed earlier. While in Fig. 2b, it can be clearly seen that MV is in new RSU's territory. Here, MV will reply with BU message containing the new CoA. Thus, CN will be able to know that MV has been moved to the new location and hence handover process should be performed. As CN got this information very late (after expiry of binding lifetime) that MV has moved, thus it will lead to suffer the issue of packet loss which may result to severe damages in case of safety-critical applications.

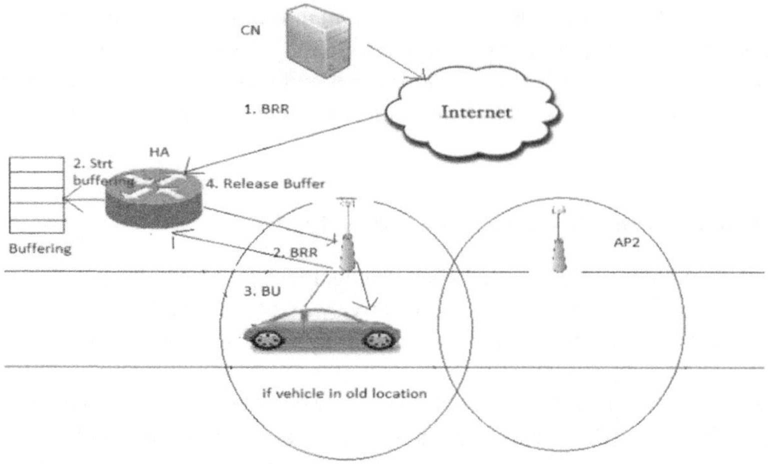

a. Mobility while MV in old RSU's territory

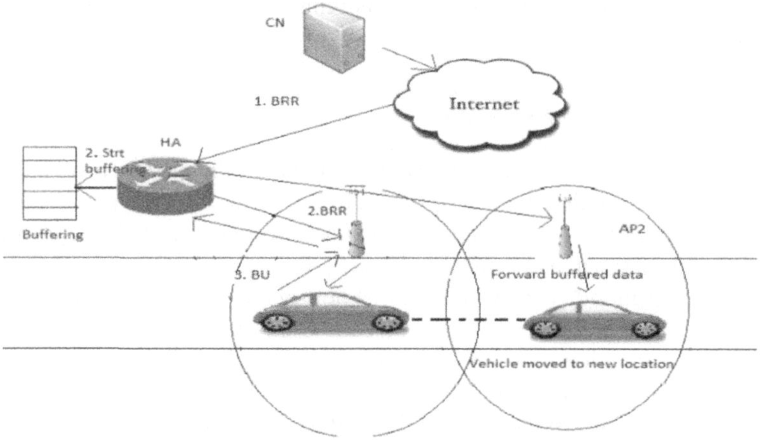

b. Mobility while MV in new RSU's territory

Fig. 2. Vehicular Networks mobility scenarios

3.4 Protocol Operation

The proposed communication optimization, to resolve the communication overhead and packet loss issues in existing mobility management protocols for vehicular networks, is based on mobility prediction of MV at CN and buffering of in-flight data at Home Agent (HA). The probability of the vehicle's movement and handover execution is calculated using the modified probabilistic scheme of Kabir et al. [16], where CN predicts the mobility of MV without depending on the layer 2 trigger.

The handover process starts when MV moves from one RSU/BS to another, changing its point of attachment. In the proposed scheme, when MV enters the range of RSU/BS it will exchange Modified Binding Update (MBU) messages and Binding Acknowledgement (BAck) messages through HA, as shown in Fig. 3. As Mobile IPv6 allows direct communication between MN and CN, therefore, after successful reception of first data packet, MV will start Return Routability Procedure (RRP) to establish a direct link with CN [17].

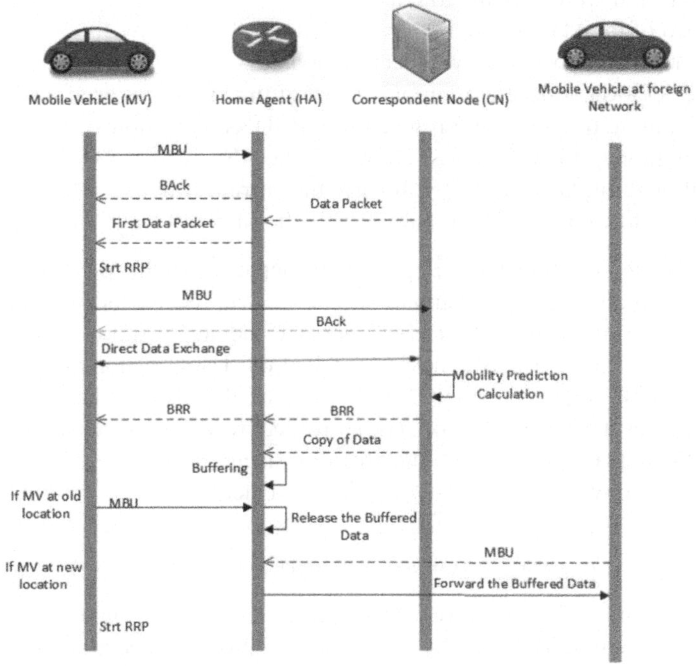

Fig. 3. Signalling messages of the proposed solution

The MBU Message also contains additional information of the vehicle's location information which is obtained through the Global Positioning System (GPS) at the time of the vehicle's entering the range of BS, as compared to the standard MBU message defined by Shah et al. [18]. Each field in the MBU message is the same as the ones in the Shah et al.'s MBU except for the location coordinates. Accordingly, the Binding Acknowledgement (BAck) message is also modified.

The first data packet sent by the CN to the MV is through the HA. Upon receiving the first data packet from CN, the MV will start RRP and send an MBU message to CN for direct communication. As mentioned earlier, the MBU message contains GPS information of the vehicle and the time the vehicle entered in the range of BS, thus based on this information CN will set its Time to Live (TTL). After, specific time, CN will start BRR and sends a copy of data packets to HA. HA will forward this BRR message to the vehicle and buffer data packets received from CN. The MV will reply to this BRR by MBU message with its CoA. If the vehicle is still attached to the current CoA as shown in Fig. 2a, HA will release buffered data. However, if CoA is new, the buffered data will be forwarded by HA to the MV's new location. This will prevent the data packets of safety-critical applications from being lost during transmission.

Handover Prediction

Below is the list of notations used.

CoA_{ti}: Care-of-Address of the MV at time ti.

$\ell_{ti}(x_i,y_i)$: Location of the MV at time t_i, where x_i and y_i are the coordinates.

D_{ti}: Distance travelled by the MV at time t_i.

V_{ti}: Speed of the MV at time t_i.

ΔT_i: Time interval between two location updates.

A_{ti}: Acceleration or deceleration of the MV at time t_i.

R_{tt}: Remaining time-to-live for the current RSU's connection.

TTL: Lifetime of the CoA registration with the CN.

P_{leave}: Probability that the MV will leave the current RSU.

Th: Threshold value for the probability that the MV will leave the current RSU.

In the proposed solution, CN will predict the departure of the MV from current CoA to new CoA through probability estimation. The CN will receive location information of MV $\ell_1(x_1, y_1)$ at time T_1 in the first MBU message and next location information $\ell_2(x_2, y_2)$ at time T_2 in the next MBU message and so on. Using historical values received previously in MBU messages, the CN will compute the distance between RSUs/BSs. The CN computes the current distance (D_c) travelled by MV, upon receiving the location update of MV and compares it with the previous distance (D_p).

The distance travelled between two updates is calculated as:

$$D_{t_{i+1}} = \sqrt{(x_{i+1} - x_i)^2 + (y_{i+1} - y_i)^2}$$

Similarly, Time ΔT between two MBU messages will be computed every time on receiving a new MBU. The velocity V and acceleration or deceleration of the MV at time t_i, of the vehicle is also computed from D and ΔT using the universal velocity and acceleration methods.

The probability P of the vehicle leaving its current CoA is calculated using "Eq. 1" and then compared with the threshold *Th* computed in "Eq. 2" [16].

$$P_{leave} = \left(\frac{a}{a+1}\right)^{\frac{Rtt}{TLL}} \times \left(1 + \beta + \frac{|A_{t_i}|}{V_{t_i}}\right) \tag{1}$$

where:

β is a weighting factor that adjusts the influence of acceleration/deceleration on the probability calculation.

$|A_{ti}|$ represents the absolute value of acceleration, capturing both positive (acceleration) and negative (deceleration) changes.

$$Th = \frac{\left(\frac{a}{a+1}\right)^{\frac{1}{TTL}} + \left(\frac{a-1}{a}\right)^{\frac{2}{TTL}}}{2} \times \left(1 + \gamma + \frac{|A_{t_i}|}{V_{t_i}}\right) \tag{2}$$

where:

γ is a separate weighting factor for the threshold adjustment, allowing flexibility in how much impact acceleration/deceleration has on the threshold.

```
Algorithm: Handover execution in the proposed solution
INPUT: Prediction Parameters
OUTPUT: Received Data at New Location
1.   Get location coordinates at MV
2.   Send MBU from MV
3.   IF the node is MV
4.       Calculate ΔT
5.       Check for expiry of ΔT
6.       Check for Candidate BS
7.       Create a link with BS
8.   ELSE                                  #node is CN
9.       Calculate P_leave and Th
10.          IF P_leave >= Th
11.              IF (D_c >= D_p) & BRR time expires
12.                  Send BRR
13.                  Send a copy of Data to HA
14.                  Receive BRR at MV
15.                  IF MV Moved
16.                      Send MBU with new CoA
17.                  ELSE
18.                      Send MBU with old CoA
19.                  END IF
20.              ELSE
21.                  Go to line no 16
22.              END IF
23.          ELSE
24.              Go to line no 16
25.          END IF
26.  END IF
```

Handover Execution

The algorithm above presents that how CN predicts to perform the handover by initiating BRR procedure from CN to MV. When the probability P becomes equal to or greater than the threshold Th, MV will check for D_c which becomes equal or greater than D_p and the time ΔT is expired or not. In case, all conditions are satisfied, BRR procedure is initiated. When BRR is generated, the parameters would be reset as a threshold $Th = 0$, D_p will be to D_c and D_c to 0, accordingly to compute the new threshold and current distance.

On receiving the BRR message at MV, it will respond with an MBU message containing the current CoA of MV. In this way, the proposed solution will reduce the number of BRR messages as compared to Mobile IPv6 and Probabilistic solution. On the other hand, MV will calculate the time difference each time it gets the GPS information and uses this time difference information to predict the handover process. Now, as MV knows the time between getting two GPS information, it is able to predict about when next handover will be performed. Before the expiry of that time, it will check for the availability of an alternative candidate BS. Upon finding, it will create a link to candidate BS and then perform the proactive handover process.

4 Simulation Results

In the case of mobility management in wireless networks like Vehicular Networks, a protocol is analysed in terms of Quality of Service (QoS). The QoS in such scenarios is measured efficiently in terms of handover delay, controlled traffic, and packet delivery cost. These metrics are very useful in the performance assessment of mobility management protocols. Simulations are performed in Network Simulator ns3 (Release 3.27). Our scenarios consist of a two-lane and two-way highway. The simulation runs for 500 s. The proposed scheme is compared with Mobile IPv6 and Probabilistic scheme [16] and the results related to the evaluation are presented and discussed here.

Figure 4 shows the comparison of different protocols for the number of binding refresh requests generated while changing the simulation time. It shows that at the start of communication, the number of BRR generated by Mobile IPv6 is not too high as compared to the other two protocols. However, as the simulation progresses the number of BRR for Mobile IPv6 increases more rapidly in comparison to the other two protocols. This is due to the fact that in Mobile IPv6, BRR procedure is executed every time after the binding lifetime got expires at the CN. In the Probabilistic protocol, the increase is small as it does not initiate the binding refresh procedure rather it checks the threshold value computed after the expiry of the binding lifetime. Therefore, the number of BRR messages generated are less as compared to the standard Mobile IPv6 but still high as compared to proposed. The number of BRR messages of the proposed solution is least affected by an increase in binding lifetime. As proposed solution has two conditions for mobility prediction, it first compares the probability with a threshold as in the Probabilistic solution. After that, it also checks the expiration of MV's time to remain in the area of RSU/BS. The proposed communication optimization improves the performance by about 34% than the standard Mobile IPv6 and about 4% than the Probabilistic solution.

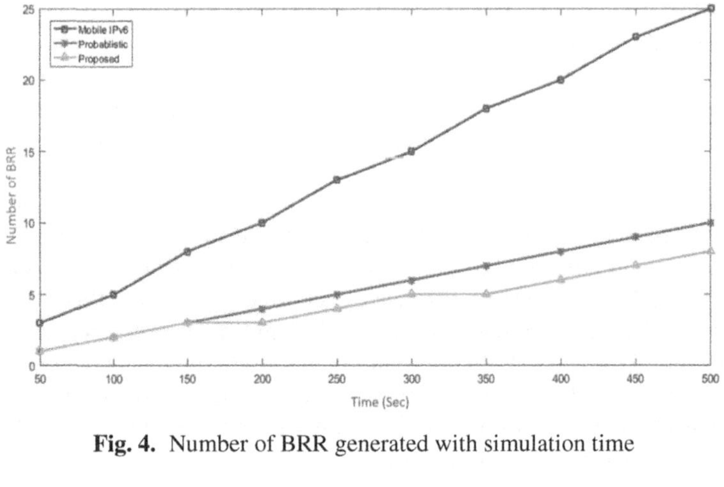

Fig. 4. Number of BRR generated with simulation time

Figure 5, shows the comparison of protocols for the cost of packet delivery with varying number of MVs. The packet delivery cost for all of three protocols increases as the number of MVs increases, because the number of handovers increase with the increasing number of MVs which results in more packet loss. However, the cost for Mobile IPv6 is much higher than the other two. In the Mobile IPv6, the number of packet loss is much higher due to the fact that CN remains unaware of the movement

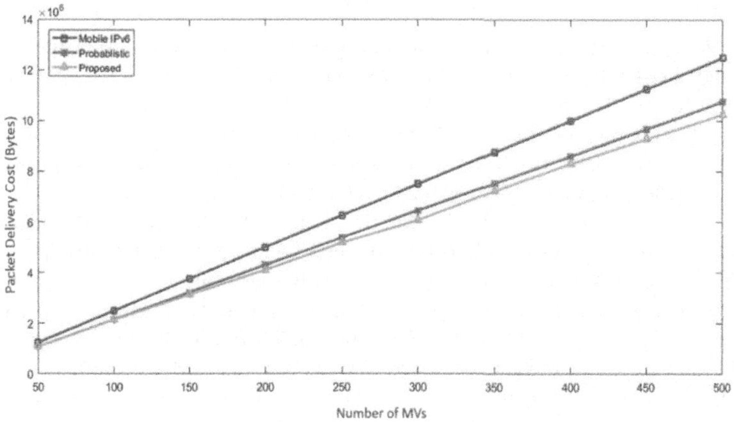

Fig. 5. Cost of packet delivery with varying numbers of MVs

of MN from the current CoA to the new CoA, therefore, CN continues to send data packets to MN's previous address. For safety-critical applications, packets that are lost need to be retransmitted at the new address of MN which involves extra cost. While the Probabilistic protocol and proposed solution performs buffering at HA during the handover process. Therefore the number of packet loss decreases and it also decreases the cost of packet delivery. Because packets are not needed to be retransmitted as packets are already stored at HA which will forward them to MV's current CoA.

5 Conclusion

This paper discussed a new dimension for a well-known issue of handover in the Internet-based Vehicular Network environment. Though existing solutions of mobility management offer seamless handover for MV, however, their route optimization becomes the reason for packet loss and communication overhead. The vehicle's handover execution is considered in a new perspective, where movement probability is computed by the CN instead of MV itself. This probability for MV's to move from the current CoA when exceeds or becomes equal to a certain threshold and the time of MV's to remain in the area of current RSU expires, which is computed by CN based on GPS information received from MV, then the handover is initiated. The new mechanism reduces the number of BRR messages which helps in reducing the control traffic which consequently reduces the signalling overhead. Also, the packet loss for safety-critical applications can be reduced during the handover process, which in turn reduces the overall packet delivery cost. The handover delay of the proposed enhancement remains low as compared to the other solutions. This work has considered only one aspect of handover communication optimization for host-based mobility management. Location management and network based mobility management operations can also be optimized for better performance.

References

1. Qu, F., Wang, F.Y., Yang, L.: Intelligent transportation spaces: vehicles, traffic, communications, and beyond. IEEE Commun. Mag. **48**(11), 136–142 (2010)
2. Ning, Z., Xia, F., Ullah, N., Kong, X., Hu, X.: Vehicular social networks: enabling smart mobility. IEEE Commun. Mag. **55**(5), 49–55 (2017)
3. Conti, M., Giordano, S.: Mobile ad hoc networking: milestones, challenges, and new research directions. IEEE Commun. Mag. **52**(1), 85–96 (2014)
4. Zhang, Y., Chen, M., Guizani, N., Wu, D., Leung, V.C.M.: SOVCAN: safety-oriented vehicular controller area network. IEEE Commun. Mag. **55**(8), 94–99 (2017)
5. Shah, P.A., Yousaf, M., Qayyum, A., Hasbullah, H.B.: Performance comparison of end-to-end mobility management protocols for TCP. J. Netw. Comput. Appl. **35**(6), 1657–1673 (2012)
6. Yang, Y., Li, H., Huang, Q.: Mobility management in VANET. In: Proceedings - 2013 Wireless and Optical Communications Conference, WOCC 2013, pp. 298–303 (2013)
7. Lee, D.: Efficient mobility management scheme to support highway environment. Int. J. Control Autom. **8**(12), 263–272 (2015)
8. Johnson, D., J. Arkko, "Mobility Support in IPv6," Internet Eng. Task Force, p. 169, 2011
9. Orsino, A., et al.: Effects of heterogeneous mobility on D2D-and drone-assisted mission-critical MTC in 5G. IEEE Commun. Mag. **55**(2), 79–87 (2017)
10. Jiang, J., Zhou, Y., Li, H.: Machine learning-driven mobility management for VANETs. IEEE Trans. Veh. Technol. **71**(2), 1234–1245 (2022). https://doi.org/10.1109/TVT.2022.3145678
11. Liu, X., Zhao, M., Chen, P.: Proactive handover management using real-time GPS in VANETs. IEEE Access **11**, 34567–34578 (2023). https://doi.org/10.1109/ACCESS.2023.4567890
12. Zhang, Y., Wang, L.: Probabilistic handover prediction in high-speed VANETs. J. Netw. Comput. Appl. **190**, 102925 (2021). https://doi.org/10.1016/j.jnca.2021.102925
13. Sun, Y., Zhang, H., Wu, X.: Buffering strategies to mitigate packet loss in safety-critical VANET applications. IEEE Commun. Mag. **62**(5), 78–85 (2024). https://doi.org/10.1109/MCOM.2024.3045678
14. Ahmed, A., Boulahia, L.M., Gaïti, D.: Enabling vertical handover decisions in heterogeneous wireless networks: a state-of-the-art and a classification. IEEE Commun. Surv. Tutorials **16**(2), 776–811 (2014)
15. Zarei, M., Rahmani, A.M.: Analysis of vehicular mobility in a dynamic free-flow highway. Veh. Commun. **7**, 51–57 (2017)
16. Humayun, K.M., Al-Farabi, K.M.: A probabilistic scheme for reducing the packet loss in mobile IPv6. J. Netw. **7**(12), 1912–1924 (2012)
17. Johnson, D., Perkins, C., Arkko, J.: RFC 3775 - Mobility support in IPv6. IETF, June, pp. 1–165 (2004)
18. Shah, P.A., Hasbullah, H.B., Lawal, I.A., Mu'azu, A.A., Jung, L.T.: A TOTP-based enhanced route optimization procedure for mobile IPv6 to reduce handover delay and signalling overhead. Sci. World J. **214**, 16 (2014)

Enhancing Course Performance Reports: Leveraging ChatGPT for Comprehensive Data Analysis

Ghazala Bilquise(✉), Sharmila Siddartha, Munther AlHassan, Bindu Sunil, and Lama Al Ibaisi

Higher Colleges of Technology, P.O. Box 15725, Dubai, UAE
{gbilquise,ssiddartha,malhassan,bsunil,llbaisi}@hct.ac.ae

Abstract. Course performance analysis is a critical process that involves the systematic review and evaluation of students' academic progress, course feedback, and learning outcome attainment at an institutional level. This analysis ensures that educational standards are met and identifies areas for improvement in teaching and curriculum. However, data analysis tends to be a time-consuming task which is susceptible to human bias and mistakes. The process is often hampered by challenges such as a lack of automation and decision support, making reviews time-consuming and prone to errors. To address these limitations, this study utilizes the capabilities of ChatGPT to analyze end-of-semester course assessment reports for three courses across seventeen campuses within a higher education institution based in the UAE. The study adopts a structured approach to analyze course performance data, highlighting the potential of ChatGPT as a tool for analyzing course performance, encompassing both qualitative and quantitative data. By leveraging ChatGPT, the study aims to streamline the course performance analysis process, making it more efficient. The insights provided by this study could be valuable for educational institutions looking to enhance their course evaluation methods and overall academic standards.

Keywords: ChatGPT · Course Performance · Higher Education · Qualitative analysis · Quantitative analysis

1 Introduction

Quality assurance in education is a fundamental requirement to ensure that academic institutions meet established educational standards and continually improve their teaching and learning processes [1]. It plays a crucial role in maintaining the integrity of educational programs and ensuring that students achieve the desired learning outcomes. Course performance analysis is a key component of quality assurance. To achieve quality assurance goals, institutions must engage in comprehensive analysis of courses, examining both quantitative metrics, such as student performance data [2], and qualitative feedback, such as student and faculty course evaluations, and faculty reports [3].

A. Safi et al. (Eds.): ISICS 2024, CCIS 2381, pp. 331–345, 2025.
https://doi.org/10.1007/978-3-031-82931-4_25

However, generating accurate and insightful course assessment reports (CARs) poses significant challenges. The process involves analyzing feedback from numerous teaching faculty and students across various campuses, assessing grade distributions of coursework, final assessment and final grades. This makes the process time-consuming, susceptible to human bias and prone to errors and inconsistencies, thereby reducing the reliability and usefulness of the reports. These challenges necessitate a more efficient and accurate approach to course performance analysis to meet the requirements of quality assurance.

In today's rapidly evolving technological era, Generative Artificial Intelligence (GenAI) has transformed data analysis methodologies, offering unprecedented capabilities for processing and interpreting vast amounts of data [4]. Therefore, one potential solution for addressing the challenges in course performance analysis lies in leveraging the power of GenAI, specifically ChatGPT, to streamline the process of course assessment analysis and reporting. ChatGPT, an advanced language model by OpenAI, stands out for its ability to process and generate human-like text, making it well-suited for tasks requiring natural language understanding and generation [5]. Beyond education, ChatGPT has demonstrated its versatility in various domains, including business, healthcare, and tourism, where its ability to understand context and generate coherent responses has proven invaluable [6–8].

ChatGPT has shown promising results in various educational applications, including teaching and learning, assessments, and evaluations. Extensive research has been conducted on using ChatGPT for educational tasks such as content creation, developing personalized learning resources, generating assessment activities, evaluating submissions and providing feedback [9–11]. Recent studies have leveraged ChatGPT for qualitative data analysis to identify and interpret patterns in data for research activities [12, 13]. However, there is a noticeable research gap in utilizing ChatGPT for comprehensive qualitative and quantitative data analysis in Higher Education Institutions (HEIs) for quality assurance purposes.

ChatGPT can analyze complex data sets, identify patterns, and provide coherent and insightful summaries of qualitative feedback [14]. This makes it an ideal tool for synthesizing diverse inputs from numerous faculty members and students across multiple campuses. Furthermore, ChatGPT can standardize reporting formats, ensuring consistency and reducing the likelihood of errors that typically arise from manual data handling. Its ability to generate detailed and accurate reports can save significant time and resources, allowing educators and administrators to focus on interpreting the insights and making informed decisions to improve educational outcomes.

Therefore, this study aims to harness the power of ChatGPT to produce an accurate and consistent analysis of CARs. As a case study, it focuses on three courses offered in the Computer Information Science (CIS) division of a UAE based HEI, spanning across 17 campuses. The objective of this research is to explore the potential of ChatGPT as a tool for automating and improving the course performance analysis process, providing a structured approach for data analysis that encompasses both qualitative and quantitative aspects. This research seeks to develop a comprehensive protocol for its use in analyzing system-wide CARs.

The rest of the paper is organized as follows: Sect. 2 provides the background of the problem, Sect. 3 presents the related work, Sect. 4 outlines the methodology of this research, while Sect. 5 discusses the results. Finally, Sect. 6 concludes the study and provides areas of further research.

2 Problem Background

This study is based on a HEI with approximately 23,000 students across multiple campuses. The HEI offers five accredited programs. To ensure consistent course delivery, a System-Wide Course Team Leader (SCTL) coordinates collaboration among course team members teaching the same course throughout the semester. Quality assurance (QA) processes are in place to ensure that courses meet educational standards and provide a uniform learning experience across all campuses.

As part of the QA and continuous course improvement efforts, both faculty and students evaluate the course and provide qualitative feedback. Each faculty member also prepares a Course Assessment Report (CAR) based on the performance outcomes of their respective classes. These reports include feedback on class GPA, drop-out rates, and grade distributions, noting any anomalies and offering course improvement recommendations. The faculty feedback is crucial to evaluate the continuity and relevance of the content within the course. The faculty member also prepares a report on the achievement of the Learning Outcomes (LO).

The SCTL consolidates these CARs into a System-Wide CAR (SWCAR) for the course. The SWCAR details the course performance supported by assessment results and the faculty course evaluations. The SCTL analyzes the overall course performance using data from multiple sources to identify areas for course improvement. Qualitative feedback and recommendations from teaching faculty are sourced from the consolidated CARs. The initial SWCAR includes quantitative data such as the system-wide GPA, dropout rates and grade distribution. However, for a comprehensive analysis, the SCTL refers to the system-wide LO attainment, previous semesters GPA, drop-out rates and grade distribution. Figure 1 illustrates the current process of producing the SWCAR.

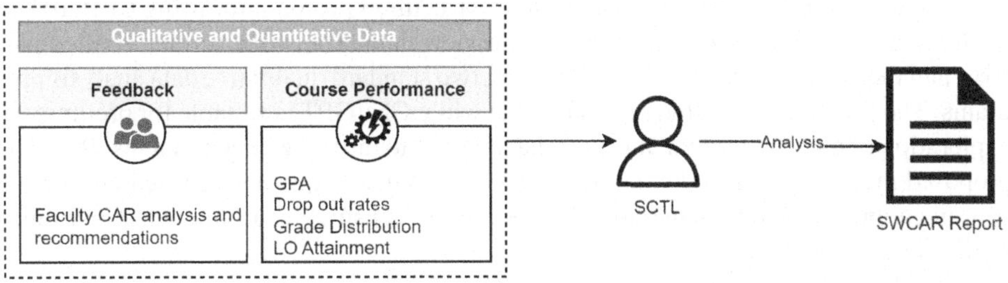

Fig. 1. Current System

The SWCAR consists of four main sections. (1) **System-Wide GPA and Drop-Out Rates:** This section includes analysis of these figures based on faculty feedback, highlighting any anomalies. (2) **Faculty and Student Course Evaluations:** This section presents evaluation results and qualitative feedback, with the SCTL analyzing the data to identify areas of concern and justifying low satisfaction rates. (3) **Grade Distribution:** This section covers the distribution of coursework, final assessment, and final grades. The SCTL analyzes performance metrics and reports any anomalies based on the expected grade distribution and faculty feedback. (4) **Course Improvement Recommendations:** This section compiles improvement suggestions from faculty members, which the SCTL analyzes to identify overall areas for enhancement.

The process of analyzing multiple data sources, including - CAR data, LO attainment, and grade distribution, into a comprehensive SWCAR is a time-consuming process prone to errors and inconsistencies. Moreover, analyzing qualitative feedback requires careful interpretation to ensure that insights are accurately captured and addressed. Furthermore, balancing quantitative data with qualitative feedback to provide a holistic view of course performance and areas for improvement can be complex. This may lead to variability in how SCTLs may interpret and report performance outcomes, anomalies, and recommendations. This in turn may affect the reliability of the SWCAR. By leveraging tools like ChatGPT for data analysis, we aim to streamline this process, reduce errors, and enhance the overall quality of the course performance reports.

3 Related Work

The application of ChatGPT for data analysis in various domains has garnered significant attention in recent studies. Numerous studies explored the thematic analysis of interview data using ChatGPT. The analytic capabilities of ChatGPT were explored by [15] to analyze interview data of thirty guaranteed income recipients. The research revealed that ChatGPT was effective in identifying themes and patterns consistent with human analysts' results. It efficiently processed large datasets, providing timely insights. However, the GenAI tool occasionally misinterpreted context-specific details, highlighting the necessity for human supervision. Similar findings were reported by [4], where the author investigated the application of ChatGPT in the analysis of focus group interview data. The study revealed that while ChatGPT could efficiently process and analyze qualitative data, it must be used correctly to produce meaningful results.

Researchers in [16] designed and tested a structured protocol for using ChatGPT in qualitative analysis of thirty participants interview data. The study further verified patterns and themes identified by ChatGPT using two standard qualitative data analysis programs. The findings of the study revealed that while ChatGPT is suitable for preliminary exploration of qualitative data, it is unsatisfactory in identifying contextual insights. The proposed protocol enhanced consistency and reliability in qualitative research, though careful calibration and human input were required to ensure the accuracy and relevance of the GenAI's analysis.

The ability of ChatGPT to mimic human reviewers in scientific medical research was evaluated by [17] using a descriptive and qualitative approach. The study's findings revealed that a significant portion of ChatGPT's comments did not align with those of human reviewers, and a smaller percentage even contradicted them. The study concluded that GenAI tools fall short in capturing the contextual aspects of medical studies that are crucial in a clinically significant research article.

Another study [18], researchers explored the potential of ChatGPT for automating the systematic review process. The study found that ChatGPT could automate parts of the review process, such as literature screening and data extraction, thereby reducing human researchers' workload. However, ChatGPT's performance was limited by difficulties in interpreting complex texts and extracting detailed information, necessitating human validation and oversight.

ChatGPT was employed by [19] to analyze open-ended student course evaluation feedback. The analysis's result was verified against the themes generated by course instructors on the same data. The research findings revealed a high level of agreement between the themes identified by instructors and those identified by ChatGPT. While ChatGPT was effective in identifying general course related themes, it faced challenges in accurately interpreting subjective comments related to course weaknesses, necessitating human review to validate the findings.

ChatGPT has also been employed for quantitative analysis. In a medical research conducted by [20], ChatGPT demonstrated proficiency in data cleaning and statistical testing with comparable performance to established analysis tools. However, limitations were noted in ChatGPT's dependency on clear prompts and difficulties with complex statistical methods. In another study, the application of ChatGPT for financial ratio analysis was investigated to assist managers in decision-making [21]. The quantitative data of fifty companies, provided in the form of balance sheets and income statements, was analyzed by ChatGPT with up to 92% accuracy. The study did not utilize ChatGPT's capabilities for interpreting the ratio analysis figures to identify trends or generate actionable insights.

Overall, the literature review demonstrated that ChatGPT is efficient at analyzing large volumes of both qualitative and quantitative data. However, it struggles to provide contextual insights for qualitative data, thereby necessitating human supervision for deeper interpretation and meaning. Furthermore, none of the reviewed studies utilized ChatGPT for both qualitative and quantitative data analysis simultaneously. This study aims to fill the research gap by employing ChatGPT for comprehensive analysis of both types of data in an educational setting to generate themes and actionable insights using course performance data.

4 Methodology

The experimental setup for this research utilized ChatGPT as the GenAI tool to conduct a comprehensive analysis of course performance data of three courses. ChatGPT was chosen due to its widespread availability, user-friendly interface, and robust LLM engine. The research team's familiarity with the tool also made it an ideal choice. Specifically, ChatGPT-4o was selected for its advanced natural language processing (NLP) capabilities, which are highly effective for processing and analyzing both qualitative and quantitative data. Its improved accuracy and advanced NLP features [22, 23] make it suitable for the comprehensive analysis required in this study. Additionally, ChatGPT-4o allows data file uploads without word limit restrictions, unlike ChatGPT-3.5 legacy.

The research methodology is divided into four main phases – (1) Course selection, (2) Data preparation, (3) Prompt generation, and (4) Querying and evaluation. Each phase is illustrated in Fig. 2.

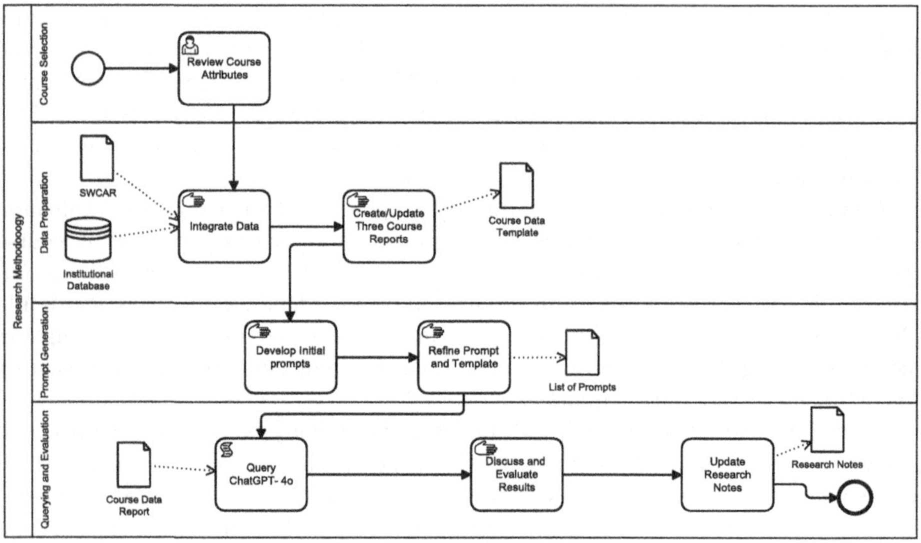

Fig. 2. Research Methodology

4.1 Course Selection Phase

In this study, three courses from the CIS division were selected for a comprehensive course performance analysis. These courses were chosen to represent the diverse nature of CIS offerings in terms of course type, teaching faculty, and student enrollment. The selected courses include one core course (Project Management) and two concentration courses (Enterprise Routing and Web Development).

The core course, offered to all CIS program students, typically has high student enrollment and is taught by multiple faculty members across the system. In contrast, the concentration courses are specific to majors like networking and application development, resulting in lower enrollments and fewer classes across the campuses offering these majors. Additionally, the nature of the courses varies, with the concentration courses providing technical content and the core course focusing on developing non-technical leadership and management skills.

The three selected courses are offered in the fourth year of the bachelor's program. Course 1, from the networking concentration, has 4 teaching faculty and 27 students. Course 2, an application development course, has 5 teaching faculty and 68 students. Course 3, the core course, is taught by 14 faculty members and has a total of 420 students system-wide. Table 1 summarizes the selected courses.

Table 1. Selected Courses.

Course #	Course Title	Course Type	Course Level	# Faculty	# Students
Course 1	Enterprise Routing	Concentration	Year 4	4	27
Course 2	Web Development	Concentration	Year 4	5	68
Course 3	Project Management	Core	Year 4	14	420

4.2 Data Preparation Phase

The data required for the comprehensive course performance analysis is spread across multiple sources. Consequently, the data preparation phase involves integrating data from these various sources to ensure it is suitable for analysis using ChatGPT. At the end of each semester, the system automatically generates a course performance document for each course, compiling performance and evaluation metrics from classes taught across the entire system. This report includes:

1) System-wide course performance metrics, such as the system wide GPA, dropout rate, number of enrolled students and number of teaching faculty.
2) Satisfaction rates from the course evaluation survey, assessed both by the student and faculty.
3) Student performance including the coursework grades, final exam grades and final grade distribution of all enrolled students.

For a comprehensive course performance analysis, each course report is augmented with additional necessary data for the respective course and consolidated into a single document. A template was created with structured headings organized into four sections for the analysis. Common data such as grade distribution policy was pre-filled in the template. Three course reports were prepared using the template to upload to ChatGPT for analysis. Table 2 presents the structure of the course report illustrating each section with the existing data, additional augmented data, source of the augmented data as well as the objective for including the additional data. It is important to note that the data used in this study was anonymized to protect the identities of the students, faculty and the institution.

4.3 Prompt Generation Phase

The augmented course report was uploaded to ChatGPT-4o. Four prompts were developed and refined in an iterative manner for analysis of each SWCAR section data. Thematic analysis was used to interpret and analyze the qualitative data in each section to interpret and identify patterns in the faculty feedback. Implicit instructions were given for quantitative analysis.

The prompts were refined in an iterative manner using an initial querying phase. Three rounds of experimentation were conducted and based on the preliminary results, the prompts were refined such as including reference to section headings of the course file such as "*Using section 1 data*", adding phrases such as "*Give insights based on themes*". Furthermore, minor adjustments were made to the data template to improve granularity. Contextual data was added in some sections such as the total number of students attempts for each assessment. Abbreviations were replaced such as "FA" with "*Final Assessment*". Table 3 outlines the prompts generated for each section.

Table 2. Data Set including existing and augmented data.

Section # Existing data	Augmented Data	Data Source	Objective
Section 1 • # Teaching faculty • # Enrolled students • System-wide GPA & drop-out rate	Course level	Course syllabus	For grade analysis based on course level
	Learning outcomes	Course syllabus	For learning outcome attainment insights
	Previous semester's GPA and dropout rate	Archived SWCAR reports	For comparative analysis of previous semesters performance
	Consolidated faculty feedback on class performance and dropout rates	Archived faculty CAR report	To generate themes and insights from the qualitative data related to system-wide performance and drop-out rates
Section 2 • Course evaluation satisfaction rates (faculty and students)	Faculty assessment of course evaluation	Archived faculty CAR report	To generate themes and insights from the qualitative data related to course evaluation
Section 3 • Coursework grade distribution • Final exam grade distribution • Final grade distribution	Expected grade distribution policy	Policy document	For a comparative analysis of course performance against the expected performance benchmarks for each course by level (specified in Section 1)
	System-wide LO attainment	Consolidated LO attainment report	For an analysis of learning outcome attainment
	Faculty feedback on grade distribution	Archived faculty CAR report	To generate themes and insights from the qualitative data related to course evaluation
Section 4	Faculty recommendations on course improvement	Archived faculty CAR report	To generate themes and insights from the qualitative data related to course recommendations

4.4 Querying and Evaluation

For consistency, the same prompts were used to query ChatGPT for a comprehensive analysis for all three courses. All tests were performed simultaneously on different machines to avoid the training bias that may arise. The output of the quantitative analysis was validated using manual calculations to ensure accuracy. ChatGPT analysis results for each prompt were evaluated by the respective course SCTLs for accuracy and quality using a 5-point Likert scale. A focus group interview with the SCTLs was used to examine the validity of ChatGPT results. The results of the experiment are discussed in the next section.

Table 3. ChatGPT Prompts.

SWCAR Section #	Prompt
Section 1	*Analyze the system wide GPA and drop-out rate using section 1 system-wide data. Summarize the faculty feedback of section 1 only. Give insights based on themes*
Section 2	*Analyze the faculty and student course evaluation survey results in section 2.1 and 2.2 respectively, taking into account the student response count and the enrollment count. Provide insights on the results* *Summarize the faculty feedback using section 2 data only and give insights arranged by themes*
Section 3	*Use section 3 data to analyze and reflect on the grade distribution considering the attainment of the learning outcomes, the expected grade distribution as per the provided directive, comparability of the final grade and coursework grade, and final exam grade. Highlight any areas of concern related to the grade distribution* *Use the faculty feedback of section 3 to uncover the main themes*
Section 4	*Using your previous analysis of sections 1, 2 and 3 data, include section 4 Faculty recommendations to suggest course improvements, Consolidate the analysis and suggestions by theme and relevance*

5 Discussion of Results and Evaluation

The outcomes and evaluation of the ChatGPT analysis was divided into four sections corresponding to each identified prompt. The section results are presented below.

5.1 Section 1 Results

In section 1 of the SWCAR analysis ChatGPT performed a comparative analysis of the system-wide GPA and drop-out rate against the previous semesters metrics. The SCTLs found the comparison relevant, well-structured and meaningful. For instance, "*The system-wide GPA has improved from 2.32 to 2.64, indicating a positive trend in academic performance The drop-out rate has decreased to 0%, showing better student retention and possibly improved course engagement or support systems.*"

ChatGPT effectively identified and summarized multiple themes that emerged from the qualitative feedback of section 1 data. While the SCTL generally agreed with the generated themes, they noted that some themes could have been combined, as there was some repetition. For instance, ChatGPT identified themes such as "*Student Performance*", "*Teaching Methods*", "*Challenges and Suggestions*". The key points under challenges and suggestions were already included in the teaching methods and student performance.

According to the SCTL, the insights generated from the themes were relevant. For instance, in course 2, section 1 faculty feedback, ChatGPT provided the insight: "*The emphasis on practical demonstrations and problem-solving significantly benefited students, resulting in higher performance.*" This insight aligns with the observed high system-wide GPA and the updated assessment strategy. However, some insights were considered too generic, such as: "*Despite the overall success, the need for more practice and better preparation for final exams was highlighted, suggesting areas for future improvement in course design and delivery.*"

5.2 Section 2 Results

ChatGPT effectively summarized the high, moderate, and low satisfaction areas from course evaluation data, highlighting areas of concern when satisfaction levels were low. Additionally, ChatGPT performed a comparative analysis of student vs. faculty course evaluations, highlighting discrepancies or agreements between satisfaction levels. For instance: "*Both faculty and a majority of students felt the course lacked clarity in some areas. This includes learning outcomes, assessments aligning with those outcomes, and overall course structure.*" and "*Faculty are satisfied with the content's relevance, but students find the academic challenge high.*"

The number of student responses was taken into account in ChatGPT's analysis to ensure the feedback's accuracy and representativeness, leading to a more comprehensive understanding of the course evaluation data. While ChatGPT effectively analyzed and summarized this data, it also provided caution regarding the interpretation of the results. For example: "*With 68 students enrolled but only 6 student responses, the feedback may not fully represent the entire student body's experiences.*" and "*Given that only one student responded, these results should be interpreted with caution as they may not be representative of the entire student body.*"

The SCTL generally agreed with the overall themes and insights generated by ChatGPT from section 2 qualitative faculty feedback data. However, they noted that ChatGPT's insights were sometimes too generic due to a lack of contextual knowledge or undocumented feedback. An example of this is: "*While students found the course challenging and expressed lower satisfaction with some resources, the high faculty ratings on the appropriateness of learning outcomes and teaching methodologies indicate a belief in the course's structure and educational value.*"

5.3 Section 3 Results

In section 3, ChatGPT conducted several tasks such as a comparative grade distribution analysis between assessments and expected final grade distribution as per institutional policy. It also conducted an LO attainment analysis to identify and reflect on areas of concern. Additionally, it analyzed qualitative faculty feedback to generate themes and provide insights. ChatGPT handled all these tasks effectively based on a single prompt, demonstrating its robust NLP processing capabilities.

ChatGPT accurately calculated the percentage of A, B, C, D, and F grades by consolidating various grade ranges such as A, A–, B, B–, and B+, etc., without explicit instructions. Furthermore, it extracted the relevant data from the uploaded course file, such as total number of students, and accurately computed the respective grade percentage. The reflection on the grade distribution highlighted areas of concerns, for instance: "*...the number of F grades is significant and suggests that many students struggled substantially with the final exam.*". Also, the discrepancy between coursework and final exams was highlighted: "*There is a noticeable discrepancy between coursework grades and final exam grades suggesting that the final exam may be disproportionately difficult or that students are not adequately prepared for the cumulative nature of the final assessment.*". ChatGPT also reflected on the course grades using correlation analysis such as: "*The correlation between coursework and final assessment grades (0.80) indicates that students who perform well in coursework generally also perform well in the final exam*".

For the comparative analysis based on the expected grade distribution policy, ChatGPT referenced course-level information from section 1. The analysis also included a reflection of LO attainment, highlighting LOs with low attainment providing insights by referencing the LOs provided in section 1, for example: "*Most students achieved the learning outcomes well, especially LO4, indicating strong practical understanding. However, LO3 shows lower attainment, suggesting difficulties in understanding and applying BGP design requirements.*"

The qualitative analysis of section 3 data revealed several themes and areas of concern, such as "*Disparity Between Coursework and Final Exam Grades*", "*Increased need for practical activities*" and more.

5.4 Section 4 Results

The objective of section 4 analysis was to consolidate the ChatGPTs previous analysis as well as the faculty recommendations for course improvement. ChatGPT synthesized data from previous sections (section 1–3) of the course file to align faculty recommendations with identified trends and statistics. The recommendations were organized by themes such as "*engagement*", "*assessment structure*", "*learning outcomes*", "*resources*", and more. ChatGPT provided reasonable actionable suggestions for course improvements. The SCTL evaluation of ChatGPT results for each section based on a 5-point Likert scale is presented in Table 4.

Overall, ChatGPT exhibited strong capabilities in quantitative analysis across all sections of the experiment and performed reasonably well in the qualitative analysis. The model accurately extracted, compared, and interpreted numerical data while also identifying and synthesizing themes from qualitative feedback. The insights and recommendations provided were coherent and relevant, demonstrating ChatGPT's potential as a valuable tool for analyzing and improving course performance data. The key strengths of the GenAI tool were accurate data extraction and comparison, identification and synthesis of qualitative themes, coherent and actionable insights and recommendations. However, it was noted that sufficient context should be provided in prompts and data template to maximize the accuracy of analysis.

The experiment confirms that ChatGPT can effectively support educational researchers and administrators in analyzing and enhancing course performance through

Table 4. SCTL evaluation of ChatGPT results.

SWCAR Section	SCTL rating Course 1	SCTL rating Course 2	SCTL rating Course 3	Average Rating
Section 1	5	4	4	4.33
Section 2	4	4	4	4
Section 3	4	3	4	3.67
Section 4	5	4	5	4.67

a combination of quantitative metrics and qualitative feedback. However, it is important to use ChatGPT with discretion, as it might generate irrelevant details or overlook themes that need to be validated and interpreted within a specific context.

6 Conclusion

This study explored the effectiveness of ChatGPT-4o as a tool for automating and enhancing the process of course performance analysis in a HEI. The primary aim was to investigate how this advanced GenAI tool could streamline the generation of course performance reports, addressing the inefficiencies and inaccuracies inherent in traditional methods. By developing a structured methodology, the study sought to create a framework that not only leverages ChatGPT's capabilities but also sets the stage for future research and application in the field of educational quality assurance.

The research employed a multi-phase methodology to achieve its objectives. Initially, three diverse courses from the CIS division were selected to represent various course types and student enrollments. The data preparation phase involved consolidating performance metrics, satisfaction surveys, and qualitative feedback into a structured template designed to reduce the explicit information required in prompts for ChatGPT. This template included enhancements such as defining grade ranges for letter grades, specifying course levels, and incorporating statements on LO attainment. These modifications enabled ChatGPT to refer to specific sections of the data for more accurate and insightful analyses.

In the subsequent phase, carefully crafted prompts were developed and refined through iterative experimentation to guide ChatGPT in analyzing the course performance data. The prompts utilized a combination of thematic analysis and implicit instructions for quantitative evaluation, allowing ChatGPT to generate detailed and consistent reports. The study found that the advanced NLP capabilities of ChatGPT-4o enabled effective analysis of both qualitative and quantitative data, resulting in valuable insights into system-wide GPA, drop-out rates, and grade distributions, as well as identifying themes from faculty and student feedback. However, it was also observed that the outputs from ChatGPT displayed slight variations across the different courses due to the tool's inherent repetitiveness and occasional inconsistencies. As a result, it was necessary for SCTLs to review and supplement the generated analyses to ensure that the course performance reports were comprehensive and accurate.

The findings of this study are consistent with previous research, which highlighted that the quality of faculty feedback significantly impacts the effectiveness of ChatGPT's analyses. The structured template developed in this research proved to be instrumental in minimizing the amount of explicit information needed in the prompts, thus enabling ChatGPT to focus on the relevant data for each section of the report.

The study also demonstrated that the process of using ChatGPT for course performance analysis is notably more efficient than traditional manual methods. While preparing the course files using the structured template required some initial effort, the time saved during the analysis phase highlighted the value of this approach. This efficiency not only streamlines the QA process but also ensures a consistent depth of analysis across different courses, thereby supporting uniform quality assurance reporting.

Based on these results, the study proposes that institutions consider automating the data consolidation process using the template and methods developed here. Such automation could further enhance the efficiency and accuracy of course performance evaluations, providing a solid foundation for future advancements in educational quality assurance practices.

6.1 Limitation and Future Work

One significant limitation of this study is its focus on a relatively small sample size, specifically three course performance reports from a single program within the CIS division. This limited scope, while manageable and intentional for the exploratory nature of the research, may not fully capture the diversity of courses across the entire institution. Future research could address this limitation by expanding the sample size to include a broader range of courses from different programs and academic levels.

Another notable limitation stems from the use of ChatGPT-4o, which, as a subscription-based tool, may not be readily accessible to all faculty members or institutions. This reliance on a specific version of ChatGPT highlights a barrier to entry for some users who might not have the resources to access advanced GenAI tools. Future work could explore the application of earlier versions of GPT, such as GPT-3.5, or alternative open-source GenAI tools like Gemini, to compare their effectiveness against ChatGPT-4o.

The study also utilized a structured template for data preparation, which proved effective in streamlining the process and improving the results. However, there is room for innovation in this area. Future research could focus on developing and testing alternative templates or automated tools, such as Python scripts, for data consolidation and preparation. These tools could be designed to further automate the data integration process, reducing the manual effort required and potentially increasing the efficiency of the analysis. Finally, the results of the study were validated by interviews with the SCTL of the selected courses. However, additional insights could be provided by comparing ChatGPT's analysis with traditional human-generated reports, using previous SWCAR reports, to further enhance the credibility of the results.

Disclosure of Interests. The authors have no competing interests to declare that are relevant to the content of this article.

References

1. Welsh, J.F., Dey, S.: Quality measurement and quality assurance in higher education. Qual. Assur. Educ. **10**(1), 17–25 (2002). https://doi.org/10.1108/09684880210416076
2. Rexwinkel, T., Haenen, J., Pilot, A.: Quality assurance in higher education: analysis of grades for reviewing course levels. Qual. Quant. **47**, 581–598 (2013)
3. Grebennikov, L., Shah, M.: Student voice: using qualitative feedback from students to enhance their university experience. Teach. High. Educ. **18**(6), 606–618 (2013)
4. Morgan, D.L.: Exploring the use of artificial intelligence for qualitative data analysis: the case of ChatGPT. Int J Qual Methods **22**, 1–10 (2023). https://doi.org/10.1177/16094069231211248
5. Hariri, W.: Unlocking the Potential of ChatGPT: A Comprehensive Exploration of its Applications, Advantages, Limitations, and Future Directions in Natural Language Processing. arXiv Prepr. arXiv2304.02017 (2023). http://arxiv.org/abs/2304.02017
6. George, A.S., George, A.S.H.: A review of ChatGPT AI's impact on several business sectors. Partners Univers. Int. Innov. J. **1**(1), 9–23 (2023)
7. Sallam, M.: ChatGPT utility in healthcare education, research, and practice: systematic review on the promising perspectives and valid concerns. Healthcare, 887 (2023)
8. Carvalho, I., Ivanov, S.: ChatGPT for tourism: applications, benefits and risks. Tour. Rev. **79**(2), 290–303 (2024)
9. Baidoo-anu, D., Ansah, L.O.: Education in the era of generative artificial intelligence (AI): understanding the potential benefits of ChatGPT in promoting teaching and learning. J. Artif. Intell. **7**(December), 52–62 (2023)
10. İpek, Z.H., Gözüm, A.I.C., Papadakis, S., Kallogiannakis, M.: Educational applications of the ChatGPT AI system: a systematic review research. Educ. Process Int. J. **12**(3), 26–55 (2023)
11. Mai, D.T.T., Van Da, C., Van Hanh, N.: The use of ChatGPT in teaching and learning: a systematic review through SWOT analysis approach. Front. Educ. **9**(February), 1–17 (2024). https://doi.org/10.3389/feduc.2024.1328769
12. Lee, V.V., van der Lubbe, S.C.C., Goh, L.H., Valderas, J.M.: Harnessing ChatGPT for thematic analysis: are we ready? J. Med. Internet Res. **26**, e54974 (2024)
13. Turobov, A., Coyle, D., Harding, V.: Using ChatGPT for Thematic Analysis. arxIv Prepr., pp. 1–14 (2024). http://arxiv.org/abs/2405.08828
14. Perkins, M., Roe, J.: The use of generative AI in qualitative analysis: inductive thematic analysis with ChatGPT. J. Appl. Learn. Teach. 7(1) (2024). https://doi.org/10.37074/jalt.2024.7.1.22
15. Hamilton, L., Elliott, D., Quick, A., Smith, S., Choplin, V.: Exploring the use of AI in qualitative analysis: a comparative study of guaranteed income data. Int J Qual Methods **22**, 1–13 (2023). https://doi.org/10.1177/16094069231201504
16. Goyanes, M., Lopezosa, C., Jordá, B.: Thematic analysis of interview data with ChatGPT: designing and testing a reliable research protocol for qualitative research (2024)
17. Suleiman, A., et al.: Assessing ChatGPT's ability to emulate human reviewers in scientific research: a descriptive and qualitative approach. Comput. Methods Programs Biomed. 108313 (2024). https://doi.org/10.1016/j.cmpb.2024.108313
18. Alshami, A., Elsayed, M., Ali, E., Eltoukhy, A.E.E., Zayed, T.: Harnessing the power of ChatGPT for automating systematic review process: methodology, case study, limitations, and future directions. Systems, 11(7) (2023). https://doi.org/10.3390/systems11070351
19. Fuller, K.A., Morbitzer, K.A., Zeeman, J.M., Persky, A.M., Savage, A.C., McLaughlin, J.E.: Exploring the use of ChatGPT to analyze student course evaluation comments. BMC Med. Educ. **24**(1), 1–8 (2024). https://doi.org/10.1186/s12909-024-05316-2

20. Huang, Y., Wu, R., He, J., Xiang, Y.: Evaluating ChatGPT–4.0's data analytic proficiency in epidemiological studies: a comparative analysis with SAS, SPSS, and R. J. Glob. Health, 14(1088) (2024). https://doi.org/10.7189/JOGH.14.04070
21. Sarvandani, S.R.: Employing AI to evaluate companies' performance - an approach to utilize Chatgpt for financial ratio analysis to assist managers (2023)
22. Wang, T., Zhu, Q.: ChatGPT - technical research model, capability analysis, and application prospects. In: IEEE Advanced Information Technology, Electronic and Automation Control Conference, vol. 7, pp. 787–796 (2024).https://doi.org/10.1109/IAEAC59436.2024.10503756
23. Kocoń, J., et al.: ChatGPT: jack of all trades, master of none. Inf. Fusion, **99**(February), 101861 (2023). https://doi.org/10.1016/j.inffus.2023.101861

Author Index

A. Safi et al. (Eds.): ISICS 2024, CCIS 2381, pp. 347–348, 2025.
https://doi.org/10.1007/978-3-031-82931-4